Human
Adaptability

Also of Interest from Westview Press

Rethinking Human Adaptation, edited by Rada Dyson-Hudson and Michael A. Little

† **Sociobiology: Beyond Nature/Nurture?: Reports, Definitions and Debate,** edited by George W. Barlow and James Silverberg

† **Biology and the Social Sciences: An Emerging Revolution,** edited by Thomas C. Wiegele

† **A Systems View of Man,** Ludwig von Bertalanffy, edited by Paul A. LaViolette

† **The Women of Rural Asia,** Robert Orr Whyte and Pauline Whyte

India: Cultural Patterns and Processes, edited by Allen G. Noble and Ashok K. Dutt

Resource Managers: North American and Australian Hunter-Gatherers, edited by Nancy M. Williams and Eugene S. Hunn

Involuntary Migration and Resettlement: The Problems and Responses of Dislocated People, edited by Art Hansen and Anthony Oliver-Smith

The Dilemma of Amazonian Development, edited by Emilio F. Moran

† Available in hardcover and paperback

Human Adaptability

An Introduction
to Ecological
Anthropology

Emilio F. Moran

Westview Press
Boulder, Colorado

To Millie

Published in 1982 in the United States of America by

Westview Press, Inc.
5500 Central Avenue
Boulder, Colorado 80301
Frederick A. Praeger, President and Publisher

Library of Congress Catalog Card Number 82-8605
ISBN 0-86531-430-6
ISBN 0-86531-431-4 (pbk.)

Printed and bound in the United States of America

Contents

Preface

The warm reception of the first edition of this book, among environmental specialists in ecology, geography, and anthropology, has encouraged me to make it available once again. Westview Press and, in particular, associate publisher Lynne Rienner supported the endeavor. When the book first appeared, in spring 1979, I was seeking to present a systems approach that would help overcome the disciplinary biases that seemed to restrict the development of holistic research and theory building. There has been a great deal of work in human adaptation since 1979, but truly systemic approaches to research remain a rarity. I believe the task of developing models that are based on fundamental problems of human adaptation and that are sensitive to the complexity of human responses is still before us. I hope that this book will continue to contribute to shaping our methods of conceptualizing research and to our growing understanding of the multiple levels of adaptation.

This book, about mechanisms of human adaptability, is unique in that it integrates findings from ecology, physiology, social and cultural anthropology, and geography around a set of problems or constraints posed by human habitats. This problem-oriented approach lends itself to the integration of data and at the same time orients the researcher toward answering the question, how do humans adapt.[1]

The answer to that question is found through the study of human adaptability, which emphasizes the plasticity of human responses to environment. This plasticity is manifested in both social/cultural and physiological terms. Social/cultural responses, such as clothing, shelter, and various forms of social organization, help to articulate the adjustment of our species to the environment. Physiological responses require changes in organic structure of function and therefore take longer to come into operation than social/cultural responses. Both types of responses provide a more rapid mechanism for improving survival chances than does genetic change, which accumulates over several generations. The presence of physiological and social/cultural responses implies that most human adjustments are reversible.

The need for a book based on this approach became apparent to me several years ago and its usefulness remains undiminished to this day. Ecological studies tend to adhere to strict disciplinary boundaries and rarely

---

[1]This book is more concerned with functional responses than with evolutionary/structural ones. There have been a few developments that may make a linkage between micro-level functional studies and macro-level evolutionary ones possible. See Moran (1983) for a review of these new directions.

explore the complex and multilevel ways in which humans adjust to their surroundings by non-biological responses. Discussions of human adaptation from a social science perspective often give only cursory treatment to the characteristics of the habitat that forms the context for human behavior. Much progress has been made in the past decade but the need remains for a book such as this that integrates bioecological, physiological, and social/cultural insights into human adaptability.[2] This work reflects the strengths and weaknesses of current research. The study of human adaptability is still in its infancy and many topics and relationships have yet to be explored. Some of the discussions of adaptability are better documented than others. In many instances, this reflects the state of knowledge in that area; in others the limitations of the author. It is my hope that readers will be challenged by these gaps and will be moved to make contributions toward bridging them.

The book features the most extensive published bibliography on ecological anthropology. Over seven hundred works, both classic and recent, are cited. In addition, a list of recommended readings is found at the end of each chapter. Because of its extensive citations and the scope of each chapter, the book can serve as a reference tool for professionals and students alike. The synthesis of ecological theory, history of the field, and discussion of research methods may be useful in advanced courses in cultural ecology, cultural geography, human biology, and environmental studies. The text is relatively free of jargon, but technical terms with precise meanings are, at times, unavoidable. A glossary at the end of the book will assist readers with some of the technical terms. (Terms that are defined in the glossary appear in boldface type the first time they are used in the text.)

The material is presented in three parts. Part 1 (Chapters 1–4) introduces the history, methods, and principal concepts relevant to the study of human adaptability. Part 2 (Chapters 5–9) synthesizes studies of human adaptability to arctic, high altitude, arid, grassland, and tropical rain forest ecosystems. Crucial constraints in each ecosystem are identified (for example, extreme cold) and responses analyzed (for example, characteristics of clothing and peripheral blood flow to the extremities). Part 3 (Chapter 10 and Epilogue) identifies new directions in ecological research and includes a brief discussion of urban ecology.

This book has been clearly influenced by research sponsored by the International Biological Program (IBP) between 1964 and 1974. Two major

---

[2] A state-of-the-art volume on the ecosystem concept in anthropology resulted from a 1982 symposium at the annual meeting of the American Association for the Advancement of Science (Moran 1983). It is an excellent guide to recent advances in anthropology and biology that address the criticisms made by some that ecosystem approaches are ahistorical, narrowly focused on energy flow measurement, and insensitive to variation and socio-political factors coming from "outside" the system under study. The papers in the book clearly show that those flaws are being corrected (cf. Moran 1981; Winterhalder and Smith 1981; Jochim 1981; Ellen 1982; and their papers in Moran 1983).

components of the IBP were the environmental management and the human adaptability projects. The environmental management projects, based on biome units, had ambitious goals of generating macro-ecosystem simulation models. The more modest human adaptability projects commonly had one or two investigators working on narrowly defined problems (Weiner 1977). Fewer than 10 percent of the projects were multidisciplinary and involved research terms. These projects focused on human adaptive responses to the ecosystem. There was little consideration of the influence of the human population on the dynamics and development of the ecosystem (Little 1982). Given the emphasis on human biology, and consequent neglect of social, economic, and political aspects of human behavior and culture in the human adaptability projects and the lack of integration of these projects with the environmental management studies by biological ecologists, it is not surprising that the macro-ecosystem models did not result in a holistic understanding of ecosystems (Worthington 1975).

The IBP was followed by the Man and the Biosphere (MAB) project sponsored by UNESCO. It built on the IBP and attempted to integrate the human component more intimately. MAB is now celebrating its tenth anniversary and there is no doubt that a more scientific basis for the rational use and conservation of resources has been developed. MAB does not aim at generating comprehensive biome models like the IBP. Rather, its aims are more site specific—recognizing that resource management problems are human problems, subject to the particularities of social, political, historical, and other factors. MAB has yet to develop, however, a strategy for project definition that is multidisciplinary in scope. The scope of projects is a product of the orientation of the country directorates rather than the result of a paradigm designed to generate a holistic approach to research.

It is my assumption that if one begins a research design by asking what factors most constrain ecosystem productivity and human choices about time and energy allocations, the product will be a hierarchy of problems (from most to least constraining) and a hierarchy of responses (from ones that use more energy and are less permanent to ones that are more efficient and more permanent) that shape the organization of individuals and society and help one understand the impact people will have on the ecosystem and vice versa (Rappaport 1979; Moran 1981).

I am indebted to friends, students, and colleagues. Conversations with Charles Wagley at the University of Florida provided the germ of inspiration. Professor Wagley encouraged me to study the writings of Julian Steward and introduced me to his colleague in environmental engineering, Professor Howard T. Odum. Coursework and discussions with Professor Odum and other ecologists (especially J. Ewel, A. Lugo, and S. Snedacker) on the Florida campus led me to an integrated view of the bioecological and the social sciences. This view was also fostered by my study of soil science and agronomy under the expert guidance of Hugh Popenoe, Victor Carlisle, and Victor Green of the Institute of Food and Agricultural Sciences at the University of Florida. They imbued their technical discussions with a strong feel for the sociological aspects of farming and resource management.

Professors Bonnie McCay (Rutgers University), Robert Netting (University of Arizona), and John Bennett (Washington University) read the entire manuscript and provided extensive comments that contributed many improvements. Professor Bennett was helpful not only as a reviewer, but also as an early sounding board for my ideas for the book. His stimulating questioning led me to rethink many of my original concepts, and for this I am grateful. Among the many others who read chapters of the manuscript in their areas of expertise were: James Eder (Arizona State University); John Hourihan (University of Maryland); Susan Lees (Hunter College, CUNY); Michael Little (SUNY, Binghamton); Robert Spencer (University of Minnesota); Alan Swedlund (University of Massachusetts); Stephen Thompson (University of Oklahoma); Robert Meier, Paul Jamison, Ivan Karp, and John Myers (Indiana University); and Robert Werge (International Potato Center, Lima, Peru). I am grateful for the thoroughness and constructive character of their reviews. I also wish to thank my students at Indiana University for their helpful discussions—especially Peggy Martin, Kathy Small, and Peter Little.

The preparation of a book requires the typing of many drafts. In this task Rita Brown, Asli Basgoz, Mary Makreas, and Penny Shaneyfelt distinguished themselves for their patience in deciphering handwritten portions and for speedy completion of the manuscript.

Despite all this assistance through the years, only the author may be blamed for any deficiencies in the book.

The task of integrating the many disciplinary strands used in this book was facilitated by the stimulating criticism of my colleague and spouse, Millicent Fleming-Moran. As a result of our many discussions of every section of the manuscript our ideas merged; thus, this book is dedicated to her in appreciation for her part in its development.

Emilio F. Moran
March 1982

References

Ellen, Roy
  1982 Environment, Subsistence and System. Cambridge: Cambridge University Press.

Jochim, Michael
  1981 Strategies for Survival. New York: Academic Press.

Little, Michael
1983 Human Biology and the Development of an Ecosystem Approach: Past Studies and the South Turkana Ecosystem Project. In The Ecosystem Concept in Anthropology. E. F. Moran, ed. Boulder, Colo.: Westview Press and AAAS. AAAS Selected Symposium Series.

Moran, Emilio F.
1981 Developing the Amazon. Bloomington: Indiana University Press.

Moran, Emilio F., ed.
1983 The Ecosystem Concept in Anthropology. Boulder, Colo.: Westview Press and AAAS. AAAS Selected Symposium Series.

Rappaport, Roy
1979 Ecology, Meaning, and Religion. Richmond, Calif.: North Atlantic Books.

Weiner, J. S.
1977 The History of the Human Adaptability Section. In Human Adaptability: A History and Compendium of Research. K. J. Collins and J. S. Weiner, eds. London: Taylor and Francis.

Winterhalder, B., and E. A. Smith, eds.
1981 Hunter-Gatherer Foraging Strategies: Ethnographic and Archeological Analyses. Chicago: University of Chicago Press.

Worthington, E. B., ed.
1975 The Evolution of the IBP. Cambridge: Cambridge University Press.

1

Ecological Anthropology: History, Theory, and Method

1

People in Ecosystems

The study of human adaptability focuses on those functional and structural features of human populations that facilitate their coping with environmental change and stressful conditions. It is a marked feature of human populations that they are amazingly adaptable. This chapter and chapter 4 present major theoretical and methodological concepts relevant to the study of adaptability. Chapters 2 and 3 outline the historical development of **ecological anthropology.**[1] As will be seen, contemporary studies of human adaptability reflect a growing interaction between the social and the biological sciences. **Cultural ecology** and **ethnoecology** represent variant forms of research wherein the concepts and methods of the biological sciences play a less significant role; most of the research in human ecology in the disciplines of anthropology, geography, and sociology has been of this kind. These social and cultural approaches to the study of human adaptability have enriched our understanding of coping behaviors. Nevertheless, in a full explanation of the adaptability of our species, it is desirable to include the physiological aspects of human responses.

The integration of social and biological approaches to the study of adaptability was facilitated by the increasing acceptance of the **ecosystem** concept. This concept, derived from the study of biological **ecology,** views all organisms as part of ecological systems and subject to the same physical laws. Using this framework, one can refer to human beings as third-order **consumers** in a food chain or view the interaction between two human populations as **mutualistic.** The ecosystem approach makes it possible to apply a greater body of data to explanatory models of human behavior than is possible from a strictly social or cultural approach.

In this chapter, we will discuss the ecosystem concept and introduce another, equally crucial concept—that is, the distinction between **adaptation** and **adjustment.** While the concept of evolutionary adaptation is certainly relevant to the understanding of human adaptability, most research with human populations has found that nongenetic forms of adaptability are much more common. Genetic adaptation involves changes in gene frequencies that confer reproductive advantage to the population in a particular environment. It is a response to prevailing environmental circumstances and lowers the population's capacity to adjust to changes in its environment. It also tends to restrict the population to certain types of habitat wherein it has a reproductive advantage. The human species is characterized by a marked degree of **genotypic** plasticity. As a result, the interaction between environment and **phenotype** brings about variations (that is, adjustments) in behavior and in morphology to adjust the organism to those conditions. These adjustments occur at the level of the individual, although the adjustments may be shared by the whole population inhabiting a given habitat. In other words, the human species is a generalized species adjusting itself to new circumstances by physiological and social/cultural means.

[1]Terms in boldface are defined in the glossary.

As we have noted, the other central concept to be discussed in this chapter is that of the ecological system or ecosystem. This fundamental unit is a heuristic tool used to describe the interaction between living and nonliving components of a given habitat. While it is possible for some purposes to view the whole biosphere as an ecosystem, scientists have found it useful to divide the biosphere into smaller and more homogeneous biogeographical regions, or **biomes.** Such biomes represent a given set of climatic, floral, and faunal characteristics. While species may differ between continents, the type of **biota** across biomes will manifest commonalities resulting from the adaptation and adjustment of species to similar ecological conditions.

For purposes of study, the ecosystem is subdivided into the three components that structure it: **energy, matter** and **information.** Energy flows into ecosystems and is converted into vegetal biomass, which in turn sustains animals and humans. Chemical energy makes possible the conversion of matter from organic to inorganic forms and the cycle of essential nutrients in ecosystems. Information makes possible control over rates of flow, changes in ecosystem structure and function, and overall adaptability to both internal and external conditions. In the study of adaptability, it is most convenient to begin by studying how humans respond to **constraints** posed by their habitat.

Human Adaptability as a Response to Constraints

The study of human adaptability tends to emphasize the plasticity of human response to any environment. Its use of a broad data base that includes physiological, behavioral, and cultural adjustments to environmental change circumvents sterile debates over whether cultural or biological studies provide the most useful tools for studying interactions between humans and their environments. The human adaptability approach deals with the specific problems faced by inhabitants of various environments rather than with environment as a static "given" that limits human possibilities. It focuses on how human populations in interacting with each other and their environments attempt to accommodate themselves to these very specific environmental problems. As a result, the environment ceases to be an overgeneralized context for human action and the scope of particular investigations is narrowed.

The identification of problems presented by environments does not imply a capitulation of the ideal of studying entire biomes. However, data available on entire biomes is still fragmentary and researchers have experienced difficulty in analyzing these broad units. Some scientists have chosen to divide the biome into species for study, while others deal with

Table 1.1   **Limiting Factors of Representative Biomes**

Arctic zones	Extreme and prolonged low temperatures
	Light/Dark Seasonal Cycles
	Low biological productivity
High altitudes	Low oxygen pressure, or hypoxia
	Nighttime cold stress
	Low biological productivity
	High neonate mortality
Arid lands	Low and uncertain rainfall
	High rates of evaporation
	Low biological productivity
Grasslands	Prolonged dry season
	Cyclical drought
	Herd size and composition
Humid tropics	Great diversity of species
	High rainfall
	Secondary succession
	Solar Radiation

specific behavior of populations. The approach used in this book advocates the identification of clearly defined limiting factors, **stresses,** or problems that elicit human responses. Problems such as extreme cold, low biological productivity, and water scarcity demand some form of adjustment by organisms occupying areas that are so constrained. Table 1.1 summarizes the major constraints of a number of ecosystems that will be studied in chapters 5 through 9.

Choosing a problem as the focus of research allows the individual researcher to get away from the debate over the appropriate unit of analysis (that is, individual, population, or ecosystem) and requires initially that *all* levels of response to the problem be considered. For example, extreme and constant forms of stress may be coped with by irreversible physiological change during the developmental period of the individual **(developmental adjustments).** Acclimatory forms of physiological response, on the other hand, facilitate the adjustment of individuals after the developmental period and are reversible **(acclimatory adjustment).** Perhaps the most common forms of adjustment are behavioral, social, and cultural **(regulatory adjustments).** The latter are more flexible than developmental or acclimatory adjustments because they involve less of a commitment by the physical organism.

A *problem approach* permits the inclusion of these multilevel responses to a particular problem—for example, cold stress. It also facilitates the conceptualization of the research by suggesting **hypotheses** to be tested and knowledge to be sought. During the investigation the focus on specific problems helps to keep the study "on track" by continuous testing of the hypotheses proposed. In the analysis stage the focus on specific problems helps guide the interpretation of data.

Adaptation and Adjustment   The term *adaptation* is at the heart of the ecological approach. Organisms, human and nonhuman, respond to structural and functional characteristics of their environment. Adaptations result from exposure to physical and chemical factors in the environment, from interaction with other species, and from the interaction of individuals within the same species. Evolutionary change through the mechanism of natural selection involves the replacement of individuals with one type of adaptation by those with another. This type of **genetic** or **evolutionary adaptation** involves a slow adjustment to environmental change and is studied at the level of populations.

Individuals, however, can respond to changes in their environment by morphological and functional adjustments. Ricklefs (1973:56) differentiates between regulatory, acclimatory, and developmental adjustments. All three types operate by a process known as negative **feedback.** This type of feedback seeks to maintain a stable relationship between the organism and the surroundings. To be effective, a response must be of the proper magnitude and occur at a time and rate that is appropriate in relation to the stimulus that elicited the adjustment.

Regulatory responses occur rapidly and reflect the physiological and behavioral flexibility of an organism. Virtually all behavior is a form of regulatory response that either serves to maintain a stable relationship to the environment or permits adjustment to changes in that environment. Cultural **strategies** of clothing and shelter are among the most common regulatory mechanisms that enhance human chances to survive and live in relative comfort in a variety of environments.

Acclimatory responses take longer to come into operation because they require a change in organismic structure. They occur when an external stimulus is present for a sufficient amount of time. They are usually reversible when the situation that produced the organismic change ends. For example, muscle enlargement as a result of frequent and demanding physical exercise is reversed when the individual begins to lead a more sedentary life.

Developmental responses are not reversible and occur during the growth and development of an individual. They are adjustments of the organism to the environmental conditions prevalent during the developmental period. During this developmental period human organisms have the ability to mold themselves to prevalent environmental conditions **(genetic plasticity).** For example, a child growing at high altitudes will

7

develop larger lungs and chest capacity to adjust to prevalent low oxygen conditions. After the growth period, a non-native will be unable to achieve a larger chest cavity. Developmental adjustments are of limited value for *short-term* environmental adjustments, but provide a more flexible adjustment to prevalent conditions than does genetic change. The developmental flexibility of the human population provides a more rapid mechanism for improving survival chances and enhancing reproduction than genetic change accumulated over several generations (Ricklefs 1973:60).

The Ecosystem The ecosystem is a fundamental ecological unit that refers to associated species of living organisms in a nonliving physical environment and to the structural and functional relationships among them. In the study of human adaptability, the ecosystem is the total situation within which adaptability occurs. Because human populations have spread over the totality of the earth, this context of adaptability varies a great deal. A population in a specific ecosystem adjusts to environmental conditions in specific ways that represent both present and past conditions. In other words, a desert population that has existed in that environment for several millenia will differ significantly in its responses to desert conditions than a population that migrated there only in the last generation. A population that has existed longer in a particular environment is more likely than a recently settled population to have developed physiological and even genetic characteristics aimed at coping with environmental constraints, such as extreme heat. The more recent inhabitants will have physiological and cultural adjustments attuned to another environment. When they begin adjusting to the new environment, a process of change will be initiated that may take several generations, and the final result may or may not be much like the adjustments of the original inhabitants. This is particularly true when native populations are available from whom to borrow a variety of forms of adjustment. The newcomers may borrow some of the practices of the original inhabitants in order to achieve a satisfactory adjustment to their new habitat.

The above scenario suggests that human adaptability can proceed along any one of many paths. In the absence of borrowing and **diffusion** of ideas, the population may innovate and develop new forms of adjustment. If the new adjustment pattern conflicts with previous practices and yet provides a workable solution that does not threaten the survival and well-being of the individual or group, some form of compromise may emerge. If the exposure to the stress is continual, physiological change of a permanent kind (developmental adjustment) may provide a more adequate adjustment than regulatory forms. The human body is able to adapt by genetic, physiological, and behavioral and cultural means. The purpose of these various levels of adjustment is to enhance adaptability through a flexible hierarchy of response.

Human adaptability, therefore, refers to ecological success as measured by demographic, energetic, or nutritional criteria. Demographic criteria often used are (1) a balance between natality and mortality, (2) morbidity or incidence of disease, and (3) the population's rate of reproduction. Energetic criteria can be relative or absolute. Relative **energetic efficiency** is used as an indication of the adequacy of a technology. Efficient subsistent technologies have been noted to be sustainable at low levels of population density. In the past it has been more common to use total energy harnessed as indicative of success. Nutritional criteria provide a good index of adaptability since food consumption reflects knowledge of resources, capability to exploit them, and capacity to achieve a given level of work capacity.

However, all these criteria are only indexes of adaptability and do not constitute any firm measure of **fitness.** Fitness refers to reproductive success. The more "adapted" a species is in its environment, the greater the opportunity for individuals of the population to survive and reproduce and then to occupy the territory. It is much easier to define energetic failure or inefficiency and nutritional inadequacy than to determine reproductive success. The problem of overpopulation raises numerous questions about the adequacy of fitness as an index of human adaptation.

Modeling

The complexity and multiplicity of factors that impinge on human adjustment to environment are such that to deal with them, we must simplify the overall situation. To this end, we turn to representations of the real world situation, or **models,** which facilitate comprehension of complex ecosystems. A model simplifies reality and is created by speculating on what processes might be involved in producing the observed facts. Once certain processes have been identified as relevant, we infer other facts that may be related. These facts can then be observed and/or measured. Next, we check our predictions against the real world and assess the accuracy of our simplified representation (that is, the model). The model may be modified in accordance with our new observations and then retested to see whether it now more accurately represents and predicts real behaviors found in the system. A model, in other words, is evaluated in terms of its ability to predict correctly other new facts about the system (Lave and March 1975:19–20). Because it provides a systematic development of conjectures, tests, and validations that help us explain and appreciate how systems work, modeling is a major tool of the natural and social sciences.

Boundaries: Closed and Open Systems   All modeling presents the problem of defining a model's boundaries. It is the researcher who must delimit the field, usually basing such a decision on an issue or problem that is to be the object of investigation. The modeling situation is particularly thorny when one is dealing with ecosystems that include people. To cope with the complexity of such a task, it has become common in both ecology and the social sciences to deal with systems as if they were closed. A **closed system** is one that is bounded for heuristic reasons and is treated as if it were unaffected by forces outside the system. Foster (1966) justified the closed-system approach in this way: "It is methodologically sound to assume for analytical purposes, a cultural situation that is contrary to fact. . . . For analytical purposes, I am making use of an ideal type that nowhere corresponds to reality."

Although this approach served the sciences well and allowed many scientists to deal more effectively with complex data, it is more realistic to view most living systems as open to outside forces. While a closed system is maintained by *internal* cycling of materials, an **open system** requires constant inputs from *outside* the system to maintain it. In ecological systems everything is ultimately interconnected and everything ultimately feeds back on itself (Miller 1975:77). (This interconnectedness helps preserve the system because of cybernetic characteristics; **cybernetic systems** are those that maintain control and adaptability by information feedback.)

The thermoregulatory functioning of the human body is a good illustration of how feedback operates (see figure 1.1). If the temperature of the surroundings rises above the normal body temperature of 98.6° F. (37° C.), sensory devices send messages to the brain, and the brain, in turn, brings on a sweating response. The evaporation of sweat cools the skin. The skin sensors feel the cooling and send new information to decrease sweating (*negative feedback*). When a system is overloaded—that is, when conditions are beyond the tolerance capacity of the organism or system—the system goes out of control and *positive feedback* takes over. Such a response can either permit reorganization to occur and a new adaptive response to emerge or it may mean death or breakdown.

This feedback process is similar to the phenomenon of revitalization movements described by Wallace (1956). In this work, Wallace describes a "mazeway," which he defines as the complete set of cognitive maps (that is, of both positive and negative goals) that characterize an individual at a given time. Mazeway content includes images of self and of the outside world and tactics and techniques for achieving satisfactory goals. Following stress upon a cultural system, there are efforts (or "revitalization movements") to find solutions and maintain steady state. Following increased stress, efforts are made to reconstitute the mazeway at a new level that can more effectively deal with the changed environment. If these efforts are unsuccessful, the system may face extinction as a result of higher death rates, lower birth rates, factional disputes, and conquest by neighbors who see an opportunity to gain territory, labor, or other resources. The similarity between the feedback process and revitalization movements emerges from the derivation of the revitalization movement

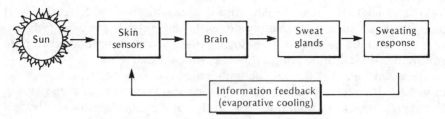

Figure 1.1   **Cybernetics and Feedback:**   A simple model

concept—an organismic analogy in which events in one subsystem are information to other subsystems.

The interest in ecological systems, modeling, and similar efforts at holism has been closely associated with the development of **general systems theory** (von Bertalanffy 1968; Buckley 1968). The systems approach is a way of thinking, an approach to problem solving. Simply stated, the systems approach is that of "(1) defining goals and objectives, (2) establishing conceptual boundaries to distinguish the system and the environment, (3) defining the range components and processes to be considered, and (4) forcing formal consideration of how each component is related to all the others." (Harris et al., 1975: 7–8)

When one pursues the practice of modeling, it is tempting to simplify reality to the point that it becomes a static equilibrium situation. Both ecologists (Slobodkin 1974; Holling 1973) and social scientists (Buckley 1967; Friedman 1974) have pointed out that the equilibrium models that came so easily in the past are not so reliable or useful as once thought. A more viable and realistic notion is to conceptualize human societies as complex adaptive systems. Closed systems have been characterized by minimal linkages with the rest of the world and a minimum internal capacity for change. Open systems, on the other hand, emphasize that the internal flows are capable of significantly changing the internal components of the system. Information flows about the state of the outside world lead to feedback loops that do not return the system to equilibrium but, rather, lead it along new paths that improve its adjustment to changing conditions. One of the challenges to modeling is to deal with how change occurs, instead of aiming at elegant models that do not represent the survival demands faced by living organisms.

Advantages of Modeling   Modeling can be utilized at any phase of a study, but it is particularly useful in the preliminary stages of an investigation. At this point modeling helps to identify knowledge gaps and to formulate relationships to be investigated. The narrowing down of objectives is crucial for most investigations, given the limited resources and time available in most research projects. During data-gathering stages, modeling can be helpful in monitoring the gradual accumulation of data and in identifying those compartments with sufficient data.

Simulation at the intermediate phases of research may also be helpful in testing the model's accuracy in representing the situation under study. Simulation refers to a technique for solving and studying problems by following a model's changes over time. Simulation is one of the most useful techniques available for studying complex systems. A simulation model attempts to represent the functioning of a system in such a way that *dynamic* interactions between system components are reproduced. Simulations are useful in planning for optimum changes in a system. This may avoid those disheartening discoveries that much of the data gathered were inappropriate to a workable model and that other data are still required. At the end of the data-gathering period, a wide range of techniques for analysis and simulation are available, such as Dynamo, Fortran, analog simulation, and many others.

Another advantage of modeling is that systemic relationships rather than detailed content receive special attention. In addition, the investigator is not bound to modeling only one type of information. If agricultural, climatic, and social variables are relevant, they can be included in the model. Their inclusion, in fact, may be vital if the model is to adequately represent the structure and function of the system. Regardless of the topic of investigation or the level of a model's complexity, the parts of a system are always linked by flows of energy, matter, and information. It is these flows that connect the components of ecosystems, and they must be understood if we are to understand the structure and function of ecosystems and human adaptability within those systems.

Energy

Modeling in ecological analyses is most often used to represent flows of energy, matter, or both. Since the writings of Leslie White (1943, 1959) and Fred Cottrell (1955), the social sciences have been aware of the relationship between humankind's social complexity and its harnessing of energy. Because energy refers to ability to do work, it is important to know what units to use in computing the energy harnessed or released by an organism. Energy can be expressed as joules, BTUs, watt-hours, foot-pounds, and **kilocalories.** The kilocalorie (kcal) is the most commonly used unit in human ecological studies. It is defined as the amount of heat required to raise the temperature of one kilogram (i.e., one liter) of water one degree centigrade at a temperature of 15° C. This unit has wide applicability and is commonly used in nutrition, physics, and chemistry. Some scientists have advocated the use of the joule as a unit because kcal cannot be defined with sufficient accuracy for certain physical purposes. A joule is, however, an

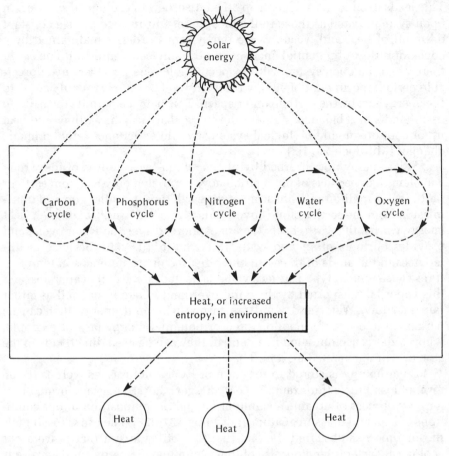

Figure 1.2 **Closed and Open Cycles in the Biosphere** Energy (dotted lines) flows in and out, matter (solid lines) cycles in a nearly closed cycle, while energy is constantly lost.

Source: G. Tyler Miller. 1975. Living in the Environment. Belmont, Cal.: Wadsworth Publishing Company.

inconvenient unit to use because it is very small: one kilocalorie equals 4,184 joules. Since many of the energy studies that involve human populations are based on nutritional assessments, the kilocalorie is the most convenient unit (Durnin, 1975:10).

How energy is stored and how it performs work are best described by the **laws of thermodynamics.** The first law states that *energy is neither created nor destroyed.* It may change form, go from one place to another, or be degraded into less usable forms. The second law is closely related to the first and states that *part of the energy involved in doing work is lost as heat* to the surrounding environment. Thus, there is a constant degradation of energy.

13

This leads to an increase in **entropy** (i.e., disorder) in ecological systems. In open systems, such as those in the biosphere, entropy occurs as a constant drain-off of heat and waste, while the system's order is maintained by a constant inflow of potential energy from the sun (see figure 1.2). The earth, therefore, is an open system with respect to solar energy. Over any appreciable period, the amount of energy received from the sun is roughly equal to the energy lost by the earth to outer space. This balance permits the earth to maintain its heat balance. Without the energy balance, the earth would heat up or cool down, and biological systems would experience lethal climatic changes (Murdoch 1971:2).

Solar energy not absorbed by plants, either because it is of the wrong wavelength or because of plant efficiency, is radiated outward from earth or participates in differential heating of the earth through reflection and transmission from the earth's cloud cover. This is referred to as *heat energy*. Heat energy warms the earth, heats the atmosphere, drives the water cycle, and provides currents of air and water (R.L. Smith 1974:30). Because of differences in the angle of the earth and other factors, differences in temperatures cause winds. When surface water is heated, some of it evaporates, and this vapor is transported by the wind over land where it may fall as either rain or snow. Water and wind are forms of natural energy that can be harnessed and transformed to stored or potential energy (as, for example, when water is accumulated in a dam) or they can be used directly (as in the case of wind-generated grist mills).

Solar energy is stored in the form of living biomass, as well as in the form of fossil fuels (for example, coal, oil, gas). Fossil fuels are formed by a lengthy process of organic accumulation and decomposition under conditions of heat and pressure (Odum and Odum 1976:28). The use of fossil fuels in our time has obscured the fact that it is still the sun that powers our ecological systems; and our use of that accumulated energy source exceeds the speed at which the processes of nature can create it.

The energy converted and stored in plant **biomass** becomes available to other organisms of the ecosystem. (Biomass refers to the mass of living organisms in a given area or population. It may be expressed in calorie terms or in weight units. It may refer to the total mass or to a portion, as in plant biomass, livestock biomass, and so forth.) The energy stored in plant biomass powers a series of organisms in what has been described as a *food chain*. A food chain is a simple unilinear summary of who-eats-whom. In nature, however, the situation is not a simple "chain," but a complex network of **trophic** (that is, feeding) relationships, referred to as a *food web* (figure 1.3). At each step in a food chain or food web, energy is lost as heat because of the expenditure of energy within the food-chain process (cf, second law of thermodynamics). Thus, as one passes from plants to higher organisms, there is an increasing loss of potential energy. This steady loss of energy can be visualized as a pyramid that represents trophic relations in the system. Figure 1.4 is one such pyramid and illustrates the dramatic declines in biomass and in a number of organisms.

14

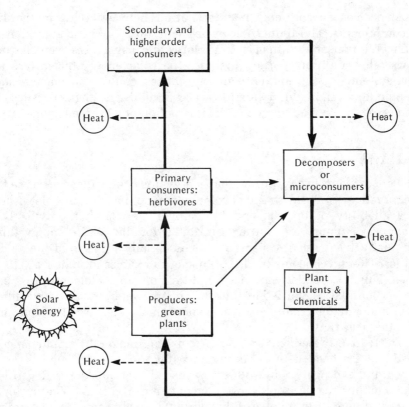

Figure 1.3 **A Simplified Food Web** Solid lines represent movement of matter, unshaded lines indicate flow of energy.

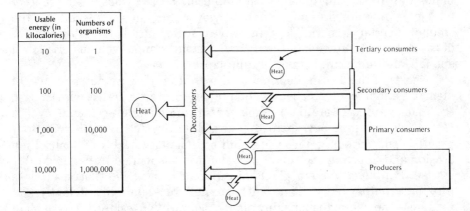

Figure 1.4 **An Ecological Pyramid Used to Describe Trophic Levels** Because of the steady decrease in usable energy, both energy and numbers of organisms decrease as one moves from producer organisms to higher order consumers.

15

An ecosystem represents the interrelations between living and nonliving components. The living portion is made up of green plants (that is, **producers**), consumers (that is, **herbivores** and **carnivores**), and **decomposers.** The nonliving portion includes the solar energy that drives the entire system, organic and inorganic substances, and physical factors such as temperature, light, wind, humidity, and rainfall. The characteristics of a given ecosystem are a function of the interaction of all these factors.

Matter

The work of plants in converting solar energy into energy that can be used by other organisms for growth and development would not be possible without the availability of organic and inorganic materials that provide both mechanical support and nutrients essential for life. While energy flows continually in and out of systems, matter essentially cycles from one state to another. There has been a tendency to speak of **cycles of matter** as closed cycles. This is essentially an oversimplification since elements cross ecosystems boundaries. Carried by the atmosphere, water, or other mechanical means and leaving in similar ways, elements make their way from one area to another (see figure 1.5).

Thirty to forty elements are known to be required for the maintenance of life. Some are needed in large amounts (for example, carbon, nitrogen, oxygen, and hydrogen), while others are needed in minute doses. Regardless of the amount required, all these elements are necessary. The cycles of materials on the earth involve pathways that take elements from organic to inorganic forms and back again. For instance, nitrogen is released from animal remains by decomposers, later to be recombined in its elemental form by nitrogen-fixing organisms in the soil, which is then utilized by plants in synthesizing their own protoplasm. These cycles go on whether human beings are present or not. However, human activity affects the amount of certain material flows in such a way that, in an increasing number of cases, the components of the natural system cannot cycle materials fast enough, and the result is toxic accumulations.

Cycles of matter can be illustrated by noting how plants make use of elements and how human beings enter into these processes. As with energy, the plant producers are the key element in the material exchange cycles. Human populations have helped control these cycles of matter. Contour planting and terracing alter water and sedimentary cycles by controlling erosion and delaying the runoff of water and suspended minerals. Multistoried cropping, wherein plants of different heights are placed in close proximity, helps to control nutrient leaching, to use sunlight efficiently, and to increase net yield. In managing plants, people often test the limits of plant tolerance and soil productivity. Sometimes the result is failure, but in other cases unexpected advantages result—as when a plant taken to another

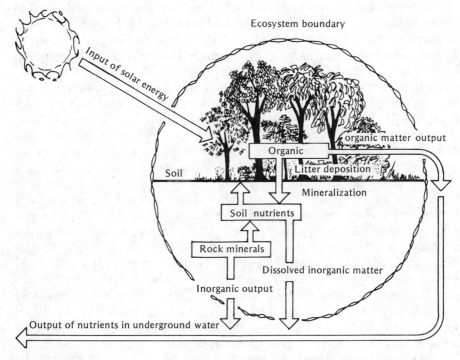

Figure 1.5   **Flow and Storage of Matter in a Terrestrial Ecosystem**

continent thrives in the absence of its natural enemies under soil and climatic conditions similar to those of its native habitat.

Information

How information flows and is transformed is of interest to an analysis of how matter and energy are transformed and work is achieved (Adams 1974:21). The effect of cognition on human value structures and the effect of those values, in turn, on the implementation of controls over natural processes have not been always empirically determined.[2] The field of semiotics has developed in recent years as an interdisciplinary attempt to deal with the complex phenomena of message exchanges and communication systems.[3]

[2]Some authors argue that such controls are responses to systemic states (e.g. Rappaport 1968), while others emphasize the role of individual choicemaking (for example, Bennett 1969).

[3]For an excellent review of the historical development, scope, and state of the art in the field of semiotics, see Sebeok (1974).

17

In the interest of formulating theories that can adequately deal with the interrelations between social, cultural, and environmental variables, several authors have recently advocated that structural analyses of the entire area of communication, meaning, and cognition be combined with energetic and/or other forms of ecological research (Alland 1975; Adams 1974). So far, these statements have been frankly programmatic, but there is evidence that students are beginning to test out the approaches. A recent book, *Energy and Structure* (Adams 1973), details how the concentration of decision making and social power at higher levels of a social system leads to the concentration of control over energetic flows "so that fewer independent decisions are responsible for greater releases of energy" (Adams 1974:29).

Similarly, Rappaport has discussed how ritual can act as a cybernetic switch that automatically adjusts the relationship between a population and its resources. While the proposition has not been thoroughly tested, there is evidence that "religious activities are primarily part of the information processes of human societies" (Rappaport 1971b:25). According to Rappaport, ritual reduces ambiguity by putting complex analogic information and more-less information into simple digital signals (that is, a *switch*). In general, one can note that religious ritual affirms group values and asks individuals to abandon their selfishness and take on the social good. Ritual is an "expensive" cultural investment, but it pays off by providing unequivocal information of value for adaptability.

Mackay (1968a:204) has suggested that semantic questions can be included in information theory only when one thinks of senders and receivers as goal-directed, self-adaptive systems. According to this view, an organism requires a certain repertoire of acts and has a selective process that is organized according to the current state of the environment. Constant work must be done to update the informational system in a *logical* sense. If one defines information as that which does logical work in orienting the organism toward better coping behaviors, then information in this sense can be measured. What is to be measured is not an *amount* of something learned, but the establishment of logical relations (that is, structure). In this view of information, both perception and evaluation are neatly included in the model. Human systems are self-organizing—that is, able to receive inputs of new information and to develop characteristic organizing sequences as a result of combining new and old information. Since the environment manifests consistent and recurrent features, an individual having a set of perceived conditions can use the notion of probability in deciding which routine is most likely to be successful (Mackay 1968b:363–364).

A number of authors have questioned the assumption that humans act according to the principles of probability. According to van Heerden (1968:20), it was Laplace who extended the concept of probability to events in which the card-game types of selection did not apply. Some argue that human choices respond to empirical experience—that is, if it worked in the past, try it again; if it did not, try something else (Ibid. p. 45). Others suggest

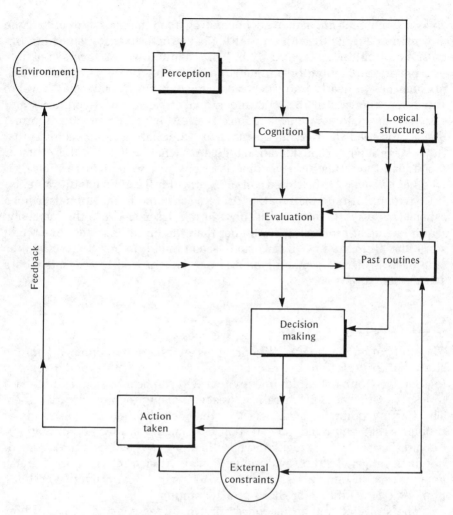

Figure 1.6   **Flow of Information**   Information flow is seen as an organizing feedback that attunes the organism to environmental and social conditions. External restraints may refer to social pressure put on the individual by the social group that steers the person in a course other than that decided on individually. Each action taken becomes part of the past routines that will, thereafter, constrain choice.

that the choices are made from a limited set of options, usually those that have occurred in the most recent past and that express the least uncertainty about outcomes (Slovic, Kunreuther, and White 1974).

Figure 1.6 presents a more realistic perception of human organization. There is sensory reception of signals and symbols some of which are ignored and some of which are perceived, depending upon the sensory quality of the information and its fit with current logical structures that result from linguistic and cultural categorization. This then allows for several possible interpretations, ambiguity, and new reorderings. When a perceived stimulus does not fit neatly into categories, the cognitive domain may develop structured analyses of the stimulus so that it can create hypotheses and assign meaning to the information acquired. After this occurs, the information is processed and put into the realm of "information-for-decision"—that is, the stage at which consideration is given to whether the stimulus is first or secondhand information, whether it elicits an immediate response, or whether it is meant to be stored as a subroutine until certain conditions elicit it. For example, upon reading that drinking the blood from animals is not a satisfactory way of coping with thirst in the desert because the metabolic requirements of processing are higher than the liquid ingested, one might store that information. Later, such secondhand information might be employed in decision making should one be stranded in a desert with a small water supply.

Summary

The study of human adaptability provides an integrating framework for the study of the interactions between human populations within, and in relation to, their environment. Studying environment can be an all-consuming task unless the relevant and generalizable aspects of environment are identified. The starting point for such a task is the identification of constraints or problems that require adaptive responses from all the affected populations. Such responses may be regulatory, acclimatory, or developmental. We will not focus on genetic (i.e., evolutionary) adaptation, although it is of course another type of human response, but will instead deal primarily with the more pliable mediums for short-term adaptation.

The study of human responses first includes considerations of how ecosystems are structured and functionally related. Flows of energy, matter, and information form the connecting links between components of the ecosystem and define both the constraints and the opportunities available to the human inhabitants. Low mean biological productivity may constrain the population densities that can be supported, call for reduced activity to minimize caloric expenditure, or even seasonally reduce the population through famine. On the other hand, human adjustments such as migratory behavior, trade linkages with more productive areas, and technological movement of resources into the region may provide just the needed energy, matter, and information expenditures to permit these populations to achieve unexpected high densities, engage in calorically expensive work, and prevent decimation from occurring. In part II, we will look at various mechanisms used by groups in a wide variety of settings to exploit, and even expand, the resources of their surroundings. Before proceeding to part II, we first need to explore the historical development of the field and to evaluate theory and method used in the study of adaptability.

Recommended Readings

Numerous useful introductions to the topic of human adaptability are available. An evolutionary perspective is found in Alland's *Evolution and Human Behavior* (1967). An excellent collection of articles with an epidemiological emphasis on human ecology is that edited by Sargent (1974). The journals of *Human Biology* and *Human Ecology* regularly publish articles of interest on human adaptability. The volumes generated by the human adaptability component of the United States **International Biological Program** make important contributions to our knowledge of particular biomes (Baker and Little 1976, on high altitude adaptability; Jamison, Zegura, and Milan 1978, on Eskimo adaptability).

Almost any modern introduction to the field of ecology will discuss the flow of energy and matter. Among the most notable are the discussions in Ricklefs (1973), R.L. Smith (1974), Kormondy (1976), Simmons (1974), Odum (1971), and Odum and Odum (1976). It is more difficult to find discussions on the flow of information. Adams (1973, 1974) and Rappaport (1971b) are among the few who have dealt with this subject. They illustrate how information is embodied in social institutions and how cybernetic controls function in a system. Patten (1971), Levin (1974), Forrester (1961, 1968, 1969), Odum (1971), Odum and Odum (1976), Pugh (1970), Watt (1968), and Wilson and Bossert (1971) contain discussions of theory and applications of systems theory and of techniques for modeling and simulation.

2

Theories of
Human/Habitat
Interaction
up to the 1950s

Contemporary theories about the nature of human physiological functioning and about the effects of human beings upon the environment and the effects of the environment upon them are only fully intelligible in the light of the historical roots of such theories. Modern notions of homeostasis reflect ancient concerns and assumptions about the order of nature. This same yearning for order keeps making its way into ecological explanations through the attribution of purposive motives to biological populations. The gloomy view of some international lending institutions about the potential of the tropics for development reflects a long tradition of environmental determinism that sees some regions of the world as ecologically bound to backwardness and others to progress. In fact, every society has philosophical or mythological explanations about the natural world and the human being's place in it. It is through such explanations that members of a society articulate both their behavior as individuals and their requirements of survival as a population. Such explanations also provide societies with a means of achieving a measure of well-being.

In this chapter we will survey the major Western intellectual currents up to the 1950s that sought to explain the interaction between people and nature. Three main themes may be noted: environmental determinism—that is, the determining effect of nature upon human society and **culture;** human adaptation to nature; and nature as a limiting factor to human possibilities. These themes represent three points on the intellectual spectrum. One view overemphasized the influence of nature, another the role of human culture. The third view helped to bridge the gap between the other two themes. The common features of all these themes is that they conceptualized the human/environment interaction as mainly unidirectional, rather than systemic, and that they emphasized stages, rather than process. The theme of environmental determinism offers the clearest example of this type of unidirectional, stage-oriented explanation.

Environmental Determinism

Determinism is a broad term referring to explanations that assign one factor a dominating influence over the whole system. From Greco-Roman times through the early part of the twentieth century, scientific theories stressed single-factor explanations to the neglect of the complex interactions of biological systems. Environmental deterministic theories served as rationales for political dominance in many guises. The format of all such theories was essentially the same: a "temperate" or "balanced" climate, ethnocentrically defined, was responsible for the virtuous qualities of the area's inhabitants. As a result, they were destined to rule and control the "lesser" domains where populations were more lethargic, less courageous, and less intelligent. Roughly, then, a predominant or technologically superior position indicated that the powerful were really innately superior peoples. This superiority was produced by "favorable" geoclimatic conditions. Ironically, the locus of the "temperate climes" or "middle latitudes" has shifted from the balmy Mediterranean to the cooler regions of Western Europe as shifts have occurred in world power over the centuries. Such ethnocentric theories served not only to explain a country's dominant position, but also to rationalize policies for ensuring its continued dominance.

Greek, Roman, and Arab Theories   The original Greek geoclimatic theories arose from observations of nature and society. At the heart of their argument lay a recognition of their own political power and of the role that their strategic location in the Mediterranean played in the acquisition and maintenance of such power. Writers rose to the the task by explaining that the "middle latitudes" (that is, Greece) were most conducive to favorable cultural developments because in that locale humans were subject to an ideal proportion of the basic four elements (fire, water, earth, air). A hot tropical climate was believed to foster idleness and resignation (Thomas 1925:227), while the climate of Greece with its seasonal changes balanced the exposure to the elements and thus was the most conducive to progress. These ideas, which were endorsed by Hippocrates, Aristotle, and other major figures of ancient Greece, set a trend that was followed by the Romans.

Roman writers confidently cited geoclimatic reasons for the Roman conquest of the rest of the civilized world. Cicero attributed this success to the strategic location of Rome itself; Vitrivius to the allround superiority of peoples located in the middle latitudes. Like Greek authors before him, Vitrivius felt the optimal location was one midway between the two extremes of hot and cold. He pointed to Rome's dominance as proof of the correctness of his judgment. In a similar, geoclimatic vein, Tacitus viewed Germanic tribes as strong, but disorganized savages. Pliny, another Roman author, added to this assertion by describing Rome's location as so salutary to human development that "the manner of the people are gentle, the intellect clear, the genius fertile and capable of comprehending every part of nature. They have formed empires which has never been done by the remote nations" (Pliny quoted in Thomas 1925:38).

Because of the protection afforded classical learning in Christian monasteries and Arab centers of scholarship, the major nature people theories of classical times survived the turmoil that followed the breakdown of Roman rule (Castaglioni 1958: 258–63). Environmental and astrological explanations, which were derived from classical speculations, dominated medieval science. These theories were relevant to understanding the medieval world and complemented the theology of the time.

Theoretical contributions of the Arab world elaborated on classical theories. The Arab conception of the human/environment relationship was twofold. One part consisted of an astrological explanation that considered humans to be part of the cosmos, as a result of which their character and outlook were determined by the ruling stars of their environment. The other

25

part was a purely geographical explanation based on climatic considerations (Alavi 1965:68). Elaborating upon the geographical explanation, Arab scholar Al-Mas'udi discussed the importance of the availability of water, natural vegetation, and topography in determining the sites of human settlements. He also correlated the climate to the humors of the body, showing how a certain climate gives rise to humoral imbalance and thus to particular virtues or vices (Alavi 1965:69-70). To quote Al-Mas'udi:

The Arabs preferred life in an open countryside, where the air was pure, wholesome and free from epidemics, and where there was refinement of intelligence and strength of body; for intelligence, they thought, was produced in the same way as fresh air. The Arabs are, therefore, marked by strength of resolution, wisdom and physical fitness. They take care of those whom they take under their protection, they are distinguished in acts of charity and possess good intelligence, for these qualities are produced by the purity of environment. (Al-Mas'udi quoted in Alavi 1965:70).

Arab scholars preserved and translated the Greco-Roman classics and, in the process, added some of their own interpretations to the texts. As a result, when the classics were read in twelfth and thirteenth century Europe, it was with the addition of commentaries by Arab and Jewish scholars from Cordoba, Seville, Toledo, Bagdad, and Damascus.

Theories of the Renaissance and Eighteenth Century   With the discovery of the East Indies and the New World, Europeans were thrust into contact with cultures and environments that differed considerably from their own. Among the adventurers, missionaries, and merchants of those days were naturalists and curious travelers; their accounts of the strange habitats and ways of native Asians and Americans excited intellectual interest in explaining cultural and environmental differences and similarities.

A new boldness, based on the discoveries of the natural sciences, fostered secular explanations for similarities and differences in plant and animal forms. Many of these explanations contributed to later evolutionary and adaptational approaches. As information on new environments continued to spread, writers of the Renaissance began to question Greco-Roman theories on the relationship between environment and human character. With a growing awareness of the oversimplifications in classical conceptions, Renaissance writers raised many questions, including whether climate had the same influence on all living things. The role of human culture in buffering the impact of environment upon society began to be appreciated, and the scope of possible explanations for similarities and differences in human populations was greatly expanded.

In the eighteenth century, climatic influences again became the focus of deterministic explanations. Bodin and Montesquieu, among others, reaffirmed the ancient notions that the middle latitudes were superior environments. (This time France was shown to be ideally located and predisposed for greatness!) The association of climate to physical and moral character was strongly made. During this period, theories were secularized as the role of religion and astrology was de-emphasized. Generalizations were rampant: whole regions were treated as uniform, and nations were seen as drawn together by the action of dominant civilizations.

Nineteenth and Twentieth Century Theories   In the late nineteenth century, a general trend toward organizing increasing amounts of archaeological and **ethnological** data resulted in an attempt to illuminate the processes by which human cultural history changes. A very simple heuristic device was quickly discovered—many cultures with similar artifacts and customs could be grouped by geographic location. Geographers and, later, **ethnographers** seized upon this notion. They viewed the interrelation of groups with their habitats as producing specific kinds of cultural traits.

Friedrich Ratzel (1844-1904), a scholar with broad ethnographic interests who was the founder of anthropogeography, emphasized the primacy of **habitat** in bringing about cultural diversity (Helm 1962:630). In his view, human society reacts to nature like any animal to its habitat. He explained human cultural evolution as being spurred by the conflicts over territory between migrating peoples. His thesis thus centered on the **migration** of groups, which promotes the diffusion of cultural traits (Harris 1968:383). While diffusion may produce divergence in the original traits, Ratzel believed that migratory peoples usually "hold fast to their natural conditions of existence [that is, culture]" (quoted in Thomas 1925:140).

Ratzel pointed out that, among other things, the "natural boundaries" created by topography and location give definition, distinction, coherence, and unity to such entities as political units. This particular politico-environmental relationship is twofold. First, similar locational conditions give rise to similar political models, as, for example, in all island societies (Thomas 1925:163). On the other hand, geographic diversity *within* a nation's territory can produce a variety of effects:

A variety of orographic [i.e., mountainous] features divides a state; ... mountains produce isolation and cultural stability, while lowlands promote racial and cultural mixture and migration; ... topography that promotes isolation and overexuberant flora [as in tropical forests] inevitably produces political and cultural stagnation. (quoted in Thomas 1925:165).

In explaining cultural similarities and differences as the result of the processes of migration and diffusion, Ratzel began a trend in both ethnography and evolutionism that viewed human beings as limited by their habitat in their range of responses.

The environmental determinist trend continued in the twentieth century with the work of geographers Ellsworth Huntington (1915) and Griffith Taylor (1951). Huntington's chief concern was to ascertain the bearing of various climatic, seasonal, and weather conditions upon human efficiency. According to this view, humans, when confronted with an environmental challenge, always take the path of least effort—for example, herding cattle in dry areas rather than farming and irrigating the land. Huntington and Taylor although acknowledging that several options may exist, believed that the best and most often utilized option is that which involves the least cost.

In general, Huntington believed that variations in temperature and humidity were beneficial, provided they were not taken to extremes. He eventually postulated what he came to regard as an ideal climate for maximum human efficiency: one with moderate seasonal changes, average humidity, and abundant storms. Although Huntington was far from naive, he formulated his generalizations as if climate were the only important factor.[1] Variations on this form of determinism are still expounded today. However, they are often tempered by a clearer awareness of the complex factors that may be involved in any human/habitat situation.

An elementary problem with these deterministic theories is their misuse of inductive reasoning. The inductive approach requires that one observe the facts and then form a generalization that will fit all the observed facts. It has been more common among determinists to formulate a generalization first and then set out to prove it with an unclear methodology and an inadequate sample. Selective sampling led to confirmation of many deterministic generalizations. At a time when so little was known about the workings of the physical world, it is striking how broad the scope of these generalizations was.

Human Adaptation to Environment

The Humoral Doctrine   Greco-Roman scientific concepts originated in attempts to cure disease and achieve a healthful balance. Disease was considered to be a disturbance of the natural harmony of the body. According to Hippocrates (460–375 BC), everything on the earth and in the universe was made up of four elements (air, earth, water, and fire) that had their analogues in the human body in the form of the four humors (blood, phlegm, black bile, and yellow bile). When the four humors were in balance, the body enjoyed health. Air was thought to be represented in the body by blood, both being hot and moist; fire by yellow bile (hot and dry); water by phlegm (cold and

[1]Reviews of the determinist tradition in geography are to be found in Minshull (1970:100–118) and Sprout and Sprout (1965).

moist); and earth by black bile (cold and dry). This theory, known as the *humoral doctrine*, significantly contributed to the development of environmental deterministic theories and also strongly influenced the development of soil theory, chemistry, and agriculture (Glacken 1967: 11–12). In addition, the humoral doctrine has also influenced psychological and physiological research on the influence of climate upon the body.

Such was the strength of humoral theory that alternative notions of human adaptation were rare throughout the Middle Ages and the Renaissance; and when such alternative theories were suggested, they linked diseases with environmental conditions. For example, Jose de Acosta (1539–1600) noted that individuals who traveled into high altitudes experienced mountain sickness, but those who lived there permanently seemed to have adjusted to the altitude (Leake 1964:4).

Purpose in Nature: The Problem of Misplaced Teleology   The eighteenth century witnessed the development of approaches that emphasized not the determining influence of environment, but the limitations that environment places upon all life. During this same period, the writings of Hume and Kant explored the question of teleology in nature. Teleology, which is the doctrine of final causes, implying purpose in the evolution of organisms, continues to be a crucial question in contemporary biology.

The great Lisbon earthquake of 1755 caused intellectuals to question the assumed order, harmony, and beneficence of nature and the validity of the wisdom of evolution (Glacken 1967:521). That disaster was probably the most catastrophic natural occurrence in western Europe since the eruption of Mount Vesuvius in 79 AD. It provoked such questions as: Why is such pain and devastation necessary? What is its purpose? Kant used the example of alluvial deposition to illustrate the weakness of teleological explanations: rivers carry soil in suspension and, during floods or high tides, deposit such soil on the banks; nature builds up soils this way to the benefit of human beings; was it the purpose of nature to benefit the farmers who would cultivate such alluvial soils?

According to Kant, use of nature does not prove that such use was intended by nature. Kant argued that the landscape and living forms on it are the result of historical events, not of final causes (Glacken 1967:535). Nevertheless, because human beings are aware of acting with purpose, projection of such purposiveness continued to make its way into ecological theories.

Evolutionary Sequences: Eighteenth Century Views   The eighteenth century was also a period when natural historians, concerned with human progress, formulated evolutionary sequences that attempted to explain human society in terms of increased human control over nature. One of these figures, Turgot (1727–1781), foreshadows the cultural ecological approach of Julian Steward (see chapter 3). In his *Universal History*, Turgot interpreted the band-organization of hunters as a response to the necessity of pursuing game over vast areas. Such pursuit resulted, in turn, in the dispersal and diffusion of peoples and ideas. On the other hand, where easily domesticated species were present, a pastoral way of life with greater population concentrations and greater control over resources might emerge.

During this period, the Scottish School (an intellectual elite in Scotland in the eighteenth century), made efforts to correlate social organization with **subsistence.** A major figure of this school was historian William Robertson. His *History of America* (1777) is a landmark for its discussion of the conditions for cultural similarities around the world. Robertson believed that cultural similarities were evidence of independent invention, arguing that similarities between the resource bases of two groups would lead to similar adaptive responses:

The character and occupations of the hunter in America must be little different from those of the Asiatic, who depend for subsistence on the chase. A tribe of savages on the banks of the Danube must nearly resemble one upon the Plains washed by the Mississippi. Instead of presuming from the similarities that there is any affinity between them, we should only conclude that the disposition and manners of men are formed by their situation, and arise from the state of society in which they live. (Robertson 1777:652, quoted in Harris 1968:34)

Whenever Robertson encountered seemingly "nonadaptive" traits, he attributed such behaviors to the group's borrowing the trait, despite its nonadaptiveness, from neighbors with whom they had had previous contact. Thus, Robertson dealt with two of the major research questions in cultural ecology: diffusion of traits vs. innovation or invention and the explanations for adaptive vs. maladaptive cultural behavior.

The Scottish School included many writers, such as Adam Smith (1723–1790), Adam Ferguson (1723–1816), David Hume (1711–1776), and James Millar (1735–1801), all of whom examined the evolution of complex societies and the cultural and materialistic forces that lead to social stratification (Voget 1975:90). These men looked at the interrelation of cultural units, especially those involved in the economics of a society, rather than the evolution of ideas per se. Some (for example, Adam Smith) emphasized the division of labor in systems of production as basic to understanding the increasing complexities of a modern nation (Ibid.: 78). Ferguson and Millar attempted to correlate various institutions, such as land tenure, marriage, and slavery, to the subsistence base found in various cultures. In so doing, they tried to correct some of the distorted accounts and explanations of primitive life by utilizing a variety of data sources and by avoiding racial and ethnocentric ideas about primitive "nature" or "intellect" (Harris 1968: 29–31).

Millar and others also emphasized control over resources and accumulation of an economic surplus as accounting for differing institutions. In the writings of these men, we see a growing awareness that any explanation of cultural diversity must include a consideration of a broad range of factors. They do not yield to single-factor deterministic explanations, nor do they overemphasize individual choice, cultural determinism, or the purposeful movement of nature towards "progress" and higher civilization. Turgot and the Scottish philosophers, unlike other eighteenth century evolutionists, emphasized adaptation rather than the evolution from one subsistence mode to another.

Buffon (1707–1788) and Cuvier (1769–1832) emphasized the functional interrelations of different parts of living things and the relevance of the study of past living forms for understanding the present. Buffon thought that change in an environment had little impact on the structures of individual living things. Lamarck (1744–1829), on the other hand, suggested that change could occur in individual morphology during a creature's lifetime as an adjustment to environmental change and that these changes could then be passed on, and intensified, through inheritance (Leake 1964:5). Advances in evolutionary theories were particularly remarkable in the nineteenth century.

Darwin's Theory of Evolution   The nineteenth century was the heyday of the naturalists. Their careful recording of the similarities and differences in living organisms impressed them and stimulated their search for explanations. The contributions of Charles Darwin (1809–1882) to ecological theory are particularly notable. Darwin found inspiration for his theory of evolution in the works of Charles Lyell and Thomas Malthus (1766–1834). Darwin took a copy of Lyell's *Principles of Geology* (1830) with him on his Beagle voyage and confided in his diary that it "altered the whole tone of [his] mind." Through Lyell's account of the geological record, Darwin saw an alternative to the narrow Biblical time-scale and was impressed by the relationship between environmental change and modifications in biological forms. Malthus's *An Essay on the Principle of Population* (1798) influenced Darwin with its idea that the natural trend of the human population was to increase unless stopped by disease, war, or famine. Darwin extended this notion to plant and animal populations.

Darwin's synthesis appeared in 1859 under a misnomer, *On the Origin of Species by Means of Natural Selection*. In this work, Darwin did not really explain the origin, but rather the mechanisms by which species develop and diversify. Darwin began by assuming that all living things are related and that the diversity of species results from a continual branching out. Such branching is a product of the process known as natural selection. According to the principle of natural selection, those organisms most fit to survive and reproduce in a given environment will outreproduce less well-adapted organisms; species not adapted to current environmental conditions will be reduced to insignificant numbers and possibly to extinction.

Evolution includes what may be termed *mechanisms of continuity* and *mechanisms of variation* (Alland, 1973:4). Mechanisms of continuity provide stability in nature, while mechanisms of variation are the product of chance and provide the variability in species that allows new solutions to be available when environmental changes occur. If **biological evolution** reflected only the process of adaptation to environment, it would be a static, nonevolutionary process. For evolutionary change to occur, there must be random changes in species that are not responses to current needs, but that under given circumstances give an advantage to individuals who share the trait in a population.

It is easy to misunderstand Darwin's view of natural selection. The process is not a product of chance. Quite the contrary. It is directional and in due time leads to adaptive solutions. Natural selection does not require that all or most variations be in adaptive directions, but only that *some* improve the fitness of organisms. Indeed, naturalists had long observed that some do. Nor did Darwin believe that natural selection was the only guiding force of evolution. He lacked, however, the knowledge of *how* favorable characteristics were passed on.

Modern Evolutionary Theory   Unlike the theory of evolution, which is very general, the knowledge required in determining how natural selection works is very specific. The science of genetics provides an exact accounting of the sources of variation and continuity in organisms. While environment has a strong influence on the individual, it cannot transform it beyond the bounds of its own heredity. Every organism is the product of its own particular environmental history and of its genetic heritage (Alland 1973:11).

Modern evolutionary theory and genetics have put to rest the simplistic notions of determinism. The functions and forms of organisms can be understood only by careful accounting of complex processes of interaction. This is best expressed in the contrast between genotype and phenotype. The genotype refers to the hereditary potential of an organism. The phenotype, on the other hand, is the product of the interaction between the genotype and the environment where the organism is located. Some species tolerate a minimum of environmental change and exhibit a minimum of phenotype variation (that is, highly specialized species). Bacteria, for one, tolerate only minute differences in habitat temperature. The human species, by contrast, manifests great phenotypic variations and can tolerate a wide range of environmental conditions (that is, generalized species).

The basic elements of evolutionary theory are, briefly: (1) all populations are capable of genetic variation through the mechanisms of mutation and recombination, (2) all populations seek to increase their numbers exponentially until restricted by environmental constraints, (3) under a given set of environmental circumstances, the best-adapted phenotypes in a population will be selected for, and (4) the effect of the environment on the genotype is indirect. Adaptive changes in all organisms, including human beings, are mediated by the genetic hereditary material passed on from generation to generation. "The evolutionary fitness of the *particular* combination of hereditary traits embodied in an organism is largely determined by interaction of the organism with its environment during its lifetime" (Ricklefs 1973:69). Since more fit individuals who possess the best-adapted traits must replace a population, evolutionary change is always slow. A population thus often reflects earlier conditions and is always in process of change—just as the environment is always changing (Levins 1968:11).

Biological adaptation is seldom perfect and is opposed by numerous factors. Among these are mutations and **gene flow,** evolutionary opportunity, physical limits, problems of allocation, and changing environments (Ricklefs 1973:71–73). No matter how well adapted a population may be, new random mutations occur and are introduced into a population, leading to change. The past history of an organism limits future changes, so that major changes in anatomy are rare and may take millennia. The range of adaptation is also limited by the properties of the natural world, and these cannot be easily altered either. Adaptation is essentially a compromise. The results are seldom the "best," but represent solutions to conflicting priorities, and if they are to be advantageous and selected, they must increase fitness over the cost (Levins 1968:35). Adaptation is never perfect because environments are always changing, and populations must constantly readjust to the new environmental conditions. Since biological change is slow, populations are rarely in perfect adaptation to their present situation—except in rare cases of long-term environmental stability.[2]

Nature as Limiting Factor: Malthus and Possibilism

Unlike deterministic theories which emphasize the influence of nature on the behavior and institutions of people, theories of nature as a limiting factor were based on an awareness that populations do not exploit their habitat to the fullest and when they begin to do so, environmental factors limit their capacity to expand in numbers. These theories view nature as a relatively static factor that prevents human growth or the performance of given actions. The idea of limiting factors seemed to appear after the Age of Discovery and continues up to the present. It is an important element of population ecology and serves to explain the dynamic aspects of community structure.

The notion of limiting factors was most clearly stated by Justus Liebig around 1840. His contribution, known as "the law of the minimum,"

---

[2]Readers will find stimulating discussions of evolutionary theory in Levins (1968), Bajema (1971), and Lewontin (1968). The journal *Evolution* is particularly recommended.

explained that organisms were limited by the factor in most limited supply. When the principle is extended to include the limiting effect of too much and the limiting effect of one thing on the rest of the system, we have a broadly encompassing concept of wide applicability. In ecological research the concept of limiting factors points the researcher in the direction of empirically accounting for nonconstant factors whose supply may be limiting. For example, nutrients like nitrogen and phosphorus may be rapidly leached from the soil under some management practices and account for declines in yield, village fissioning, fallow cycles, and even choices of crops.

The most memorable effort to show the limitations of the earth as an abode for human beings is that of Malthus in the late eighteenth century. He was neither interested in how environment molds culture, nor in how human cultures have modified the environment. According to Malthus, all living things have a tendency to increase geometrically if they have enough food. However, once good soils have been put into production, populations find increasing difficulty in providing enough food for the rapidly growing population. Disease, war, famine, and other forms of population control enter to reduce the pressure on resources. His views continue to have relevance today. The notion of Spaceship Earth and of the limited resources of the biosphere were clearly in evidence in the writings of Malthus.

A very different view of environmental limitations was proposed by Franz Boas (1858-1942). His approach has been called one of **historical possibilism**—that is, nature circumscribes the possibilities for humans, but historical and cultural factors explain what possibility is actually chosen. Boas rejected the idea that the environment was a primary molder of culture (Boas 1896:901-908) and sought explanation for cultural differences in the particular cultural history of a people. Boas did not come to this position immediately but, rather, after initial acceptance of the environmental deterministic views of his day. He read Buckle and Ritter, major exponents of deterministic views. He was also influenced by Adolf Bastian (1826-1905), the well-traveled German ethnographer who wrote about folkways around the world. Bastian saw variation in geographical conditions as the basic source of cultural variations. When Boas went on his trip to Baffin Island to study the Eskimo, he did so "with a strong presumption in favor of the primacy of geographical factors in the life of the Eskimo" (Harris 1968:265). His account, *The Central Eskimo* (1964, originally published in 1888) is a lucid portrayal of life in the arctic, stressing the interrelationship between geographical and cultural factors.

Thereafter, however, Boas gave the geographical setting only a perfunctory role in his work. For Boas, people use what they want in nature, and it is such cultural decisions not nature, that dictate the direction of cultural change. In other words, culture is environmentally selective (Bennett 1976:165). In Boas's scheme, culture takes precedence over environmental settings. The ethnological inquiry began with the perceptions, interests, wants, and actions of humans as conditioned by their social milieu. The Boasian approach set out to correct environmental determinism, but in so doing introduced a strong culture-centeredness. The environment is seen not as a dynamic influence, but only as a limiting one in which cultural forms are "manifested and stabilized in a distinct geographical milieu at the moment of study" (Ibid.: 162). Culture as the basis of human behavior became such a dominant outlook in anthropology that even recent discussions of human adaptation (for example, Cohen, 1968; Sahlins, 1964) continue to state this as a given, rather than as a subject of inquiry.

In *The Mind of Primitive Man* (1911), Boas pointed out that the environment furnishes the material out of which people shape and develop the artifacts of daily life as well as their theories, beliefs, and customs (Thomas 1925:278). Yet while he granted that the environment had a general influence, Boas criticized the one-sided notion that the same type of environment will in a given stage of culture produce the same results everywhere. He noted that, in the arctic, Eskimo subsistence is based on hunting and fishing, while the Siberian Chukchee derive their support from the breeding of reindeer. At the opposite climatic extreme, the Hottentot follow a pastoral life, while the Bushmen rely on hunting in a semitropical environment (Thomas 1925:279). Boas and his students pointed out that customs that may have originated in one habitat can be perpetuated by "cultural inertia" after the group has moved to a new location in which the custom is no longer appropriate. Examples cited are the expensive and complicated tents of the Chukchee—a survival from the time when they were permanent dwellers on the coast (Goldenweiser 1937:446-447).

Boas's emphasis on the particular circumstances of a population led him to fruitless efforts at explaining cultural similarities in terms of geographical proximity or economic forces. In the data he collected, he found no significant law to cover the relationship between social organization and industrial activities. He even denied any causality between religion and art forms. Boas did not deny that all these factors could have a determining influences, but instead maintained that they were determinative in an unpredictable way and in a manner unique to each case. Such eclecticism was a natural reaction to the facile systematization and assignment of causality that were the hallmarks of his deterministic predecessors. Boas, like Francis Bacon before him, glorified the inductive method as correcting the lack of data behind scientific doctrine (Harris 1968:287). He demanded from his students careful collection of data, suspension of generalization, critical analysis of materials, and conservative excursions into the general.

While the followers of Boas insisted that there was no Boasian school, there was a certain common ground that they shared. Regarding the environment, their approach was a reaction to environmental determinism and, therefore, iconoclastic in character. Lowie (1883–1957), for one, in his *Cul-*

ture and *Ethnology* (1917) set out to disprove the deterministic notions that "culture reaches its highest stages in temperate regions"; that the concept of liberty is directly correlated with altitude; and that island inhabitants are accomplished seafarers. Lowie argued that under the same geographical conditions, radically different cultures have developed. As examples, he pointed to the differences between the native cultures of North America and the modern civilization that quickly arose in that same environment. He sought to tighten his argument by studying racially and culturally related populations (i.e., the Hopi and the Navaho) within comparable environments. Despite their occupation of similar regions in the Southwest, Lowie showed their cultures to be markedly different. Lowie attempted to demonstrate that the availability of a resource does not predispose a population to use it in any particular manner. North American Indians did not domesticate the buffalo, nor the Eskimo the reindeer. Like Boas before him, and Goldenweiser thereafter (1937:443-454), Lowie showed how culture defines what is a resource or, in other words, "a culture assigns revelance to particular external conditions" (Sahlins 1964).

Goldenweiser's view was similar to Lowie's and Boas's in that he saw the environment as a static force and culture as the dynamic element that shaped the use of natural resources. He also suggested the important argument, later to be used by Ferndon (1959), that man changes the natural environment (for example, he turns forests into cultivated fields) and as a result man makes his own environment instead of being determined by it (Goldenweiser 1937:452-3).

The "cultural area" approach also accounts for the little effort spent on establishing direct relationships between aspects of cultural systems and the environment. In this approach, continents were divided into culture areas based on shared linguistic characteristics and a mixed bag of cultural traits. This emphasis on shared traits was based on the strong assumption that diffusion may have occurred. The basis for that assumption can be traced to the work of the German and British diffusionists and, more immediately, to the work of Wissler (1870-1947). Wissler had noted that maps of geological and ecological features matched areas of cultural features. From this observation he postulated the diffusionist **age-area concept.** According to this principle, traits tend to diffuse outward in all directions from their point of origin. The more widely distributed a trait from its origin, the older it is. Environment in this scheme is an inert configuration and at its most active is seen as passively setting limits to cultural development (Wissler 1926).

Kroeber (1876-1960), like other anthropologists of his day, subscribed to the Boasian credo that the physical environment is there merely to be acted upon by human culture. However, unlike the other Boasians, Kroeber completely subordinated the individual to his cultural milieu. Kroeber elaborated this idea in his notion of the "superorganic in culture." According to this idea, in all cultures the individual is subordinated to the cultural pattern and is an agent of inevitable cultural forces. The implication of this view is that scientific understanding of historical processes and social evolution is impossible.

In his 1939 book *Cultural and Natural Areas of Native North America*, Kroeber briefly departed from his usual approach and followed the scheme earlier proposed by Wissler. Kroeber organized his descriptive material into regional categories developed from data on subsistence systems, habitat characteristics, and population densities. In this work he momentarily admits that "no culture is wholly intelligible without reference to . . . environmental factors with which it is in relation, and which condition it" (Kroeber 1939:205). He gives extensive examples of how environmental factors limit and define such cultural practices as maize farming, population concentration, and tribal and linguistic boundaries.

Kroeber's approach in *Cultural and Natural Areas* can be likened to that of his contemporary, British geographer/anthropologist C.D. Forde (1902-1973). Both of them emphasized the need for collecting ecological data and viewed such data as *potentially* valuable in explaining cultural similarities. Both, however, eventually returned to a possibilist stance. Forde, for example, after summarizing the history of economic systems in relation to ecology and social organization, concluded that neither an evolutionary sequence of "economic stages" nor the nature of the subsistence base will explain the changes in a group's culture (Forde 1934). He therefore warned other geographers against racial, geographical, and economic determinism (Minshull 1970:18). Economic and social activities, he concluded, are products of the long, but largely unpredictable, processes of cultural accumulation and integration.

Kroeber's conclusions in *Cultural and Natural Areas* resemble those of Forde's in *Habitat, Economy and Society* (1934). With that effort, Kroeber's fleeting use of technoenvironmental explanation ended, and he turned his idea of culture area increasingly towards the Wisslerian notions of diffusion and "areas of culture origins." In regard to his culture/environment explorations, he became baffled and wrote: "The interaction of culture and environment become increasingly complex when followed out. And this complexity makes generalization unprofitable, on the whole. In each situation or area, different natural factors are likely to be impinging on culture with different intensity" (1939:205).

Despite this inability and/or unwillingness to deal with irregularities in human/environment interaction, Kroeber's *Cultural and Natural Areas* is of major importance in that it forms the backdrop to the formulation of the cultural ecological approach. Although Kroeber was unwilling to accept the idea that modes of subsistence are causally and functionally related to social structure, his efforts demonstrated a comprehensiveness that remains impressive to this day.

Summary

From Greco-Roman times through the 1950s, ideas about the relationship between people and nature emphasized three main themes. One was the notion that the environment exercised a determining influence on human society. According to Greco-Roman conceptions this influence took place through the action of climate upon the body—favoring health, intelligence, and good government. Such a view was generally accepted well into the eighteenth century. In the nineteenth and twentieth century the focus of explanation shifted to the role of geographical features and their influence on society. While writers admitted that differences in response were possible, they emphasized that humans usually took the path of least effort and thereby yielded to the forces of environment.

The second theme was that of human adaptation to environment. These views emphasized the interaction of human beings with nature. Greco-Roman theories expounded on the effect of environment upon the humors of the body and on the characteristics of people living in unbalanced climates. Eighteenth century writers addressed the problem of teleology and causality in nature and proposed stages along which human society progressed. With each stage, human beings gained increased control over resources and greater independence from the environment's weighty influence. The development of evolutionary theory and genetics gave further impetus to the adaptational approach by providing a theory and a method that simultaneously helped explain change and continuity. This approach was fundamental to the emergence of a modern theory of people/nature relationships.

The third theme was that of environment as a circumscribing or limiting factor. This view, which was espoused by Malthus and then by Boas and others, demonstrated little sensitivity about nature, but a clear awareness of the human side of the equation. The Boasian approach must be understood as a reaction to the broad generalizations of determinists and as an effort to return scientific investigation to empirical and more modest goals.

The three themes are not totally distinct, and the same authors emphasized one idea over another in different contexts. Determinism and possibilism are really the two ends of the spectrum of human/habitat interaction. One overemphasizes nature, the other people. They are not so much contradictory, as overzealous efforts at explanation. The adaptational/evolutionary approach served as the mediating model between the two extremes. The efforts up to the 1950s to provide a more satisfactory explanation of observed facts exercised an important intellectual influence on the more recent development of theories. These will be taken up in the next chapter.

Recommended Readings

Numerous articles and chapters in books review the history of anthropological interest in ecology. The most scholarly source on the history preceding the eighteenth century is Glacken's *Traces on the Rhodian Shore* (1967). Glacken discusses the development of ideas about nature and culture in Western thought and finds three dominating concerns: the earth as designed for human beings alone; the environment as a modifying influence on human beings; and human beings as a modifying influence on nature. The book is based on research of primary sources and serves as an excellent starting point for analyses of the evolution of ideas in cultural ecology.

The other essential source on this early period is Thomas's work, *The Environmental Basis of Society* (1925). It is weaker than Glacken's on the Greek, Roman, and medieval periods. However, its discussion of the period from the eighteenth century to the 1920s is very useful. Glacken's book is organized chronologically and within each period by the three ideas around which he organizes the material. Thomas's book is strictly chronological. Brief surveys on the theoretical development of the period up to Julian Steward are found in Helm (1962); Geertz (1963:1-11); Sahlins (1964); Netting (1968:3-25); Vayda and Rappaport (1976); Bennett (1976); and Netting (1977).

From Cultural
Ecology to
Ecological
Anthropology

The period since the 1950s has been a productive one for ecological approaches. Julian Steward began to formulate his themes in the 1930s, but his research strategy was not implemented until the 1950s. Unlike Kroeber, who sought general theory in his research efforts, Steward aimed at what has been called *middle-range theory*. Steward delimited a range of phenomena and sought to explain the cause-and-effect relations between such phenomena. His use of the **comparative approach** to verify these connections is essentially that of anthropology: to compare societies across time and space in search of valid generalizations about human behavior. Steward's approach, which has come to be known as *cultural ecology,* led young scholars into the field and is responsible for the correction of many assumptions about human society. A more biological approach to cultural ecology followed in the 1960s. This approach, which relied heavily on evolutionary and ecological theory, has come to be known as *ecological anthropology* to indicate the importance assigned to the ecological system. The multidisciplinary approach of ecological anthropology emphasizes the study of human populations within ecosystems. Its research has focused on relatively stable societies.

In this chapter we will first discuss Steward's approach and then how it was applied by researchers. The cultural ecological approach was helpful in reconsidering the subsistence system of **hunter/gatherers, pastoralists,** preindustrial **cultivators,** and even that of modern farmers. The approach, however, neglected many ecological variables, such as disease, physiological change, genetics, and energy quantification. Critics have even found that crucial cultural variables could be neglected as a result of the a priori importance assigned to subsistence activities. The rest of the chapter will explore the approaches of ecological anthropology and **ethnoecology,** each of which represents efforts to overcome these deficiencies.

Steward's Cultural Ecology

Julian Steward's early writings broke with both determinism and possibilism by rejecting general theory and emphasizing the use of the comparative method to test causal connections between **social structure** and modes of subsistence. Steward saw social institutions as having a functional unity that could not be diffused or imitated as wholes—except insofar as they provided solutions to recurrent subsistence problems or when the recipient society already had all the prerequisites for that change. Steward's approach was a **functionalist** one, concerned with the operation of a variable in relation to a limited set of variables, not in relation to an entire social system. Unlike the British functionalists who emphasized the role of institutions in the maintenance of structural equilibrium at a given point in time (that is, they employed a **synchronic** approach), Steward limited his scope within one system. However, his interest in evolution led him to study change in time and across societies (that is, he used a **diachronic** approach). Steward's functionalism was not so much concerned with equilibrium as with change and the causal connections that led to it.

The cultural ecological approach proposed by Steward involves both a problem and a method. The problem is to test whether the adjustments of human societies to their environments require specific types of behavior or whether there is considerable latitude in human responses (Steward 1955a:36). The method consists of three procedures: (1) to analyze the relationship between subsistence system and environment; (2) to analyze the behavior patterns associated with a given subsistence technology; and (3) to ascertain the extent to which the behavior pattern entailed in a given subsistence system affects other aspects of culture (Ibid.: 40–41). In short, the cultural ecological approach postulates a relationship between environmental resources, subsistence technology, and the behavior required to bring technology to bear upon resources.

The crucial element in Steward's approach is neither nature nor culture-bearing humans. Rather, it is the process of resource utilization, in its fullest sense, that interested him. The reasons for the priority he gave to subsistence are clear: obtaining food and shelter are immediate and urgent problems in all societies, and patterns of work at a given level of technology are limited in their ability to exploit resources. The approach is best illustrated by his study of the Western Shoshoni.

The Shoshoni inhabited the Great Basin of North America, a semiarid land with widely dispersed resources. The Shoshoni were hunter/gatherers with simple tools who relied heavily on the collection of grass seeds, roots, and berries. Steward showed how almost every resource could best be exploited by individuals—except rabbits and antelope which required seasonal group hunting. Each fall the Shoshoni gathered pine nuts that were stored for the long, cold winter. Although in winter they formed larger population concentrations, they did not form stable social units because pine nuts were not available in the same places each year, and groups therefore had to remain fluid to adequately exploit the Basin. Thus, the requirements of subsistence produced fluid and fragmentary social units that were lacking in distinct patterns of leadership.

To Steward, the Shoshoni presented an extreme case of the limitations placed by environment on the workable options available to a culture. Like the adaptational writers discussed in the last chapter, Steward hypothesized that the immediate impact of environment upon behavior decreased as techological complexity improved the human capacity to modify the environment. He even suggested that in complex societies social factors may be more important in explaining change than subsistence technology or environment (Steward 1938: 262).

The research strategy proposed by Steward is all the more striking if one considers its historical backdrop. Until Steward's time, human/habitat theories either dealt in broad generalities lacking a firm grounding in empirical research or emphasized lists of cultural traits. Cultural ecology put the emphasis on the study of behavior patterns—careful analysis of social interaction, recording of movement, timing of work activity, and so forth. Through such research it was possible to more effectively delimit the field of study and arrive at cause-and-effect relationships.

In an earlier study (1936), Steward compared hunter/gatherers in extremely varied environments. The groups chosen lived in territorially based bands and were also characterized by patrilocal residence, patrilineal descent, and **exogamous** marriage. The environmental determinist approach had long been baffled by the social similarities between groups as different as the Kalahari Bushmen, the Australian aborigines, and the rain forest pygmies. Steward showed that the ecological parallels between these groups were low population density, reliance on foot transportation, and the hunting of scattered nonmigratory animals. The requirements of knowing the resources of a territory anchored each population to it. Their limited means of transportation reduced the range that could be effectively exploited and favored the maintenance of low densities. Although not totally correct in his conclusion, Steward motivated others to study the interactions of hunter/gatherers with their habitats. Some of the results of those studies are discussed in the next section.

Steward has been criticized by some scholars because his approach is difficult to operationalize in the field and because it assigns primacy to subsistence behaviors. The focus on subsistence is essential to the cultural ecological approach, but it does not deal adequately with every research situation. There are cases when other factors may have far greater control over a social system, and over the years Steward expanded the scope of cultural ecology to include political, religious, military, and aesthetic features of culture (1955a: 93). Geertz (1963) concluded in his study of Indonesian agriculture that historical and political factors are part of the total environment to which populations adapt and must not be dismissed as secondary. Rappaport, a few years later, showed how ritual could play a central role in the maintenance of a society's balance with resources (1968).

While revolutionary in his emphasis on human/environment interactions, Steward seemed to have slighted several environmental phenomena that could well affect the cultural development of human groups. For instance, he had little to say regarding the influences of demographic makeup, epidemiology, competition with other groups in a given area, or human physiological adaptations (Vayda and Rappaport 1976: 16–17). These phenomena, however, were only recognized as "appropriate" for anthropological study after Steward had formulated the concept and method of cultural ecology. More serious is the charge that the comparative approach cannot yield cause-and-effect relationships. Vayda and Rappaport question whether correlations between adaptations and cultural traits can be translated into causes and effects (Ibid.: 14). Steward never followed a clear statistical sample, and his correlations left out the number of cases in which the correlation did not hold. Steward usually succeeded in demonstrating functional relationships, but not in establishing causality.

The contribution of Steward was to delimit, more than anyone before him, the field of human/environment interaction. He did so by emphasizing behavior, subsistence, and technology. The weaknesses of such an approach became apparent within a decade and spawned other research strategies. Few contemporary students of the relationship between people and enviroment can deny the influence of Steward upon their thinking.

Application of the Cultural Ecological Method

In the 1950s field-workers began using the cultural ecological method to study old and new problems. It is sometimes hard to identify the intellectual thrust of scientists. Those following the Stewardian style of cultural ecology tend to utilize a culturally defined human population as their unit of study, to focus on cultural rather than biological adaptations, and to personally acknowledge a direct debt to Julian Steward (Netting 1968: 11).[1] These studies tend to concentrate on culture, rather than on the environment or even the interphase of the two. Most of these authors do not claim to be anything else but cultural anthropologists—who use an ecological approach to cultural study. The danger in this approach is that it claims to be "ecological," but in fact mainly discusses cultural factors. The method of cultural ecology has been applied to the study of hunter/gatherer, preindustrial farmers, pastoralists, and contemporary rural societies.

Hunter/Gatherers Cultural ecological research has led to a revision of our understanding of hunter/gatherers. Earlier, they were viewed as populations at the mercy of unpredictable resources, constantly under threat of starvation, and primarily concerned with subsistence. Field research since the time of Steward has demolished that simplistic notion. A rich variety of social forms, complex adjustments to neighbors and resources, and, in some cases, a life of relative leisure and security have been revealed. Important in this respect are *Man the Hunter* (Lee and DeVore 1968), *Hunters and Gatherers Today* (Bichieri 1972), and the work of the Harvard Kalahari Research Group (cf., Lee and DeVore 1976; Yellen 1977).

These new interpretations of the lives of hunter/gatherers resulted from the careful gathering of data on labor time and on the weighted yields from hunter/gatherer efforts. Important, too, were improved data on the prehistoric distributions of hunter/gatherers. Such investigation showed

---

[1]This section on cultural ecological applications owes a great deal to Netting (1977). Readers wishing greater detail on these discussions are urged to consult Netting's work or his older module (1971).

Figure 3.1   **Female Gatherers of Wild Plants**
Photograph from Anthro-Photo by M. Shostak.

hunter/gatherers to be present in most of the habitable globe in 10,000 BC and particularly concentrated on the areas that later supported populations of agricultural peoples. By 1900, however, their range had shrunk to extremely marginal areas, and their way of life had been threatened with extinction. It was under these later conditions that most ethnographic research was conducted, and it comes as no surprise that the first impressions were of an impoverished way of making a living. In the early years of anthropology, field-workers used the recollections of informants to reconstruct the ancient ways of life, paying particular attention to ideology. Later, more attention was given to the study of observed behavior, and contrasts were drawn with the stated norms of the population (Lee and DeVore 1968: 5).

Since hunting/gathering is essentially a mode of subsistence, it was a particularly attractive topic for cultural ecologists. Steward had formulated his classic comparison of patrilineal bands using hunter/gatherers as samples. Because these populations are in most intimate contact with their habitat, the interaction between nature and humans is very explicit among them. Hunter/gatherers also form relatively small groups so that quantification of relevant variables is more feasible among them than among other groups, such as those found in terrace-irrigation societies.

Although the hunter/gatherers' way of life is highly flexible and complex, it is still possible to make some generalizations. Hunter/gatherers appear to live in small groups and to be fairly mobile. They operate in territories, but do not appear to have closed social systems. From the very beginning, reciprocal visiting and marriage alliances appear to have operated to form larger breeding and linguistic communities than those found in small, localized bands. Male hunters and female gatherers of wild plants fan out from base camps and bring back foodstuffs that are shared by all (see figure 3.1) Because mobility is important, personal property is kept to a minimum and egalitarian conditions predominate. Generally groups are kept small to prevent deterioration of the primary producers (i.e., plants) or game depletion. Bands, however, are flexible in size so that they can adjust to the fluctuating availability of food sources. Such variations in food supply seem to have encouraged the development of reciprocal visiting and food sharing with guests. Conflict is generally avoided, and *fission* (that is, partitioning of the group) is a common response to social friction when it does arise.

From this basic social outline, specific cultural features are likely to have developed in response to the particular conditions of a habitat or the history of a population. W. Suttles (1968), for example, has pointed out that the fishermen of the Northwest Pacific Coast of North America may have started as nomadic bands, but were led into surplus accumulation, stable settlement, and larger population concentrations in response to the peculiar abundance of their salmon supply.[2]

Preindustrial Cultivators The cultural ecological literature on cultivators is even more extensive than the literature on hunter/gatherers. All the subfields of anthropology have attempted to explain the origins of agriculture and the contemporary worldwide patterns of food production. Writings on farming societies that preceded the development of cultural ecology dealt only briefly with farming behavior and production. When the farming methods of preindustrial peoples were discussed, they were

---

[2]Much of the work that permitted these new views on the hunting/gathering way of life occurred during the 1960s and 1970s. Our brief discussion does not do justice to the large number of workers involved and the data they generated on this ancient subsistence mode. Readers are encouraged to consult the sources previously mentioned (Lee, 1968 1969; Lee and DeVore, 1968, 1976; W. Suttles, 1968), as well as the works of Woodburn among the Hadza (1968); of Damas (1968) and Laughlin (1963) on Eskimos; of Peterson (1975) and Yengoyan (1968, 1976) on Australian aborigines; of Flannery (1968) on the prehistoric bands of the Tehuacan valley; of Bishop among the Ojibwa (1970) of Hudson Bay; and of Yellen in the Kalahari (1977).

often unfavorably compared with modern agricultural methods. The comparison also pitted tropical cultivators against temperate cultivators and assigned a higher value to the latter's emphasis on grain crops and domestic animals. The revision of the anthropological view of agricultural societies and productivity began with the work of Harold Conklin (1954, 1957, 1961) among the Hanunóo of the Philippines.[3] What he discovered was an intricately complex agricultural system based on shifting agriculture that exhibited sound agronomic management and achieved high levels of productivity per unit of labor spent. *Shifting agriculture* refers to a mode of cultivation in which fields are cropped for fewer years than they are allowed to remain fallow.[4]

Geertz (1963) demonstrated that two models were dominant in Indonesian agricultural systems. He showed how traditional shifting agriculture in the outer islands produced an imitation of the natural forest vegetation. The system supported low population, but was also low in labor costs. The other model, the increasingly complex irrigated rice paddy system of the inner islands, was described by Geertz as a response to the historical and cultural experience of colonialism. In the rice paddy system, ever greater amounts of labor were spent to sustain the demands of a colonial power. Carneiro's important studies of the Kuikuru Indians of Brazil (1957, 1961, 1970) showed that large settlements could be maintained in the tropical forest by using shifting agriculture, and, most importantly, by planting the high-yielding root crop manioc *(Manihot esculenta* Crantz).

While the development of agriculture has been commonly associated with the diffusion of sophisticated tools from a few centers of cultural innovation (Childe 1951), the new cultural ecological research has pointed out that intensive cultivation was often practiced with only rudimentary tools. Netting (1968) described the complex **intercropping** practice of the Kofyar of Northern Nigeria and showed that it was very efficient even though the group lacked draft animals and modern farming technology. Farming practices have thus been interpreted as adjustments to the particular ecological situation in which a group finds itself (Carneiro 1957; Conklin 1957; Moran 1976; Sanchez and Buol 1975).

---

[3]The British functionalists produced valuable studies during the 1930s and 1940s in which excellent descriptions of agricultural systems were made (see Richards 1939). However, their efforts to fit the data into equilibrium models limited the cultural ecological value of these studies. Equilibrium models are discussed in the next chapter.

[4]Shifting agriculture is a dominant land preparation technique in 30 percent of the world's cultivable soils, especially those covered by tropical forests. It is also known as *swidden, slash-and-burn, milpa, citemene,* and innumerable other names (Conklin 1963). Some of these are special forms of **swidden agriculture** that represent adjustments to local conditions. Citemene is an adaptation to the soil conditions, limited vegetation, and low labor areas of Central Africa (Allan 1965). Citemene includes the clearing of an area larger than that which will be cultivated and the piling up of the vegetation into a restricted area. In other words, since fallow periods have been reduced, the amount of vegetation is inadequate for a good burn, and added areas must be cleared.

Cumulative evidence has begun to show that the move from extensive shifting cultivation to a more intensive labor system only occurs when increasing population density puts too much pressure on current resources (Boserup 1965; Clarke 1966). A study that supports this view showed that a given area of irrigated land could support fourteen times as many families as it could with shifting agriculture—but only with a great increase in labor cost (Palerm 1968). A volume by Spooner (1972) contains useful articles on the arguments and merits of this causal explanation of agricultural intensification. Opposite views have been aired by Bronson (1972, 1975), Moerman (1968), Geertz (1963), and Rawski (1972). Bronson argued that cultivators may seek to invest labor for prestige, even at the expense of labor efficiency (1972). Moerman emphasized that social rewards or values may influence preferences in labor utilization (1968). Geertz convincingly showed that intensification could be a result not of population pressure, but of political domination and colonial exploitation (1963). Intensification may also result simply from economic opportunity, as producers seek to improve their exchange rates and income (Rawski 1972). The debate is far from concluded, and readers may wish to join in research efforts that may some day give us a clearer view of the processes of agricultural intensification.

Since cultural ecologists are, above all, cultural anthropologists, they have shown great interest in the relationship between farming practices and social organization. For example, Sahlins (1957) showed how extended family units predominated in an area of widely separated food sources. Netting (1968) found that where cultivation involves small areas of land but demands continual care, the nuclear family may be sufficient to supply the necessary labor. Researchers have also shown that rights to resources "are not simply correlates of particular stages in social evolution, manifestations of cultural values or legal creations. Rather, such rights are bound up with the *way* a resource is used and the degree of competition for it" (Netting 1977: 75).

An indication of the increased sophistication of cultural ecological analyses is evident in a statistical comparison of seventeen Highland New Guinea populations (Brown and Podolefsky 1976). This analysis showed that a shift took place in the ownership pattern as the population density increased and agriculture intensified. The authors generalize that individual land tenure occurs in societies with a fallow period of six years or less and that group ownership is found in areas with longer fallow periods. Although this statistical correlation does not demonstrate causality, it does show the close interaction between demography, technology, and cultural practices.

It is obviously impossible to review all the works relevant to the cultural ecology of farming societies in this chapter overview. Possibly the best review of the literature on agrarian ecology is that of Netting (1974a). It is clear, that the direction of studies is toward increased sophistication in data collecting and increased concern with the processes of decision-making among cultivators. Party to this evolution is the growing interaction between economic anthropology and cultural ecology—evident in the work of Johnson (1971, 1974), Bennett (1969), and Netting (1968) to name but a few. Such interaction is also apparent in the adoption of a new brand of ecological analysis within anthropology—*systems ecology*—which will be discussed later in this chapter.

Pastoralists   The interest of cultural ecologists in pastoralist societies has also lead to the revision of some hallowed assumptions of the past. This can best be seen in the reinterpretation of the East African cattle complex. The *cattle complex* refers to dominant cultural values among East African pastoralists that lead to alleged inefficient and irrational use of cattle. According to the original interpretation (Herskovits 1926), the peculiar characteristics of the East African Cattle Complex—for example, the herdsman's strong attachment to cattle—simply represent an irrational use of cattle, rather than rational use of cattle for economic or social purposes.

Cultural ecological and economic analyses have substantially changed this view. The new interpretations see the East African devotion to cattle keeping and to maximizing the number of cattle as an effective utilization of a biome that is marginal for agriculture and where pastures scattered over a large territory are subject to periodic **drought.** Rainfall is low and unpredictable and diseases can decimate cattle herds in very little time (Ford 1977:146-149). Cattle, though they do not provide the bulk of subsistence in normal times, are an important insurance factor in bad times and crucial to the nomadic pattern of settlement followed by these human groups. Evans-Pritchard (1940) gave a detailed analysis of how the environment of the Nuer determines most aspects of their culture. The cycle of seasonal migrations determines the settlement pattern, the sociopolitical role of segmentary lineages, and the social relations. Gulliver (1955) discussed how the differences in the habitat of the Jie and the Turkana affected their herding practices, their practice of agriculture vis-à-vis herding, seasonal migrations, and inheritance patterns.

The economic analyses of Schneider (1957, 1970, 1974a) present convincing arguments for the adaptiveness of the East African pastoralist pattern. The Turu, for example, aim at converting their agricultural surplus into cattle, which are less subject to climatic vagaries and can reproduce themselves, thus yielding interest on the Turu's initial investment. Ultimately cattle wealth is sacrificed, like money, to gain social status. In periods of grain scarcity, however, cattle provide a major food source (Dyson-Hudson and Dyson-Hudson 1969). Even the apparently uneconomic practice of maximizing herd size, rather than quality, has been shown to be an appropriate adjustment to local conditions. Spencer (1965) pointed out that during dry spells a large percentage of the herd will die, so the more cattle units a man owns during normal times, the better off he is. Cyclical droughts are sufficiently frequent that one could say the East African herder must maximize, because he can seldom, if ever, optimize his production. Before he can reach an optimum herd size, another dry spell decimates his herd.

Several insightful studies of pastoralism have involved discussions of the interaction between pastoralists and cultivators, as well as historical explanations for the changing relationships between the two groups. One of the crucial works in this vein is Barth's analysis of the relations between ethnic groups in North Pakistan (1956). Barth tried to show that the economic and political organization of neighboring ethnic groups could be best understood in terms of the **niche** concept—" . . . the place of [each] group in the total environment, its relation to resources, and competitors" (Ibid: 10-79). Barth showed that the niches occupied by three neighboring groups (Pathans, Gujars, and Kohistanis) reflected adjustments to the habitats occupied by each, as well as changing relations over time between the three groups. While two groups could use an area with equal effectiveness, a group with greater military strength could drive the other one to a different area and force it to adjust to a different set of resources. The merit of Barth's study lies in his careful blending of historical data with ecological concepts and cultural data. In another study, among the Persian Basseri (1961), Barth provided an excellent analysis of the cyclical shifts between pastoralism and agriculture. Populations turn to farming on the basis of the success or failure of pastoralist activities, and there appears to be a new exodus from pastoralist societies in the direction of farming communities. (This view has been recently questioned with convincing arguments by Lees and Bates [1977].) Greater detail on this issue is provided in chapter 7.[5]

A key contribution to the study of pastoralist/farming adaptations has been made by Edgerton (1965, 1971) as part of a large collaborative effort known as the *Culture and Ecology of East Africa Project*. Of particular interest are the hypotheses and methods used. Instead of traditional behavioral observation and ecological data collection, the study makes heavy use of psychological testing and other projective techniques in combination with the collection of life histories and interviewing. Such methods were emphasized, but behavioral observations have not yet been integrated because of the time limitations of the project. Edgerton attempts to show that people's thoughts, feelings, and actions can be predicted for the most part by tribal affiliation and by subsistence mode. He adds that individual innovation is important in cultures, since both minor and substantial changes in human social organization, ideology, and technology derive from it. This approach to cultural ecology is significant

[5]Spooner, in an excellent module on "The Cultural Ecology of Pastoral Nomads" (1973) integrates the available data on this subsistence mode and provides a general model for analyzing it. Readers are encouraged to read this module with care and to consult the literature cited there.

because in its effort to understand the locus and mechanisms of adaptation, it focuses both on individual adjustments and on the adjustments of the culturally defined group.[6]

Edgerton's research among four East African tribal groups (the Hehe, the Kamba, the Pokot, and the Sebei), each of which was composed of pastoralists and farmers and exploited highland and valley resources, was directed at a search for covariance in the attitudes of groups with different subsistence modes. He sought to explain "how and why farmers and pastoralists became different" (Edgerton 1971: 294). He predicted that the attitudes, values, and personality characteristics of farmers and pastoralists would vary because of certain differences in their subsistence mode. However, he found that individual responses were more likely to express past environments than present ones—a finding he explained by suggesting that the environment exercises a causal influence on attitudes that operates over a period of years. Although an environment may change overnight, the attitudes developed in response to it adjust more slowly. Edgerton concluded that a person's tribe or "culture" was dominant over his subsistence mode—that is, persons of different subsistence modes (farmers and pastoralists) of one tribe were more alike than were persons of the same subsistence mode (farmers) from the four tribes. Nevertheless, he also found impressive differences between farmers and pastoralists— for example, open vs. closed emotions, direct vs. indirect action, social cohesion vs. social negativism. Edgerton believes that these differences can be traced back to the environment.[7] Each milieu makes different demands on its inhabitants, who are thus subject to different constraints. In time, the individual adopts a particular set of attitudes and values appropriate to his environment, and even his personality type is affected.

The conclusions of studies such as those of Edgerton lead us to reflect that "culture" is the result of situation-specific adjustments, reflecting the interaction of people adapting to particular environmental circumstances, by particular technological means, at a given point in their history.

Culture, as such, does not adapt. The process of adaption can only be studied through the close examination of individual action and specific items of behavior. . . . the grand schemes of cultural evolution may be seen as an epiphenomenon to the process of ecological adaptation; similarly, I think it is reasonable to see ecological adaptation as a generalized statement of the process of individual adaptive acts. (Goldschmidt in Edgerton 1971: 303)

[6]Statistically analyzed data from Edgerton's work is available in the 1971 volume.

[7]This is somewhat surprising given the relatively scant attention paid by Edgerton (1971) to ecological data gathering and reporting. However, Porter (1965), as a geographer, may have provided such data for the project.

Modern Farmers   Ecological studies in contemporary societies have thus far been few. Cultural ecologists have concentrated on tribal and peasant groups because of the more immediate interaction evidenced in less complex social systems. However, there is increased evidence that many more anthropologists are considering complex societies as a research focus. Bennett's studies in this area (1969, 1976) have been among the most notable, both because of his ability as a practitioner and his presentation of a program for a policy-oriented cultural ecology.

Bennett attempts to show that controls over resources can be the result of rational choices and not necessarily of built-in, culturally embedded patterns as has been suggested by studies of tribal societies (Rappaport 1968; Nietschmann 1973). In the case of the Amish, self-imposed constraints are placed on consumption and on the use of modern machinery. These "taboos" are designed, according to Bennett, to shield the Amish from what they perceive to be corrupting influences from the majority culture all around them. A number of these restrictions prohibit the use of environmentally damaging techniques, including chemical fertilizers, powered implements, and pesticides. The Amish obtain substantially lower crop yields than their neighbors, but because of their simpler consumption standards and low-cost technology, they are able to live at a higher economic level than their non-Amish neighbors who have comparably small tracts of land. (Bennett 1976 : 277).

The communal Hutterites, farming the low-productivity northern plains of Canada, exercise similar controls over consumption by individuals, but use a full range of sophisticated technological implements and support a larger number of people than the Amish could. Their communal lifestyle allows them to have some of the benefits of economies of scale and more efficient use of farm equipment. (*Economies of scale* refers to a reduction in cost per unit of production as a result of large-scale operations.) Both the Hutterites and the Amish maintain a separation from the outside culture, but have different economic arrangements, social organization, and densities of population.

The Approach of Ecological Anthropology

Dissatisfaction with the research approach of cultural ecology led some field-workers to search for more satisfactory methodologies, data collecting techniques, and analytical tools. The major influence on this new research approach came from general, or biological, ecology. Ever since the time of Darwin, the field of biological ecology has grown in theoretical sophistication, and many of its concepts now lend themselves to application in human/habitat studies. Ecological study, in its broadest sense, applies to the dynamic relation between living and nonliving parts of an ecological system. The ecosystem concept provided a conceptual framework more satisfactory to some scientists than the behavior/social structure equation stressed by Steward. By studying human population as parts of ecosystems, attention can be paid to human adaptability—physiological, cultural, and behavioral. The research strategy of ecological anthropology is to study a wide range of human responses to environmental problems, to social constraints, and to past solutions to environmental problems. Little and Morren have succinctly expressed the strategy: "We are concerned with those cultural and biological responses, factors, processes and cycles that affect or are directly connected with the survival, reproduction, development, longevity or spatial positions of people. This set of questions rather than the traditional division of scientific labor defines the subject matter" (1976 : 5).

Although references to the interdependence of biological organisms can be found throughout most of the nineteenth century, the ecosystem concept was not actually articulated until 1935 when A. G. Tansley proposed it in an effort to emphasize the dynamic aspects of populations and communities. An ecosystem includes "all the organisms in a given area, interacting with the physical environment, so that a flow of energy leads to a clearly defined trophic structure, biotic diversity and material cycles" (E. Odum 1971 : 8).

Ecosystems are said to be self-maintained and self-regulating, an assumption that has affected ecosystem studies and that has also been recently questioned by both biologists and anthropologists. The concept of **homeostasis,** which in the past has been defined as the tendency for biological systems to resist change and to remain in a state of equilibrium (Ibid.: 34), has led to an overemphasis on static considerations and to an evaluation of man's role as basically disruptive. More recently, Vayda (1974), Slobodkin (1968, 1974), and Bateson (1963) have defined homeostasis as the maintenance of system properties (for example, resilience).

The cybernetic quality of ecosystems leads naturally to the use of systems analysis techniques.[8] Systems analysis has become a useful approach for anthropologists since it begins with a holistic model of the components and interrelations of an ecosystem, essentially a qualitative and descriptive process with which anthropologists feel at ease. However, it then proceeds to simplify these complex interactions so that it can quantitatively study the behavior of both the whole and particular parts of an ecological system (E. Odum 1971 : 276–292).

Systems theory provides a broad framework for analyzing empirical reality and for cutting across disciplinary boundaries. By way of limitation, system approaches still have to rely on other theories and develop measurements based on criteria other than those suggested by the system itself.

[8]The use of systems theory has been more common in archaeology than in ethnology. For a recent review of the use of systems theory in archaeological research, see Plog (1975). Its uses in social/cultural anthropology have been reviewed by Rodin, Michaelson, and Britan (1978).

Essentially, systems theory is a perspective that bears a great deal of similarity to anthropological holism: a system is an integral whole and no part can be understood apart from the entire system. At first, studies focused on closed systems, understood through the negative feedbacks that maintained functional equilibrium. The current thrust of systems analyses is to deal with open systems reflecting positive feedback, nonlinear oscillating phenomena, and the purposive behavior of human actors. Such purposiveness is unevenly and differentially distributed leading to conflict over goals and to system behavior reflecting the internal distribution of power.

Clifford Geertz, influenced by his reading of Dice (1955), Marston Bates (1953), and Eugene Odum (1959), was perhaps the first anthropologist to argue for the ecosystem as a viable unit of analysis in cultural anthropology. In his *Agricultural Involution* (1963), Geertz uses the ecosystem concept to test the validity of Steward's emphasis on subsistence and technology. In taking a whole-systems approach, Geertz notes that historical and political factors must also be included, if one is to explain Indonesia's agricultural development. Thus, Geertz stresses that a historical perspective helps explain Indonesia's economic stagnation as largely a result of the economic patterns established during the era of Dutch colonialism.

Geertz's *Agricultural Involution* is notable for several reasons. He does not give a mere typology of Indonesia's subsistence activities, but also describes both the processes within that economic system and how the various parts form an interrelated whole. Moreover, his diachronic approach to the case study adds information on how the economic system has developed and changed (Ibid. : 3). From his study, Geertz concludes that technoenvironmental features are not sufficient to explain the facts—in this particular instance, at any rate.

Roy Rappaport and Andrew Vayda have given the strongest impetus to an ecosystem approach in the field of cultural anthropology. In fact, they prefer the term *ecological anthropology* because they feel that the emphasis on "culture" suggested by the term *cultural ecology* obscures the applicability of principles from biological ecology to the study of human adaptation (Vayda and Rappaport 1976 : 20–21). Given that humans are but one species in nature, subject to the same laws as other species, use of the principles, methods, and analytical tools of the ecological sciences would greatly add to our understanding of our own species. Vayda and Rappaport believe that anthropologists should not hesitate to adopt biological units (such as population, community, and ecosystem) as units of study since this allows a more comprehensive approach to ecological studies. Even the topics of research can be couched in terms that make sense across both disciplines. Vayda and Rappaport point out that ecologists have shared various areas of interest with anthropology: ways of defining territorial rights, ways of establishing group identity, and mechanisms for establishing buffer zones. All these can be viewed "ecologically" as regulating behavior or serving a homeostasis function. To test ecological hypotheses properly, a wealth of information is required and no single researcher can expect to succeed in gathering it all.

The advantage of using a common unit of analysis, similar methods, and a common paradigm is that it facilitates team research and systems analysis (Ibid. : 23).

Vayda's study of how warfare in New Guinea is related to population fluctuations, changes in man/resource ratios, and the competition of different highland clans for gardens and pigs is a notable example of the ecological approach (Vayda 1974, 1976). Rappaport, working in the same region, is more concerned with how ritual serves to regulate: (1) the size of the pig herd, (2) the frequency of warfare, (3) the availability of horticultural land within reasonable walking distance of the village (4) the length of the fallow cycle, and (5) the military strength and alliances of a tribe and the likelihood that it will hold on to its claimed territory.[9] Rappaport is not really concerned with the individual decisions of the Tsembaga Maring as they see their pig herd increase to the point that they become a threat to the human ecological system. Rather, he finds that the system "senses" the increased burden of having too many pigs. When a system threshold is reached, the elders call for a ritual pig slaughter. The ritual reduces the number of pigs and facilitates the creation of alliances between neighboring groups. Warfare follows, and its occurrence serves to distribute the population over the landscape and to return the system to "initial conditions" or a state of equilibrium.

Bennett has criticized Rappaport's approach for its use of biological analogies, but concedes that Rappaport's study is important "as a concrete demonstration of the fact that the behavior of men toward each other, as well as toward Nature, is part of ecosystems" (1976 : 182). The major difference between Rappaport and Bennett lies in the former's emphasis on the fact that the systemic nature of the feedback loops can be found in culturally patterned behavior, such as the ritual/warfare complex. Bennett agrees that such patterned behavior may indeed be pervasive in technologically simple cultures. However, he argues that if this fact is always taken as a "given," the role of individual decision making can be overlooked. Such decision making, he feels, plays a great role in the technologically complex cultures of our day. Today human decisions about the use of the environment are predicated on institutional and technological considerations that can be overshadowed by emphasis on cybernetics.

Bennett finds the distinction between cultural ecology and the ecosystem approach artifical. The choice of one approach over the other depends on the size and complexity of the group under study. Among small tribes with primitive technologies, the ecosystem approach can be employed since much of the human/environment interactions in such tribes are embedded in cultural traditions (Rappaport 1968). On the other hand, in larger, complex, and technologically advanced cultures, institutions and technology have

---

[9]More details on the Tsembaga Maring studies by Rappaport can be found in chapter 9 of this book and in Rappaport's ethnographic account (1968).

created a distance between the population and its environment. Studies of modern societies must investigate these institutions and the processes of decisions that affect nature and humans. In these contexts, Bennett argues, the ecosystem approach does not work well because it cannot research the dynamic processes of institutions and the conscious processes of choice among alternatives due to the complexity of the systems.

An important issue raised by Rappaport's study (1968) is the utility of the concept of homeostasis. As used by Rappaport, the concept was equivalent to equilibrium—a view shared by some biological ecologists and reminiscent of the Greco-Roman search for order in nature. In equilibrium models, attention is paid to how cultural practices help maintain human populations in a stable relationship with their environment. This view is the prototype of neo-functionalism and it has its drawbacks. It views the current state of the system as the norm and overemphasizes the functions of negative feedback to the neglect of the dynamics of change accelerated by *positive* feedback. This viewpoint tends to preclude the possibility that behaviors might be maladaptive—which they surely are in certain situations (Alland 1975).

Adaptation to environment is, however, not a simple matter of negative feedback. System correction through negative feedback operates most effectively at lower levels in a system. Higher levels operate at a more general level wherein ambiguity and vagueness permit constant reinterpretation and restructuring of system properties as responses to perturbations. Homeostasis and **dynamic equilibrium** do not imply changelessness. On the contrary, they require constant adjustment of system parts and even some change in structure (in response to perturbations) (Rappaport 1977: 169). In other words, while systems have lower order mechanisms geared at the maintenance of stability, they also have higher level, less specialized mechanisms that can reorder the system to assure its survival.

Thus far studies with an ecological anthropological approach have concentrated on isolated populations of Alaskan Eskimos and Aleuts, South American Yanomamo Indians, New Guinea tribesmen, and Miskito Indians of Central America. The choice of such small isolated groups was made because it permitted easier monitoring of the interaction between the human population and their environment. Monitoring the complex relationships between such environmental stresses as disease, low energy and food availability, heat, cold, and altitude in technologically complex societies would be a far more difficult task. It is likely that once a clearer understanding of the human ecology of simpler cultures has been reached, ecological anthropologists will be able to more easily study human response to environmental degradation, urban pollution, and other contemporary stresses.

To date, the best research using the ecosystemic perspective has been conducted at the microlevel (see Rappaport 1968; Clarke 1971; Kemp 1971; Waddell 1972; Nietschmann 1973; Thomas 1973; Baker and Little 1976). Although these geographers and anthropologists have shared much substantive content, differences do exist among them. As might be expected, the geographers consistently show a greater sophistication in their analyses of the physical environment, while anthropologists deal with cultural components of the analyses with greater insight and facility. Although anthropologists have no difficulty dealing with the microscale, since it has been their traditional unit of research, there is concern over the applicability of these microstudies to the large context of human behavior and human adaptation. Criticisms of the exclusive use of this level have concentrated on the neglect of the elements of human control and human choice over ecosystems (Chorley 1973; Bennett 1976). However, as we have tried to point out, this neglect probably results from the focus on simpler cultures wherein the multiple system variables can be more easily measured and controlled.

It is certainly premature to expect the ecosystem perspective to resolve most of our questions about how humans adapt. Close cooperation will be required between biological and behavioral scientists to generate an integrated study of people in ecosystems. In the future, studies are likely to be most fruitful when they integrate the general systems approach with the study of how actors develop their own individual strategies. There is no reason why both perspectives cannot be used, and there is evidence that researchers have already begun to balance a concern for the individual with a concern for the population. One way to overcome the tendency towards static equilibrium models might be to study how populations adapt to certain kinds of stress. By studying the response of individuals to hazards, we can answer such questions as: Who responds? Does stress lead to changes in the structuring of the population? Are cultural patterns changed? How do people perceive the severity of the stress to which they are responding? How does the human population adjust to termination of the stress? These questions are more likely to be productive in outlining systemic interrelations in populations experiencing changing situations than in those with stable situations. This, however, presents even greater challenges to researchers (see Vayda and McCay 1975). As a way of dealing with these challenges, Alland has proposed what he calls *structural ecology*, which integrates cognitive/structural and bioecological aspects of human adaptation (1975).

The Ethnoecological Approach

A very different approach to the study of human/environment relations grew out of developments in the field of sociolinguistics. This general approach has been termed *ethnoscience* and deals with the study of various cultural perceptions of the world and how people order those perceptions through their given language (see Sturtevant 1964). Ethnoscience has given rise to subfields dealing with specific domains of culture, such as ethnobotany, ethnozoology, and ethnoecology. The aim of ethnoecological research is to provide a better understanding of how people perceive their *environment* and how they organize these perceptions (Frake 1961, 1962). A basic assumption of the approach is that "taxonomies of native terms either comprise in themselves standards of ethnoecology or provide the information necessary for inferring ethnoecology" (Vayda and Rappaport 1976: 18). The emphasis is clearly on the cognitive, rather than on the behavioral, aspects of cultural study. By uncovering the organizing principles behind native **taxonomies** (that is the system of classification of items by natives of a given society), ethnoecologists claim that it is possible to overcome the tendency to impose an outsider's a priori structures upon the data.

Data collection in the ethnoecological tradition aims at eliciting native terms for plants, animals, insects, soil types, and so forth. An effort is made to deal exhaustively with the distinctive criteria that are used to make up the "labels" that go with things and to relate the terms within one domain to each other. This should then lead to the development of taxonomies or a hierarchical arrangement of terms according to levels of generality (see table 3.1). Items are assigned to the taxonomy in accordance with their distinguishing features—that is, on the basis of how they contrast with one another. From these contrasts, it is possible to arrive at which features are perceived and considered "important" and which are not. The ethnoecological approach operationalizes the seemingly obvious fact that what people know about the environment and how they categorize that information will affect what they do to their environment. As such, the approach helps identify those variables that are amenable to empirical investigation—variables that must, therefore, be identified early on by the field-worker (Ibid.).

This approach is, however, fraught with problems for the ecological anthropologist. As Burling (1964) pointed out, the ethnoecological rules tell us only about verbal or culturally agreed-upon rules, but not about what people actually do when able to use their own initiative. More recently, Harris (1974a) showed that the neat categories elicited by ethnoscientists cannot predict behavior because "cultural rules characteristically contain 'except and unless' clauses." Harris adds.

What mentalists in general fail to realize is that the rules for breaking rules are also subject to rules for breaking rules and that the conditions defining occasions as appropriate for one rule rather than another are expressed by means of inherently ambiguous vernacular categories. Thus the rules elicited to explain, justify or predict behavior contain an irreducible residue of interpretation, judgment, and uncertainty . . . . [this] can only lead to one conclusion: people have a rule for everything they do. No matter how deviant or unexpected the act, a psychologically intact human being can always appeal to a set of rules which someone else will recognize as legitimate, although perhaps misinterpreted or misapplied. (Harris 1974a: 244–245)

Table 3.1   **A Folk Taxonomy.** A hypothetical taxonomy of the domain "trees" indicating diagnostic questions used to elicit the categories and pursuant of the diagnostic features between categories.

Diagnostic Questions
What kinds of plants are there?
What kinds of trees are there?
What is the difference between evergreen and deciduous trees?
What different kinds of coniferous trees/rain forest trees are there?
What is the difference between a hemlock and a pine, and a spruce? Between a spruce and a pine?

Plants

Trees				Grasses
Evergreen		Deciduous		
Coniferous	Rain Forest	Fruit	Non-Fruit	
Hemlocks / Pines	Spruces / Sequoias / Cypresses	Apple / Pear	Maple / Oak / Willow	

←————————————Contrast————————————→

Inclusion

Vayda and Rappaport (1976: 19–20) also point out that an ethnoecological approach fails to consider "latent functions"—i.e., functions or consequences of behavior that are not intended or consciously recognized by the behaving people. Yet these behaviors, such as ritual pig feasting, might be precisely the ones that are crucial to a population's survival (Rappaport 1968).

Very little of the ethnoecological work to date has tried to demonstrate the correspondence between cultural categories and behavior. One exception is the analysis of planting behavior among Northeast Brazilian sharecroppers by Johnson (1974). Establishment of the categories progressed in the manner we have described. The first question Johnson asked attempted to establish the types of land categorized by the population. The researcher found fifteen terms used, eight of which were stable ones (that is, not synonyms for other terms). He then sought the dimensions of contrast between the eight types of land. Contrast was based on relative fertility and relative moisture. Table 3.2 illustrates the categories as distributed along a fertility and moisture gradient. The degree of correspondence between cultural categories and planting behavior was found to vary in accordance with the extremeness of the categorization. Land that was extremely poor was found to remain unplanted, with a perfect positive **correlation.** On the best

Table 3.2   **Categories of Land along a Fertility (Strong-Weak) and Moisture (Hot-Cold) Gradient.**   Crops associated with different types of land are indicated in the center of the table.

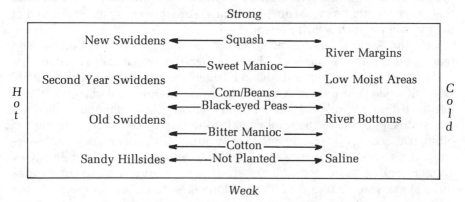

Source: Based on Allen Johnson. 1971. Sharecroppers of the Sertao. Stanford, Cal.: Stanford University Press.

soils found in the area, as identified by the categories, there was 87 percent correspondence. However, in the middle-range soils the correspondence was only 50 percent. It is in this middle range of soils that individual experience and ability play an important role in agricultural performance. At the extremes, the cultural categories serve to reduce the total area that must be identified by individual actors in the culture.

The value of research such as Johnson's (1974) is twofold: in addition to using ethnoecology to focus on the relationship between cultural knowledge and social behavior, it also generates knowledge that can be tested by other than ethnoscientific means. The ethnoecological approach, in the hands of ecological anthropologists, is a field tool for examining the knowledge constraints upon a population's use of available resources. However, as the Johnson study demonstrated, one should expect correspondence between categories and behavior only in the unambiguous extremes of a domain, and great variability at the center. Ethnoecology may serve simply to bound the system, but not to specify resource use.

Summary

The theoretical developments in human/habitat studies since the 1950s have significantly advanced the quality of ecological studies. The cultural ecological approach proposed by Julian Steward provided a framework that more clearly delimited the scope of research. The emphasis on the comparative method and on the primacy of behavioral considerations in subsistence technology were the trademarks of the cultural ecological approach. This type of study attracted researchers throughout the 1950s and 1960s and led to major revisions in our understanding of hunting/gathering, pastoral, and agricultural societies. The rationale for the evolution of society from hunting/gathering through agriculture became less obvious as studies showed that hunters/gatherers were not peoples at the margin of subsistence, but that they in fact enjoyed relative leisure.

At the same time, appreciation for the sophistication of cultivation techniques, such as slash-and-burn, generated important questions for research. However, these studies neglected to consider some potentially relevant aspects of human ecology: disease, physiological changes, ritual, political domination, and other factors. Out of dissatisfaction with these oversights, and due to the intellectual influence of the developing field of biological ecology, researchers began to adopt a broader ecological framework. This approach, commonly referred to as *ecological anthropology* or *systems ecology*, adopted units of study from biology and in some cases units of measurement as well. Population replaced culture or society as the unit of study. A number of the studies chose to focus on the flow of energy in human society as a way of understanding the use of the environment. Another reason this focus was chosen was that it allowed for comparability in data. The study of energy flow is still relatively new and has not yet proven its full utility. Nevertheless, the union of human biologists and social scientists under the same ecological framework can only be predicted to advance our understanding of human adaptability to environment.

The ethnoecological approach sought to integrate into ecological study knowledge of how populations perceive resources. The search for native categories has added an important dimension to ecological study, particularly in the early stages of field research. How resources are categorized defines how they are utilized, especially at the extreme points of a domain. However, most domains include ambiguities which allow for considerable variation in behavior.

The themes that were discussed in chapter 2 have not been abandoned in the past decades. The reductionism represented by determinism will continue to make its appearance in various forms in our intellectual discourse, and the limitations of the earth as an abode for human beings constitute a particularly lively notion in our time, when exponential rates of population growth make the pressure on worldwide resources increasingly stressful. The concept of adaptation is central to contemporary approaches to human ecological study. These approaches are characterized by increasingly sophisticated scientific methods of observing behavior, controlling variables, and generating theory on human adjustment to environment. Some of these useful concepts and methods will be reviewed in the next chapter. The knowledge and experience accumulated by the researchers whose work has been the subject of chapters 2 and 3 make the task of contemporary ecological anthropology more precise and more rewarding.

Recommended Readings

Useful evaluations of recent work in cultural ecology, ethnoecology, and ecological anthropology can be found in Damas (1969b), Heider (1972), J. Anderson (1974), Vayda and McCay (1975), Vayda and Rappaport (1976), and Grossman (1977). Consulting the original writings of major authors may be more profitable than reading evaluations. Steward's classic comparison of hunter/gatherers (1936) provides a good starting point. It might be followed by reading his Shoshonean Great Basin study (1938) and his contribution to volume 5 of the *Handbook of South American Indians* (1946). One of the most faithful efforts to use the Stewardian approach is Damas's analysis of Central Eskimo society (1969a). Similar in approach is the excellent study of a farming population by Netting (1968). The symposium on *Man the Hunter* reevaluated the explanations given by Steward and advanced the state of knowledge of these populations (Lee and DeVore, 1968).

There is no better example of the ethnoecological approach than the work of Conklin among the Hanunóo of the Philippines (1957). More recent efforts by Johnson (1974) further affirmed that the approach can have positive contributions in some domains of knowledge about the environment.

Studies with a more systems ecology orientation began to make their appearance in the late 1960s. The one that set the mood for these is the study of a New Guinea population by Rappaport (1968). Studies by Waddell (1972), Nietschmann (1973), and others continue in this tradition. A simple introduction to this approach is provided by H. Odum (1971) and H. Odum and E. Odum (1976). The most sophisticated of the energy flow studies to date is that of Brooke Thomas (1973) on an Andean highlands population. Less ambitious, but nevertheless revealing, attempts to trace the flow of energy were carried out by Rappaport (1971a) and Kemp (1971).

Fundamental
Concepts
and Methods

The methodology of human adaptability studies is firmly rooted in both the human and the biological sciences. Investigations must, therefore, include considerations of ecosystemic relationships, human physiological responses to environmental stresses, and social/cultural adjustments. Chapter 1 presented a brief overview of the role of energy-matter-information flows between system components, or **state variables**. This chapter begins with a discussion of ecosystemic relationships in which we will examine the ecology of populations, differential primary production, the importance of soils in plant productivity, and the flow of energy in communities. Later in the chapter we discuss aspects of human thermoregulation, work capacity, biological rhythms, major categories of cultural adjustments—for example, clothing, shelter, diet, mobility, and settlement pattern—and information for decision making.

Ecosystemic Relationships

Population Ecology   Ecosystems are heuristic units that help us carry out holistic (that is, whole) ecological research on given problems. They do not, however, represent a real physical unit in biology, and they are sometimes too complex for research questions. Biological research more commonly focuses on the organism, the population or the community. Ecological research has been primarily concerned with the study of populations. If we are to understand thoroughly the subject of human ecology, we should familiarize ourselves with measurements of population characteristics. Although not all the measures discussed in this section are used in this book, they have been included to introduce the novice to these elemental concepts. The field of population ecology and demography is highly sophisticated, and numerous comprehensive treatments are readily available. Some of the principal ones are cited at the end of the chapter.

A **population** is a group of individuals of the same species that occupy a given area and interbreed with each other. Populations are units through which energy flows and matter cycles, and since they are self-regulating, they help to maintain overall stability in ecosystems. An important strategy of most living systems is the maintenance of flexibility. Populations respond to changes in the environment by physiological and behavioral adjustments and, less often, by genetic adaptation. The strategy is to change only what is necessary to maintain flexibility for future environmental changes. Intrapopulation variability enhances this flexibility and stability. Through variability the population can maintain individuals with different genetic and behavioral capability whose resources may become crucial under conditions of environmental change.

In the study of the ecology of populations, it is important to understand the factors that impinge upon population structure and process. Basically a population can do one of three things: increase, decrease, or remain stable. The relative contributions of births and deaths are of primary importance in understanding these processes. Migration is also a factor, but is less often the subject of population ecology study. In some cases, one may also wish to decompose the general figures on births and deaths into age-specific rates (for example, the birth rate for women fifteen to nineteen years old) or relate such rates to socioeconomic factors (for example, race or education-specific birth rates). By breaking down the general figures on death, birth, and migration, one may get more information on the factors that determined a given growth pattern in the population under study. Table 4.1 lists the more important measures in the study of mortality and **fertility** and the formulas appropriate to estimating each rate.

Populations grow geometrically, —that is, their potential growth follows a typically exponential pattern. This ideal situation seldom occurs, and the balance between **birth** and **death rates** (that is, *the rate of natural increase*) determines the actual growth of populations. If births exactly equal deaths, we have, in effect, no growth. When this situation occurs we refer to the population as *stationary*. However, should there be even a slight excess of births over deaths, we have a situation of exponential growth (that is, the population is said to be *expanding* at a compound interest rate). When the rate of natural increase is 1.0, population is said to double in seventy years. A 2 percent rate will double it in thirty-five years, and a 3 percent rate will achieve it in only twenty-three years. A negative rate of natural increase means that the population is *declining* and, in the past at least, has been taken to be an indicator of maladaptation and potential extinction.

Given the great potential for exponential growth of human populations, it is surprising how long our species' population remained low. Since a female can become pregnant roughly between the ages of fifteen and forty-five, it is theoretically possible for an individual female to produce slightly more than forty offspring. In actuality, many social and cultural practices reduce that number. Many populations do not wean a child from the mothers's breast for a period of up to five years. In some populations this might inhibit ovulation and reduce *fecundity* (that is, the potential birth rate). During this period the population may also restrict sexual intercourse. These two practices alone would reduce the reproductive potential of females from over forty offspring to about nine. If life expectancy was less than forty-five years, the number of births would be further reduced. Infant mortality would reduce the number to a mere two or three per woman. Even if these mechanisms to reduce potential fecundity were inoperative, cultural practices like infanticide could have played a temporary role in reducing population. In other words, the rate of natural increase would approximate zero under these conditions.

The recent explosive or exponential rates of growth appear to have resulted primarily from a drastic reduction in mortality, especially infant mortality. Reductions in adult mortality have increased life expectancy and

Fundamental Concepts and Methods 4

Table 4.1   The Principal Measures of Mortality and Fertility

Measure	Formula[a]
1. Crude death rate (CDR)	$k\left(\dfrac{D}{P}\right)$
2. Age-specific death rate (ASDR)	$k\dfrac{Di}{Pi}$
3. Infant mortality rate (IMR)	$k\dfrac{Do}{B}$
4. Crude birth rate (CBR)	$k\dfrac{B}{P}$
5. Crude rate of natural increase	$k\dfrac{B-D}{P}$
6. General fertility rate (GFR)	$k\dfrac{B}{F\ 15\text{-}44}$
7. Age-specific fertility rate (ASFR)	$k\dfrac{Bi}{Fi}$
8. Total fertility rate (TFR)	$5\sum_{i} ASFRi$
9. Gross reproduction rate (GRR)	$5\sum_{i} ASFR_{Fi}$
10. Net reproduction rate (NRR)	$\sum_{i}\left(ASFR_{Fi}\right)\left(\dfrac{5^{L_x}}{l_o}\right)$

[a]k equals 1,000
D equals number of deaths
P equals population at the midpoint in the year
i equals the age-group interval
o equals dead under the age of one year
B equals number of live births
F equals number of females
$\sum$ equals sum total

$\dfrac{5^{L_x}}{l_o}$ equals mortality rate for cohort

the number of years women can participate in reproduction. Reduced periods of breast-feeding and elimination of postpartum taboos on sexual intercourse have further limited the factors that in the past effectively reduced the rate of natural increase of the human population.

Because death occurs only once, it is a particularly useful measure of population and the one most often available with a high degree of accuracy.

Several measures of mortality are commonly used: the crude birth rate (CDR), age-specific death rate (ASDR), standardized crude death rate (SCDR), and infant mortality rate (IMR). The crude death rate is the number of deaths per 1,000 people per year. It is calculated by taking the population at midyear, (that is, the number of people in January and December) and dividing by two in order to eliminate variations resulting from factors such as births, deaths, and migration. The range for the CDR varies between a low of about 5 per 1,000 to a high of about 30 per 1,000.

Age-specific death rates provide a more accurate mirror of a population than crude death rates because they can reflect population-specific differentials in age structure. For example, Taiwan's crude death rate is 5 per 1,000 while that of the United States is 8.9 per 1,000. Does this mean that Taiwan really has a lower death rate? The lower Taiwan rate results from the fact that the population of Taiwan is very young and that young people have a generally low death rate after age one. In other words, older or stable populations tend to have a higher CDR than younger populations. To get a more accurate picture of the status of a population, it is useful to rely on age-specific death rates. ASDR is calculated by taking the number of deaths in each age group and dividing by the population at midyear of each age group (that is, in five to five year intervals, zero to four, five to nine, and so forth). However, such data may be unavailable among some populations of interest to anthropologists and geographers, and in these cases the only approximation possible may be CDR.

Because the age structure of a population has a pronounced effect on the CDR, the technique of *standardization* has been devised. In standardization, one seeks to compare two populations by using one population's age structure as the standard or constant. Any standard demography book discusses the derivation of this adjusted death rate, which is too complex for inclusion in this brief discussion of methods. (See suggestions for additional reading at the end of the chapter.)

Infant mortality is a useful demographic measure in that children up to the age of one are particularly susceptible to environmental stresses and experience an unusually high mortality. Sources of very early infant deaths (that is, in the first month of life) tend to be congenital defects, injuries at birth, prematurity, and other factors beyond the control of normal health practices. Subsequent infant deaths tend to result from infectious diseases, nutritional problems, and the like. Neonate deaths have some relation to the conditions of the mother during pregnancy and during the birth process. Subsequent deaths are more a reflection of the overall living conditions of the population. Infant mortality is calculated by taking the number of deaths occurring among children under one year of age and dividing by the number of live births in the year per 1,000 population. Rates vary anywhere from a low of about 11 to a high of 200 per 1,000.

These measures (CDR, ASDR, SCDR, and IMR) can give useful information about mortality in the absence of unusual sources of fluctuations.

69

Among such major sources are epidemics, famine, and seasonal fluctuations. Disease epidemics can have a major local effect upon a population's structure, and evidence of their effects can be seen in the age structure long after their occurrence. The same is true of famine whether it results from natural hazards or from political blockading of food movement across frontiers. Populations dependent on a single crop for their subsistence are particularly sensitive to market fluctuations and crop blights.

Several sociological factors affect death rates: age, sex, marital status, social status, and occupation. Age is the most important factor coloring mortality. The human mortality curve is U-shaped. Rates are high in the first year of life, they decline rapidly and remain low through middle age, and they then rise rapidly with "old age." The definition of old age varies according to the life expectancy of a population. Nevertheless, the shape of the mortality curve is the same whether life expectancy is thirty-two or seventy-five years. Sex also accounts for differences in mortality. Males have higher age-specific death rates than females. Surprisingly, the gap between male and female rates actually increases with rises in living standards and sedentarization. Married people appear to have lower mortality than single, widowed, or divorced people. This may reflect a better adjustment to surroundings, especially where it is normal to be married. Social status and occupation affect death rates as a result of differential work demands, nutritional level, settlement pattern density, and overall living standards.

While mortality measures are useful in the study of population ecology, fertility measures are a necessary supplement. Studies of human fertility are far more complex than those of mortality. Death is a singular event, unlike fertility which can occur many times and is heavily influenced by intermediate variables (that is, intrinsic factors), such as age-specific participation in sexual unions, frequency of intercourse during unions, use of contraceptive techniques, and gestation variables (that is, fetal mortality). Figure 4.1 summarizes these and other interactions relevant to the structure of populations.

Several measures of fertility are commonly used: the crude birth rate (CBR), general fertility rate (GFR), age-specific fertility rate (ASFR), and total fertility rate (TFR). The crude birth rate is estimated by taking the number of live births per year divided by the population at the midyear per 1,000 population. The highest recorded CBR is 60 per 1,000 for a Hutterite population. The lowest CBR is that of West Germany with 10.1 per 1,000. However, CBR, like CDR, is significantly affected by the population's age structure. A young population will have a higher CBR than older or more stable populations—especially if the population has high numbers of persons in their late teens and early twenties.

The general fertility rate is a more accurate measure than the CBR because it includes only women during childbearing years. It is measured by taking the number of live births in a year and dividing this figure by the number of women between the ages of fifteen and forty-four, per 1,000

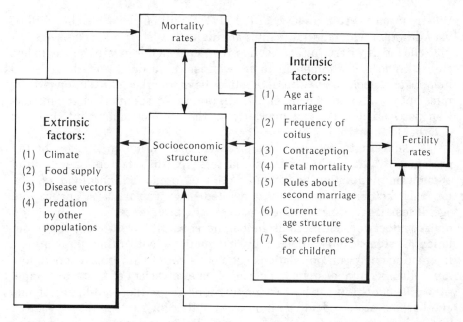

Figure 4.1 **The Complex Interactions between Extrinsic and Intrinsic Factors** These interactions result in given rates of mortality and fertility in human populations.

population. Such a breakdown may not be available for some populations.

Another measure that seeks to overcome the limitations of the CBR is the age-specific fertility rate. It is estimated by taking the number of live births per age group divided by the number of women in that age group per 1,000. As with death rates, the rates may be standardized for the purpose of interpopulation comparisons. The importance of age-specific rates is evident when one notes that 50 to 60 percent of all births occur between ages twenty and twenty-nine. Differences exist between populations according to patterns of marriage and especially because of age at the time of marriage.

The total fertility rate serves to estimate completed family size by giving the total number of children a woman would have in a lifetime if the age-specific rates were continued indefinitely through the reproductive years. A problem with this rate is that it does not take into account the effect of infant mortality or mother mortality. A modified form of this measure is the *gross reproductive rate* (GRR) which refines TFR by including only the number of female births —that is, it gives the average number of daughters a cohort of 1,000 would bear if all these women survived their reproductive years. Because the GRR, like the TFR, does not control for mortality, it is preferable to use another measure: the *net reproductive rate* (NRR). NRR is the number of daughters a cohort of new female babies would bear given the continuation of a fixed fertility schedule and a fixed mortality schedule.

When mortality rates are low, NRR and GRR will be close, but they will be very different when mortality rates are high.

The fertility curve by age has an inverted U-shape: low in the mid to late teens, highest for women in their twenties, then declining slowly until menopause. Social and cultural practices have a marked effect upon fertility rates but not upon this general pattern. Figure 4.1 summarizes the interaction between fertility and mortality as they reflect factors internal and external to the population.

To sum up, then, population size and distribution are affected by the presence of intrinsic and extrinsic factors. Extrinsic factors operate from outside the population and include climate, predation, and food supply. Intrinsic factors are internally generated—e.g., social class, occupation, age at marriage, contraceptive practices, sex preferences in children, and dietary allocation within households. Moreover, the well-being of a population is significantly affected by its relations with other populations. Interactions between populations can take a variety of forms: cooperation, mutualism, commensalism, amensalism, and a variety of forms of competition. In *cooperation* the two populations favor the well-being of one another, but are not dependent on one another for survival, as they are in *mutualism*. In *commensalism* one population remains relatively unaffected by its interaction with the other, while in *amensalism* one population actually inhibits the growth and survival of the other. *Competition* refers to a vying for resources by either individuals or populations.

Forms of intraspecific competition, such as territoriality, are also significant in population size and distribution. Territorial size tends to vary with habitat—for example, where food or water are scarce, the size of the territory tends to be larger. Organisms also require a certain amount of personal space. When they are denied this needed space, they experience stress and a set of bodily reactions, usually referred to as *general adaptation syndrome*. If the syndrome is long lasting, the result may be decline in reproductive capacity or death. With increased population density, there are increased social density and increased intrusions upon personal space. Although social stress is not an important regulator of human population size, it does have numerous negative effects that involve physiological and behavioral consequences, which can in turn lead to individual and offspring marginality. The lower classes in most stratified societies have higher rates of infant and adult mortality, limited access to resources, and an inadequate food supply. These factors affect mortality and fertility rates.

No one of these factors can be said to predominate at all times and in all places in population regulation. Moreover, the human population seems to have lost any biological homeostatic mechanism for population regulation—if, in fact, it ever had any. At any one time, specific factors such as drought, war, and disease may come into play. These factors form

Table 4.2   Net Primary Production and Plant Biomass of Major World Ecosystems

	Net primary productivity unit area in dry g/m²/yr		Net primary production (10⁹ dry tons)	Biomass/ unit area (dry kg/m²)		World biomass (10⁹ dry tons)
	range	mean		range	mean	
Tropical rain forest	1000–5000	2000	40.0	6–80	45	900
Tropical Savannas	200–2000	700	10.5	0.2–15	4	60
Temperate Grasslands	150–1500	500	4.5	0.2–5	1.5	14
Tundra/Alpine	10–400	140	1.1	0.1–3	0.6	5
Semiarid	10–250	70	1.3	0.1–4	0.7	13
True Desert	0–10	3	0.07	0–0.2	0.02	0.5

Source: Adapted with permission of Macmillan Publishing Co., Inc. from *Communities and Ecosystems* by Robert H. Whittaker. Copyright © 1970 Robert H. Whittaker.

the subject for much human ecological research.[1] The role of social and cultural factors in the regulation of population also requires further exploration.

Soils and Plant Productivity   The crucial biological organisms in nature are the green plants, which are able to convert diffuse solar energy into concentrated energy in the form of plant biomass. Plant growth and production are dependent on a number of factors, including temperature, water availability, soil nutrients, and soil texture. Human utilization of plants depends upon the production by plants of a net yield. Because energy transfers are inherently inefficient, plants must absorb and convert far more energy than they can yield. A major portion of this energy goes into keeping the plant alive so that it can reproduce. These processes of energy transfer, usually called **respiration,** always involve a loss of energy or heat. This loss is significant because only the difference between the total energy assimilated by the plant (i.e., its **gross primary production)** and its respiration requirements becomes available to people. Human populations are particularly concerned with this balance, which is referred to as **net primary production.** The more complex the ecosystem is, the greater the portion of gross primary production or overall plant growth that will be invested in maintenance, and the smaller the proportion that will be available as net yield. Table 4.2 illustrates the range of variation in gross and net primary production of the major ecosystems

[1]Readers may wish to consult Little and Morren (1976: 29–45) for a brief but useful overview of human responses to stresses. The texts on ecology by Smith (1974), Odum (1971), and Ricklefs (1973) have readable sections on population ecology. The best short manual for population ecology is Wilson and Bossert's *A Primer of Population Biology* (1971). After reading this, readers may wish to do mathematical modeling with help from Pielou (1969) and Watt (1968).

that will be discussed in part II of the book. The difference in production and productivity results from basic constraints present in each area—such as lack of water in deserts and extreme cold in tundras. Soil characteristics may also be important in understanding the productive potential of ecosystems.

The study of how human populations make use of plants is intimately tied to the nature of the **soils** upon which plants grow. While temperature, rainfall, and other climatic factors are as important as soil, there is very little humans can do to manage or control these forces of nature. On the other hand, soils can be and often are managed by human groups who have acquired sophisticated knowledge over time. Most populations (particularly farming populations) possess ethnoecological expertise about soils and their characteristics.

The soil is not an undifferentiated medium, but is, rather, a dynamic one that is constantly in formation and undergoing transformations. Soils are distinguishable from bedrock and unconsolidated debris by their relatively high content of organic matter, an abundance of roots and soil organisms, and the presence of clearly distinguishable layers, or **horizons** (Buckman and Brady 1969: 3–4). Soils may vary even within short distances of each other. These differences may be the result of variations in surface, slope, weathering conditions, and the impact of plant activity. For example, soils originating from chemically basic **parent material** (bedrock) will have a **pH** close to neutral (7.0), while those originating from acid bedrocks will tend to be acid. Soils on steep slopes will be shallower than those on gentler slopes if the steep slopes are not covered in a vegetation capable of breaking the impact of water and light.

The field investigator with interests in human agricultural activities or water control, for example, should note a soil's texture, structure, color, the depth of its humus layer, the vegetation that grows on it, and the horizons that it presents. **Soil texture** refers to the arrangement of soil particles. **Soil structure** is influenced by soil texture and chemical status, by the plant cover, the soil microorganisms present, soil management, and climatic conditions.

Soil color is an important indicator of various characteristics, but is not a foolproof indicator of soil type. When weathered, a red shale or sandstone may yield a red-colored soil even though the oxidation of iron is not the major process in this case. In interpreting the nature of the soil, color must be used in conjunction with broader knowledge of the weathering factors in a given climatic zone. In temperate regions dark-colored soils are high in organic matter. In the tropics, however, dark clays may be poor in organic matter. Bright red and yellow soils in the tropics may suggest high levels of iron oxides, but they also indicate good drainage and aeration—both important factors to consider in interpreting plant performances and in planning management approaches in an area. In poorly drained areas where oxygen is deficient, reduced iron yields bluish gray colors; sites of good drainage lead to oxidation of iron, producing red colors.

Because chemical weathering, slope, and other influences vary at different depths, distinctive layers or horizons develop in most soils. These horizons, when taken as a group, form what is known as a **soil profile,** which expresses the types of processes experienced by the soil in the past and indicates the factors important to the use of that soil in the future. Profiles are two-dimensional slices through a soil. Soils, in general, have four major horizons: an organic or 0 horizon and three mineral horizons (A, B, and C).

Of all the horizons, the organic layer is the most critical for plant growth (see figure 4.2). This layer usually contains a disproportionately large portion of the total humus in a soil. **Humus** is important because it is so highly **colloidal,** a factor that both promotes a longer retention of water and nutrients and facilitates exchange of bases (Buckman and Brady 1969:144). Organic matter is also responsible for the loose, friable condition of productive soils. It is the source of phosphorus, sulfur, and nitrogen inputs. Organic matter increases the capacity of soils to hold water and provides most of the sustenance for soil microorganisms. The majority of the domesticated plants utilized by the human population rely primarily on this humic layer for their nutrition (Buckman and Brady 1969:7). This is why most soil sampling for agricultural purposes takes place in the top few inches of soil.

The mineral horizons are characterized by lesser concentrations of organic matter and varied particulate structure. The A-horizon is richer in organic matter than B or C. It is also characterized by the presence of granular, platy, or crumb structures. The B-horizon is characterized by alluvial concentrations of silicates, clay, iron, and aluminum and by the development of blocky, prismatic, or columnar structures. The C-horizon lies above the consolidated bedrock and has even larger particulate matter. It is the zone of transition between the B-horizon and the bedrock proper.

Soil sampling may take either of two forms, each of which reflects different research objectives. These forms are known as *core sampling* and *profile sampling.* In core (or surface) sampling, a soil sample is taken to a depth of between ten and twenty centimeters. Since this is the zone from which most domesticated plants obtain their nutrients, core sampling is the method commonly used to assess the soil nutrients available to plants. The sample is taken with the use of a core sampler. A single soil sample consists of fifteen to twenty "cores" collected in a random manner in an area. A zigzag pattern is usually used. The cores that make up a single soil sample are deposited in a bag and thoroughly mixed before being sent to the laboratory for analysis. Each sample should be numbered and described in terms of where the sample was taken; what vegetation was in the area; what texture the soil had; what color is was (using available

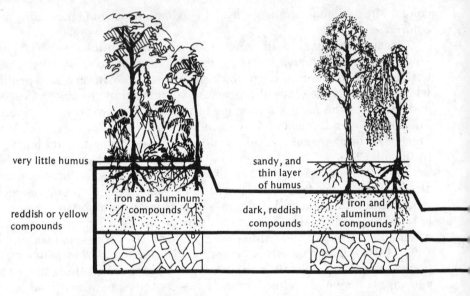

very little humus

reddish or yellow
compounds

iron and aluminum
compounds

sandy, and
thin layer
of humus

dark, reddish
compounds

iron and
aluminum
compounds

Tropical rain forest soil
(latosol or oxisol)
wet, warm climate

Temperate coniferous forest soil
(podzol or ultisol)
wet, cool climate

color charts such as Munsell color charts); and what the past use of the
soil was (if known). Any other remarkable features (for example, drainage
problems and slope) should also be noted.

Profile sampling goes to greater depth. One to three meters provides a
fairly comprehensive cross section of soil horizons applicable to the study
of land uses, such as tree farming or the use of special plants with deep
tap roots. In profile sampling a soil auger is commonly used. The aim in
this type of sampling is to establish the various horizons and their characteristics. As the auger is turned, each layer is laid out on a sheet of plastic
or other material in the order in which it was extracted. Each horizon is
then described in terms of the same information that is noted in core sampling descriptions. Such descriptions help to assess the alternatives open
to cultivators and can serve to test the accuracy of the ethnoecological
knowledge of populations.

Knowledge of soil properties is useful when ecological investigation
includes a focus on human management of land resources. Soil phenomena are of such complexity that a system of classification can be helpful in
grouping soils that share natural properties. Native systems of classifying
soils exist in many human groups. Over four thousand years ago, the
Chinese developed one that was based on color and structural characteristics (Steila 1976:64). The Hanunóo of the Philippines used vegetative
cover criteria (Conklin 1957:39), while the Kekchi of Guatemala used
color, texture, drainage, root content, as well as vegetational criteria

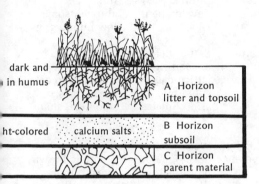

dark and
in humus

A Horizon
litter and topsoil

ht-colored   calcium salts

B Horizon
subsoil

C Horizon
parent material

Figure 4.2

Grassland soil
(chernozem or mollisol)
semi-dry climate

**Three Characteristic Soil Pro-
files** Note the differences in the
depth of the organic horizon, coloration, and mineral content.

(Carter 1969:21).

In the chapters that follow, reference will be made to a system of soil
classification based on the current properties of soils. Each order of soils
is characterized by diagnostic features (see table 4.3). **Oxisols,** for example, are characterized by a clay or argillic horizon and by the presence of
high proportions of iron and aluminum oxides. The latter have resulted
from **leaching** due to intense weathering of soil silica. Although oxisols
present favorable structural conditions, such soils are relatively acid (low
pH) and may contain aluminum levels that are toxic to some plants. Manioc, cowpeas, and other crops do well in oxisols, while corn and beans do
poorly. **Alfisols,** on the other hand, are less acid, richer in nutrients, and
present more favorable conditions for agriculture. If crops that are appropriate to soil conditions are to be chosen, human populations must solve
the problems of distinguishing among soils and relating soils to crop
management. This requires that they devise a system for categorizing
soils.

The distribution of major soil orders affects what forms of agriculture
are possible and what levels of productivity can be achieved. Since soils
are the product of the weathering of rock materials, the prevalent climatic
conditions play a crucial role in the formation of soils and in their characteristics. Thus, oxisols are dominant in wet, humid areas, **mollisols** are
characteristic of temperate grasslands, and alfisols are common in boreal
or deciduous forests.

Table 4.3   **Soil Orders According to the Comprehensive Classification**

Order	Formative syllable	Derivation	Meaning	Diagnostic features	Older equivalents
1. Entisol	ent	Coined syllable	Recent soil	Very weak or no profile development	Regosols, lithosols, alluvial, some low humic gley
2. Vertisol	ert	Latin: *verto,* turn	Inverted soil	Self-mulching; expanding lattice clays; subhumid to arid climates	Grumusol, regur, black cotton, tropical black clays, smonitza, some alluvial
3. Inceptisol	ept	Latin: *inceptum,* beginning	Inception, or young soil	Weak profile development but no strong illuvial horizon; cambic horizon present	Brown forest, subarctic brown forest, tundra, ando, and some lithosols, regosols, and humic gley
4. Aridisol	id	Latin: *aridus,* dry	Arid soil	Soils of arid regions; often have natric, calcic, gypsic, or salic horizons	Desert, red desert, sierozem, reddish brown, solonchak, some regosols, and lithosols
5. Mollisol	oll	Latin: *mollis,* soft	Soft soil	Thick, dark A_1 horizon; usually develops under grassy vegetation	Chernozem, brunizem (prairie), chestnut, reddish prairie, some humic gley, rendzinas, brown, reddish chestnut, and brown forest soils
6. Spodosol	od	Greek: *spodos,* wood ash	Ashy (podzol) soil	Illuvial horizon shows accumulation of iron and organic collodids; weak to strongly cemented pan	Podzols, brown podzolic, groundwater podzols

Table 4.3   **Soil Orders According to the Comprehensive Classification (Cont.)**

Order	Formative syllable	Derivation	Meaning	Diagnostic features	Older equivalents
7. Alfisol	alf	Coined syllable	Pedalfer (alfe) soil	Argillic horizon of relatively high base saturation (>35%); usually under boreal or deciduous broad-leaf forest	Noncalcic brown, gray-wooded; many planosols, some half-bog soils
8. Ultisol	ult	Latin: *ultimus*, last	Ultimate (of leaching)	Argillic horizon of low base saturation (<35%); plinthite often present; humid climate; usually forest or savanna vegetation	Red-yellow podzolic, reddish-brown lateritic, rubrozem, some gley and groundwater laterites
9. Oxisol	ox	French: *oxide*, oxide	Oxide soils	Argillic horizon very high in iron and aluminum oxides	Latosols and most ground water laterites
10. Histosol	ist	Greek: *histos*, tissue	Tissue (organic) soils	Organic surface horizon (>30% organic matter) more than 6 inches thick	Bog and some half-bog soils

Source: After *Soil Classification, a Comprehensive System.* Soil Conservation Service. 1960 (revised 1964).

Figure 4.3 illustrates the distribution of soils on a worldwide scale. Although the association is not perfect as pockets of unexpected soil types may be found anywhere, the association of soil orders with ecosystem types is remarkable. **Tundra** regions are dominated by inceptisols, **deserts** by aridisols, temperate **grasslands** by mollisols, tropical **savannas** by ultisols, and **tropical rain forests** by oxisols. This close association suggests that in any study of human adaptability to ecosystems, the soil

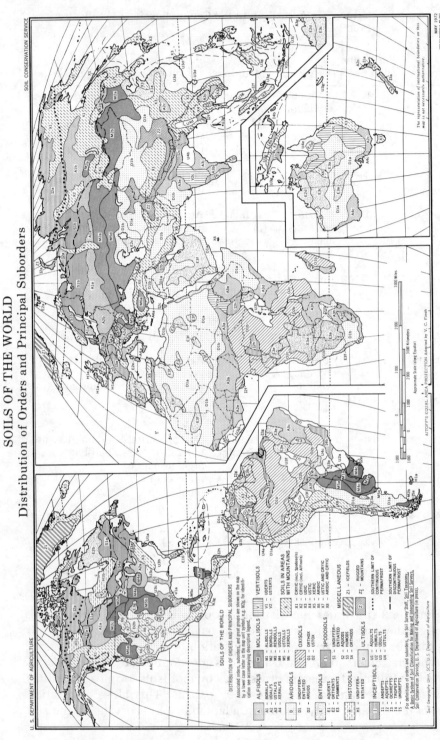

Figure 4.3   World Distribution of Soils
Source: Courtesy of the Soil Conservation Service, U. S. Department of Agriculture.

Table 4.4   Areal Significance of Soil Orders

	% of total world soils[a]	Rank (according to total area)
Entisols	12.5	4
Vertisols	2.1	9
Inceptisols	15.8	2
Aridisols	19.2	1
Mollisols	9.0	6
Spodosols	5.4	8
Alfisols	14.7	3
Ultisols	8.5	7
Oxisols	9.2	5
Histosols	0.8	10

[a] An additional 2.8 percent of the total includes ice fields and unclassified lands.
Source: Donald Steila. © 1976 *The Geography of Soils*. Englewood Cliffs, N.J.: Prentice-Hall.

component needs to be considered if for no other reason than to understand ecosystem structure and plant productivity. Note, too, that the areal significance of soil types is highly variable (see table 4.4). **Aridisol** soils, which present problems of high salt levels and high concentrations of other minerals, are the most extensive. Some of these soils can be made productive if water is provided in adequate and regular amounts. **Inceptisols** rank second in extent and are also problematic for farming uses. These are soils with rocky, gravelly horizons still in process of development. It is only in moving to the third most of the ten categories of soils that one begins to encounter fertile, easily workable soils. This suggests that a crucial problem of farming populations is to locate those areas of land with the best possible soils. Location of such land requires knowledge of soil characteristics and their effective management.

Knowledge of soils, plant productivity, and population ecology would not be helpful in the study of human adaptation unless they were integrated into larger schemes. In chapter 1, modeling was suggested as a useful means of summarizing interrelationships between ecosystemic components. In the chapters that follow, we will use the type of energy flow modeling proposed by H. T. Odum (1971) to summarize the systemic interaction between people and environment.

One Type of Modeling: Energy Flow   If we accept the laws of thermodynamics, the concept of trophic levels, and the notion that systems tend toward some sort of equilibrium, we have all the requirements for studying the flow of energy through ecosystems.[2] The special value of **energy**

[2]Energy flow models were first used by R. Lindeman in 1942.

81

flow models is that they help us to compare ecosystems and to identify their functions despite ecosystemic differences—as, for example, the difference between ecosystems of grasslands and arctic tundra. By translating the biomass and rate of energy flow into common units (usually kcals), a general model can be built that describes life processes, quantifies dynamic relationships, elucidates functional relationships, and provides a basis for the comparison of ecosystems (Shugart et al., 1975).

The usefulness of this type of analysis was demonstrated by R. B. Thomas's study of energy flow in the high Andes (1973), by Kemp's study of Eskimo hunters (1971), and by Rappaport's study of a New Guinea population (1968, 1971). The major difficulties with an energy flow approach to ecological study seem to be the difficulty in quantifying all the relevant data (see table 4.5) and in deciding which are the major functions and which are less significant; the possibly false assumption of stability in the ecosystem; and the temptation to try to reduce every aspect of ecosystems to caloric equivalents. Nevertheless, the approach can be useful for numerous types of ecological investigations, particularly where energy seems to be available in limited amounts. Where energy itself is not limiting, other factors may be more important—e.g., water flow in desert ecosystems.

To understand energy flow through ecosystems, one should know something of how energy flows through the *populations* that make up the ecosystem and be able to relate this information to the flow of energy between trophic levels. This presents a unique problem: to date, energy estimates for major ecosystems are based largely on assumptions, rather than on carefully collected energy budgets. The interactions between ecosystem components are very complex, and energy flows are likely to change in accordance with numerous variable conditions that may be hard to monitor over time. Studies to date have neither proven nor disproven the general utility of an energy flow approach. Used with caution, such an approach can provide a more solid basis for comparison of human interactions with nature.

A systems approach making use of energy flow modeling involves a three-step procedure. First, the investigator develops diagrams that contain factors that are perceived as important and the interrelationships among these factors. Second, the investigator identifies sample studies that provide a basis for quantifying each of the essential processes and state variables. If no data exist, the investigator makes a note to collect such data or makes "guestimates" based on reasonable assumptions. It is now that the investigator notes the kinds of measurements and units that he or she must collect in the field. Finally, the investigator employs simulation to refine the model so that it is a good expression of the real system and is suggestive of the most sensitive aspects of the system. In other words, a model is a useful summary of what is understood, both factually and theoretically, about the structure and function of the system in ques-

Table 4.5   **Some Methodological Considerations**
in Measuring and Analyzing Energy Flow

I. Energy production
   A. Data collection
      1. regional survey of production
      2. questionnaires and conversations
      3. direct measurement
         a. production/land unit or animal, production/time unit
         b. measurement of food stores
         c. wastage and loss preceding consumption
         d. experimentation with production techniques
   B. Conversion to caloric values
   C. Evaluation of the measurement period
      1. representativeness of annual production
      2. annual variability in production

II. Energy consumption
   A. Data collection
      1. weighing of food consumed
      2. questionnaires concerning food use
      3. daily recording of food items consumed
   B. Conversion to caloric values
   C. Establish consumption by sex-age group
   D. Adequacy of energy consumption
      1. comparison with international standards
      2. presence of deficiency related symptoms
      3. indicators of caloric balance

III. Energy expenditure
   A. Survey daily activity pattern
   B. Determine key activities
      1. importance in subsistence pattern
      2. extent to which activity is relied on
      3. performance effort necessary
   C. Testing procedures
      1. in field measurements
      2. standardized testing conditions
   D. Estimate energy cost of activities not tested
   E. Time-motion studies
   F. Physiological strain in performing activities

Source: R. B. Thomas, "Energy Flow at High Altitude." Reprinted, with permission, from *Man in the Andes: A Multidisciplinary Study of High-Altitude Quechua,* Baker and Little, eds., © 1976 by Dowden, Hutchinson & Ross, Inc., Stroudsburg, Pa.

tion (Moran 1973 : 13–14). This final process sometimes requires revisions in both model and hypothesis. After field research is carried out and a final model is drawn up, simulation serves to deny or confirm the hypothesis. Figure 4.4 illustrates the process.

There are numerous mathematical and symbolic languages for representing ecological systems and energetic relationships. The energy flow

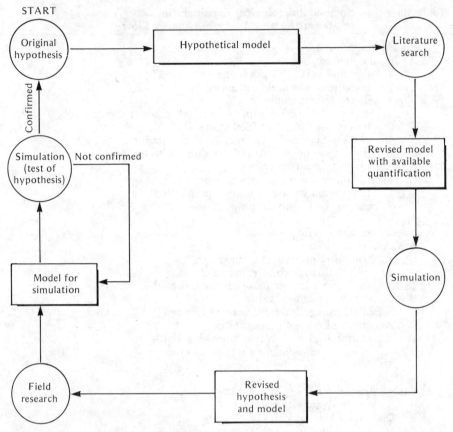

Figure 4.4   Process of Modeling

language suggested by H. T. Odum (1971) is among the most comprehensive. It describes energy availabilities, causal actions, state variables, flows and pathways, and multiplier effects. It can be used both qualitatively and quantitatively. From qualitative diagrams it is relatively simple to translate the symbols to differential equation equivalents for simulation in analog and digital computers. Input variables that originate from outside the diagrammed system (for example, solar energy) are termed *sources.*

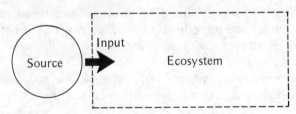

Energy moves along *pathways* that connect the system parts and express rates of flow.

Pathway

A *passive storage* identifies state variables (or system components) in which no new potential energy is generated, but in which work must be done (at a cost) to move energy in and out of the storage compartment. An example of such a state variable is the moving of a harvested crop into a storage area.

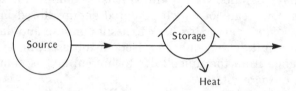

Source Storage Heat

The energy cost just described is represented by a downward arrow or *energy sink*, which, as the second law of thermodynamics suggests, is the result of all processing.

Heat sink

Whenever a function is unspecified because of lack of information, it is indicated by a box or black box. The identity of the box (that is, what it is—for example, a market) is written within and its internal details may become an important aspect of the field investigation.

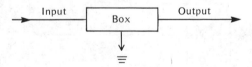

Input Box Output

Workgate symbols express a variety of processes in which one flow controls the rate of flow of another. (A *multiplier effect* is a type of workgate and is shown by that symbol.)

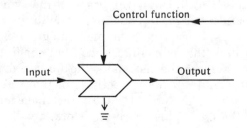

Control function

Input Output

For example, to express the impact of human energy on harvesting a crop from a field, one would diagram it in the following way:

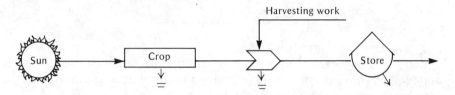

Another useful unit symbol is the *self-maintaining consumer*. In the illustration we have detailed its workings: it is a combination of a workgate and a storage by means of which potential energy stored in one or more sites within a subsystem is fed back to assure growth and development of the consumer unit. This symbol is used in representing animal populations that range from the unicellular to human and is commonly represented by a hexagon only.

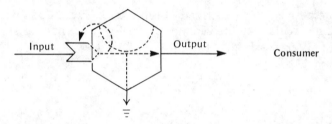

To represent the producers in the food chain, one uses the *green plant module*. This symbol is a combination of a self-maintaining consumer with a pure energy receptor. It is seldom symbolized in such detail and commonly appears with only its bullet shape (see the darker lines).

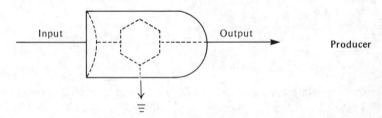

Figure 4.5 serves to illustrate the usage of the symbols we have just discussed. The sun's energy, in combination with the rain falling on an area planted in crops, is used by green plants to grow. Some of the energy is lost as respiration (that is, maintenance), but some of it goes into net productivity. To increase the net yield, the human managers weed the fields to eliminate undesirable competitors of their crops—for example, corn and beans. When the crop is ready, the managers must invest in labor to harvest the crop. This process is work, and some energy is thus

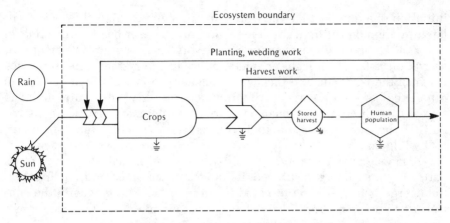

Figure 4.5   **Simplified Energy Flow Model**   Figure illustrates the elementary symbols: sources, pathways, workgates, storages, and self-maintaining module.

lost in the process. The gains are stored in an area from which amounts are periodically removed to feed the human population. In this process, there is some energy loss resulting from spoilage, food preparation, and decline in nutritive value.

Since in most societies the human population engages in *economic transactions*, there exists a symbol to express the process.

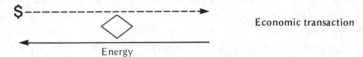

The broken line describes money flows, the solid one energy flows. The flow is in opposite directions to indicate the payment of one for the other.

Flows need not always be operative—when "off," they are turned "on" in response to a signal or *switch*.

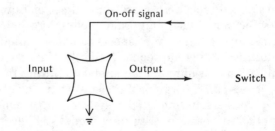

For example, to begin an agricultural flow, an appropriately timed signal is required to initiate land preparation, plowing, planting, and so forth. Such signals embody information on the conditions appropriate to the initiation of a flow. Unlike the workgate, in which the rate of flow is regulated by the controlling flow, the switch mechanism has an unequivocal on or off state, in which usually a relatively small amount of energy for activation has a significant energetic effect in the system. The difference between the workgate and the switch mechanism is best illustrated by the difference between a standard light switch and one with a dimmer. The former (like the switch mechanism) turns simply on and off, while the latter (like the workgate) is able to do that as well as regulate the flow of current while on.

Some signals are expressions of stress upon the system or one of its parts. When a system is stressed, its flows are disrupted and much potential energy is lost. It is represented by an inverted workgate with the control factor being a *stress factor* that drains energy out of the system at a rapid rate.

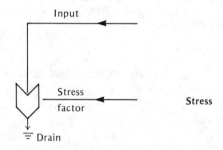

Models can be designed that describe the workings of a whole ecosystem. Their advantage is that one can visualize the whole system and concentrate on major functions. Such an approach, however, can lead to models so general as to be barely useful. More commonly, models are drawn up to study not only the whole system, but, even more importantly, its parts as well. Figure 4.6 is an illustration of a general model of shifting agriculture. However, a simulation of such a model could be very time-consuming. Through simplification and elimination of detail, we might end up with a general model of the type shown in figure 4.7. This type of model concentrates on a more limited set of flow and state variables. While some potentially important details are left out, efforts are made to summarize all important aspects in major functions of the system. The usefulness of this approach lies both in its conciseness and its potential applications for quantitative analysis. During the early stages of investigation, it serves as a way of representing the available knowledge and the current understanding of the system. Such a use represents a qualitative application of an energy flow model, which is the way these models are applied in the chapters that follow. Such qualitative applications do, however, permit computer simulations.

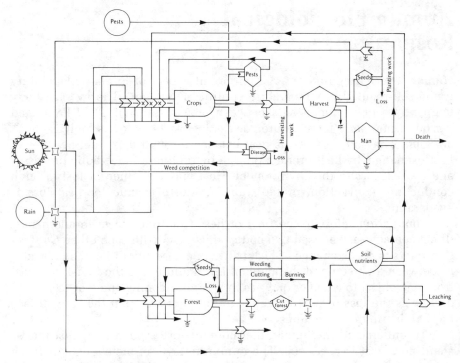

Figure 4.6   **Slash-and-Burn Agriculture Model**

Source: Emilio Moran. 1973. Energy Flow Analysis and *Manihot esculenta* Crantz. Acta Amazonica 3(3):31.

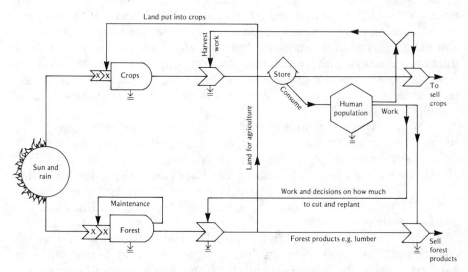

Figure 4.7   **Simplified Model of Swidden Agriculture**   Model assumes that pests are not a major factor and the erosion is not a cause of important fluctuations or changes in the ecosystem in question.

Human Physiological Responses

Human Thermoregulation   An important aspect of human adaptability is the self-regulating temperature control of humans. The average body temperature of a human falls between 36.5° C. and 37.5° C. Prolonged periods when body temperature goes as low as 24° C. or as high as 45° C. are fatal. The body maintains heat balance through two chief avenues of heat exchange: by heat production as a by-product of metabolic processes and by heat loss to the environment. Heat may be gained or lost through conduction, convection, or radiation. A fourth avenue for heat loss is evaporation.

Conduction refers to the flow of heat from one object to another by direct contact—as between two bodies in contact with each other. *Convection* refers to the exchange of heat between a gas or liquid and an object—as between a person and the ambient air. *Radiation* is the transfer of heat from one object to a cooler one—as in a hand touching snow or ice. *Evaporation* is the loss of heat by vaporization of sweat from the skin surface or of moisture from the lungs.

To understand the human thermoregulatory system one must understand how heat is produced. The minimum level of metabolic activity of the body during complete rest and after fasting eight hours is known as the **basic metabolic rate** (BMR). An average value for young adult males is about forty kcals of heat per m² of body surface per hour. Heat may also be produced by the dynamic action of food, especially protein; by increased muscle tone and shivering; and by nonshivering or chemical **thermogenesis.** Shivering can increase heat production up to five times above BMR, and extraneous exercise about thirty times. Heat loss by convection, conduction, radiation, and evaporation depends on: (1) the transfer of heat from the core or interior of the body to the surface; (2) the body composition, especially fatty deposits; and (3) the proportion of surface area to weight of the body.

The circulatory system is the chief transferrer of heat within the body. Blood flowing through deep body organs picks up heat and can channel it either to the core or to the surface of the body. This is accomplished chiefly by vasomotor constriction or dilation (**Vasoconstriction and dilation**) of vessels at the surface. Direct heat conduction also occurs, but is slower. When the body is exposed to cold, the **body core** shrinks and the **shell** expands (limbs, skin, fat, and other peripheral structures) as a result of constriction of peripheral blood vessels. Heat is passed on largely by conduction. The opposite occurs during exposure to heat. In adaptation to cold, two mechanisms are particularly relevant to heat transfer: *countercurrent heat exchange* and *cold-induced vasodilation*. In countercurrent heat exchange, heat is conserved by the precooling of blood flowing to the periphery, while heat is added to blood flowing to the interior of the body. This exchange is supplemented by a cold-induced vasodilation (or peripheral blood flow), which is a cyclic response of a protective nature. It refers to the spontaneous rewarming of fingers and toes during cold exposure as a result of dilation of specialized vessels. It provides protection to vulnerable parts of the body, like the fingers.

During the course of normal human growth, a number of morphological and physiological changes (particularly changes in height, weight, and surface area) take place that influence temperature regulation. The infant is poorly protected against cold stress because of a low BMR, inadequate subcutaneous fat deposition, poor development of muscular tissue, small size, and high rate of heat loss. By way of protection, infants turn to nonshivering thermogenesis. This form of heat production is related to the presence of **brown adipose tissue** in the infant. This tissue is found not only in infants up to age one year, but also in cold-acclimatized adults. Infants are able to elevate their metabolism by 170 percent over BMR. Cold temperatures also affect infant growth. In experiments, children raised at 2° C. cooler temperatures and fed the same diet as a control group experienced smaller weight gains. This reflects a diversion of calories from storage or growth to heat production aimed at maintaining temperature at normal levels.

Circadian Rhythms   The casual observer, without devices to measure the timing characteristics of behavior, is unlikely to identify biological rhythms even when looking for them. Gross features of a daily cycle can, however, be noted. Daily rhythm or **circadian rhythm** indicates that the period during which these features appear is approximately, though not exactly, twenty-four hours in length. Circadian rhythms have been identified in the simplest single cell animals, such as amoeba and paramecium; they are universal to living things (Chapple 1970:24). With the aid of measuring devices, the activity rhythm of living organisms—(that is, the occurrence of physical activity, its onset, duration, and cutoff) is directly observable, as are the major physiological and biochemical functions of the body. With a chemical thermometer, the circadian path of body temperature becomes evident—higher at midday, lower in the morning and at nighttime. Blood sugar, liver glycogen, white corpuscle counts, adrenal activity, RNA and DNA synthesis, cell division, and drug-specific sensitivities have also been shown to follow circadian rhythms.

The newborn lacks a fully developed nervous system and so cannot fully manifest circadian periodicities. Not until the sixth week of life do differences between day and night begin to appear in the infant's rhythm, and the typical pattern seen in the adult does not develop until age one. Similar rhythmical change is manifested in body temperature rhythm.

Given the universality and constant properties of the circadian rhythms themselves, it seems reasonable to assume that the total amount of activity and inactivity is constant for the individual animal. Duration of activity and duration of inactivity are under the control of remarkably accurate biological clocks. When an animal is barred from its required activity, compensatory increases in activity need to be taken to restore the balance between activity and inactivity. Biological clocks help synchronize the organism to the changing properties of the environment (Ibid.: 26). Their role in survival requires little elaboration.

In experiments in which animals are placed consistently in the dark or light, it has been shown that circadian rhythms are innate and repetitive. In other words, the rhythm is endogenous. The organism anticipates each stage of adaptation, reacting in advance in terms of its own internal organization. It is always prepared and this allows it to survive. Given the existence of these various rhythms, there have to be ways of setting each clock to the external environment.

Three synchronizers have been identified as important in setting biological clocks: light, temperature, and social interaction. Light is the primary clock setter and affects all species. It is the only synchronizer that is well understood. The pineal body, a small somewhat conical body situated behind the third ventricle of the brain, translates the energy of light into a fundamental secretion, melanin, that acts directly on the hypothalamus (that is, the autonomic correcting center) to maintain body rhythm. Temperature is important for clock setting in some species, but in most species circadian rhythms are temperature-compensated – that is, significant alterations in rhythms occur only when the limits of thermoequilibrium have been breached. It is presumed that interaction rhythms of animals are part of the clocksetting—that is, that animals adjust their periodicities in response to other animals with whom they interact. However, little controlled work on this subject has been done.

Just as light, temperature, and social interaction can set a biological clock, they can also desynchronize it. When circadian rhythms are desynchronized, the individual can suffer serious damage. As a result of radical disorganization of endocrine activity, rapid growth of tumors can occur, extreme susceptibility to disease can be **endemic,** and even death can come suddenly.

In studies in the arctic, light emerged as the most significant factor in the biological clock of arctic Indians. In winter the Indians followed regular routines; in summer irregular ones. Yet, excretion of potassium and other nutrients were out of phase in winter (that is, there were dramatic changes in the excretion of these nutrients) even though interactional patterns were normal (Chapple 1970:28). Above the Arctic Circle, daylight changes dramatically with seasons. In late June the sun never sets, but moves 360 degrees around the horizon. In late December the sun never comes above the horizon and offers only a deep red glow in the sky for several hours. Thus, in the arctic, light as a synchronizer of human physiology is subject to dramatic and rapid year-round change. The most clearly documented studies suggest that vitamin D autosynthesis declines in winter. This results in lowered intestinal capacity to absorb calcium, thus rendering the Eskimo hypocalcemic for part of the year.

Work, Diet, and Subsistence   Human physiological functioning requires that calories be provided on a regular basis to make up for the calories spent on body maintenance, physical activity, and growth and reproduction. The cost of body maintenance is usually measured by taking the basal metabolic rate of the individual at rest. The procurement of food and other activities add to this cost in accordance with the exertion involved. While the energy requirements of the body vary according to activity, and to a lesser extent according to body size and climate, ecosystems vary in their ability to produce energy per unit of labor invested in obtaining that energy. A useful, though crude, index for measuring the relative efficiency of a foraging strategy is to take the number of man-days of work and divide it by the number of man-days of consumption. Among the !Kung San (see chapter 7), the efficiency rate is about 25 percent, while among New Guinea horticulturalists it is 10 percent (Harrison et al. 1977:402).

Among the many activities of the human population, probably none influences the structure and function of social groupings more than the procurement of food.[3] Human populations have long exhibited an intimate knowledge of their habitat—what is edible and what is not, what is available in drought and what emerges from the ground with the first rains. In the previous chapter we noted how this knowledge has been of interest to ethnoecologists. The consumption of insects by some populations makes all the difference in a diet that, without such dietary contributions, would be marked by fat and protein deficiencies. Kalahari Desert and Amazon tribes alike consume insects, as do Australian aborigenes and some populations of western Africa. If toxic plants have properties that make them desirable and a process can be found to detoxify them, these plants are not necessarily avoided. The best-known illustration of this is the use of manioc (*Manihot esculenta*). Through soaking and heating, the toxic cyanogenetic acid is destroyed, and the **carbohydrate**-rich flour of manioc can then be safely consumed. Remarkable yields have been noted (Moran 1973, 1976).

Preparation, storage, and consumption of food often reveal remarkable practices that enhance the nutritional value of the food. Many fermented foods have high antiscorbutic (that is, high vitamin B) and mineral value. Where carbohydrates are in abundance, such fermentation

---

[3]Two excellent studies on food and nutrition are the classic by Audrey Richards (1938) and the excellent collection edited by Margaret Arnott (1976).

expands the range of nutrients made available. Soaking of corn in lime water enhances the calcium content of the manufactured tortilla and improves its food value. It should be noted that not all food practices are adaptive. Food taboos in many cases appear to deprive segments of the population of foods that they particularly need. In parts of Brazil, children with gastroenteritis are not given liquids for fear of causing further diarrhea, which results in an increase of dehydration. Imitation of western practice has led to a decline in breast-feeding in areas where access to protein-rich bottle formulas is not easy. This has resulted in caloric and protein deficiency and a high infant mortality rate.

Until relatively recent times, most populations experienced periods of marked food scarcity. When able to supply themselves with enough calories, hunter/gatherers seem to have achieved an adequate balance in diet. The uncertainty of the hunt was balanced by the more secure harvesting of seeds, roots, and other plant materials when available. The cultivator has a more secure food supply, but it is seasonally variable and during times of heavy farm work may be inadequate. Harrison et al. (1977: 416) noted dramatic weight losses during periods of heavy work and low caloric intake. Farming populations sometimes have an inadequate supply of high quality proteins and fats. Mixed agropastoral economies and economies that combine utilization of marine/riverine resources with horticulture represent responses to the problem of securing a balanced diet of protein/fat and carbohydrates.

Human populations have great metabolic flexibility. When one contrasts the average dietary intake of British, Bikuyn, Eskimos, and Bulador Islanders, one cannot help but marvel at the great differentiation between the food supplying the bulk of the calories and the health status of the respective groups. The proportion of fats and carbohydrates ingested varies significantly between populations. However, all ingest a minimum of protein—except the Eskimo who lacked access to carbohydrates until recent years. Protein, carbohydrates, and fats have important metabolic functions. The **amino acids** that form part of the ingested protein are necessary for tissue repair and growth, as well as for the synthesis of special proteins. Fat provides insulation and caloric storage. Carbohydrates are the main substance in body energy balance. Both protein and fat can be broken down into energy-producing carbohydrates. High carbohydrate intake can make up for deficiencies in fat intake up to a point. Foods supplying animal protein tend to have higher biological value because they have a more complete set of essential amino acids than do vegetable proteins. Most populations satisfy amino acid requirements by a combined diet of animal and vegetable proteins (Ibid.: 404).

Human survival often depends on the ability of individuals to perform muscular work under given environmental conditions. The human species possesses a flexible system that is capable both of continuous hard work and sudden bursts of intense activity. The work capacity of individuals is usually assessed by measuring the ability to transfer oxygen from lungs to muscle and to utilize oxygen. This measurement is called the *maximum aerobic capacity,* or VO₂ max. Among all populations measured, there is a dramatic decline in VO₂ max with age. This may be partly the result of decreased activity levels. By progressive intensifications of muscular effort, VO₂ max can be increased up to 20 percent. Subsistence-oriented populations have a higher VO₂ max than urban populations. Both genetic and nongenetic factors are involved in determining the range of **work** (or **aerobic**) **capacity** (Ibid.: 455–456). (Studies of twins show that genetic factors help to account for over 80 percent of the variance in VO₂ max.)

When it is not feasible to carry out field measurements of energy expenditure, it is possible to estimate these expenditures by the use of time/motion studies. The only things needed are a stopwatch and a tally counter. This technique requires that activities and types of body movement be recorded over time. Thus if one is measuring planting behavior, one records how many times per minute the body bent over, what sort of hand motion the planting required, any rest periods taken, and the weights, ages, and sexes of the workers. This data are then used to estimate energy expenditure by consulting calorimetric studies of the various types of motions recorded per unit of time for such persons (Edholm 1967; Passmore and Durnin 1955). Data on populations outside of western Europe are sometimes hard to locate.

Social/Cultural Regulatory Adjustments

Cultural adjustments include a broad repertoire of knowledge about nature. Under this category, one can include knowledge of house construction, clothing styles, subsistence technology, and ritual. Social adjustments mainly include forms of social and economic organization. In conjunction, these adjustments provide flexible, yet infinitely variable adjustments to changes in the habitat and to changes in relations with other human groups.

Cultural adjustments to climatic conditions occur mainly through knowledge about housing, clothing, and technology that enhances individual cooling or heating. House form, which is constrained but not determined by available materials, represents a compromise between behavioral, religious, and other values of the environment. The Eskimo winter dwelling is a good illustration of the role of climate in house form. A deep entrance pit and a long tunnel permit the gradual heating of cold air that enters the home. The dome design enhances surface area exposed to sun and reduces the drag resistance to wind. Bodily heat and oil lamps serve to maintain a cozy temperature inside the dwelling, and overheating is prevented by manual central air vents.

Housing in dry hot regions presents a very different sort of problem. The goal here is to reduce human heat production and heat gains resulting from radiation and convection. Thick-walled construction is used among sedentary peoples to slow down the buildup of heat. This type of construction also provides a warm dwelling in the evenings when temperatures drop. Nomadic populations require a different solution: they depend on ventilation to reduce heat gains. Clothing follows much the same pattern as housing. In hot areas cooking occurs outside the dwelling to reduce heat gains; in cold areas it occurs inside.

Religion can affect the form, layout and location of houses. The height of a house, the size of rooms, and the meaning of house parts may be related to elaborate cosmological interpretations. The special underground houses for menstruating women among the Nez Perce Indians make no sense apart from their religious and, therefore, social significance.

The settlement patterns of the human population reflect adjustments to both the distribution of resources and to associated social and cultural factors. Thus, marriage patterns influence the residential pattern, and available materials and climatic factors influence the type of house form and the proximity between dwellings. In desert areas semi-subterranean or highly overlapping houses (for example, pueblos in the southwestern United States) cut down on the surface area exposed to the hot sun and reduce heating of the interior. In most cases, patterns of residence and marriage are likely to be supportive of this pattern of house construction, rather than contradictory. The predominant subsistence strategy is significantly related to the pattern of settlement: populations that are nomadic build makeshift structures or carry their housing on their animals, while agricultural peoples are more sedentary.

One topic that has long interested anthropologists is the organization of social groups into units of production. Each type of social organization represents a strategy for subsistence. Flexible forms of social organization have been noted among hunter/gatherers in the arctic, in the Great Basin of North America, and in the Kalahari Desert of Africa. Units tend to be based on **bilateral** affiliation—that is, they trace their descent through males and females—and are of variable composition seasonally. Various **quasi-kin** mechanisms are used to enlarge the cooperative group that individuals have access to. This is accomplished by reciprocal visiting, patterned resource sharing, intermarriage, and patterned trade between groups with differential access to resources. Resource sharing is enhanced by patterns of generalized reciprocity. The hunting/gathering strategy depends upon the maintenance of the primary productivity of this territory. Work effort and population are kept low when the group is optimally adjusted to the resources. Since there is no hierarchical allocation of prestige, effort is not spent on overproduction for the purpose of redistribution and prestige seeking. On the contrary, gift giving is frequent and accumulation is eschewed. The hunting/gathering strategy would not long be viable without either controls over population size or without mechanisms that lead to **group fissioning** when densities reach a threshold level.

When these small local groups are linked together by ties of marriage, blood, and shared territory, we have what is known as a tribal form of **social organization.** Tribes are not significantly different from the more atomized bands that we have just described except that they represent an adjustment to the presence of aliens. This unity, which is elicited by an outside force, may lead to the formation of more complex forms of organization, or ranked societies. Such societies represent a significant departure from the egalitarian structure of hunter/gatherers and some horticultural societies. Prestige is differentially shared in ranked societies, as is access to resources. The chief is far above his fellows and has the power, usually enforced by a military elite under him, to enforce payment of tribute, to allocate privilege, and to organize systems of redistribution. Part of the prestige and power of the chief is assured by generous redistribution among the population at large of goods taken from them.

Forms of redistribution are tied to other aspects of a society. Among some populations, conspicuous display of wealth may be a way both of redistributing wealth and food, as well as a means of improving one's social status. Among New Guinea populations, yam feasts function to redistribute production, to improve status, and to gain allies for warfare and raiding. The warfare complex is crucial to the maintenance of appropriate man/land ratios and to the stability of the system. Particularly in areas subject to natural hazards, such as forest fires, flood, or drought, these forms of redistribution enhance survival by rewarding industrious individuals who produce surpluses. When disaster strikes, such "surpluses" may be sufficient to prevent famine among the population. Populations practicing redistribution have been more successful in the long run than those lacking it.

The emergence of markets or "negative reciprocity" as a context for the redistribution of goods marked a significant change in social organization. It further permitted individuals to climb the social hierarchy by manipulating the flow of goods into the market, by creating artificial pricing, and by creating demand for unnecessary products. Although all these things are not necessarily associated with markets, there is little doubt that the ideal model of supply-and-demand pricing markets is but a neat heuristic device for studying economics. It bears little resemblance to real situations, except as an approximation.

Information and Decisions

In chapter 1 some elementary principles of information flow in self-regulatory systems were introduced. In this section the discussion is extended and applied to special problems in human decision making. These principles represent a new frontier in research since they have seldom been applied to resource management and adaptability problems.

Research in the field of psychology has yielded some valuable observations on how a self-organizing system develops and functions. If information stored and past routines are simple and small in number, simple groping can be effective in decision making. In groping, the organism goes through its repertoire of activities until the proper response is elicited (Mackay 1968b:362). Although groping is used by people and is, at times, a major source of new and inventive solutions to problems, it is largely an ineffective system. This is particularly true if the situation is complex or the external conditions (that is, the social or physical environment) change rapidly and unpredictably. If one can establish any regularity (that is, redundance) in the statistical structure of a situation, then one can use such redundancy to save time by the use of "imitative organizers" or control sequences based on the statistical characteristics of redundant phenomena (Ibid.:363). These allow the organism to induce the correct adaptive response without major investments in groping.

Groping and control sequences assume that one knows in advance the range of options available and constraints present, but this is not often realistic. Human systems are self-organizing—that is, they are able to receive inputs of new information and to develop characteristic organizing sequences as a result of new and old information.

The human informational system probably works at various levels, depending on the level of difficulty in making choices. Decisions can be made in a climate of certainty, uncertainty, or risk. Certainty exists when one can predict what will happen in the period relevant to the decision. Uncertainty describes a situation wherein one cannot specify the probability of outcomes. Risk refers to situations where one can specify the probability distribution of several possible outcomes. (Levin and Kirkpatrick 1975:106.)

Under conditions of certainty about a situation (for example, at breakfast I have a choice between cereal and eggs, with coffee in either case), a set of simple rules or pathways may be followed in arriving at a decision. As certainty decreases and there is a greater possibility of inappropriate or maladaptive choices, increasingly complex logic and structure must be used to help sift the information and allow for decision making under conditions of risk and uncertainty. Solutions may be elicited from the use of simulation, probability, and "judgment heuristics" (that is, nonprobabilistic methods that make use of consensus between knowledgeable people). Effective research tools for dealing with conditions of risk have not achieved the sophistication of those dealing with uncertainty. Both areas offer fallow ground for new contributions given the paucity of analytical tools available and the importance of this aspect of human systems (Levin and Kirkpatrick 1975:529–530).

Methods developed in microeconomics and in the field of management and decision theory can be usefully applied to the problem of choosing from different possible courses of action. If one has too many choices in a given set of circumstances, one may be immobilized by indecision. Thus, one of the typical responses of information flow systems is to have complex rules to simplify the number of options. Over time, social scientists have presented a variety of theories that seek to give primacy to one factor or another. Perhaps dominant for many years has been the assumption behind the behavior of economic man (that is, maximization of expected utility). Much of the behavior has been simplified so that economists can focus on those aspects of behavior that are aimed at advancing the interests of business, households, and so forth. However, both theorists and field-workers have seriously attacked those assumptions. The key assumption that the decision maker's objective is maximization of expected utility is useful for analysis, but does not represent the actual behavior of actors.

Critics have shown that economic men sometimes seek to maximize "noneconomic" things, such as prestige (Cancian 1972; Schneider 1974), or that they simply try to minimize risk and uncertainty (Johnson 1971). Leibenstein in his book *Beyond Economic Man* (1976) has called for an overhaul of economic theory that takes into account "selective rationality"—that is, choice making that reflects a compromise between what one might do in the absence of constraints and what one does when they are present. One's preference reflects social, cultural, and psychological standards of behavior that may be in direct conflict with the calculus of maximization. Similar theories have been proposed by business psychologists (March and Simon 1958; Lindblom 1964; Cyert and March 1963) and geographers (Heijnen and Kates 1974; Slovic, Kunreuther, and White 1974). The emphasis of these studies is on how decision makers do not necessarily maximize utility, but aim instead at *satisfactory* solutions to problems—often invoking simplified "programs" that lack the complete knowledge often assumed in economic analysis.

Figure 4.8 illustrates a simplified decision tree that formalizes the process of decision under conditions of drought for a rancher. The tree represents relevant events and the expected consequences of each course of action. Such decision models allow for representation of alternative courses of action under varying conditions and very closely resemble energy flow models. The major difference is a reduction in the slope of the model. It is best used in combination with other approaches. Figure 4.9 represents a modified model with decision making components, but takes into consideration other aspects as well.

Barlett (1977) found in a study of peasant decisions that access to land was the critical criterion for understanding land use patterns, although other factors, such as age of the farmer, were also important. Figure 4.10 illustrates, in flow chart manner, the way in which these deci-

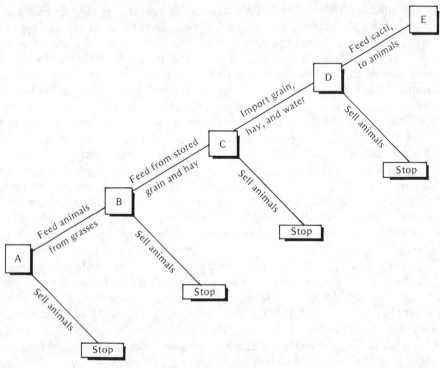

Figure 4.8   **Decision Tree Summarizing Options Open to a Cattle Rancher during Drought**   In time *A* the situation is best summarized as a "dry spell." If the rancher keeps his animals and the spell continues, he will be unable to feed his livestock from standing pastures. In time *B*, if he stays in the game, he will have to feed them from stored grain or hay. As drought increases in seriousness, he will have to import grain, hay, and water to keep his animals alive (time *C*) and will resort to feeding them cacti, after burning off the spines, as a last resort (time *D*). Usually ranchers get out of the game by selling all or part of their herd before reaching points *C* or *D*. The decisions made reflect perception of drought, frequency of drought episodes in the habitat, and opportunity costs.

sions were reached. Tobacco planting was a major distinguishing feature between farmers. Landless farmers planted primarily grains and did not plant tobacco and coffee. This was a rational choice given their lack of control over land. They chose less remunerative crops to minimize risk (Ibid.:298).

To integrate relevant information flows into matter/energy models, we must be able to assign a *logic* to human acts. This logic is derived from the sorts of decision models we have just described. In addition, considerations of space and time play a role in human decision making. Human

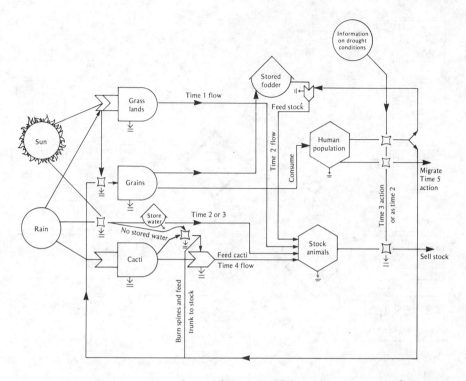

Figure 4.9   **Energy/Matter/Information Model Using Energy Flow Language**   The model represents the situation of a rancher in a drought zone. Numerous switches are required to signal changes in management strategy. In time 1 the stock feeds on the grasslands and surface water. In time 2 the grassland begins to show signs of drought, and the cattle must be fed from stored grain and hay. In time 3 the rancher must decide whether to sell stock or expend considerable income and labor to maintain it (see figure 4.8). In time 4 the rancher has lost his natural grasslands and his stored water and feed. He then burns the needles off the cacti and feeds the cacti to the cattle. In time 5 if the drought still persists, he migrates from the region.

strategizing is usually sequential in nature, a characteristic that is evident when one looks at human responses to changing levels of stress. Each time a decision is made, it limits the set of options available at the next time period. For example, a drought can be short-lived (that is, a "dry spell") or it can be an extended one. In incorporating the logic of the rancher into a more general energy flow model, one can mathematically describe the alternatives so tht each decision point (for example, A, B, C) define the location of a logic switch. Thus, at a given perception of drought conditions, one must choose among available courses of action.

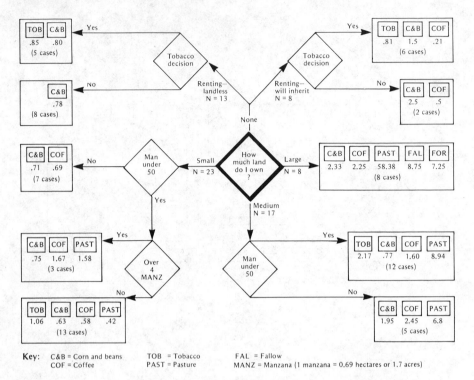

Key: C&B = Corn and beans   TOB = Tobacco   FAL = Fallow
      COF = Coffee   PAST = Pasture   MANZ = Manzana (1 manzana = 0.69 hectares or 1.7 acres)

Figure 4.10   Flow Chart of Decision Making in Reference to Land Use

Source: Peggy Bartlett. 1977. The Structure of Decision-Making in Paso. Reproduced by permission of the American Anthropological Association from the *American Enthnologist* 4:297, 1977.

Note: C&B = corn and beans
       Cof = coffee
       Tob = tobacco
       Past = pasture
       Fal = fallow
       Man = manzana (1 manzana = 0.69 hectares or 1.7 acres)

Summary

In this chapter we have tried to cover a number of basic concepts and methods that will be applied in the following discussions of human adaptability to various ecosystems. Because excellent texts on population biology and ecology are available, we have chosen to make only passing reference to these subjects, both in chapter 1 and here. On the other hand, we have highlighted subjects that are often neglected—such as concepts and methods of soil science and soil management, energy flow, thermoregulation, and circadian rhythms. Thermoregulation is particularly important in human adaptability to a variety of climates. Circadian rhythms are relevant to understanding human scheduling in general and human adaptations to arctic conditions in particular. Soil management is a constant concern of human populations and helps to explain phenomena such as slash-and-burn agriculture, mobility of villagers, crop associations, and distances between planted fields and villages.

The discussion of population ecology introduced basic terms and measurements used in population level studies. Such knowledge is useful in understanding trends in populations, the relative adaptability of populations, pressure exercised on resources, and health and disease. The energy flow approach is much broader. As a technique, it helps to summarize understanding of the system and to generate possible hypotheses for investigation. It can also be a quantifiable systems model, although it is not used in that way in this book. A brief discussion of cultural and behavioral adjustments served to introduce concepts, such as the connection between social structure and subsistence, the role of clothing and shelter in buffering the effects of environment, and mechanisms for redistribution of resources and populations. The discussion on information and decision theory served to tie together key concepts from psychology, management, and economic theory and to suggest their relevance to the study of human adaptability. These considerations have been too often neglected in ecological studies in the past and represent a fertile field for future studies.

The tasks of human adaptability research can be either broad or highly specific. In this chapter and the rest of the book, the material fluctuates between these two complementary approaches. Broad problems are defined and major adjustments are discussed. However, it should be noted that there is great variability between and within populations. This variability enhances stability and resilience, both of which are crucial factors in maintaining adaptability in human responses to environment.

In the next five chapters the theories and methods that we have discussed find expression in concrete studies of human adaptability. Each of the chapters in part II begins with a characterization of a particular type of environment. This is followed by the identification of problems that are particularly constraining or limiting in that ecosystem. Conditions such as extreme cold, low biological productivity, and water scarcity demand some form of adjustment by organisms occupying areas that are so constrained. In their process of adjustment, populations must face the conflict arising from having to choose optimal solutions while maintaining the flexibility necessary to cope with future conditions.

Recommended Readings

Among the standard reference works on demographic methods that readers may wish to consult are Barclay (1958), Jaffe (1951), Bogue (1969), and Whelpton (1954). More advanced discussions can be found in Spiegelman (1968), Keyfitz (1968), and in Shryock et al. (1971). For basic demographic data by nations, it is useful to consult Keyfitz and Flieger (1968) and the

United Nations Demographic yearbooks. Several readers provide excellent supplements to the introductory discussion in this chapter: Nam (1968), Heer (1968), and Freedman (1964). A particularly insightful volume is the reader by Harrison and Boyce (1972). It breaks disciplinary barriers and integrates relevant considerations from genetics, demography, ecology, sociology, and social anthropology into its discussions of the structure of human populations.

For further study of soil science with a view to broader understandings of the relationship between humans and plants, the essential book is Buckman and Brady (1969). Also useful are the short discussion in Steila (1976) and the extensive discussion of crops in Janick et al. (1974). The best two treatments of soils of the tropics are the collection of articles in National Academy of Science (1972) and the complilation of research by Sanchez (1976). The latter is the most thorough and up-to-date evaluation of soils of the tropics. On soils of the United States and temperate areas, there are numerous publications from the Soil Conservation Service and the United States Department of Agriculture. Consult a recent list of publications for the area of your interest.

The best source on primary production and productivity is still Whittaker (1970) and Whittaker and Likens (1975). Most standard ecology texts have comparative evaluations of ecosystem productivity. Additional information on energy flow modeling can be found in H.T. Odum's (1971) study or his more concise text of 1976 (Odum and Odum). Lugo and Snedacker (1971) edited a useful reader on ecological systems that compiles the classic articles on the flow of energy.

Two useful compilations of methods in the study of human physiology are Yoshimura and Weiner (1966) and Weiner and Lourie (1969). The edited volume by Damon (1975) on physiological anthropology is an excellent collection and could be read along with this book to their mutual benefit and that of the reader. The volume on work capacity by Edholm (1967) is now a classic on the topic. Standard books on nutrition are numerous, but one with a strong applied bent that makes it particularly useful in the study of diets is that by Williams (1973). The most concise treatments of human thermoregulation are the module by Little and Hochner (1973) and the more extensive discussion in Folk (1966). Their bibliography can guide the reader to more advanced studies. Specific studies of hot or cold environments are cited in the appropriate chapters of this book. Circadian rhythms and their behavioral component are discussed in Chapple (1970).

Social and cultural aspects of human ecology are treated in Alland (1975), Alland and McCay (1973), Bennett (1976), Netting (1977), and many other works cited throughout this book. There is currently no concise book on methodology for ecological anthropology. A useful discussion on methodology is found in the last chapter of Damas (1969b).

Among the quantitative methods dealing with decision making that may be helpful in modeling are: probability, expected utility, linear programming, and matrix algebra. Probability concepts are useful in dealing with conditions of uncertainty and limited information. The broad category of decision utility methods includes approaches that combine probability theory and economic data to generate decision algorithms. The decision tree method combines probability and expected utility in the solution of complex problems that involve both uncertainty and a large number of alternatives. This approach has been useful in management studies and in economic anthropology (Plattner 1974; Raiffa 1968). Linear programming and matrix algebra can be helpful in dealing with large bodies of data and efforts at optimization strategies.

Excellent books on these methods are available. Aoki's *Optimization of Stochastic Systems* (1967) contains a useful bibliography and makes use, throughout the book, of models in which "perfect information" is not available. Hadley's *Introduction to Probability and Statistical Decision Theory* (1967), on the other hand, assumes knowledge of prior probabilities. Schlaiffer's *Analysis of Decisions under Uncertainty* (1967) shows in great detail how one can structure apparently realistic problems. It is written in a how-to-do-it style and requires no more than an understanding of basic algebra. Readers may find this among the most useful of books on the subject. Raiffa's *Decision Analysis* (1970) provides prescriptive models of how to scale preferences according to utility values based on probabilities. It attempts to deal with subjective probabilities by scaling them—in an effort to bridge what it calls the "judgmental gap" between models and reality.

Part

2

Studies
of Human
Adaptability

5

Human
Adaptability
to Arctic Zones

The study of human adaptation to arctic conditions has engaged scholars in many fields since the late nineteenth century. In this chapter we will focus on the problems posed by the arctic environment of northern Alaska and on the strategies for adaptation used by the Inuit population. (The term *Inuit* [that is, "the people"] is preferred by the native peoples over *Eskimos* and will be used throughout this discussion.) Human populations inhabiting these regions must cope with extreme cold, low biological productivity of the terrestrial ecosystem, periods of prolonged light and darkness, and the dangers of working on snow and ice. Housing and shelter provide effective regulatory adjustments to cold stress, while acclimatory and developmental adjustments protect human extremities from damage during hunting activities. Particularly significant in such protection are a high rate of peripheral blood flow to the extremities, rapid warming of the body, and nonshivering forms of heat production.

The low biological productivity of the tundra made the Inuit turn to the rich ocean resources fed by **upwelling** and to animals that migrate between the arctic tundra and the subarctic taiga. Flexible forms of social organization extend the network of individual households through non-cousin marriage, adoption, spouse exchange, and meat-sharing partnerships. Hunters are taught animal **ethology** that give them skills in observing, stalking, and killing game. Inuit animistic religion helped reduce anxiety during winter, and the feasts that accompanied religious rituals served to reduce hostilities and to provide an artificial schedule during the perpetual darkness of winter, as well as contexts in which to socialize the population. The following section will detail some of the characteristics of the environment within which the Inuit must cope.

The Arctic Ecosystem

Arctic ecosystems are relatively young—probably going back to mid to late Pleistocene times (thirty thousand to eight thousand years ago). The flora and fauna of the arctic probably evolved in highland areas of central Asia and the Rockies and then colonized the tundra (Bliss et al. 1973:360). The tundra is the northernmost frontier of vegetation. The landscape is treeless and the temperatures bitterly cold. Summers are cool and short, but summer days are long. The vegetation resembles that of the high mountain alps, the area between the tree line and permanent snows. The situation is even harsher in Antarctica. The Antarctic continent covers 14.24 million square kilometers of which only 10,350 square kilometers are estimated to be suitable for sustaining life. The largest permanent inhabitant is a tiny fly. There are no land vertebrates, no birds, no amphibians, no reptiles, no freshwater fish, no mollusks, and no earthworms. Only lichens, mosses, and fungi in protected coastal areas are able to exist (Natani and Shurley 1974:90–91).

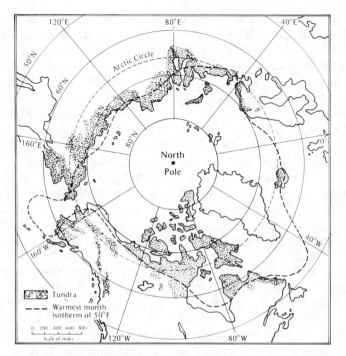

Figure 5.1 **The Tundra Areas and the 50°F. Isotherm**

Temperatures, particularly summer temperatures, are the usual means of defining tundra ecosystems. The definition most commonly used in Köppen's boundary line of the 50°F. (10°C.) isotherm for the warmest month of the year (see figure 5.1). However, other factors besides actual temperature are involved in the formation of tundra. Throughout the arctic, tundra vegetation can be found south of the 50°F. July isotherm (Mackay 1969:327). Wind is an important factor because of the absence of trees. At ground level the wind can have a rapid effect both in terms of dehydration and of frostbite.

Like other biomes, the tundra is not wholly undifferentiated. From the margins of the subarctic boreal coniferous forest, or **taiga,** to the polar desert one may note at least three types of tundra vegetation. The *bush tundra* represents the ecotone that borders the taiga and is characterized by dwarf trees. The bush tundra grades off into the broader expanse of *grass tundra,* which is composed of a nearly continuous mat of mosses, lichens, and bushes that tend to lie prone on the ground. When the soil surface thaws out in summer, the water does not drain but is soaked by the spongy vegetation. The depth of thawing may vary from only a few inches to a depth of about two feet. Below this, the ground will remain frozen and impermeable to both water and plant roots (R.L. Smith

1974:578). Tundra soils may contain high accumulations of peaty organic matter caused by the slow breakdown of plant material (Tedrow 1977). Closer to the poles is the *desert tundra*, an area characterized by lack of vegetation, except in protected hollows (James 1966:362). These differences are associated with the depth at which permafrost begins.

Tundra occupies a total of about eight million square kilometers of land or one-twentieth of the earth's land surface (Webber 1974). To date, it is an area with a sparse population—that is, between .02 and .08 persons per square kilometer. In 1972 there were ninety-five thousand Inuit scattered in Greenland, Canada, Alaska, and Siberia (Zegura 1978).[1] In addition, several Eurasian peoples inhabit the arctic of whom the Lapps, Samoyeds, Yakuty, and Chukchi are the most numerous (Irving 1972:23). The most comprehensive studies of Inuit groups are those of Spencer (1959) and Oswalt (1967), and both emphasize that cultural distinctions in Inuit lifestyles are a result of ecological adjustments to either coastal or inland resources.

Spencer (1959) divided the Inuit populations into *nuunamiut* (people of the land) and *tareumiut* (people of the sea) in accordance with the predominant subsistence strategy. Each group practiced a well-defined strategy consonant with the resources available in their respective environments. These groupings are not restricted to the Alaskan Inuit, but are paralleled in the contrast between the maritime and reindeer Chukchi (Spencer 1959:126). The nuunamiut and tareumiut were economically interdependent, but they avoided intermarriage and quasi-kin ties. The distinctiveness of the two groups was reinforced by the difference in skills that made marriage between them impractical. Other ethnographers have also noted this tendency of both groups[2] toward *endogamy* (Campbell 1968) resulting from the specialization required to exploit their respective resources (Burch and Correll 1972:24). Among the coastal population the village was a more stable unit because of the stable residence of the whaling crews. The caribou hunts of the inland Inuit never played this sort of stabilizing role.

The inland adaptation, based on caribou hunting, ended once in the 1920s and again in the 1950s. In the 1920s the outmigration was due to shifts in caribou migratory routes, whereas in the 1950s new weapons and overhunting reduced the size of the herds to the point that the human population could no longer be sustained (Spencer 1959:28; Gubser 1965; Shelford 1964:183). Since then, inland Inuit have joined the maritime

[1]Inuit populations are difficult to divide into unambiguous subgroups because of contradictory linguistic, cultural, and biological evidence. Zegura (1978) discusses the various boundaries offered by these three perspectives. Kraus (1973) summarizes the linguistic evidence; Spencer the cultural basis (1959); and Laughlin (1975) the recent archaeological evidence.

[2]Oswalt (1967) has referred to these two groups as "tribes", but few have adopted this suggestion.

Inuit in increasingly larger and fewer coastal villages (Jamison 1978; Arima 1975:175).

Tundra ecosystems are heat-limited ecosystems (Bliss et al. 1973), which results in low species diversity, low productivity, and the largely insignificant nature of plant **succession.** The short growing season in the arctic inhibits levels of production capable of supporting a large herbivorous population. Mosses yield the highest proportion of total phytomass, followed by phanerogams and lichens (Matveyeva et al. 1975:67). Tundra and desert ecosystems share similar problems; the crucial difference is that one ecosystem is limited by water availability, the other by extreme cold.

Plants have numerous physiological adaptations to cope with arctic conditions: prolonged seed dormancy and rapid germination, vegetative reproduction and metabolic systems able to capture, store, and use energy in a short time (Billings 1974:417). A large proportion of the plant biomass is below ground, protected from arctic wind, cold, and herbivore pressure (Webber 1974:457). The environment has been described as fragile because it is biologically rather simple and because of the long time lapse required for its return to steady state. Damage to tundra vegetation by tracked vehicles alters plant cover and reduces both surface insulation and **albedo.** As a result, more heat is absorbed, which leads to deeper thaw and greater erosion (Webber 1974:465). Erosion is difficult to control because of the slowness of plant succession. Once an eroded niche becomes empty, there are few species than can occupy it. This is a result of the low species diversity (Bliss et al 1973:360–361.). Arctic soils are of recent origin and tend to be **hydromorphic.** Most of the soil nutrients are not available for plants because of permafrost. To survive, therefore, plants use complex internal cycles that retain and reincorporate nutrients rather than relinquishing them to the decomposers. Phosphorus appears to be a limiting factor to arctic plants' productivity (Bunnell et al. 1975:117).

Many of the land animals, such as reindeer in Eurasia and caribou in North America, migrate over vast expanses of tundra territory in summer and exploit the richer boreal forests to the south (that is, the taiga). Caribou and reindeer are essential resources to the inland arctic populations. This has been documented by Gubser (1965), Balikci (1970), and Arima (1975). The musk ox was important at one time, but it has been brought to near extinction. Herding, specifically reindeer herding, is about the only other effective way of supporting human populations in the inland tundra areas (Kallio 1975:219).[3] Smaller fauna is found in greater densities. Insects are restricted to a few genera, but are abundant in midsummer. Black flies, deer flies, and mosquitoes are so numerous that Inuit in many areas must continue to cover most parts of their bodies, despite the pleas-

---

[3]Recent studies of reindeer herding and its modernization include those by Pelto (1973), Ingold (1974), and Müller-Wille (1974).

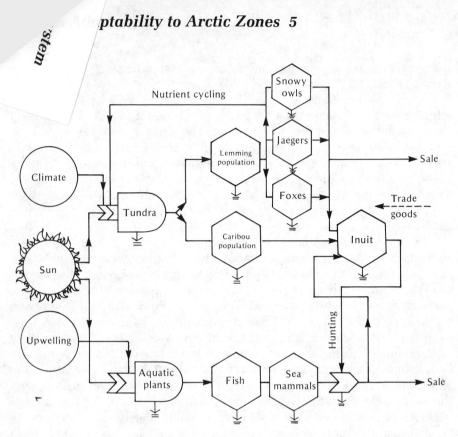

Figure 5.2   **Energy Flow Model of an Arctic Ecosystem**   The Inuit population plays a dominant role in controlling population densities of
land and sea mammals. Lemmings speed up the nutrient cycling,
and upwelling makes the aquatic environment rich in resources
for the Inuit.

ant temperatures, to avoid their bites. Arctic birds have a fast life cycle,
similar to that of rodents. The ptarmigan and the redpoll have heavy fat
layers and dense feathers for protection against cold. Ducks and geese are
also important wild fowl resources to the Inuit. Most bird and insect species, however, leave the tundra for more southern regions as winter
approaches (R. L. Smith 1974:587).

Ocean fauna has always been more important to the arctic human
population than land fauna. Ringed seals (*Phoca foerida*), barbed seals
(*Erignathus barbatus*), walruses (*Odobenus*), whales (especially bowhead,
white, and fin types), and fish and shellfish varieties are among the most
important maritime resources exploited. Other seals, such as the spotted
seal (*Phoca vitulina*), the bladdernose (*Cystophora cristata*), saddleback
(*Phoca groenlandica*), fur seal (*Arctocephalus ursinus*), sea lion (*Eumeto-
pias jubatus*), and ribbon seal (*Histriophoca fasciata*) avoid firm ice and
are less available in winter to Inuit hunters. Seals provide many raw mate-

rials that make Inuit cold adaptation possible, such as mittens, boots, summer coats, trousers and sinew thread.

There has been a tendency to overemphasize the importance of the larger fauna to the neglect of smaller animals that may play a more important ecosystemic role. For example, the brown lemming *(Lemmus sibericus)* is the dominant herbivore of the arctic. Unlike other arctic animals which leave the tundra seasonally, the lemming is active year-round. Researchers have noted that lemming densities vary in cycles of three to five years. Its population "booms-and-busts" mark significant cycles in standing crop, in soil temperatures, in depth of thaw, and in rates of organic decomposition (Bunnell et al. 1975:95). Numbers decline in summer as a result of predation, but steadily increase over time until overgrazing and natural increases in the predator population bring on a sudden decline. Following such a "crash," lemmings and their predators remain at low densities, thus permitting a recovery in tundra vegetation.

The spatial distribution of nutrients can be altered by the grazing habits and consequent fecal deposition of lemmings. During the yearly melt off, they facilitate a flush of nutrients that tends to collect in crevices and ponds. Figure 5.2 illustrates some of the crucial energy relations in the arctic and the important role of lemmings in the ecosystem. The feedback of nutrients from the lemming population to the soil and to plant components is crucial to the system's productivity. Even though this flow is determined by the timing of the thaw, coastal Inuit rely for up to 83 percent of subsistence on marine and freshwater aquatic resources, rather than on terrestrial production. The inland population rely on a more evenly balanced seasonal exploitation of both aquatic and terrestrial animals.

Adaptation to Cold Stress

Inuit adaptations to cold stress involve both physiological and cultural adjustments. For a while it was thought that the Inuit had unique genetic adaptations that facilitated cold adaptation. One common misconception was that they had a great deal of body fat when, in reality, they are relatively lean (Laughlin 1966). Other factors often cited as morphological adaptations to cold stress were eyefold characteristics and facial flatness. It has been shown that these morphological characteristics offer inadequate protection (Steegman 1967, 1970). Laughlin noted that the frequent use of slit goggles and visors during travel is a demonstration of the inadequacy of these Inuit morphological characteristics (Laughlin 1966:476).

Failure to protect against cold stress can result in cold injury, frostbite, **hypothermia,** and eventually, death (Carlson and Hsieh 1965:16). (Failure of the thermoregulatory system occurs when body core temperature is near 33°C., and death occurs at 25°C.) Among the cultural practices that facilitate Inuit adaptation to cold are clothes, shelter, use of seal oil lamps, sharing of body heat and diet. Recent writings have described the exposure of the Inuit to the arctic cold as chronic, but moderate. In fact, the **microclimate** of men in arctic clothing was found to be the same as that of men working in temperate zones with light clothing.

Cultural Regulatory Adjustments   Adequate insulation is an important way of preventing cold stress. The insulation problem is dual: how to provide for continued warmth and how to prevent overheating during periods of strenuous work. If the latter problem is not properly solved, sweat-soaked or frozen insulated clothing results in a loss of its cold protection effectiveness. Irving (1972:181) noted that this sometimes occurs. He described how the Inuit hang their clothes so the moisture will freeze and then beat out the frost with a stick. Eventually they must scrape the leather to restore its pliability.

Two methods are commonly used to prevent overheating. In summer when the Inuit must do heavy work, they remove their impermeable "outside" parkas and remain relatively cool in the outside temperature. The more important method, however, is the actual design of the Inuit clothing. The traditional clothing of the arctic has many vented openings through which air can constantly flow in and out. Figure 5.3 illustrates some of the venting areas of arctic fur clothing, which can be released or closed by drawstrings (Folk 1966:123). This is one way in which the traditional Inuit adapted their clothing to ambient conditions. The other major insulative factor is that the clothing has numerous layers that trap and warm the air and act as an insulator; and, with the outside layer being windproof and impermeable, the clothing holds the heat in and keeps cold and wetness out (Edholm and Lewis 1964:436). Because of the difficulty of matching activity and weather to clothing while on the move, it is common to tolerate moderate degrees of thermal discomfort under these conditions (Budd 1974:33-34). The solution to this problem is to dress too warmly and to tolerate sweating during work periods and shivering during rest periods.

Boots (*kimik*) call for special attention. The sharp ice at subzero temperatures can cut the best footgear and extreme care must be taken to protect such clothing. Traditionally the soles were made of carefully prepared bearded seal skin, while the uppers were made from split ringed seal skin. They were sewn with sinew, but the sewer avoided making needleholes all the way through the skin layers to assure its waterproofness. Stockings were made from the fragile fur of the arctic hare and were kept dry by inserting a pad of dry grass between the sole of the boot and the sole of the stocking. This pad absorbed any moisture that penetrated from outside or moisture from feet perspiration (Ekblaw 1927:181–182). Similarly, seal skin mittens were filled with grass pads to protect the hands on long trips.

Figure 5.3   **The Chimney Effect in Inuit Fur Clothing**   Vents in the clothing can be opened by release of drawstrings during exercise to
prevent accumulation of sweat.

Like clothing, Inuit shelters must hold heat in and be windproof.
Cold-adapted housing must avoid loss of heat through compact design,
minimum exposure of external surface areas, use of insulating materials,
and the encouragement of heat reflection from internal heat sources (for
example, lamps, stoves, and body heat) (Rapoport 1969:95). While
engaged in nomadic activities in the pursuit of subsistence, Inuit build
snow shelters. Snow shelters (that is, igloos) have been described as
excellent insulators by virtue of the myriad of small air cells in the ice.
The igloo offers minimum wind resistance, provides maximum volume
with the least surface area, and is effectively heated by a seal oil lamp,
which also provides interior light. The heat of the lamp causes minor
melting of the inside snow surfaces which refreeze during the night, thus
forming a smooth reflecting surface that conserves radiant heat. The outside surface becomes encrusted with snow and forms an airtight seal.

In summer *tupik* (sealskin tents) are used. The tents, made of dark-
colored skins to absorb solar energy, are double-layered and provide a

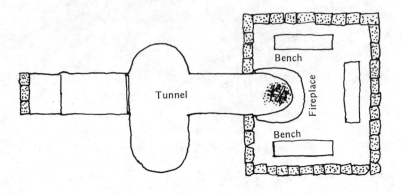

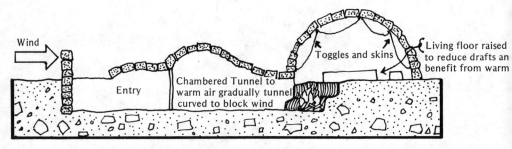

Figure 5.4 **Features of Inuit Housing** Three architectural features are particularly significant: the presence or absence of fireplaces, the
positioning of benches, and the depth of the tunnel doorway.
Presence or absence of fireplaces was associated with availability
of wood in winter. If the tunnel were not subterranean, floor temperatures could drop below freezing.

Source: Amos Rapoport.© 1969. *House Form and Culture.* Englewood Cliffs, N.J.:
Prentice-Hall.

comfortable temperature in the warmer periods (Edholm and Lewis
1964:436). The tupik is made of many seal skins sewn into a continuous
cover. Large tents require well over sixty skins. An inner tent and outer
tent create an area of dead air that facilitates warming during cold
periods, but can be opened during the summer months (Ekblaw
1927:161).

For more permanent habitation, northern Alaska Inuit also build
semi-subterranean stone or driftwood housing, covered with turf and
snow for insulation. They are frequently located in protected hillside
spots. These houses consist of walls five feet in height, with narrow
underground entrances and with the living area at a higher level than the
entry (see Figure 5.4). Like Inuit clothing, these stone and sod houses
always have ventilation holes to allow circulation and to prevent over-

heating. The interiors are covered in seal skins. Thus constructed, the subterranean winter home is warm, keeping temperatures between 15.5° and 21°C. (Ibid.:169). (Analogous housing solutions may be noted among the Yakuty of Siberia. They use a timber frame covered with wood and then with a heavy layer of sod [Rapoport 1969:96].)

The Inuit diet is high in fat and protein and delivers significant amounts of calories. To keep warm and to carry out strenuous activities, such as sledging, Edholm and Lewis (1964:441) estimated that a man requires approximately five thousand kcals daily. Seasonal fluctuations in body weight have been noted: body weight and subcutaneous fat rise in winter and decrease in spring and summer. This may be a biological rhythm that enhances adaptability to cold, but it may also result from the relative inactivity of winter as compared to the vigorous exercise of spring and summer (Ibid.).

Physiological Adjustments Although clothing and shelter can provide warm microclimates, the Inuit are exposed to extreme cold during winter seal hunting and ice fishing. To maintain body core temperatures within a permissible range, a number of systems may be activated (see figure 5.5). Of these the most important are shivering, vasoconstriction, increase of basal metabolic rates (BMR) and oxygen consumption, acclimatizational changes, and behavioral responses (Van Wie 1974:815).

The most rapid and effective way to increase heat production is by vigorous exercise, but this response cannot be maintained for long periods of time (Hanna 1968:216–217). Shivering is a frequent response, which can increase heat production up to threefold, but it does not increase the total heat content of the body to any significant degree (Folk 1966:102). More useful and effective is the activation of nonshivering thermogenesis. This chemical response refers to increases in cellular metabolism without any accompanying muscular movement. Adults are able to elevate metabolism 25 percent over basal levels, while infants are able to increase it by 170 percent over BMR (Little and Hochner 1973:6). Nonshivering thermogenesis is more effective than shivering in protecting the body since it is located in the body core, rather than the skin surface. It is associated with the presence of brown adipose tissue in all human infants, and this response is apparently maintained in adults native to cold areas (Ibid.: 6–7). The nonshivering metabolism of all Inuit is 30 to 40 percent greater than in control groups (Folk 1966:110).

There is some evidence that Inuit exhibit a kind of metabolic acclimatization (Hammel 1964:425). Their 20 to 40 percent higher BMR reduces the risk of hypothermia, cold discomfort, and pain. It is still not clear whether this is a physiological response to cold or a result of their protein-rich diet. (Ibid.:430–433); Edholm and Lewis 1964:444). In either case, the result is a slightly warmer core temperature.

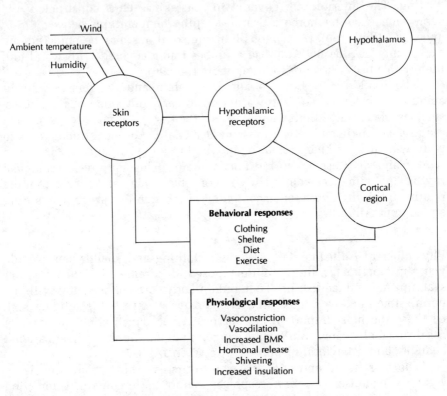

Figure 5.5   Cold Thermoregulation in Human Beings

Inuit have also been noted to have a high rate of peripheral blood flow to the extremities when exposed to cold. This has been measured by high finger temperatures in cold water immersion tests (Hanna 1968:230). Figure 5.6 compares response to cold in Inuit with the response of other test subjects. The warmer finger temperatures maintained by the Inuit occur in persons habitually exposed to cold at the extremities, thereby preventing injury and allowing greater hand dexterity in cold environments (Ibid.:220). Harrison et al. (1977:429) have noted that this localized response is cyclical: intense vasoconstriction is followed five minutes later by vasodilation and then a return to vasoconstriction and so on. This response at the extremities prevents tissue temperature from dropping to frostbite levels.

The higher BMR of the Inuit is complemented by their ability to respond quickly to cold exposure, both in the extremities and throughout the body. This ability is the result of *high core to shell conductance*, which refers to rapid response when exposure to cold occurs. This response is as much as 60 percent faster among Inuit than among white controls. The mechanism is commonly associated with a high rate of

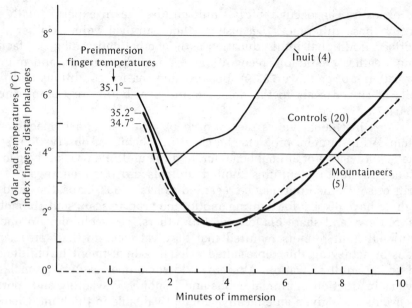

Figure 5.6   **Vascular Responses to Ice Water Immersion**   The response to cold of finger vessels of Inuit is different from that of other outdoor people. Inuit retain warmer fingers, which assists dexterity.

Source: C. J. Eagan. 1963. Introduction and Terminology: Habituation and Peripheral Tissue Adaptations. Fed. Proc. 22:930–1933.

blood flow to the extremities. High heat conductivity, combined with high heat production, enables Inuit to temporarily expose body parts without experiencing frostbite (Hanna 1968:229–230). Although this type of response consumes a great deal of energy, this has not normally been a problem among the Inuit as their diet provided them with adequate calories.

In summary, then, although localized acclimatory adjustments to cold are noted in the extremities, the evidence does not suggest a general adaptation to cold by Inuit and other arctic natives. This may be due to the protection provided the body by cultural adjustments that prevent exposure. The extremities, however, cannot be as effectively protected.

Coping With Snow and Sea Ice

A great deal of the ecological knowledge of the Inuit centers around the identification of minute differences in ice and snow characteristics. Such knowledge is essential to survive in an environment where death from cold exposure can occur rapidly. Inuit children learn experimentally to identify these differences because of their survival value. Collier has described traditional Inuit education as nonverbal and ecological, facilitating weather prediction, recognition of blizzard warnings, and migratory patterns of game (1973:39). Boas related sea ice conditions and the habits of ringed seals to the demographic distribution of Central Inuit (1964:417).

Laughlin (1968a) views the training of a hunter as a biobehavioral system. Adult hunters program the child into habits of observation, systematic knowledge of animal behavior, and the multiple uses of the game. Because in hunting cultures hunted animals are often endowed with spirits or souls, the hunt may be regarded as hazardous. Thus, the child is taught to have respect for hunting and for the prey, to scan, stalk, immobilize, retrieve, and share his fortune with others. The technology of more traditional Inuit hunters required that they get close to their prey, and means of achieving this represented a lengthy investment in childhood and young adult education. Adults would sometimes capture animals to serve as instruction in animal habits and anatomy. Playacting and sportslike events were given an educative content valuable in the hunt (Chance 1966:74). Perseverance, toughness, and generosity were desirable traits (Nelson 1969:375–576). Generosity, particularly towards kin and meat–sharing nonrelatives, plays an important adaptive role in regions such as inland Alaska where resources are irregular in both quantity and quality.

Inuit on land must intimately know the behavior of game, but on sea ice they must also know the behavior of the ice itself (Ibid.:9). Such knowledge comes about slowly, mainly through the childhood **socialization** process described above. Inuit, for example, know that young salt ice (that is, the state of the ice in the autumn) is flexible rather than brittle. When sleds begin to sink, they know that it is best to keep the sled moving and "ride out" the thin ice spots. The Inuit make use of color as a distinguishing feature between different types of ocean ice. Unsafe thin ice tends to be very dark, as it thickens it becomes gray, and from this point to darker color gradations, it is safe enough to support a man and a loaded dog sled (Ibid.: 16). Color distinctions are particularly useful since they allow an Inuit to determine conditions ahead of time and to lead his dog appropriately. This method is said to be nearly 100 percent effective— although not infallible. In inland lagoons, for example, color is deceptive as a result of suspended sediment.

The Inuit avoidance of risky situations and knowledge of ice serve them well, but accidents still occur. In the past, the Inuit went on ice prepared for many types of emergencies. Hunting partnerships helped to provide protection and assistance in emergencies. The *unaak*, or ice probe, is a safety aid in avoiding being swept by the current underneath the ice and helps to spread one's weight on thin ice. If one falls through the ice and gets out soaked, it is customary to run back to the village to keep warm. If too far from a settlement, the hunting partners may lend extra items of clothing until the soaked garments dry. The skin and fur clothing is relatively waterproof, and if powdery snow is available nearby, it can be used to blot out the moisture before it soaks in and freezes (Ibid.:24–28).

Weather prediction is important and, at least in northwestern Alaska, relatively easy once the indicators are known. Changes in barometric pressure are reliable indicators in winter storm predictions. Strong winds are forecast by elongated clouds and by ice mirages resembling low clouds. The behavior of the wind may forecast the continuation or end of a storm. Periodic subsidence in wind indicates an end to the storm, while strong gusts followed by normal wind speeds suggest continuation of the storm. Dogs traditionally provided excellent weather forecasting. They howled more frequently right before winter storms and predicted the end of it by similar behavior. Today the Inuit increasingly rely on the radio for weather forecasting (Ibid.:29–47).

In addition to extensive knowledge of the environment, the Inuit is in good physical condition, although not unusually so for an active person. Shepard (1974) has reviewed work performance among Inuit and Ainu populations. There appear to be no appreciable differences between mean values for Inuit VO_2 Max and those for other populations. However, in Inuit performance, patience, experience, and skill in interpreting small signs are more important than a superior oxygen transport system (Rennie 1978). There has been a steady deconditioning in physical capacity in recent years as a result of changing lifestyles. Young Inuit are much less willing to face up to the rigors of the hunting way of life (Nelson 1969).

To cope with snow and ice cover, Inuit rely greatly on observation both to avoid unnecessary expenditures of energy, and to circumvent unnecessary dangers. Foresight is particularly crucial to the Inuit and is evidenced by their unwillingness to travel onto sea ice in winter unless they have carefully excluded all potential signs that they might be set adrift on a loose floe. Nelson has noted than Inuit seldom act in the Western manner of doing something for the excitement of taking a chance (Ibid.:377). Instead, the Inuit carefully avoid percentage risks, even when the risk may be as low as 20 percent. Alertness is also valued. Seldom do they give their full attention to a single activity, but instead commonly glance around to survey their surroundings. Such alertness minimizes the danger of being carried away by floating ice, presents opportunities of hunting animals other than the one being stalked, and familiarizes each person with his surroundings. When crises arise, Inuit hunters exercise unusual experimentation. In one case noted by Nelson they constructed an emergency sled from pieces of frozen meat (Ibid.:378).

Cooperativeness in hunting also enhances the survival chances of the individual through pooling of physical effort and environmental knowledge. Laughter rather than anger is the typical reaction to a mistake, and this helps to alleviate the frustrations that surely occur frequently in an environment where so much can go wrong. Many of these traits have begun to disappear with the steady acculturation of the Inuit to Western culture and with the adoption of time-saving technologies.

Adaptation to Prolonged Light and Darkness

Arctic populations are subject to fluctuating cycles of light and darkness in the spring and fall and to no cycling at all in midsummer and midwinter (Foulks 1972:83). Above the Arctic Circle daylight changes dramatically with the seasons. In late June the sun hovers around the horizon and does not set. By contrast, in late December the sun never comes above the horizon. This unusual pattern is believed to have a negative effect upon the well-being of populations. Human physiological functioning is, to an extent, regulated by the pattern of light and darkness in a twenty-four-hour period. Numerous physiological functions in human beings are known to vary according to a circadian rhythm synchronized to a twenty-four-hour scheme. Body temperature, blood pressure, pulse, respiration, blood sugar, hemoglobin levels, amino acid levels, levels of adrenal hormones, and levels of minerals excreted in the urine all follow a daily rhythm. The development of this pattern may be associated with human phylogenetic development in equatorial regions. When man moved to arctic zones, which are subject to twenty-four hours of light in summer and twenty-four hours of darkness in winter, adjustments had to be made. Antarctic psychological researchers have noted that insomnia, disrupted sleep, anxiety, depression, and irritability are common during winter. The problem, however, is believed to be largely social and related to prolonged confinement (Natani and Shurley 1974:92).

Physiological Disturbances Bohlen et al. (1970) have shown that the extreme seasonal changes in arctic light/dark patterns seriously disturb Inuit physiological functioning. They found that body temperature and urinary excretion of potassium maintain twenty-four-hour rhythms, but that urinary excretion of calcium leads to mild anxiety and depression. In individuals with psychological predispositions for anxiety, this phenomenon can have a cumulative effect and precipitate behavior characteristic of "arctic hysteria," or *pibloktok*. Arctic hysteria is a temporary mental disorder characterized by alterations in consciousness, memory loss, psychomotor seizures, and other symptoms typical of epilepsy. Arctic hysteria encompasses two general types of behavior: imitative mania and frenzied disassociated states. The former is confined to Siberia, while the latter is found throughout the arctic. Figure 5.7 illustrates the type of seizure associated with arctic hysteria. A role model for the frenzied behavior manifested in arctic hysterias is said to be shamanistic spirit possession (Foulks 1972).

124

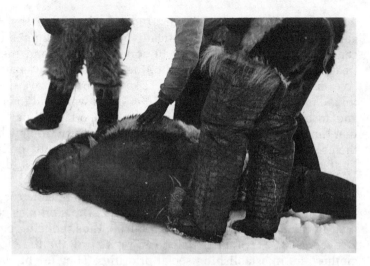

Figure 5.7   **An Inuit Experiencing Arctic Hysteria**
Courtesy American Museum of Natural History

Cases of arctic hysteria have been noted for as long as outsiders have known Inuit populations. They were said to be more frequent among women than men, but no one ever gave the matter sufficient attention to permit any assertions on the subject (Ibid.:17). Nachman has suggested that such attacks may have served as social expressions of role demands (1969:7–11). He explains that for women the attacks might have provided an opportunity to acknowledge sexual threats and temptations normally not permitted. By the same token, men might have been able to express fears about their inability to fulfill the responsibilities of married life. Gussow (1960) argues that arctic hysteria was a basic way in which the Inuit reacted to intense stress. Such stress might have been associated with the low and steadily depleting food supplies of winter. Wallace (1960) has suggested that numerous factors were probably implicated: shamanistic outlets for hostility, hypocalcemic levels resulting from a low calcium diet and low vitamin D synthesis during winter darkness, and anxiety over subsistence.

Religion as a Regulatory Adjustment   A great deal of the stress that is implicated in arctic hysteria was relieved through religious practices. Inuit religion was essentially animistic, with animals, the moon, and other environmental features being imbued with supernatural will and power. Religion, therefore, sought to create a meaningful and peaceful relationship between Inuit and game animals through taboos, ceremonials, and practices that prevented excess slaughter of animals, provided release from tensions, and defined human roles and actions (Martin 1976:18).

125

Inuit groups regulated the use of animals and the distribution of game and defined hunters' obligations through religious taboos. Rituals centered around economically important animals and their spirits. The treatment of animal corpses and of the human dead was markedly similar (Weyer 1932:336), and animals, like the people, were divided along inland/maritime lines. Sea and land animals were said to enjoy separation and to be displeased by contact with each other. Rituals helped assure that the spirits of the animals killed would return, in new bodies, to offer themselves again to the hunter. However, the Inuit believed that if a hunter killed too many animals, the animal spirits would withdraw and not offer their bodies to the hunter.

Religion also helped the Inuit explain bad weather or reduced game supply (Chance 1966:35). Personal guilt and misfortunes could be attributed to the machinations of angry spirits, thus reducing personal anxiety (Weyer 1932:231). Taboos helped in regulating the time for making new clothes and in establishing social priorities. They might also have helped to establish a **circannual rhythm** than could have alleviated the disturbances caused by the light/dark arctic pattern.

In the regulation of social activity, the shaman played a crucial role. A shaman who could successfully forecast the weather, help cure the ill, bring good luck to hunters, and make game receptive to hunters could achieve a measure of respect and even wealth. However, if his powers failed to improve the group's life-chances, he might be deposed or killed (Weyer 1932:451–452). The group, then, selected individuals who manifested skills in forecasting crucial factors involved in survival and who could educate the population into the proper behavior required for well-being.

One means of socially coping with winter stress is to hold ceremonial feasts where foods and other goods are distributed to the less fortunate in the group. The Bladder Festival was held in west central and southwestern Alaska. Its rituals ensured that the bladders of the animals caught in the past year would return to the animals and enhance future hunting chances. Shamanistic seances, the mimicking of hunting dramas, and purifications were also a part of the ceremonies. The poor and the elderly received special treatment, as well as a substantial portion of the food and goods distributed (Lantis 1947:60–62).

Ceremonies that provided relief from sexual tension were also common. The Inglalik Feast for the Dead and the western Alaskan Asking Feast included exchange of favors and sex and ritual exchanges of male/female roles and dress (Ibid.:74). Although their purpose was to stimulate animal reproduction and enhance hunters' chances in the next season, they probably also helped to relieve social and psychological tensions (Martin 1976:36). The Messenger Feast was a high point of winter and served to facilitate social and economic exchange (Spencer 1959:216–228). It manifested numerous similarities to the potlatches of the northwest coast.

Changes in Regimentation and Diet   Western regimentation and diet have facilitated Inuit adaptation to the light/dark pattern. The Inuit have acquired watches, and schools have introduced a scheduling element that strongly socializes the child into the twenty-four-hour rhythm. The introduction of milk products into their diet has enhanced the calcium levels of the Inuit and facilitated calcium homeostasis. The adoption of wage labor requires being at work at stated times, often according to a schedule more familiar in New York than in the arctic. These socially prescribed schedules have improved the physiological performance of the Inuit. However, not all the changes have been for the better. Concentration in villages has led to abandonment of traditional housing and adoption of less healthy shelters. Instead of the sod and snow igloos, Inuit now live in plywood shacks or government-built prefabricated homes heated by coal stoves where air is not properly humidified. As a result, the population is all the more susceptible to respiratory infections. Chronic respiratory ailments surely affect the emotional profile of the Inuit and foster susceptibility to nervous disorders similar to arctic hysteria. Such impairment may also be implicated in problems of foreign language learning and school performance (Foulks 1972).

Coping With Low Biological Productivity

The low net productivity of the tundra imposes on the human population of that zone a constraint that, using flexible forms of social organization, they overcome by seasonally exploiting coastal and more southerly taiga resources. Interdependence between coastal and inland groups was created by the need of each to trade for the resources of the other (Spencer 1959:76). The coastal Inuit lived in small, but relatively permanent settlements oriented to the seasonally regular appearance of large numbers of sea mammals, which were used not only for food, but also for clothing and fuel. Inland Inuit, on the other hand, were more nomadic, following the herds of caribou and exploiting the fish of the rivers and, in their excursions to the coast, sea mammals. The inland population depended on the coast for supplies of seal oil and other fuels, while the coastal population depended on the interior for caribou skins and plant products, particularly vitamin-rich berries. Not much has been made of the Inuit use of plant foods, but it is known that when berries were available they stored them in seal oil or kept them stored in the permafrost (Nickerson et al. 1973).

Social Adjustments   The maintenance of interdependencies among Inuit was facilitated by flexible alliance systems. The Inuit recognized membership in two lineages. Because of bilateral, or bilineal, descent, individuals

127

could count on many kinsmen. Kinship bonds assured cooperation, mutual aid, and responsibility for each other's actions. Essentially, the basic principle of the Inuit social organization was to extend, by kin and quasi-kin ties, the sphere of social obligations. Although intermarriage across the inland/coastal boundary was rare, an elaborate quasi-kin system evolved that allowed the extension of hospitality and protection, and encouraged trade (Spencer 1959:95). The flexible Inuit kinship system also permitted inclusion of new members into the network whenever appropriate (see the review of alliance practices in Guemple 1972).

The flexibility of Inuit settlements was a response to scattered resources, aimed at an increasingly secure subsistence. The single **nuclear family** unit was maintained year-round, but other **affinal** and **consanguineal** ties may have been present as well. Aggregation, when such groupings maximized hunting chances and provided greater security at uncertain periods (that is, winter), also occurred and was facilitated by the yearly cycle of religious feasts.

Winter sealing fostered the formation of relatively large winter villages made up of several **extended families,** whereas summer fishing was a time for the efforts of small families. Seal meat-sharing patterns reflected precise rules of cooperation:

The seal-meat sharing system functioned as follows: every hunter had a number of sharing partners for each part of seal meat and blubber. . . . Ideally, there were twelve and they were chosen by the hunter's mother either shortly after birth or during his childhood. Whenever the hunter killed a seal his wife cut up the animal and gave the appropriate parts to each one of his partners' wives. (Balikci 1970:135).

Partners named each other by the name of the part of the seal exchanged, and this reinforced the sense of cooperation required during the long, dark winter months. What is of great ecological and social interest is that close relatives and members of the same commensal unit could not become partners. Only distant kin or nonkin were eligible, thereby extending the network of subsistence and overcoming the hostility that was often directed at those outside the extended family (Ibid.: 138). Yengoyan (1976:129) points out that *any* society inhabiting an environment with marked fluctuations in resources requires structural devices, such as meat-sharing partnerships, that allow local populations to expand and contract in response to resource availability. Having a broad network of partnerships allowed individual households to move without losing the security of having help in new areas.

Exploitation of the scarce and sometimes fluctuating resources necessitated that the Inuit use population controls to adjust the size of families to the capacity of the provider and to enhance the survival of the living and productive members of the group (Balikci 1968:81). The most common population control practice was female infanticide. During times of stress, however, infanticide—regardless of the sex of the infant—also took place. Such an act freed the mother and others in the group from the emotional and physical costs of a dependent child. The long-term effect of this practice may have been to increase the proportion of older individuals in the population, thereby bringing about a more stable population structure (Freeman 1971).

Female infanticide was based on the cultural preference given to boys and on the fact that girls were considered less productive than their male siblings who became the hunters. Thus, families tried to maximize their number of boys. The practice of female infanticide also may have taken into account the higher death rate of males who, while hunting, froze to death or were killed in disputes. While among juveniles, males numerically predominated over females, by adulthood females were more numerous than males. Schrire and Steiger (1974) have gleaned from ethnographic accounts incidents of female infanticide and tried to test the effects of such a practice on the population. The evidence suggests that the rate of female infanticide had to be below 8 percent to ensure the survival of the group. The greatest likelihood is that infanticide was an opportunistic response to short-lived crises and intense periods of stress, rather than a normal cultural practice manifesting preference for boys.

Suicide, senilicide, and invalicide also served as means of eliminating unproductive members of society—a task that the nonproductive individuals often allocated to themselves through voluntary abandonment (Spencer 1959:92). One should not assume that female infanticide and other population controls were evenly practiced throughout the arctic. In areas where winter ice prevents access to intertidal areas, the old, the infirm, and the young became potential candidates for abandonment and exposure to the elements. These practices were less frequent in areas where the nonproductive subgroups could obtain a sizeable portion of their own food supply, in particular shellfish (Laughlin 1968b:242). When such intertidal areas or coastal resources were not available, a feedback process may have been effected by which the population adjusted to the leanest months of the year and to the areas with the least resources. The population may also have used prolonged nursing[4], abortion, sexual abstention, as well as infanticide, to limit its numbers.

Four social features appear to enhance the adjustment of the arctic population, particularly to the inland areas: marriage practices, adoption, child betrothal, and spouse exchange (Damas 1969a:32). The goal of Inuit marriage appears to have been to extend, as far as possible, the bonds of mutual aid and cooperation. Marriage between cousins was discouraged,

---

[4]In humans, prolonged lactation only incompletely suppresses ovulation. Birdsell has suggested that the demands of nursing a previous child and of mobility may have made it necessary to kill 15 to 50 percent of the children born (1968:243). Compare with Schrire and Steiger's maximum figure of 8 percent (1974).

and no **levirate** or **sororate** was practiced. Even marriage between quasi-kin (for example, trading partners) was viewed as undesirable. Through adoption, the population could be redistributed according to sex, as well as number, into viable units adjusted to current environmental conditions. The value of child betrothal is tied to the practice of female infanticide. A male could assure himself of a spouse by arranging to marry a female infant. This arrangement might also be said to have freed him from devoting time to searching for eligible females and to have allowed him to give full attention to hunting. Child betrothal may have also reduced the incidence of female infanticide. Spouse exchange is cited as a means of extending one's quasi-kin network and of expressing mutual aid and cooperation (Spencer 1959). Damas (1969a) suggests that it might also have alleviated the tensions of monogamous sexual life. All four of these social features helped to regulate the size of groups, their reproduction, and their distribution and to affirm their bonds of cooperation.

Implicated in the practice of senilicide may be a pathological condition in aging Inuit known as *bone resorption*. Aging Inuit appear to lose bone mineral content at an accelerated rate, possibly as a result of high protein, high phosphorus, low calcium diets and marginal vitamin D intakes (Mazess and Mather 1978; Zegura and Jamison 1978). While the causal factors are not well established, the condition is known to lead to bone resorption and to increased frequency of vertebral fractures. Such increased impairment of the aged put a major drain on seminomadic communities. Coastal populations were able to store food for lean times, and their sedentariness permitted the old and infirm to continue contributing to group subsistence instead of becoming burdens (Spencer 1959:92–95). Laughlin has pointed out that the richness of the Aleut intertidal ecosystem permitted greater longevity than elsewhere in the arctic and that older Aleuts played an important role as "consultants and cultural librarians" (1972:386). Table 5.1 illustrates the greater number of persons who survive to ripe old age in the Aleutian islands vis-à-vis Labrador Inuit populations. While these are not northern Alaskan samples, they do suggest the need for further research on arctic demography.

Diet　Despite the absence of plants in their barren tundra surroundings, the northern Alaskan Inuit practicing a traditional subsistence pattern had a nutritionally adequate diet. The major portion of the native diet consisted of seal, walrus, caribou, and fish. It was a diet high in protein and fat, but very low in carbohydrates. This native diet, when prepared in a traditional manner, was able to furnish all essential nutrients (Draper 1977). From meat, Inuit obtained protein and an adequate supply of vitamin K and the B-complex vitamins—the latter usually associated with enzyme proteins. The oils of fish and marine mammals supplied vitamins A and D. For a long while it was thought that Inuit diets were deficient in vitamin C, but, surprisingly, no symptoms of such a deficiency were

Table 5.1   **Age at Death in Populations of Aleuts[a] and Inuits[b]**

| | Aleut | | Inuit | |
Age	Number	%	Number	%
1–15	150	30.55	38	34.55
15–25	41	8.35	10	9.09
25–45	103	20.98	29	26.36
45–65	117	23.83	20	18.18
65–80	58	11.81	13	11.81
80–100	22	4.48	0	0.00

[a] Aleuts of the Aleutian Islands.
[b] Inuit of Labrador
Source: William Laughlin. 1972. Ecology and Population Structure in the Arctic. In The Structure of Human Populations. G. Harrison and A. Boyce, eds. Oxford: Clarendon Press.

noted. Some have suggested that the Inuit must have obtained vitamin C by consuming caribou rumen that was still full of undigested plant materials (Nickerson et al. 1973). Studies of cattle, however, have shown that vitamin C is rapidly destroyed in the rumen. It is now believed that the ascorbic acid was derived chiefly from fresh meat consumed raw or only slightly cooked (Draper 1977).

The diet of the Inuit was traditionally high in phosphorus and low in calcium. This high phosphorus intake is not only associated with bone loss, but also is implicated in the abnormalities of calcium homeostasis that were discussed earlier. A total concentration on protein consumption raises a potential problem in glucose homeostasis. If the diet includes only minimal amounts of carbohydrates (about 2 percent), glucose homeostasis would seem to be impaired. An all-meat diet provides about ten grams of glucose per day in the form of glycogen, but the adult brain consumes well over one hundred grams of glucose per day. The body obtains the glucose it needs by protein digestion and release of amino acids for conversion to glucose, thereby providing the needed amount (Draper 1977:311). The high fat content of the Inuit diet was thought to be associated with highly saturated body fats. However, native animals contribute mainly polyunsaturated fats to the diet, and this is implicated in the typical health profile of the traditional Inuit population, which is characterized by low blood pressure, low blood cholesterol, and lean body mass.

The well-being that this native diet provided is dramatically illustrated by recent changes in Inuit health status. In the last twenty years, there have been rapid changes in Inuit diet. Today it more closely resembles the diet of Western industrial nations than that of the traditional Inuit. A greater proportion of the calories are now derived from carbohydrates—especially from breads, cereals, rice, and sugar. Over half of the fat currently used is imported, primarily in the form of hydrogenated shortenings and margarine. Vitamin C is in greater scarcity than before, as a result of changes in cooking patterns. **Anemia** is now a frequent nutritional problem. Obesity, especially among females, is found with greater frequency. Hypercholesterolemia is increasing throughout the population, particularly among the aged (Bell and Heller 1978; Way 1978; Zegura and Jamison 1978). Increased opportunity to obtain sweets and less frequent use of the teeth as tools have led to a rapid increase in periodontal diseases and dental caries. On the other hand, the new diet has perhaps contributed to the accelerated growth trend noted by Jamison at Wainright—a trend that reflects an increased alienation of Inuit from the environment and increased dependence on subsidies from outside (1978).

Changes in the diet have not been physiologically easy because of a relatively high incidence among Inuit of both **lactase** and **sucrase deficiency** (Bell et al. 1978). Symptoms of lactase deficiency are gastrointestinal distress, flatulence, and mild diarrhea. This phenomenon is rather common in populations who do not have a long history of dairying. Inuit have a limited capacity for lactose digestion. More than 80 percent of the population tested were intolerant of a fifty gram dose of lactose, which is the equivalent of the lactose in one liter of cow's milk. Most Inuit adults were able to tolerate smaller amounts of dairy foods when taken at intervals of several hours. Sucrose utilization is a problem primarily for children who have taken on the Western delight in candy.

Change in the Arctic

Ever since the first Inuit came in contact with whaling ships in the 1870s, their culture has been changing. However, it is only in the last twenty years that whaling has increased as a way of life while hunting has declined. Since then, a steady erosion of Inuit adaptive practices has taken place. The acquisition of rifles has meant that subsistence can be secured at a faster rate. As a result of their desire for Western goods and the necessity of having money to pay for them, the Inuit now work for wages. However, despite the boom conditions in Alaska, most jobs have gone to skilled outsiders. The result has been an annual unemployment rate, adjusted for seasonal factors, of close to 70 percent (Bureau of Indian Affairs 1971:60).

Several factors have contributed to the process of change, but the most significant are Western education and technology. Instead of the experimental ecological education of yesteryear, modern Inuit attend schools where education focuses on literacy gained by reading the wisdom of non-Inuit. Especially influential are boarding schools that separate children from parents at a crucial time in their education as hunters. To a large extent, the influx of outsiders to the arctic and the presence of non-native teachers have caused children to lose respect for their traditional social and cultural values and practices. Rather than a guarded disapproval of change, they have learned an appreciation of technological innovations and Western ways of achieving success.

Technological Adjustments   The Inuit, like the Laplanders, adopted the snowmobile with astounding rapidity. The snowmobile was first developed in 1962, and since that time sales in North America have grown 2,500 percent. Fifty manufacturers now market four hundred different models to supply the persistent demand (Ives 1974:908). Osburn (1974) studied the adoption of snowmobiles among the nunamiut Inuit of Anaktuvuk Pass, Alaska. Before the 1960s the population had been seminomadic caribou hunters. In 1964, the first snowmobile appeared and caused intense jealousies among the group. The snowmobile was advantageous for caribou hunters because the caribou appeared to be less afraid of its noise than of the dog teams. By 1969 the switch from dog sledding to snowmobiles was complete.[5] Dogs were neglected and slowly disappeared. Inuit stopped walking and drove everywhere in their machines, even if their destination was only one block away in the village. Such overuse eventually took its toll, and the machines began to fall in disrepair. Lacking the capital to replace them and the expertise to fix them, they were increasingly dependent on outside handouts and wages.

The transition to snowmobiles was just as rapid among the Finnish Lapps (Müller-Wille 1974; Pelto 1973; Linkola 1973). As was the case with Inuit dog sledding, reindeer sledding was abandoned within a couple of years, and the snowmobile became universal. The major difference was that the Lapps continued to herd reindeer and, in their mind, could do so more effectively with their snowmobiles. Before the arrival of the snowmobile, Lapps had year-round contact with herds and could easily make herd management decisions. With the adoption of the snowmobile, there has been increasing pressure to hold several roundups throughout the year, instead of only one. This represents a response both to market demand for their product and to their need to meet payments on their snowmobile equipment. Linkola (1973:130) estimated that the profits from one-third of the reindeer sold yearly go toward the purchase of snowmobiles and the maintenance of existing ones. The result has been a steady depletion in the size of the herds (see table 5.2). The snowmobile has enhanced class distinctions and economic differences between people in the arctic, with the small herder having to abandon his occupation and become a full-time wage earner to sustain his family and new machinery. In addition, the snowmobile scars the arctic. Ecologists have noted that

---

[5]Bliss (1975:56) estimates the annual cost of a dog team at $12, while a snowmobile costs $1,075 in depreciation and operating costs. However, Inuit expended considerable effort on hunting meat to feed to their dogs. When the transition to snowmobiles was made, all the hunted meat became available for consumption or sale.

Table 5.2   **Patterns of Reindeer Sales and Herd Growth in a Lapp Community, before and after the Use of Snowmobiles**

Period	Reindeer slaughtered and sold	Net increase in herds
1956–61		
By Owner A[a]	25.5%	1.7%
By Owner B[a]	15.5%	34.4%
By Owner C[a]	22.7%	13.5%
By All 104 Members	23.7%	7.8%
1963–69		
By Owner A	43.7%	−16.8%
By Owner B	32.6%	−17.4%
By Owner C	43.0%	−20.2%
By All 111 Members	32.7%	−10.0%

[a] Owners A, B, and C have the biggest herds in Utsjoki.
Source: Ludger Müller-Wille and Olavi Aikio, "Die Auswirkungen der Mechanisierung der Rentierwirtschaft in der lappischen Gemeinde Utsjoki (Finnisch-Lappland), Terra 83:179-185, 1971.

plant recovery is slow and damage still evident even when ten years have elapsed since the snowmobile tracks were first cut (Bliss 1975:57).

Energy Relationships   Kemp (1971) has studied the flow of energy among contemporary Inuit (see figure 5.8). Although he limited his energy measurements to two families, his model sheds lights upon systemic relationships and Inuit success in coping with productivity. Considerable energy subsidies from outside the region (for example, store-bought food, gasoline, wages, and cash from art objects sold) are used. These subsidies permit the maintenance of a larger population, a decreasing amount of time spent hunting, and ever increasing amounts of energy processing (much of it lost as heat). Hunting with motorized vehicles is reasonably efficient. Kemp found that for an expenditure of 1.75 million kcals, the Inuit whom he studied obtained 5.29 million kcals—a three to one energetic efficiency. However, most of the calories today come not from hunting, but from wage labor, the carving of sculptures, and skin and fur preparation—activities that give an even better return per unit of energy invested. At the time of Kemp's study, the impact of the Trans-Alaska pipeline had not yet begun to be felt, but it has surely spelled an increased flow of energy in and out of the system—much of it probably bypassing the Inuit. Kemp does not share the pessimism of some observers regarding social and cultural changes in the arctic. While the emergence of wage earners and entrepreneurs is notable, so is the persistence of the hunter. The continuation of the hunting way of life seems predicated on the shift by many Inuit to other occupations and on the consequent reduction of hunting pressure on game.

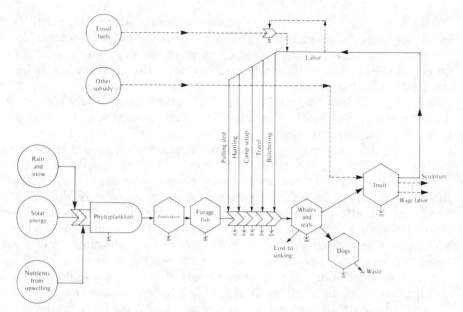

Figure 5.8 **Energy Flow Model of Two Inuit Households** Dotted lines indicate recent additions to the system. Fossil fuel inputs have allowed greater total catches, but have increased losses due to sinking, waste, and distance. Flows of meat to dogs have been almost eliminated. Labor previously spent on hunting is now spent on crafts and extractive industrial activities.

Source: Based on William Kemp. 1971. The Flow of Energy in a Hunting Society. Scientific American 224(3): 104–115.

The development of the arctic in the foreseeable future will follow an **extractive** path, and it can only be hoped that its effect will not resemble the results of the Amazon Basin rubber boom of the late nineteenth century, which ended with that region still undeveloped. An evaluation by the Bureau of Indian Affairs on the impact of the proposed Trans-Alaska Pipeline concluded that, although the pipeline did not cut across a sizable number of Inuit villages, it would increase the pace of acculturation and absorption of Inuit into Western culture (Bureau of Indian Affairs 1971:39).

Maintenance of Tradition Although Inuit interpersonal relationships have changed a great deal, recent events have sparked a renewal of Inuit traditions. The transitional period during which Inuit kinship networks broke down as families settled among strangers in villages was so lengthy (1850s to 1960s) that it is amazing any aboriginal customs survived. Modern communications equipment that is available to the mass consumer has facilitated a return to wider kin networks. Most Inuit in northwestern

Alaska have tape recorders and use them to communicate with relatives in distant villages. Even relatives who have never met are included in these tape networks, which serve to integrate the population. Another crucial change has been the construction in most villages of landing strips from which flights are chartered to attend, en masse, cultural events in other villages. Although Inuit economic behavior is increasingly Western, a great many of the kinship obligations still function and in fact appear to be on their way to a revival. (For a full discussion of these changes, as seen among the northwestern Alaskan Inuit, consult Burch [1975].)

A recent Inuit Circumpolar Conference evidenced the efforts of the arctic peoples to act jointly to preserve their cultural heritage, gain a voice in how their environment is exploited, and establish conservation measures that will allow them to sustain a hunting way of life in the modern world (Morgan 1977). Despite initial difficulties in communication, the Inuit arrived at unified resolutions. Whether this growing unity is translated into growing control over their destiny remains to be seen, but the goal of a renewed Inuit lifestyle more closely attuned to the opportunties and limitations of the arctic environment is a hopeful one. The influence of outsiders has thus far meant a replacement of adaptive behavior by technological subsidy. Such a subsidy can be expected to continue only as long as the area yields high value, nonrenewable resources. Once they have been extracted, the arctic will once again need the ancient strategies of the Inuit population. We can only hope that the adaptive value of such a lifestyle is recognized and nurtured by both Inuit and outsiders.

Summary

Most of the mechanisms for human adaptation to arctic areas are regulatory, rather than acclimatory, developmental, or genetic. Housing and shelter provide effective regulatory adjustments to cold by creating microenvironments of relative comfort. These cultural solutions are supplemented by acclimatory adjustments that protect the extremities: nonshivering thermogenesis; a high rate of peripheral blood flow to the extremities; and a high core to shell conductance. The higher basal metabolic rate of the Inuit, although not well understood, facilitates cold adaptation.

Adjustments to the other stresses of the arctic are regulatory in nature. The traditional education of the Inuit trained them in acute observation, knowledge of animal ethology, and careful avoidance of risk. In combination, these adjustments enhanced the population's chances of survival. Social and cultural adjustments to the potentially disruptive effects of prolonged arctic nights and days may have helped to reduce the incidence of arctic hysterias and other cases of mental and physiological maladjustment. The traditional animistic religion alleviated anxiety over resources, gathered the population into larger social aggregates, provided an opportunity to redistribute goods and reenforce social obligations, and increased the flow of information among the otherwise scattered population.

The low biological productivity of the terrestrial environment was dealt with by exploitation of coastal and migratory inland resources. Marriage practices, adoption, spouse exchange, and meat-sharing partnerships helped extend the networks of friendships and reciprocity. These networks helped to ward off the random probability of famine, thereby improving the life-chances of individuals and households. Population controls were used to reduce the burden of newborns during times of stress. They also served to stabilize the population structure—enhancing the number of providers and reducing the number of prereproductive and nonproductive members.

The impact of change, in its initial stages, is seldom kind, and thus far its impact on the Inuit, from a cultural and ecological point of view, can only be said to have been unfavorable. The health status of the Inuit has declined (as evidenced by the increase in anemia, obesity, high blood pressure, hypercholesterolemia, and loss of teeth) without any marked improvement in the persistent problems of otitis media, gastroenteritis, respiratory ailments, and eye damage (Zegura and Jamison 1978; Way 1978). There has, however, been a sharp decline in the incidence of tuberculosis. In schools Inuit children are slow to learn as a result of chronic hearing impairments, passive teaching techniques, and lack of respect by non-native teachers for their Inuit pupils (Collier 1973).

The technological improvement of the snowmobile was adopted before adequate knowledge of engine repair and vehicle maintenance were provided. The result has been a neglect of traditional means of transportation and increased dependence on wages to maintain an expensive technology. Yet most Inuit are unemployed. According to Smith (1972), Inuit can still live off the land by hunting on weekends and keeping a job during weekdays. However, other problems arise: because the snowmobile permits more distant trips, there is greater danger of being stranded in an area so remote that it is impossible to get back on foot. The speed of snowmobiles increases the danger of frostbite by adding the effect of wind from the speeding vehicle to that of cold. The driver of the snowmobile cannot see if anyone traveling on the sled behind him has fallen, and there have been cases in which companions have frozen to death after falling from sleds.

Human adaptation to arctic conditions, and especially to cold, suggests that regulatory adjustments can successfully insulate a population from the selective forces of the environment. The Inuit manifest no evident developmental or genetic adaptations to arctic conditions. Instead, their physiological adjustments are local in nature (for example, protection of the extremities). The core of Inuit adaptations to northern Alaskan conditions is social and cultural—a remarkable and somewhat unexpected conclusion. By the same token, such adjustments can be very easily disrupted by adoption of social and cultural lifestyles inappropriate to the area. The arctic today presents a fascinating natural laboratory for studying how flexible the newly imported social and cultural systems might be in coping with polar environments.

Recommended Readings

Students of the human ecology of tundra ecosystems should consult the rich and rapidly growing literature being produced by investigators. These ecosystems were recently the focus of research efforts by the International Biological Program (IBP). The Swedish component of the IBP/Tundra Biome has published a useful collection of papers, *The Structure and Function of Tundra Ecosystems* (Rosswall and Heal 1975). The best recent synthesis article on tundra ecology is that of Bliss et al. (1973).

Fortunately for human ecologists, the Tundra Biome/IBP research also included a human adaptability component. The synthesis volume from that research project makes important contributions to the gaps in knowledge identified a decade ago (Jamison, Zegura, and Milan 1978). Hildes and Laughlin in 1966 summarized the knowledge of arctic human ecology and provide the background for the recent synthesis. An out-of-date, but still useful, bibliography by Culver (1959) should be consulted on matters relating to cold thermoregulation. Important surveys of human adaptation to cold stress may be found in Folk (1966), Carlson and Hsieh (1965), Edholm and Lewis (1964), Van Wie (1974), and Little and Hochner (1973). Given the lack of terrestrial living forms, the conditions in Antarctica are even more inimical for human habitation than in the arctic. Research on human adaptability to Antarctica has appeared in Budd (1974) and Natani and Shurley (1974).

There is solid archeological and genetic evidence that human occupation of arctic zones began between 8,000 and 15,000 BP when hunters from Siberia crossed the Bering Land Bridge (Hopkins 1967). However, there is indirect and growing evidence that migrations as early as 28,000 BP may have occurred (Müller-Beck 1967; Irving and Harington 1973). Laughlin has suggested that both the present day Inuit and the Aleuts derived from a common sea-oriented mongoloid population (1975). Those who reached Nikolski Bay became Aleuts, while those who migrated further north became Inuit. Bandi (1969) has a fine discussion of Inuit prehistory. McGhee (1974) concentrates on the occupation of arctic North America. The recent volume by Fitzhugh (1975) is an effort at comparative prehistory across the arctic zones.

The human ecological studies of social and cultural anthropologists have also been important. Most recently, the study by Nelson (1969) provided finely detailed descriptions of hunting behavior. Although his sample was very restricted in size, the geographer Kemp (1971) provided the only effort at quantifying the flow of energy through Inuit society. Damas (1969a) attempted a comparative study of Central Inuit society using a Stewardian cultural ecological research model. His analysis is both enlightening and suggestive of new questions to pursue in the study of Inuit adaptations. The classic study of Inuit society is still that of Spencer (1959). Lantis (1947) probably has left the most detailed descriptions of Inuit ceremonial life, and she blends description with suggestive ecological possibilities. A stimulating volume is the psychobiological study of arctic hysteria by Foulks (1972).

What is most needed now is an effort comparable to Spencer's in the late 1950s. Much research has been carried out in the arctic since that time, and a blending of physiological, social, and cultural analyses should provide a more complete picture of what life is like in the arctic and how the Inuit have coped with their surroundings over time.

Human
Adaptability
to High Altitudes

Research on human adaptability to high altitudes is among the most advanced and well-integrated work in ecological anthropology. In this chapter the reader will be introduced to the crucial problem faced by populations inhabiting high altitude zones: **hypoxia,** or low oxygen pressure. Other problems also associated with high altitude are cold stress, aridity, low biological productivity, pulmonary disease, and reduced reproductive success.

As in the arctic, researchers have found little evidence of genetic (that is, evolutionary) adaptation in high altitude zones. Most of the mechanisms for coping with the biological stress of low oxygen pressure are physiological. Some of them are regulatory, as is the case with increased pulmonary ventilation. Others are acclimatory and developmental: increases in the number of red blood cells and in total hemoglobin, enlargement of the capillary network, and chemical-enzymatic changes related to internal respiration that enhance oxygen utilization at the tissue level.

Cold stress is handled by regulatory adjustments, such as use of warm clothing and shelter, and by scheduling activities to allow maximum time out in the sun. Developmental adjustments also improve the degree of adaptation of native populations to the cold of high altitude. Chief among these are nonshivering thermogenesis and increased blood flow to the extremities when these are exposed.

High altitude populations cope with low productivity by seasonal migration, by marriage prescriptions that serve to distribute the population, and by interzonal trade. To minimize energy costs at the population level, children are assigned the tasks of herding, thereby reducing the caloric requirements of households. Preservation techniques play an important role in providing food stores for lean times. This chapter will focus on the adjustments made by an Andean population coping with high altitude stresses. Before proceeding it is essential that one understand the characteristics of mountain ecosystems.

Mountain Ecosystems

Since prehistoric times, human populations have occupied high altitude zones despite the numerous problems initially encountered by persons entering such areas.[1] Anyone who has grown and developed at sea level will, when first exposed to high altitudes, experience symptomatic discomfort, reduced work capacity, accelerated breathing, higher hemoglobin levels, and higher arterial pressure. It is not surprising to find relatively small numbers of peoples living at high altitude. Some ten to twenty-five million people (that is, less than 1 percent of the earth's population) cur-

---

[1]The Ute occupied a zone at three thousand meters in Colorado prehistorically, and since 7500 BC, populations have lived in the Peruvian highlands at altitudes above four thousand meters (Grover 1974:817).

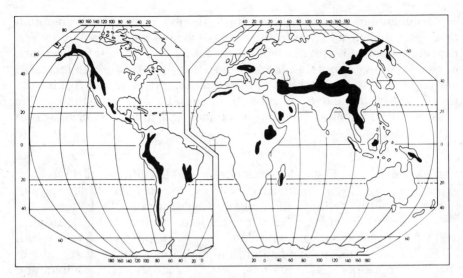

Figure 6.1   **Tropical and Mid-Latitude Highlands of the World**

rently make it their home (Grover 1974:818; DeJong 1968).[2] The majority of the areas occupied are within forty degrees of the equator where solar insolation is greater and, all things being equal, biotic productivity is higher. These areas include the South American Andes, the mountains of Ethiopia, the Caucasus of southern Russia, the Asian Himalayas, and the Rocky Mountains of the United States (see figure 6.1).

High altitudes have been the subject of intensive research in human biology and ecology. In most other biomes, cultural practices can play a major buffering action, but in the high altitude biome, hypoxia provides one of the few situations in which behavioral regulatory adjustments play a secondary role to acclimatory and developmental adjustments (Baker 1976a:2). Human biologists saw in these regions an ideal setting to study potential genetic and physiological adaptations. These studies were stimulated by the important writings of Carlos Monge (1948) who postulated that Andean natives were biologically different from, and possessed adaptive characteristics not found among, lowlanders. Since that time numerous workers have sought to test the validity of Monge's hypotheses.[3]

---

[2]Ninety percent of the world's population is concentrated at elevations below three thousand feet (Heintzelman and Highsmith 1973:185).

[3] Other useful works are Hatcher and Jennings 1966; Chernigovsky 1969; Hart et al. 1969; Pan American Health Organization 1966; Porter and Knight 1971; Van Liere and Stickney 1963; and Weihe 1963. Among the major synthesis articles are those of Hurtado (1964), Baker (1969), and Mazess (1975). Much of the following material is drawn from the studies of high altitude Quechua from southern highland Peru. This is the region best known from a multidisciplinary human ecological perspective. Some of the adaptations found in the southern highlands are not present in the northern highlands– for example, llamas are not found and chuño is not widely made.

143

Mountainous regions have complex distributions of **biotic communities**. Three major ecological features are relevant to human habitation: vertical biotic zonation, irregular biotic distribution, and geologic features such as slope and rugged terrain (Rhoades and Thompson 1975). With increased elevation rapid changes take place in vegetation and animal life, commonly distributed in distinctive life zones or biomes. On a given mountain it is possible to have four or five major biomes and numerous **ecotones**, or transitional zones.

Vertical Zonation   Figure 6.2 illustrates general conditions that might be expected in a variety of mountain ecosystems. Note that the latitude plays an important role in defining the biotic characteristics at the bottom zone. Natural vegetation may go from tropical forest to tundra in the tropical highlands, but in temperate latitudes it may begin with coniferous forest. Climatic factors, such as temperature and moisture, play dominant roles in species composition, as do highland features such as slope, contour, and differential exposure to wind and light (Dettwyler 1977; James 1966: 379–420).

Although there is a greater chance of biota interchange in mountain ecosystems than in other types of ecosystems, the narrowness of each mountain life zone and the isolation created by the rough topography make the species of each area at times unique in the whole world (E. Odum 1971:402). Native fauna is distributed in accordance with zonal characteristics. Animals inhabiting lower levels move one or two zones up, but usually no further. Some of the animals have characteristic adaptations, such as rock-dwelling rodents (Andean vizcacha) and the furry yak of the Himalayas, the vicuña, llama, and guanaco (Andean camelids). Agriculture is also zonally distributed according to changes in altitude (see figure 6.2) and there seem to be broad world patterns in the nature of the agropastoral economy. Rhoades and Thompson (1975) note that the parallels in subsistence are based on the success of the vertical oscillation of cultivators, herders, and beasts that follow the zonally available productive areas.

Geoclimatic Characteristics   Rarely are vertical zones the neat layers shown in figure 6.2. A variety of geological features, such as angle to sunlight and valleys, lead to the creation of microhabitats. The amount of rainfall depends both on altitude and on exposure to air currents. Exposed slopes receive greater rainfall than areas shielded by some geologic feature. Ruggedness and slope can make some mountain areas useless for agriculture or herding.

Most of the human ecological research in high altitude areas has been concentrated in the Andean region of South America and has been systematically pursued since the early 1960s. An important component was the intensive study of human adaptability in the district of Nuñoa, department

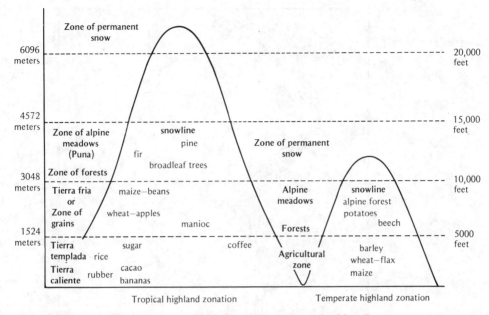

Figure 6.2   **Zonation in Tropical and Temperate Highlands**

of Puno in Peru. This was part of the International Biological Program's human adaptability studies (Baker and Little 1976). Nuñoa is an area that ranges from four thousand to forty-eight hundred meters above sea level in the altiplano. The altiplano is the treeless portion of the Central Andes above thirty-six hundred meters altitude surrounding Lake Titicaca and Lake Poopo. (The term *altiplano* and *puna* are sometimes used interchangeably both in this chapter and in the literature [Thomas and Winterhalder 1976:22].)

Figure 6.3 shows the location of the altiplano in South America. (See also figure 6.12, p. 159 for a view of the landscape.)

At the time the IBP study began, there were over eight thousand Quechuas living in Nuñoa and pursuing a traditional pattern that combined pastoralism based on camelids and sheep with seasonal agriculture in lower altitudes. As is typical of tropical highlands, mean annual temperatures are relatively constant, but there is a considerable range between maximum and minimum temperatures. Mean annual temperature is about 8°C., but the variation between maximum and minimum can be 20°C. Frosts occur frequently and are the result either of rapid loss of lower air and ground heat at night or of movement by cold air masses (Thomas and Winterhalder 1976:31). Precipitation is seasonal and averages eight hundred and thirty millimeters on this portion of the altiplano. Little or no precipitation falls four to five months out of the year, and droughts lasting one year or more occur randomly. Productivity is low and highland populations must trade

145

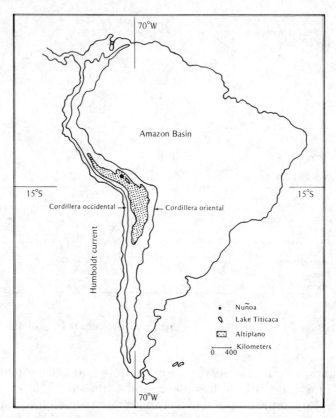

Figure 6.3   **Location of the Andes (approximately the 2,000-m isograph) and the Altiplano (shaded area)**

with lowland areas to cope successfully with the scarcity of energy of the altiplano.

Plant Productivity   The frost zone in the Andes begins at about twenty-five hundred meters and marks a significant change in plant cover. Below this zone are tropical montane forest and patches of tropical savannas (see figure 6.2). Above twenty-five hundred meters, the tropical trees grow shorter and are replaced at about four thousand meters by scrub and grass steppes. The steppe thins out and becomes a frost desert between forty-five hundred and forty-nine hundred meters. Higher still are permanently frozen areas. The human population is concentrated on the altiplano. Three major vegetation zones (moist, dry, and desert puna) are distinguished according to the moisture they receive. The moist puna is characterized by bunch grasses and some shrubs, and the dry puna by **xerophytic vegetation**. The desert puna is an area without vegetation except where scant precipitation collects

146

(Thomas and Winterhalder 1976:39). Deserts are created on the **lee side** of mountains because of the blocking of clouds, while bounteous precipitation falls on the windward slopes (Heintzelman and Highsmith 1973:368). A disproportionate number of altiplano plants are low and compact, with growth organs below or only slightly above the ground. These features provide protection against cold, drought and frost. Some vegetation is in the form of **cushion plants**, which are able to minimize exposure to the elements, keep a relatively warm interior, and absorb and retain moisture longer. They are often characterized by spines that provide protection against herbivores (Thomas and Winterhalder 1976:43).

The plant productivity in the Andean altiplano is low because of atmospheric and soil aridity, cold temperatures, and low levels of soil organic matter. High levels of solar radiation, however, permit surprising levels of net production, aided by reduction of the costs of respiration during cold nights. Harvestable biomass in one estimate was only eighty kilograms per **hectare** per year for the moist puna (Thomas and Winterhalder 1976:43). Much of the productivity of plants is stored below the ground, away from the elements and from the grazing population. Animal biomass is, therefore, also low (Fittkau 1968:641). Both the animal and the human population must adapt to the constraints of a high altitude zone. Among these constraints hypoxia is particularly important.

Adaptation to Hypoxia

Physiological Adjustments Hypoxia, or low oxygen pressure, is the most important stress with which populations living at high altitude must cope. Cultural practices are not able to increase the amount of oxygen available to human subjects, but some of its associated problems (for example, reduced ability to carry a fetus to full term and high rates of neonate mortality) have been minimized through appropriate diets, work patterns, and cultural attitudes towards reproduction. It was thought at one time that populations native to high altitude had genetic adaptations that permitted them to reproduce and live with no apparent difficulty where outsiders experienced serious malfunctioning (Monge 1948). It now appears that there is no direct evidence of population-level adaptation to hypoxia in man, but only indirect evidence, based on inferences from individual and infra-individual adaptations (Mazess 1975:193). Human adaptations to hypoxia appear to reflect the general genetic plasticity common to all of mankind, rather than distinctive genetic attributes.

The partial pressure of oxygen decreases with increasing altitude. Hypoxia results whenever either physiological, pathological, or environmental conditions cannot deliver an adequate supply of oxygen to the tissues. Since air is compressible, air at high altitudes is less concentrated and under less pressure (see figure 6.4). At forty-five hundred meters the partial pressure of oxygen is decreased by as much as 40 percent, in com-

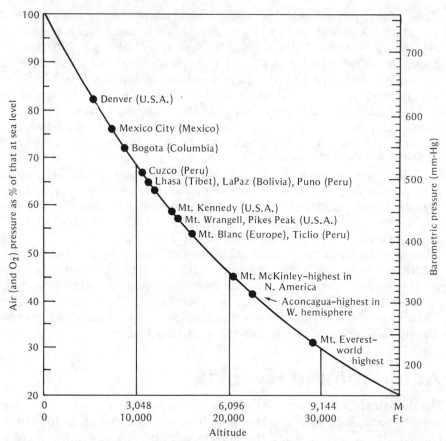

Figure 6.4   **Barometric Pressure and Oxygen Pressure at High Altitudes**   With increases in altitude, there is a marked percentage decrease in both air and oxygen pressure.

Source: R. Frisancho. 1975. Functional Adaptation to High Altitude Hypoxia. Science 187:313–319. Copyright 1975 by the American Association for the Advancement of Science.

parison to pressure at sea level. This reduces the amount of oxygen finally available to the tissues (Frisancho 1975).

Adaptation to high altitude hypoxia results in a series of modifications in body functioning that are oriented toward increasing the supply of oxygen. Because some of the adjustments to hypoxia are developmental, it is not surprising to find different adaptive mechanisms in sea level and highland populations. Figure 6.5 is a schematic representation of these two patterns of adaptation. Sea level or lowland populations utilize the less efficient response of increased pulmonary ventilation, in contrast to the developmentally acquired advantage of increased lung volume, to achieve the same adaptive result.

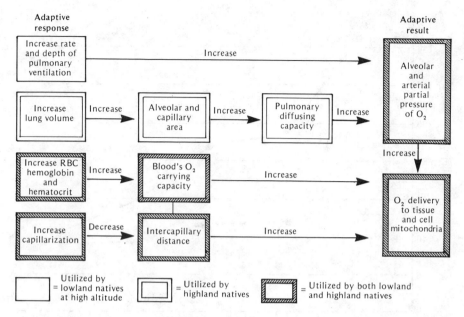

Figure 6.5 **Schematic Summary of the Adaptive Responses (Physiological) to Hypoxia**

Source: R. Frisancho. 1975. Functional Adaptation to High Altitude Hypoxia. Science 187:313–319. Copyright 1975 by the American Association for the Advancement of Science.

The adaptive responses to hypoxia are directed toward increasing both the availability of oxygen and the pressure of oxygen at the tissue level. Some of the physiological mechanisms that facilitate adaptation to hypoxia operate along the oxygen pressure gradient in the body and permit oxygen to reach tissues despite the low atmospheric pressure. Other mechanisms operate at the level of the tissues and include enlargement of the **capillary** bed and chemical-enzymatic changes related to internal respiration (Hurtado 1964:844).

At high altitudes oxygen pressure can be 40 percent or more below sea level pressure (Baker 1968:9). Without adaptive mechanisms, the tissues of a man living at 4,540 meters would have an oxygen tension inadequate to diffuse oxygen and make it available for cell metabolism. Figure 6.6 illustrates the remarkable economy of the oxygen pressure gradient among natives of high altitudes as compared with that of sea level peoples. This economy is possible mainly because of increased lung ventilation, decreased alveolar-arterial oxygen gradient, and polycythemia (Hurtado 1964:845). Because oxygen is consumed as it goes through successive layers of tissues, partial oxygen pressure tends to drop. At high altitude, where that pressure is already low to start with, the organism adjusts by shortening the distance the oxygen must travel. This is accomplished by an increase in the number of capillaries.

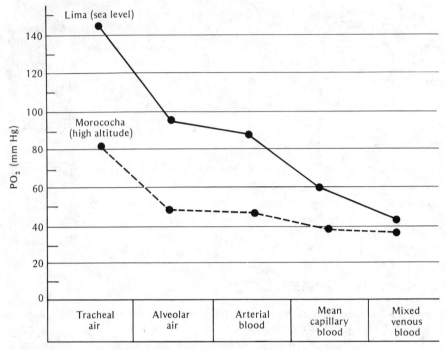

Figure 6.6   **Mean Oxygen Pressure Gradients from Tracheal Air to Mixed Venous Blood** Values are derived from a sample of sixteen healthy adult subjects, eight of whom reside at sea level and eight at an altitude of 4,540 meters.

Source: Alberto Hurtado. 1964. Animals in High Altitudes: Resident Man. In Handbook of Physiology: Adaptation to the Environment. D. B. Dill, ed. Washington, D.C.: American Physiological Society.

An *increase in pulmonary ventilation* is a common response to high altitude. Natives have a moderately higher breathing rate (that is, 20 to 40 percent) than sea level populations, and newcomers to high altitudes will quickly begin to **hyperventilate** (breathe rapidly). Surprisingly, the higher breathing rate of the native population is accomplished without an increase in metabolic rates. It is not clearly understood why this happens, but in experimental situations it appears to be related to chemical stimulation by the blood carbon dioxide level (Hurtado 1964:848). The high altitude resident is almost constantly in a state of *hypocapnia* (that is, low carbon dioxide), and adaptation to this condition is achieved by avoidance of excessive hyperventilation.[4] Newcomers to high altitude sometimes suffer from hypocapnia, if their travel to high altitude is too abrupt

[4]This is possibly because of the low pH of the cerebrospinal fluids resulting from increased anaerobic glycolysis in the brain (Ward 1975:147–8).

and their activity not reduced during a brief period of adjustment.

The *decreased alveolar-arterial oxygen gradient* results from greater residual volume in the dilated alveoli of the lungs and from the permanent dilation of the capillary bed in the lungs of natives (Hurtado 1964:849). Highland natives have a larger lung volume and greater residual lung volume (that is, the volume of air that remains in the lungs after maximum expiration). This increased volume is a developmental adjustment accomplished by the proliferation of alveolar units and an increase in alveolar surface area during childhood (Frisancho 1975).

Polycythemia refers to an increase in the number of red blood cells and in the amounts of hemoglobin in persons acclimatized to high altitude. It does not appear to be present in uterine life, but develops rapidly within a few days after birth (Hurtado 1964:850). Prolonged exposure to hypoxia has a stimulating effect on bone marrow growth. As a result, more red blood cells are produced and there is an increase in the total volume of red blood cells in the body (that is, thickening of the blood) (Grover 1974:823). Associated with the increased production of cells, there is a decrease in blood plasma so that blood contains a larger volume of red blood cells and hemoglobin. This means that a greater quantity of oxygen can now be carried—which helps reduce the oxygen gradient between arterial and venous blood and aids the buffer capacity of blood for carbon dioxide (Grover 1974:823; Hurtado 1964:851).

Adaptive processes along the oxygen pressure gradient are not entirely successful. Additional adaptive mechanisms at the tissue level that facilitate the diffusion of oxygen from blood to tissues are needed. One major mechanism is an increase in the density of the capillary bed so that the ratio of capillaries to muscle fiber is elevated (Hurtado 1964:853; Mazess 1975:175). This, as we shall see later, is also advantageous in protection against cold temperatures. Also important is the increased activity of the mito-chondrial DPNH-oxidase system and trans-hydrogenase and of the TPNH-cytochrome c reductase. This suggests a higher rate of oxygen utilization through enzymatic pathways linked with the production of high energy phosphate bonds (Hurtado 1964:854). This mechanism permits the organism to save energy or to produce more chemical energy with the same oxygen consumption (Frisancho 1975). The importance of adaptation at the tissue level is perhaps best illustrated by the contrast between the work capacity of native high altitude residents and the reduced work capacity of newcomers to these zones (Baker 1968:2).

Work Capacity and Diet Accounts of the great physical capacity of natives at high altitudes are somewhat exaggerated. Although there is little doubt that natives perform better than newcomers at high altitudes, carefully designed experiments have not shown any significant superiority in natives when they move to lowland areas. Baker (1968:16) notes that good physical training and lifelong exposure to high altitude act to

151

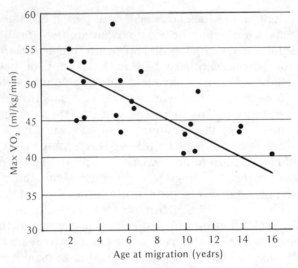

Figure 6.7   **Relationship between Adult VO₂ Max at 3,400 Meters and the Age at Which the Individual Migrated from Low to High Altitude**

Source: Paul Baker, "Work Performance of Highland Natives." Adapted and reprinted, with permission, from *Man in the Andes: A Multidisciplinary Study of High-Altitude Quecha*, Baker and Little, eds., © 1976 by Dowden, Hutchinson & Ross, Inc., Stroudsburg, Pa.

increase maximal oxygen consumption (VO₂ Max). Grover (1974:826) finds the Andean native physiologically similar to the athlete: both share a high aerobic or maximal work capacity. The native accomplishes this by exposure to atmospheric hypoxia and an active life, and the athlete by subjecting himself to strenuous exercise that subjects the muscles to tissue hypoxia.

Hurtado (1964:854) noted that at sea level natives have a higher ventilation rate, lower pulse rate, and smaller increases in blood pressure than athletes.[5] This is related to the high altitude native's efficiency, at the tissue level, in oxygen diffusion and the marked economy of the oxygen disassociation curve (see figure 6.6). Short-term acclimatization does not seem to contribute significantly to an increase in work capacity at high altitude, although modest increases in VO₂ max occur (Baker 1976:308). Childhood development at high altitude, on the other hand, enhances adult work capacity. Figure 6.7 illustrates the relationship between age at the time of migration from sea level to altitude and VO₂ achieved. The data in figure 6.7 are based on a small sample, but suggest

[5]Baker (1976:302) notes that the technique for determining output versus oxygen consumption may explain the different results. Some of the studies used a bicycle ergometer. Natives were unfamiliar with bicycle riding and may have experienced unusual conflict in muscle reactions.

that there might well be a critical age at which migration must occur if the individual to achieve a high VO₂ max as an adult (Ibid.: 310–311). Whether there is a genetic factor involved remains unresolved. Mazess attributes the higher work capacity of natives to their lower body weight, their vigorous life in the pursuit of subsistence, and their characteristic high carbohydrate diet. It has been shown that a high carbohydrate diet enhances endurance of hard work through increases of muscle glycogen (Mazess 1975:177).

Natives claim that chewing coca leaves enhances their work capability, and many of them refuse to work unless coca *(Erythroxylon coca)* is provided. Hanna (1976:370) found a slight elevation in heart rate while coca leaves were chewed during work, but he also determined that the effect was no different than it would be from ingestion of caffeine or other psychostimulants. Coca is also implicated in a mild vasoconstriction of blood vessels in the extremities. This results in reduced heat loss and slightly high core temperatures and is advantageous when outside work must be performed and there is potential cold stress.

Picón-Reátegui (1976:234–5) found no major nutritional deficiencies in the Andean population and no advantage in coca chewing from a nutritional point of view. Burchard, on the other hand, suggested that coca chewing, in combination with a high carbohydrate, low protein, and low fat diet, is an important strategy for managing problems of hypoglycemia (that is, low blood glucose) and carbohydrate malabsorption (1976:27).

Body tissues require a constant dietary supply of carbohydrate to provide energy. Absorption of ingested carbohydrate in the intestine is dependent on the time the carbohydrate is in contact with the absorbing surface, and on the supply of enzymes for the oxidation of carbohydrate. Once oxidized, carbohydrate is absorbed into the bloodstream as glucose, galactose and fructose. The last two are later transformed to glucose in the liver. Glucose is stored as glycogen for storage and reconverted to glucose when needed by the body.

Bolton found that "coca chewing has immediate effects in raising glucose levels, probably by stimulating the transformation of glycogen stores" (1973:253). Figure 6.8 illustrates the change in blood glucose after chewing coca leaves. Note that even after four hours glucose levels were still moderately higher than the levels of those who had not used the leaves.

Low levels of glucose and problems of carbohydrate malabsorption are apparently widespread health problems in highland Peru and are related to undernutrition, especially a lack of protein (Gray 1973:70–71). It is not clear, however, to what extent the general reduction in food utilization is a result of hypoxia or to what extent it is due to anorexia and hypohydration (Mazess 1975:182). Gray points out that atropine, an amino alcohol found in coca, increases contact time between carbohydrates and the intestinal mucosa (1973:122–123). Burchard notes that coca

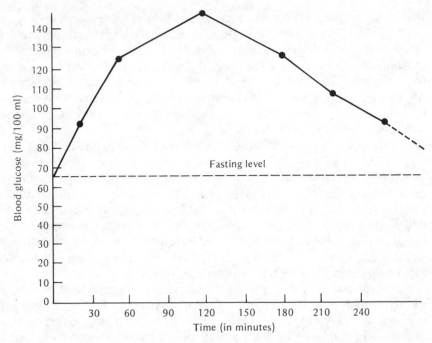

Figure 6.8   **Blood Glucose Levels in Coca Chewers after Chewing 1—1.5 Ounces of Leaves**

Source: Based on Roderick Burchard. 1976. Myths of the Sacred Leaf: Ecological Perspectives on Coca and Peasant Biocultural Adaptation in Peru. Ph.D. dissertation, Department of Anthropology, Indiana University.

is chewed often before and after meals, which relaxes the small intestines and facilitates absorption (1976:266–267). If this is the case, it might explain the ability of natives to perform well at work, despite diets that meet only the minimum recommended dietary requirements. Coca-induced intestinal absorption of food may help individuals meet the increased costs of keeping warm in a cold environment, of heavy work schedules, and the needs of pregnancy, lactation, and growth (Picón-Reátegui 1976:235).

Reproduction and Maturation   Hypoxia appears to affect reproduction. Monge (1948) found Spanish documents from the early colonial period that explained, and probably exaggerated, that no European woman could carry a child through term at high altitude. They attributed the problem to the "thin air" and justified their move from the highland capital to sea level Lima on those grounds (Baker 1968:2). Newcomers to high altitude do experience a reduction in fertility, reduced ability to carry a fetus to full term, and high neonatal mortality. Mazess, however, found that the moderately high altitudes where most Andean populations live have only

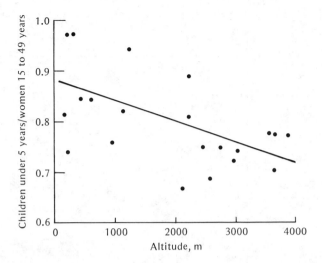

Figure 6.9   **Fertility and Altitude in Twenty-One Peruvian Provinces**

Source: Instituto Nacional de Planificación Económica. 1964. Buenos Aires, Argentina.

a mild effect on fecundity and reproductive performance. A more dramatic effect on reproduction is reflected in lower birth weights and increased postnatal mortality (Mazess 1975:185). Although short-term difficulties in spermatogenesis and menstruation are experienced upon moves to high altitudes, men and women native to the area appear normal in these respects. There appears to be no hypoxic stress on the fetus during pregnancy, possibly as a result of an increase in the size of the placenta (Hoff and Abelson 1976:130–131). There is also a decrease in the birth weight relative to the placenta, which facilitates delivery of oxygen to the fetus without unduly increasing the demands on the mother.

Although the explanation for this phenomenon has not been clearly demonstrated, there is a clear relationship between higher altitude and reduced fertility (see figure 6.9) (Ibid.:134). To overcome this threat to the existence of the population, the Quechua share an ideology that aims at maximizing births. As a result, despite high rates of abortion and neonatal mortality, Quechua females at Nuñoa, have a high rate of complete fertility (that is, 6.7 births per woman). This is accomplished by incorporating almost all women into the breeding population, by cultural preference for large families, and by the increase in placental size, which provides a more favorable uterine environment by minimizing hypoxic stress on the fetus.

In addition to birth weight being low, the growth and development of children at high altitude is slow. This may be related to the demands of chest and bone marrow development during growth (Frisancho 1976:199). During childhood important changes occur in alveolar area and diffusion capacity that facilitate the diffusion of oxygen. Maturation is delayed at

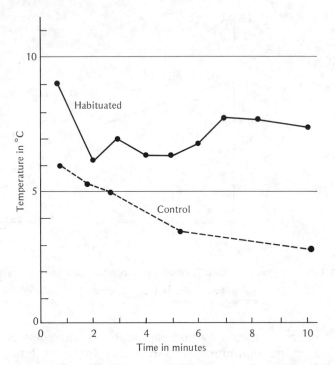

Figure 6.10   **Finger Temperatures during Ice Water Immersion in Acclimatized and Unacclimatized Englishmen**

Source: J. D. Nelms and D. J. G. Soper. 1962. Cold Vasodilation and Cold Acclimatization in the Hands of British Fish Filleters. Journal of Applied Physiology 17:444–448.

high altitude, and sexual dimorphism (that is, differences between males and females as manifested in body size and muscle size) appears to occur only after the sixteenth year. Hypoxia alone is not sufficient to explain the differences in morphology between inhabitants of different altitudes. Cold and hypoxia may be jointly implicated in the slower development of children at high altitude. It appears that a diversion of calories to heat production, instead of to storage or growth, is involved in the slower development of Quechuas (Little and Hochner 1973:17). Hypocaloric stress and, possibly, genetic factors are also involved in the slow growth and development of the Andean population.

Maladaptations   Not all individuals native to high altitude adapt to hypoxia, and some lose their adaptation. This is known as *chronic mountain sickness* and involves loss of normal stimulation of breathing, which leads to low oxygen pressure in the lung alveoli and in arterial blood. To compensate, the body experiences excessive polycythemia (that is, thickening of blood). The only cure involves bleeding the person every two or three weeks, but the best solution is to leave the high altitude zone (Grover 1974). Since high altitude natives also sometimes engage in seasonal migration to lowlands, they may also experience *pulmonary edema* on returning to altitude (that is, buildup of fluid in the lungs which interferes with the transfer of oxygen from the air to the bloodstream). Following several weeks at sea level, even natives may experience this temporary illness upon return to high altitude (Ibid.:827).

Adaptability to Cold Stress in the Andes

Next to hypoxia, cold is the most significant stress felt by high altitude populations. However, it is more amenable than hypoxia to management by appropriate cultural practices. The cold stress felt by the Andean population is unique in character: it is nonstressful during daytime because of high solar radiation and relative dryness, but, for the same climatic reasons, heat escapes rapidly from the ground and at night the population may experience significant cold stress (Baker 1966:276).

Physiological Adjustments   Long-term exposure to cold stress may lead to acclimatization. Figure 6.10 illustrates the response of habituated and nonhabituated persons to immersion of fingers in iced water. The responses of the habituated demonstrate an increased peripheral blood flow to the extremities (Hanna 1968:220) that prevents cold injury, limits heat loss through the hand, and permits easier hand functioning in cold conditions.

Such a difference in response to cold appears to be developmental. Studies of foot exposure to cold air at 0°C. in the Andean highlands showed that both native adults and children maintain warmer skin temperatures than whites, but the differences between the young and the adult Quechua studied suggest that this ability increases through the developmental period (see figure 6.11). If this is the case, the neonate may experience unusually severe cold stress. Researchers have found that brown adipose tissue (BAT) is present in human infants and plays important roles in maintaining high core temperatures and in promoting non-shivering thermogenesis. Normal fat as a percentage of body weight is at its lowest at birth. Between birth and age one, however, it increases six-fold, while the stores of brown adipose tissue are slowly depleted (Little and Hochner 1976:6).

Cultural Adjustments   Despite the lack of hand and foot protection used by Andean natives, there is no measurable cooling indicative of cold stress. The major reason for this is the success of native cultural practices

157

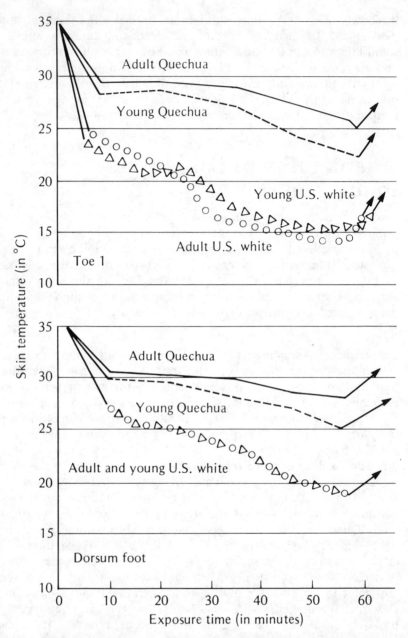

Figure 6.11   Foot Temperatures in U.S. Whites and Andean Quechas

Source: Reprinted from "Population Differences and Developmental Changes in Extremity Temperature Responses to Cold among Andean Indians," *Human Biology,* Vol. 43, No. 1 (1971) by Michael A. Little, R. Brooke Thomas, Richard B. Mazess, Paul T. Baker by permission of the Wayne State University Press. © 1971 by the Wayne State University Press.

Figure 6.12   **Adobe House Type in the Andean Highlands** On the bitter, treeless altiplano in southern Peru near Lake Titicaca, peasants have traditionally built their houses of sod and adobe block. Lacking wood even for beams, the corbeled structures of mud nevertheless withstand the freezing nights and driving rains of the weather at 4,000 meters. Each building is a room of the "house," with the surrounding wall forming the protective compound.

Photograph by Paul L. Doughty.

in creating a microclimate considerably warmer than the ambient temperatures.

Housing and shelter are the most evident means by which Andean populations deal with potential cold stress. Two types of houses are seen in these regions: one made of piled stones with a grass roof, the other made of **adobe** with roof of grass, straw, or metal (see figure 6.12). The stone houses are chiefly found at higher altitudes and are used by the pastoralist population. Although easily constructed, they offer less protection from cold—the temperature inside is only 2° to 3°C. higher than the temperature outside at nighttime (Baker 1968:18). The adobe houses, by contrast, are 7° to 10°C. warmer than outside ambient temperatures, but construction of the foot-wide adobe walls is time-consuming.

Clothing increases body temperature by 4°C. (Hanna 1976:329). The

159

outer garments are made of wool and tend to be of dark colors that provide maximum heat gain during daytime (Hanna 1968:309). Wool is an ideal material for clothing insulation since it resists crushing and tends to maintain its original volume of trapped air. The trapped air is only insulative if it can be kept from escaping, and this is achieved by wearing outer garments of such a tight weave that they are almost watertight (Hanna 1976:328). Under the tightly woven garment, open weave clothes are worn in layers to provide added dead air spaces for insulation. During heavy physical work, natives remove some of the layers that normally prevent cooling, and perspiration can escape. Once the work is complete, the layers are replaced. Men's wear often includes trousers, a shirt, a sweater, a vest, a short jacket, and a poncho. A cap or hat is also worn. Women wear anywhere from two to seven skirts, a blouse, a vest, a shawl, and a derby hat (Little 1968:376). In all, despite their lack of footwear and gloves, the Andean natives are well protected from the cold.[6] (See figure 6.13 for an illustration of women's clothing and p. 140 for men's clothing.)

We have already seen that blood flow to the extremities affords some physiological protection from exposure to cold. Hanna (1976:329; 1968:308) explains that although the Quechuas could manufacture footgear made of hides, such gear would actually be detrimental during the rainy season. At that time, the whole land is mired, and sodden footgear would increase heat loss and cooling of the extremities. Because of their impermeability, shoes or boots would also hold in sweat during periods of hard work and promote a harmful cooling of the extremities. Bare feet and open sandals, on the other hand, do not become water-soaked and dry rapidly. The protection provided by greater blood flow to the extremities is sufficient to protect them from injury.

Scheduling of work activities also helps protect Andean populations from cold. People rise sometime after dawn and go to bed at sunset (Baker 1966). Most of the daytime is spent outside, taking advantage of the solar radiation. Women and children do most of the herding, which primarily involves walking. Men do either agricultural work or work for wages in copper and tin mines. (Mountain areas have long been exploited for their minerals. Copper and tin are particularly important in the Andes.) At night, natives sleep in their own clothing with added layers of hides on sleeping platforms. Native bedding is adequate to meet minimum temperature levels that prevent shivering and cold stress. Although during daytime children had higher rectal temperatures than adults (probably as a result of higher physical activity), at night their temperatures dropped below those of the adults (Little and Hochner 1973:15).

[6]Comparable protection is experienced by the Sherpas of the Himalayas, who use sheepskins and wool as clothing. Their houses are partially heated by the body warmth of the animals. The people live on the upper story, while the animals are corraled at night on the lower story. Hearth fires also help keep the house warmer (Pugh 1966).

Figure 6.13   **Clothing in the Andes** A woman of Vicos, Peru keeps busy as
she walks through the fields. She is spinning the wool that her
husband will later weave into heavy clothing for the family. In
protection against the high altitude cold, she wears two heavy
skirts, a woolen shawl in which her baby rides, and a thick felt
hat.

Photograph by Paul L. Doughty.

Because children are more subject to cold stress, many of the child
care practices of Quechuas center on efforts to reduce cold stress in the
infant and young child (T. Baker 1976:90). Children are placed in the sun
to absorb maximum solar heat in daytime, or next to a fire, and at night
they are bedded with siblings where the heat levels are more appropriate
to their needs. A complete wrapping of young infants, as well as infrequent diaper changing, helps maintain a warm, humid microenvironment
that protects the infant against both cold and dry air. Demand feeding
provides a constant supply of needed nutrition to the child (Ibid.:91).

Aridity and Low
Productivity

It was earlier noted that increasing altitude imposes increasing limitations
upon plant productivity. At the highest altitudes, the combination of high

161

Table 6.1 Production Zones in Three Mountain Areas

	S. Switzerland		Andes		Nepalese Himalayas	
	Altitude	Products	Altitude	Products	Altitude	Products
Low altitude	less than 1000 m.	vineyards	less than 1500 m.	sugar cane, coca, fruits, rice	less than 1500 m.	rice, fruit
Mid-altitude	1000–2000 m.	cereals, hay, gardens	1500–3000 m.	cereals	2000–3000 m.	cereals, tubers
Mid/high altitude	2000–2300 m.	forest	3000–4000 m.	tubers	3000–4000 m.	forest
High altitude	2300–3000 m.	pasture	4000–5000 m.	pasture	4000–5000 m.	pasture

Source: Compiled from Stephen Brush, 1976, "Man's Use of an Andean Ecosystem." *Human Ecology* 4, (2) 128–132, 147–166.

winds, high levels of solar radiation, a largely treeless landscape, and low moisture conditions most severely limits plant productivity. Human occupation of highlands has involved a sensitively coordinated ecological verticality (that is, biotic zonation) (Brush 1976; Troll 1958). Pre-Incan populations sought access to "islands of resources" by sending their own people to colonize the various zones up and down the mountain and then trading with these people of their own ethnic group (Murra 1972:431). Ecological verticality, therefore, allowed groups to exploit resources from a variety of ecological zones located at different altitudes (Burchard 1976:37).

Types of Subsistence Strategies The limitation of low productivity is overcome in human societies through trade, **exchange networks,** and seasonal migration to more productive zones. Trade, for example, is important in Tibet, where even the religious system is partially supportive of its demands (Downs and Ekvall 1965:173). Summer migration of people and herds to higher slopes where they can take advantage of the excellent pasture of alpine meadows is still common in many mountainous regions today (James 1966:401).

In a stimulating comparison, Brush (1976) found that four zones could be distinguished in the Swiss Alps, the Andes, and the Nepalese Himalayas on the basis of products and production regimes (see table 6.1). Subsistence strategies in each area were designed to provide access to the products of the differing zones. Among the notable cross-cultural and cross-ecological similarities were reliance on an agropastoral economy, the use of trade to maintain linkages between zones, and the utilization of similar crops and animals. Netting (1976:137) has suggested that the corporate forms of land tenure commonly encountered at higher altitudes may be related to harsh environmental conditions and subsistence requirements that are more effectively controlled by group consensus than by individual effort.

Animals and Exchange The utilization of domestic animals is regulated by their capacity to live at different altitudes. In the central Andes, alpaca and llama are concentrated at very high altitudes, sheep occupy an intermediate zone, and cows and horses the lower elevations. Natives cite the lower fertility of the cattle and the low viability of the young as reasons for their absence at high altitudes. Cattle also lack the thick insulative furs of the sheep and camelids.

In the Tibetan Himalayas the high altitude animal is the yak *(Poephagus gruniens)* which provides meat, milk, blood, butter, cheese, hides, hair, fur, horns, and transport to the Tibetan population (Downs and Ekvall 1965:173). Horses and cows are found at middle altitudes and at the lower levels, the donkey. To overcome potential problems in trade

163

and mobility that the limited capacity of domestic animals presents, Tibetan populations have produced intermediate hybrids capable of moving up and down the Himalayas with less stress and with a greater capacity for useful work. The *dzo*, a cross between the yak and the cow, can carry one-third more weight than a yak, and is faster and more tractable and capable of moving into lower altitudes than the yak (Ibid.: 176–77).

In the Andes, neither wild plants nor wild fauna provide much food. Fishing is infrequent, but during certain periods provides an important food supplement. Human occupation has depleted the native population of vicuña, guanaco, and deer, and domesticants have been introduced to replace them. Alpacas, llamas, sheep, cows, horses, and guinea pigs now supply a variety of resources that are essential for life as it presently exists in the Andes.

The llama has long been a necessity of life in this region. In pre-Incan times, it was a basic right of the peasant household and a keystone of the economy (Murra 1965:211). The reason for its importance lies in the variety of resources it provides the highlander: transportation, hides, wool, dung, and food. The mobility required in a zonal environment like that of the Andes makes the use of llamas for transporting loads essential. The animal is well adapted to the bunch grasses that predominate in the moist puna and to the high altitude and cold. Llamas and other grazing animals concentrate the dispersed energy of the pasture grasses in the form of dung. The dung from the camelids (that is, alpaca and llama) is preferred as a cooking fuel. Part of the reason for this preference may be that the dung is easy to collect because camelids have special sites for defecating which facilitates collection (Orlove 1977:93). The dung also appears to have 10 percent more potential energy than that of sheep (Thomas 1976:394). A lot of the weight that llamas must carry across zones is dung, but it is sheep dung that tends to be carried the greatest distances because of its importance as fertilizer.

One important exchange that goes on in the Andes, and which has important human ecological implications, is the transfer of dung to lower altitudes and the reciprocal transfer of coca to higher altitudes. This seasonal exchange of dung for coca is an important economic activity of the southern highland population of Peru. Coca has been mentioned already as a possible factor in improved carbohydrate absorption and temporary relief of hypoglycemia. It also provides a stimulating effect comparable to that of caffeine. Dung is an important resource of the highland pastoral areas and absolutely essential to the productivity of agriculture.

Winterhalder et al. (1974) have shown that the soils of Nuñoa are deficient in nitrogen, phosphorus, and organic matter, in addition to having drainage and erosion problems. The addition of dung to the fields increased organic matter by 31 percent. It is well known that organic matter improves the physical aspects of the soil: aeration, soil moisture relationships, and the water-holding capacity of the soil. In a generally arid

Figure 6.14   **Sheep Grazing in the Andean Highlands** A woman pastures her sheep on the puna near the Peruvian city of Huancayo. The treeless plain rolls over mountain tops some 4,100 meters high.

Photograph by Paul L. Doughty.

environment this is an important consideration. In the area studied, camelid dung was primarily used as fuel in household cooking. The manure from sheep, on the other hand, was used for fertilizing fields. This is an appropriate choice since sheep manure is higher in nitrogen, magnesium, calcium, and potassium content.

For the whole ecosystem, dung is a crucial commodity: it represents concentrated energy previously scattered in the sparse vegetation of the highlands (see fig. 6.14) and converted into a form quickly utilizable by plants. Without the inputs of manure, it was found that fallow fields were not sufficiently fertile to grow potatoes (Ibid.:100). Figure 6.15 illustrates the flows of the Andean ecosystem and highlights the role of dung in maintaining the stability of the system.

The products of the vertical ecological zones in the Andes are so specialized and there is so little overlap between them that there is an abundance of products to be traded or exchanged. Despite this abundance, coca is the major facilitator of interzonal exchange. It is the universal social lubricant and is necessary for most social transactions: one needs coca to marry, to borrow, to buy, and to sell. Coca is closely tied to altitude: it only grows at lower altitudes, but its use increases with altitude (see table 6.2). High altitude dwellers, therefore, must obtain access to

165

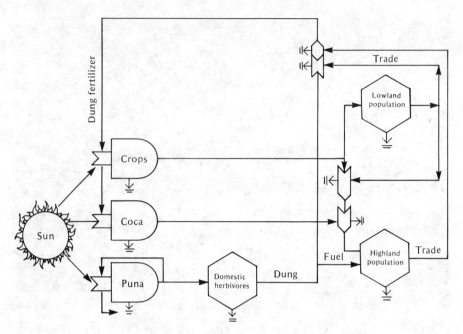

Figure 6.15 **The Role of Dung in the Andean Flow of Energy** Model high-lights the importance of dung flows in the maintenance of trade, productivity, and availability of food and coca.

coca leaves either through direct cultivation (that is, seasonal migration to the lowlands and getting paid in coca) or through purchase and exchange. Exchange is facilitated by kinship, compadrazgo (that is fictive kinship), and friendship ties (Burchard 1976:40).

The practice of village exogamy and regional endogamy facilitate both seasonal migration and exchange. Burchard suggests that this prac-tice may be seen as a spacing strategy which acts to distribute kinsmen over a broader ecosystem than that of the local village (Ibid.: 520). Although this hypothesis remains undemonstrated, it presents a testable problem for researchers.

Agricultural Practices The Andean population has overcome the limita-tions of the poor productivity of wild plants by using productive domesti-cants. Domesticated plants do not grow above forty-five hundred meters. Those grown near human habitations of four thousand meters are of ancient use: the grains quinoa (*Chenopodium quinoa*) and cañihua (*Chen-opodium pallidicuale*) and tubers, which include oca (*Oxalis crenata*), olluco (*Ollucus tuberosa*), isano, and three types of potatoes (*Solanum tuberosum, S. juzepozukii* and *S. curtilobum*). The last two types of pota-toes are frost-resistant varieties grown at highest elevations where agricul-ture is practiced.

Table 6.2   Relationship between Incidence of Coca Chewing and Altitude

Village	Altitude (in feet)	% Males	% Females	Mean
1	377	2.8	2.5	2.7
2	2,130	35.7	21.8	28.7
3	6,150	45.4	10.4	27.9
4	11,500	68.7	74.4	71.5

Source: Based on Roderick Burchard. 1976. Myths of the Sacred Leaf: Ecological Perspectives on Coca and Peasant Biocultural Adaptation in Peru. Ph.D. dissertation, Department of Anthropology, Indiana University.

The population practices a very precise form of cultivation using the numerous microenvironments found within close proximity to plant a large variety of plants that are capable of making full use of each area. Wet slopes are commonly planted while the dry slopes usually remain uncultivated. Less than 2 percent of the total land area is suitable for agriculture, which at these heights is both uncertain and of low productivity (Thomas and Winterhalder 1976: 55–56).

Crops are protected by planting them on protected slopes where there is least danger of frost (Orlove 1977:93). In addition to frost, dryness can also prevent food production. A number of practices have been noted that enhance retention of soil moisture. Manuring has a beneficial effect (Winterhalder et al. 1974). Making furrows in fields, as well as digging shallow depressions (qochavina) that retain water longer and make it available for crops, facilitates water retention while preventing waterlogging (Orlove 1977:95–96). There are good years, as well as bad ones, and during the good years the Quechua utilize preservation techniques that allow them to store production for several years. One technique of special significance is the freeze-drying of bitter potatoes to make chuño. Chuño is said to keep for several years without spoilage (Ibid.:94).

Four major stages occur in the yearly cycle of subsistence: the planting/shearing period; the growing period; the harvest period; and the post-harvest/slaughter period (Thomas 1976:383). During the planting period, work input and food intake are high, but stored food is sufficient to sustain such demand. In the growing period, food stores are at their lowest, but it is also a period when work is not intensive or arduous. Some food can be bought during this period from the proceeds of wool sales, and the meat of young herd animals that die is also consumed. During the harvest, work is hard, but food is abundant and a portion of the herd (10 to 20 percent) is slaughtered. In the post-harvest/slaughter period, food consumption is at its highest, although work is relatively light.

The annual energy consumption of the Quechua is adequate and no severe deficiencies have been noted by researchers (Baker 1969). However, during periods of drought, frost, and excessive rain or hail, crop fail-

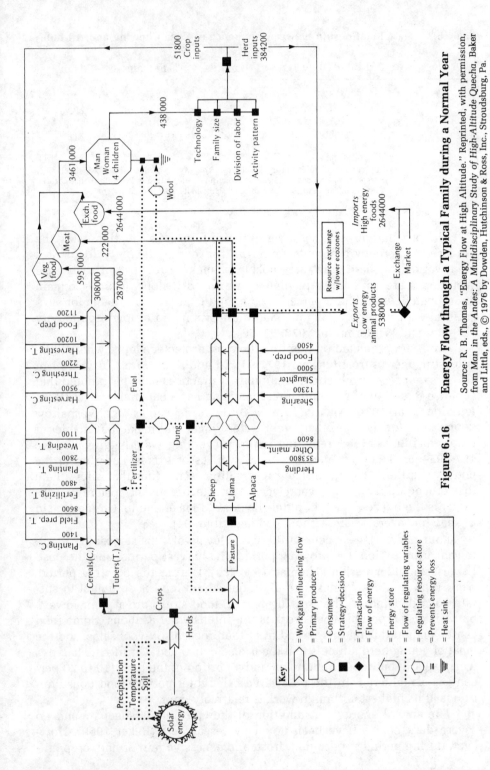

Figure 6.16   **Energy Flow through a Typical Family during a Normal Year**

Source: R. B. Thomas, "Energy Flow at High Altitude." Reprinted, with permission, from *Man in the Andes: A Multidisciplinary Study of High-Altitude Quecha,* Baker and Little, eds., © 1976 by Dowden, Hutchinson & Ross, Inc., Stroudsburg, Pa.

ure can cause severe hypocaloric stress. During these times, the survival of the Andean populations depends on the exchange networks that we have already described. The creation of obligations (that is, social capital) across altitude zones allows inhabitants of one zone to call for assistance from other populations to whom they have been generous in the past (Burchard 1976:572). Godparenthood bonds are used to reinforce family relationships and, more commonly, to create bonds of obligation with wealthier individuals.

Labor and Energy Use   The division of labor is a successful manipulation that enhances the energetic efficiency of the population as a whole. Herding is not hard work, but does require extended and continuous expenditure of energy on walking. Children by the age of twelve can perform the tasks of herding almost as well as an adult, and they are assigned the task of herding the camelids. A child of this age was estimated to spend 30 percent less energy per day than an adult. In the course of a year, this could mean a net energy savings of one hundred thousand kcals for the family. The participation of children in moderate subsistence activities would seem to contribute to the energetic efficiency of the population and to minimize the danger of hypocaloric stress (Thomas 1976:397). A great deal of the activities engaged in by all members of the population is relatively modest in energy cost and may be an adjustment to hypoxic stress aimed at preventing hypocapnia.

Thomas (Ibid.:390) has presented an energy flow model of the typical family at Nuñoa (see figure 6.16). The population plays an important role in modifying the natural puna vegetation by replacing the less productive nondomesticated vegetation with Andean plants that give a higher yield to the human population. The model also accounts for the costs of maintaining such a system, although it does not give us the energetic efficiencies involved. The efficiency of horticulture is said to be 11.7:1, while that of herding is only 1.6:1. However, when dung is traded for food products the energetic value of the dung raises the energy gained by herding to 10:1. The model represented in figure 6.15, which highlights the role of dung/coca exchange, is an expansion of the lower portion of the Thomas energy model in which all exchange with lower ecozones is lumped together and coca is not explicitly dealt with. Coca may play the role of a switch in several physiological mechanisms that enhance the well-being (nutrition, work capacity, and so forth) of the Quechua.

Summary

Human adaptation to high altitude zones involves a combination of behavioral and physiological adaptations that have made it possible for populations to survive in this vertically zonated environment. The major constraint is hypoxia and numerous developmental adaptations are particularly valuable. An enlarged capillary bed, polycythemia, decreased alveolar-arterial oxygen gradient, and other mechanisms are involved in facilitating survival in an oxygen-scarce environment.

Cold is a further constraint and is handled by both physiological adjustments and cultural practices that modify the stress before it can reach the organism. Most of the body is protected from cold stress by effective clothing and at night by the provision of shelter. The exposed hands and feet are protected by increased blood flow to the extremities, increased capillarity in these areas, and moderately elevated core temperatures.

The low productivity and aridity of the high altitude puna has been modified to yield more calories to the human population: herbivores concentrate the energy dispersed in the puna bunch grasses in the form of dung. Dung, in turn, increases the productivity of agriculture at lower altitudes and permits a flow of various foods to the pastoral area. Such a process is facilitated by interzonal exchange networks. These patterns are closely tied to resource management, to cultural history, and to social status. Andean populations rely on a multiple resource base that will, in the long term, assure survival.

It is unlikely that the stable system that Baker and his associates have described and analyzed will remain unchanged by the process of modernization. However, the resiliency of the Andean population through the centuries and the adaptive value of their practices make one optimistic that newcomers have more to learn from the Quechua than the Quechua from the newcomers.[7]

Recommended Readings

The literature on human adaptation to high altitudes is among the most extensive and thoroughly synthesized. A decade ago a bibliography of four thousand items was gathered by Wulff et al. (1968) and serves as an excellent guide to research on the topic. Since that time, there has been a proliferation of research on high altitude adaptability. Mazess (1975) wrote a thoughtful critical review of research. Two synthesis volumes generated by the International Biological program provide fresh insights into both South American Quechua and Asian adaptability (Baker and Little 1976; Baker 1978).

For a comparative exposure to the major issues in human adaptation to high altitudes, without the heavy emphasis on biological adaptation of

[7]The increasing pressure of population on the scarce resources of the highlands has led to a steady migration to the lowlands in recent years (Crist 1964; Hegen 1966) An interesting attempt at improving the native system is being made at the International Potato Center in Lima. Research includes study of the management practices of the highland population and their marketing behavior.

the above references, readers may wish to turn to the special issue of *Human Ecology* on human adaptation to mountain ecosystems (Brush 1976) and to the comparative article by Rhoades and Thompson (1975).

Interesting analyses on human responses to disaster at high altitude have been generated in the past few years by the catastrophic mud slides in the Callejón de Huaylas in Peru. Fortunately, a baseline study was made before the disaster (Doughty 1968). Subsequent studies have followed the affected populations through the period of readjustment (Oliver-Smith 1977).

More so than in other ecosystems, high altitude populations seem to have long maintained a fine balance between exploitation of their immediate habitat and reliance on trade and exchange with lower zones. Unfortunately, few studies have made this a major aspect of research. Exceptions are found in the work of Murra (1972), Burchard (1976), Netting (1976), Downs and Ekvall (1965), Orlove (1977), and Thomas (1973).

Despite the abundant literature on adaptation to altitude the topic still offers a fertile area for new work. Research to date has been heavily concentrated in the Andes, and in one restricted area of the Andes at that (the southern highlands). Integration of social/cultural data with biological data has not been as complete as is desirable. The rapid emigration of highlands peoples to the lowlands and the cities raises important questions that merit testing by careful research on human adaptability.

E. Moran

Human
Adaptability
to Arid Lands

Arid lands would have greater potential productivity for human populations than arctic and high altitude regions were water in more abundant supply. How populations have adjusted to a scarce supply of water will be the central focus of this chapter. Arid lands, or deserts, are characterized by low and random distribution of rainfall, high levels of solar radiation, high daytime temperatures, high levels of **evapotranspiration,** and a consequent scarcity of plant cover during most of the year.

Human populations appear to have neither genetic nor developmental adaptations for living in dry heat areas. They depend instead on acclimatory and behavioral adjustments to facilitate their occupation of these regions. Acclimatization to desert conditions actually occurs within a week or two. However, it is the problem of locating water, storing it, and minimizing its loss, that is central to human adaptation to arid conditions.

In ancient times arid lands served as "cradles of civilization." Today they include both the richest and the poorest regions of the earth, examples of which are the productive Imperial Valley of California and the impoverished interior of northeastern Brazil. Of the earth's surface, 20 to 30 percent is classified as arid land (Lee 1964:552), and some areas that were once fertile have been turned to deserts in our own time (Glantz 1977).

The present chapter begins with a brief discussion of the characteristics of desert ecosystems and the special adaptations of desert plants and animals. This section is followed by a discussion of the physiological and cultural adjustments of human populations to the problem of dry heat. Even more important is human adjustment to the scarcity of water resources.

In our consideration of human behavioral adjustments to arid conditions, we will discuss human **management** of surface water and underground water. The low primary productivity of these regions has evoked the responses of migration and long-distance trading. Surface water resources are exploited in various ways by hunter/gatherers, pastoralists, and farmers. Our discussion will just focus on the exploitation of surface resources by the hunting/gathering !Kung populations of the Kalahari Desert. We will then examine the exploitation of the Nile River over time by farming populations. Brief discussions of the exploitation of surface runoff and **groundwater** follow. Throughout the chapter our main concern is how populations organize socially and culturally to establish a viable system of water utilization.

Desert Ecosystems

Deserts are not homogeneous, but vary a great deal in characteristics. Generally speaking, they can be said to be areas of very low rainfall and high evaporation where vegetation is scanty. Not only is the precipitation low, it is infrequent and largely erratic as well. True, or extreme, deserts are said to be those with less than 100 mm of rainfall. They lie beyond the equatorial rainfall belt and in latitudes where drying trade winds blow throughout the

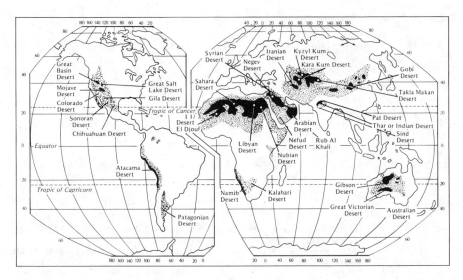

Figure 7.1   Deserts of the World

year (see figure 7.1). Deserts may also appear in areas dominated by the subtropical high pressure belt on the leeward side of high mountains where moisture-laden air is blocked from crossing; in areas far removed from sources of oceanic moisture; and in locations on the leeward side of cold currents. Winds that pass over cold water reach land with lowered temperatures, but are warmed as they pass over the land and act as drying agents when they pass over moist land (Heintzelman and Highsmith 1973:152–153). Each type of desert is characterized by unique variations in daytime temperatures, level and seasonal distribution of rainfall, and vegetation. Table 7.1 outlines some of the major types of arid ecosystems and their respective levels of primary production. Walter showed that the annual production of dry matter in the desert is a linear function of rainfall (1973:87). Moisture levels indeed may be said to control the system.

Deserts can be areas of surprising contrasts. In daytime temperatures may rise to over 43°C., while at night they may drop to an uncomfortable 0°C. Surface heating is rapid, but cooling is just as rapid when the sun sets because of high albedo (that is surface reflectivity) and clear skies. The topography is reminiscent of a region in formation. Weathering is slow and the absence of vegetative cover makes every detail visible. Large and small closed basins dramatically cut by surface runoff and erosion are common. During rare episodes of rainfall, water may be carried to the center of a basin, forming a temporary lake called a *playa*. The ever-changing stream beds, or **wadis,** along which the rushing waters run are characteristic of deserts. During a sudden rainfall, the water runs down the surrounding slopes, along old gullies or etching new ones, until it reaches the wadis where the now raging flashflood forms **alluvial fans** rich in sediment. The more gently

175

Table 7.1   **Classification of Arid Ecosystems**

Type	Mean annual precipitation	Above ground primary production	Below ground production
Extremely arid or "true desert"[a]	less than 60–100 mm.	less than 30g/m^2	less than 100g/m^2
Arid[b]	from 60–100 mm. to 150–200 mm.	30–200g/m^2	100–400g/m^2
Semiarid[c]	from 150–250 mm. to 250–500 mm.	100–600g/m^2	250–1000g/m^2

[a] In true deserts, vegetation is restricted to favorable areas only.
[b] In arid areas, one finds diffuse natural vegetation.
[c] In semiarid areas, it is possible to carry out diffuse dryland farming, but its success is highly unreliable.
Source: Compiled from pp. 25, 44, 45 of Imanuel Noy-Meir, "Desert Ecosystems: Environment and Producers." Reproduced, with permission, from the *Annual Review of Ecology and Systematics*, Vol. 4. © 1973 by Annual Reviews Inc.

inclined slopes have greater water-capturing capacity, and the runoff there is more likely to create conditions favorable for human populations (Steward 1938:12).

Lack of rain is not the only factor in the creation of desert conditions. Low air humidity is also important in that it affects the distribution and behavior of plants and animals. Because the rate of evaporation is high, an organism can become rapidly stressed by aridity. Although it is very difficult to measure actual evapotranspiration, potential evapotranspiration is commonly used to determine the water balance of a region and to arrive at an estimate of which plants may be able to grow in the area.

Desert Plants   Desert plants cope with moisture deficits either by drought avoidance or drought resistance, or both. *Drought avoidance* refers to adaptational features by which plants remain **dormant** during the dry season, but rapidly respond to seasonal rains. It also refers to plants with compressed life cycles that permit them to reproduce during brief rainy periods and to plants that drop their leaves during the dry season in order to conserve water. *Drought resistance*, on the other hand, refers to numerous physiological features that enable plants to collect, store, and retain water. Some of these plants exhibit extensive subsurface root growth or deep tap roots that reach the water table. Drought-resistant plants are also able to reduce water loss from leaves because of waxy coverings, hairiness, or angle of the leaves; and some are able to utilize water more efficiently.

Figure 7.2 lists most of the features of desert plants. Succulents store considerable water in their fleshy leaves and stems. Waxy leaves are able to

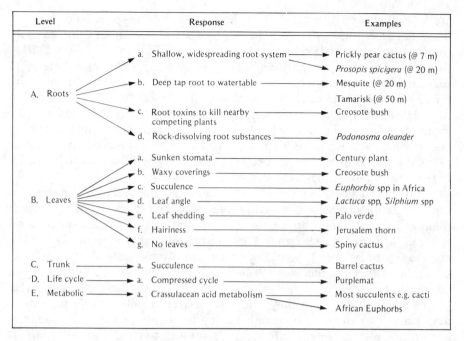

Level	Response	Examples
A. Roots	a. Shallow, widespreading root system	Prickly pear cactus (@ 7 m)
		Prosopis spicigera (@ 20 m)
	b. Deep tap root to watertable	Mesquite (@ 20 m)
		Tamarisk (@ 50 m)
	c. Root toxins to kill nearby competing plants	Creosote bush
	d. Rock-dissolving root substances	*Podonosma oleander*
B. Leaves	a. Sunken stomata	Century plant
	b. Waxy coverings	Creosote bush
	c. Succulence	*Euphorbia* spp in Africa
	d. Leaf angle	*Lactuca* spp, *Silphium* spp
	e. Leaf shedding	Palo verde
	f. Hairiness	Jerusalem thorn
	g. No leaves	Spiny cactus
C. Trunk	a. Succulence	Barrel cactus
D. Life cycle	a. Compressed cycle	Purplemat
E. Metabolic	a. Crassulacean acid metabolism	Most succulents e.g. cacti
		African Euphorbs

Figure 7.2 **Levels of Adaptation of Desert Plants** As evident even from the examples, desert plants use more than one adaptation to cope with the scarcity of water in arid environments.

reflect heat and keep the leaves cooler. Hairiness helps the leaves break up the flow of drying air near the tiny leaf openings **(stoma)** through which carbon dioxide and oxygen are exchanged during **photosynthesis** and thus helps to prevent excessive drying. Some desert plants orient their leaves to minimize the leaf area exposed during the hot hours of the day by changing the angle of exposure.

Efficiency of water use is also possible through Crassulacean acid metabolism. This strategy is usually found in combination with other features, such as hairiness or waxiness. Plants with this form of metabolism open up their stoma only at night to take up carbon dioxide and avoid loss of water. They then convert carbon dioxide to malic acid. By dawn, they close their stoma and during the day avoid losing water, while malic acid is internally converted to carbohydrates (Parkhurst, personal communication).

Desert Animals Desert animals possess biological rhythms that lower their potential water loss. Special physiological adaptations (such as size) or behavioral adjustments (such as inactivity and migratory habits) improve their life chances in the desert. Most species are nocturnal in habit and spend most of the day burrowed in holes, rock shelters, or other retreats. Those that are active in daytime retreat once the temperature reaches 50°C. Most of these daytime animals are birds and large mammals. In addition to daily rhythms, some animals rely on estivation for survival in the desert. **Estivation** refers to dormancy during the hot, dry summer and is often related to **diapause**—that is a state of suspended development accompanied by greatly decreased metabolism (Cloudsley-Thompson 1977:74). Animal fertility is carefully timed to the arrival of the rains. During the dry season, reproduction may be totally interrupted, but rapid bursts of population occur within weeks after the arrival of winter rains. A common physiological adaptation of many desert species, particularly of rodents, is their ability to survive on moisture obtained from solid food.

Burrowing animals form an important food source for hunting/gathering populations because burrowing minimizes the effort required to catch them and because their high rates of reproduction guarantee a secure food source. The larger desert animals, such as antelopes, camels, and gazelles, are too big to be able to avoid daytime conditions. Instead, they rely on adaptations that reduce water loss and thermal stress. Camels excrete a concentrated urine and nearly dry feces. Their coarse hair insulates them from solar radiation, and they can tolerate greater dehydration than most mammals. The camel can recoup its liquid losses very rapidly when it encounters water. Thus, while small desert animals avoid extreme conditions, larger ones resist them by reduced surface/volume ratios and by physiological adjustments that reduce water loss, improve insulation, and permit rapid gain of body fluid losses.

Soil Conditions   The limited amount of rain in deserts falls in ten to fifty rainy days. On only five or six of these days is the amount of rain sufficiently large to affect the biotic parts of the system (Noy-Meir 1973:28). However, most of the rainy days affect soil formation. Despite the common denominator of low rainfall and high potential evapotranspiration, desert soils are quite variable in physical, chemical, and biological characteristics. Exposed rock experiences rapid daily temperature variations. When moisture is present to expand or contract in small fissures, rocks may be broken up. Wind also exercises a powerful and abrasive force—as do the torrential flashfloods in wadis, where there is a general lack of protective ground cover. The rapid flow of water over the surface prevents the formation of soils of much thickness in any given area—except in alluvial basins at the end of wadis (Cloudsley-Thompson 1977:15). Over time, such basins may become filled with alluvial deposits and form salt flats with saline crusts. (When the water stands in a basin and forms shallow lakes, slow evaporation removes the water but leaves behind the mineral salts carried from the surrounding hills. The end result is a saline crust.)

Saline soils present special problems for agriculture since they can only be made agriculturally productive by flushing out the salts. Such flushing requires an intensive use of water, and this scarcest resource of arid lands may not be easy to obtain in the necessary quantities. Nonsaline alluvial basins, when irrigated, can be very fertile because of the deposition of nutrient-rich sediment. Extremely youthful soil forms also exist. "Rocky desert soils," known as *hammada* in the Sahara, exhibit denuded solid rock, smoothed and polished by the wind. "Stony desert soils," (regs) are formed by wind erosion of the smaller particulate matter, leaving only larger particles behind. Finally, "sandy desert soils," (ergs) consist of vast, sandy wastes of windblown dunes. The largest erg in the world is located in the southern Arabian desert.

Adjustments to Dry Heat

Before a human population can exploit the resources of a desert, its individual members must be able to cope with the hot and drying stresses of the ecosystem on their organisms. An individual in the desert is constantly threatened with dehydration and physiologically dangerous heat loads. Thermal sweating helps reduce heat gain through evaporation of moisture at the skin surface. When air and ground temperature are below 92°F. (33.3°C.) human beings can lose heat by radiation to cooler ground or by convection to cooler air. In the desert, however, daytime temperatures are often higher and sweating is the only effective mechanism. To become cool, we pay with loss of body water (Adolph et al. 1947:3). The human body appears dry in the desert because evaporation is so rapid that as sweat nears the surface, it disappears (that is, insensible evaporation). No changes in the human metabolism are needed to maintain this cooling system, but one must obtain an equal amount of liquid to replace what is lost.

Water requirements cannot be represented by an absolute figure, but are a function of ambient temperature, air humidity (or vapor pressure), diet, and level of activity. A body at rest (that is, basal metabolism only) that is protected from the sun requires at least five ounces of water per hour to remain in body fluid equilibrium. Less water intake means the body would utilize stores of tissue liquid, eventually resulting in dehydration and thermostatic deregulation. Exposure to solar radiation adds to this equilibrium requirement an extra sixteen ounces per hour; and walking an additional twelve ounces per hour (Ibid.:8). Water requirements increase proportionately according to increase in activity level and temperatures. Reduction of activity and adoption of a relaxed posture that increases surface area help compensate for increases in heat load in the human body. Figure 7.3 plots daily water requirements at three levels of activity and at various temperatures.

Physiological Adjustments   To date, physiological studies tend to agree that human populations acclimatize to desert conditions within a week or two (for example, Lee 1964, 1969; Adolph et al. 1947). Very little difference in heat adaptation has been noted between desert natives and non-natives. A

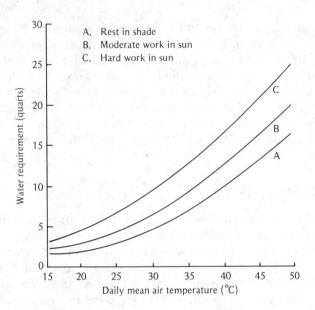

A. Rest in shade
B. Moderate work in sun
C. Hard work in sun

Figure 7.3   **Daily Water Intake in Relation to Air Temperature and Level of Activity**

Source: D. H. K. Lee. 1968. Man in the Desert. In Desert Biology. G. W. Brown, ed. New York: Academic Press.
Note: One quart = 0.95 liter.

diminished pulse rate, lower rectal temperatures, increases in the rate of sweating, and ability to work in the heat are remarkably similar among human populations (Wyndham 1966:237). Acclimatized individuals show a reduction in the salt concentration of sweat, which prevents deficiencies associated with cardiovascular inadequacy and violent muscular cramps. Urine volume is also reduced as a homeostatic compensation for increased dehydration (D.H.K. Lee 1969:239; Newman 1975:87). These few factors represent the bulk of physiological changes that occur. Adolph et. al. (1947:34) raised questions about the limitations of the desert ecosystem on the amount of physical work that could be achieved, but concluded that these limitations are not severe as long as people have enough water. Further work is needed to establish whether alleged limitations on the amount of work that it is possible to achieve might not be associated with work schedules that are inappropriate to desert living.

Body size, shape, and composition can also influence the heat exchange process. The "ideal" body type for desert conditions is tall, with long, lean extremities and low subcutaneous fat. Tallness maximizes the surface area-to-weight ratio for enhanced cooling, while lean body composition minimizes the presence of insulating fat that may limit heat flow from core to shell to cool the body. The Nilotic peoples of the Sudan are often cited as an example of optimal human form for desert environments. However, one could also argue that such greater surface area would also maximize evaporation of sweat and expose those individuals to dehydration unless other factors intervened to ameliorate that possibility. In fact, social and cultural patterns enter in to provide exactly such protection.

While there is some positive correlation between ideal body types and different body temperatures (Harrison et al 1977:435), factors such as migration, nutrition, and disease preclude a perfect association between body shape and environment (D.H.K. Lee 1964:563).[1] In desert areas today, we find peoples of all shapes, sizes, and degrees of leanness. The major adjustments of human mammals are not small size and nocturnal habits, nor complex physiological adjustments as among camels; they are cultural and behavioral in nature. The problem of how to cope with aridity may be overcome by activity patterns, clothing, shelter, diet, and other similar adjustments.

Cultural Adjustments While it is essential that human beings find and manage water in the desert, it is no less important that they conserve it once it enters their bodies. In this process, the cultural adjustments of clothing and shelter play a crucial role. Clothing helps cut the incidence of direct solar radiation. The same may be said of shelter. The "ideal clothing" style depends on the prevalent environmental conditions and the load of physical work. At rest and at moderate levels of activity, loose fitting, loosely woven clothes are best, while during hard physical work, little or no clothing is best (Ingram 1977:100). Loose fitting, loosely woven clothing allows free passage of evaporation from skin to atmosphere and also assures that a layer of insulating air is maintained between cloth and skin. Clothing soaked with sweat gives little protection (Briggs 1975:116).

Clothing is particularly important in coping with hot desert winds. This is one of the recurrent and most serious stresses faced by desert populations (Leithard and Lind 1964). A hot wind lowers the threshold of resistance to dry heat by accelerating the dehydration process. If this occurs quickly enough, the victim collapses, loses consciousness, and dies. Heatstroke (that is, sun stroke) results from a breakdown in the thermoregulatory system and consequent hyperpyrexis (high fever) when sweating fails. The spectacularly sudden deaths that have been noted in deserts appear to be a result of sandstorms and subsequent rapid dehydration (Briggs 1975:97). In addition, driving rapidly across the desert with inadequate protective clothing can cause heatstroke and dehydration equivalent to a hot desert wind.

Briggs points out that Saharan peoples conform to the established rules governing adaptive clothing (see table 7.2). Ordinary clothing, including turbans, is loose and of lightweight material. Trousers are long and baggy, with a narrow opening at the ankle—barely wide enough for one's foot to go through—which acts as an excellent dead space insulator.

---

[1]Surface/mass studies tend to ignore the fact that from birth to adulthood these ratios may change threefold (Newman 1975:83).

Table 7.2   Principles of Clothing and Shelter in Hot, Dry Conditions

Objective	Clothing	Shelter
1. Reduce heat production	1. Lightweight, absence of constriction; functionally convenient	1. Use of semi-subterranean shelters; cooking devices that do not concentrate heat
2. Reduce radiation gain	2. Provide shade; reflect shorter wavelengths; insulate by use of multiple layers	2. Cubical design; trees and bushes conveniently located to shade; light colored exteriors; heat insulation
3. Reduce conduction gain	3. Insulate by use of multiple layers; wind-excluding	3. Controlled ventilation; free flow of air
4. Promote evaporation	4. Sufficient perflation	4. Openings closable on hot days and capable of opening on cool nights; use of evaporative cooling devices

Source: D. H. K. Lee. 1964. Terrestrial Animals in Dry Heat: Man in the Desert. In Handbook of Physiology: Adaptation to the Environment. D. B. Dill, ed. Washington, D.C.: American Physiological Society.

Sandals with soles that project one inch in all directions are the usual footwear (Ibid.:122–127). The heat reflecting from the ground does not touch the feet as a result of the projections.

Housing in hot, dry areas is most adequate when it delays the entry of heat into the living quarters as long as possible. This is best achieved by use of high heat-capacity materials, by compact geometry, by closely spaced units, by use of subterranean constructions and high reflectivity colors, and by removal of heat-generating sources (for example, cooking fires). High heat-capacity materials, such as adobe, mud, and stone, are able to absorb heat in daytime and to reradiate it at night. Compact design minimizes surface area exposed to the outside. This may also be achieved by building houses close together, which both reduces ventilation and increases the time it takes for heat to build up. Reduction of ventilation is effective only if the walls and roof are thick enough to delay heat penetration. The pueblos of the Southwest are an excellent example (see figure 7.4). The Arab tents cannot provide this type of insulation and must therefore promote ventilation. Subterranean and semi-subterranean dwellings are built in extreme deserts to take advantage of the heat capac-

Figure 7.4   **The Pueblos: An Example of Adaptive Desert Housing**
Photograph by Arthur Rothstein from the Library of Congress collection.

ity of the earth itself. Rooms in Matmata houses in the Sahara are under thirty feet of earth and are comfortably cool (Rapoport 1969:89–93).

Deserts cool rapidly at night. Populations inhabiting thickwalled dwellings maintain a comfortably warm microenvironment. Hunter/gatherers, on the other hand, do not build complex dwellings and are exposed to extreme body cooling at night. Central Australian aborigines sleep naked with no apparent discomfort at air temperatures of about 0°C. They appear to be able to endure a greater drop in skin temperature without shivering (Harrison et al. 1977:430). Kalahari hunter/gatherers build fires and sleep around them with their feet towards the flames, huddled under their cloaks and close enough to one another to share body warmth. Researchers have noted that in this manner they create a microclimate close to the **thermo-neutral temperature** of 25°C. (Wyndham 1966:206–207). Steegman suggests that tropical hunters may be employing very ancient cold adaptation mechanisms not found among the more recently adapted temperate and arctic populations (1975:157)[2] Further research is needed, however, to explain this mechanism.

Utilization of Resources

The most important exploitable resource in a desert is surface water. It is also the one that requires the least technological sophistication. It is for

[2]In northern cold, peripheral adaptations were selected since the core was well protected by clothing and shelter.

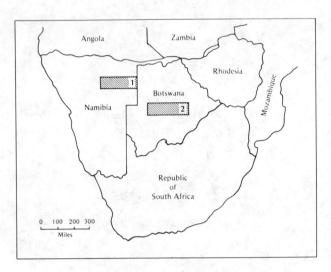

Figure 7.5   Location of the Dobe !Kung (1) and the Kade San (2)

this reason that hunter/gatherers, with relatively simple tool kits, have relied on surface water for their subsistence. The Kalahari Desert is the habitat of the !Kung San. (The *San* is the term preferred by the population over the older term of *Bushmen*.) Numerous human ecological studies of the !Kung are now available and from them a comprehensive view of !Kung use of resources is possible. The !Kung inhabit an area where resources are scattered, where water is available in varying amounts throughout the year, and where vegetation varies from shrub savanna to arid desert. In our discussion of !Kung adaptations to the Kalahari, we will refer to the Dobe !Kung and to the Kade San to the south (see figure 7.5).

Utilization of Surface Water   The Dobe area of the Kalahari lies on the northern fringe of the desert and is part of a transitional zone between the drier shrub savanna to the south and the lush region of the Okavongo river to the north. The Dobe area is a **semiarid area** with a hot summer from October to March, in which the temperatures can reach 35° to 45°C. and sweat losses are severe. On the other hand, between June and August the temperature falls below 5°C. Fortunately all the rainfall is concentrated in a four to six month rainy season during the hot summer months, but, as in other deserts, rainfall is erratic. Ranges of 239 to 597 millimeters per year have been noted and, in addition, month-to-month and locational variation further increases the uncertainty of precipitation. Drought conditions characterize about half the recorded years (Lee 1972:132).

The !Kung rely on three types of standing water sources: large collecting **hardpans** in dry river channels, smaller depressions between

Figure 7.6   **Hunter Dipping Water out of Tree**
Photograph from Anthro-Photo by R. B. Lee.

dunes (*molapo* pans), and holes in large trees. Hardpan sources are by far
the most important since some hold water year-round. The molapos offer
a varying water source that depends on the size of the catchment and the
length of the rains. The water from the tree trunks is important not so
much for its quantity, but because it is usually the only water source in
food-rich dune crests. (See figure 7.6.) Water from roots is also used, but it
is costly to obtain. The root must be dug from depths of up to forty centimeters (15 inches), and over twenty roots are necessary to provide the
fluid needs of one person per day (Ibid.:134). In choosing which water
resources to use, the !Kung must sort out the costs from the benefits of
gaining access to food and water in a given location at a given point in
the yearly cycle.

The Dobe territory actually has only nine "permanent" water holes,
and this limits the area that the Dobe !Kung can exploit. During the rainy
season, groups move away from the permanent water holes and disperse
over the territory. With the approach of the dry season, however, bands
congregate first at the larger seasonal pans, and, with increased aridity, at

185

the nine permanent water holes. Life is difficult, but—unlike the southern Kade San—they do have permanent waterholes to assure their basic needs.

Access to waterholes is maintained by widespread sharing between groups. While a group is normally associated with an area of land and a specific waterhole, rarely does a group's association with a given waterhole go back any further than fifty years (Ibid:129). Moreover, rules of reciprocity ensure that any relative or visitor can share equitably in the camp's resources. Such reciprocity and hospitality have often been observed among hunter/gatherers and pastoralists inhabiting desert areas. Cole (1975:68) notes that hospitality is adaptive in areas where resources are widely spaced and of uncertain reliability.

In the rainy period camps are evenly spaced over the Dobe region, but as the summer heat evaporates the standing water, groups begin to converge at the few permanent waterholes (see figure 7.7). The settlement pattern of the !Kung reflects the ecological principle that settlements reflect people's decisions, both conscious and unconscious, about how they will relate to their environment and to one another (Yellen 1976:48).

Unlike the San of the Dobe Area, the Kade San have no standing water sources and must obtain most of their water from plants. The environment is rich in a variety of vegetable foods. For the Kade San the primary concern in migrating is not the location of water per se, but the location of the plants that supply them with their water requirements. The amount of work they devote to subsistence is relatively small, even though it is nearly twice that of the neighboring Dobe San. Unlike the Dobe San, the Kade San cannot rely on a major nutritious food source, such as the mongongo nut, that is available to the Dobe San, but must diversify with a variety of foods throughout the year (Tanaka 1976).

After rainfalls, some water collects in pans and molapos, creating shallow water holes. The Kade San move their camps to take advantage of this water, which is available thirty to sixty days out of the year. On the other three hundred days, they are obliged to look for their water in plants, particularly two species of melons (*Citrullus lanatus* and *C. naudinianus*), two species of tubers (*Raphioonacme burkei* and *Coccinia rehmanii*), and an aloe (*Aloe zebrina*). Blood from animals is not a useful water source because of the water required to process the ingested protein. The major and most dependable water source is *Citrullus lanatus* or "bitter melon" since it keeps for most of the year and is comparable to our watermelon in water content. Tanaka (1976:104) estimated that the Kade San obtain three thousand five hundred milliliters of water per person per day from melons.

Utilization of Groundwater Groundwater occurs below the surface in what is known as a *zone of saturation*. In this zone permeable rocks become saturated under hydrostatic pressure (that is, the pressure of a liq-

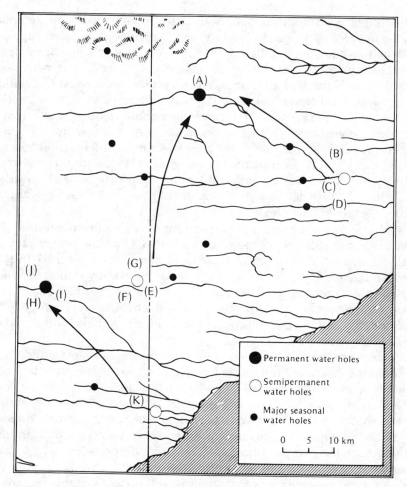

Figure 7.7   **Movements of San Bands in Times of Drought**   The bands (A)–
(K) each have their traditional water holes, but (as shown in the
figure) they may regroup in different patterns when some water
holes become dry.

Source: Adapted from p. 141 of R. B. Lee, 1972, !Kung Spatial Organization: An
Ecological and Historical Perspective, *Human Ecology* 1(2), 125–147.

uid at rest) with water that flows between impermeable layers of soil or
rock (Cantor 1970:5). Ground water acts as a replenishable reservoir that
can raise the water table during wet periods. It can also sustain considerable exploitation.

Groundwater can be a product of both local rainfall and extraregional
sources. Water can originate in areas far beyond the desert and arrive
there by flowing underground for great distances. In places, oases form as
a result of folds in the underground strata (Evenari et al. 1971:151). Oases

187

are important water sources, but are usually too far apart to enable noma-dic human groups to depend solely on them for their water supplies. Local sources for underground water include rain that seeps through the gravel beds in the wadis during or immediately after local flash floods. Since the wadi beds usually overlie a less permeable limestone formation, the water that infiltrates remains trapped underground and becomes a "perched water table" with the gravel bed acting as the **aquifer.** After flash floods have swept down the wadis, the bed of the wadis is left pud-dled and muddy, and animals can be seen drinking there. After the sur-face of the bed dries, animals may dig to a depth of up to twenty centimeters to reach the underground water. Human groups also learned this lesson. To this day, Kalahari and Australian desert hunter/gatherers obtain water in this manner.

Wells are probably next in the evolution of groundwater use. The Bedouins today still use a type of primitive well, which is characterized by shallowness (three to six meters deep) and a narrow throat (fifty to sixty centimeters in diameter) that is usually capped by a rock. A refine-ment of this form consists of a chain of wells across the face of a slope. In this system, a number of wells are dug into the aquifer and from there the water is led gradually away through underground tunnels until the lower level surface is reached.

A larger version of the chain well, which uses the same principle, is the *kanat,* or drainage tunnel (see figure 7.8). A kanat may vary in length from a few hundred meters to many kilometers. Its water yield is as high as five hundred gallons per minute. Excavation is made from vertical shafts, which have to be driven to a depth of twenty to one hundred meters on alluvial fans. Kanats are found from western China through Afghanistan. They were introduced into the Atacama Desert of South America as well. Although labor costs of contruction are high, the kanat provides a secure water source in areas where surface water is in extreme scarcity. Since it uses the force of gravity, the system is not energy-inten-sive and reduces capital and maintenance costs.

A final refinement in the use of groundwater is the deep well. This type requires an understanding of the relationship between the water-bearing layer and the impermeable stratum. It also requires a great deal of labor and technological capacity. The !Kung, for example, are unable to excavate wells to tap deep sources of underground water because they have only digging sticks, which cannot pierce the underlying hardpan. The labor required in constructing deep wells has only been justified when large populations have had to be supported.

Utilization of Plants and Animals   Even in the Kalahari, life depends on more than water supplies. As they look for water, both San groups exploit a variety of other resources. The management of wild plants and animals, as practiced by hunter/gatherers, appears simple, but the body of knowl-edge brought to bear is extensive. The !Kung name and recognize almost

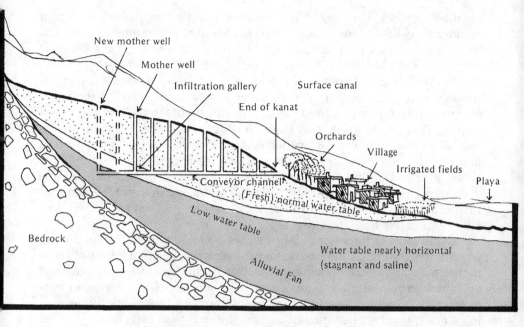

New mother well

Mother well

Infiltration gallery

Surface canal

End of kanat

Orchards

Village

Irrigated fields

Playa

Conveyor channel

(Fresh) normal water table

Low water table

Bedrock

Water table nearly horizontal
(stagnant and saline)

Alluvial Fan

Figure 7.8   **Diagrammatic Cross Section of a Kanat**   This ancient,
laboriously hand-constructed water supply system brings life to
thousands of sun-parched acres in the dry lands of North Africa
and Asia. It is found to a lesser extent in South America. In construction, the water supply is located by first digging the horizontal tunnel on a gentle grade from where water is desired to
the source. Vertical shafts are spaced along the line to bring the
excavated material to the surface. The greatest distribution is in
Iran, where the system has tended to promulgate a semifeudalis-
tic organization of agriculture because construction and maintenance costs are beyond the means of the peasant class.

Source: O. H. Heintzelman and R. M. Highsmith, *World Regional Geography*, 4th
ed., Prentice-Hall, 1973, as adapted from George B. Cressey, "Qanats, Karez, and
Foggeras," *The Geographical Review*, Vol. 48, No. 1, p. 28. Adapted, with permission, from the American Geographical Society.

five hundred species of plants and animals in the Kalahari. Out of these,
they use one hundred fifty species of plants and one hundred species of
animals. Like nearby pastoralists, they have an accurate knowledge of animal behavior that amazed even the ethologists who interviewed them
(Blurton-Jones and Konner 1976).

   The diet of both San groups is rich and varied. In the Dobe area, however, the people concentrate much of their effort on the collection of the
abundant mongongo nuts (*Ricinodendron rautanenii*). Although this
choice may be based primarily on the relative abundance of this food,
nutritionally the mongongo nut is an excellent choice as well. It has a 27
percent protein content and six hundred calories per one hundred grams

of edible portion. The Baobab fruit (*Adansoma digitata*), which is rich in vitamin C, calcium, and magnesium, is also used. *Bauhinia esculenta*, a bean, is also a rich food and is available in the drier areas of the Kalahari where the Kade San live.

In their drier environment, the Kade San follow a varied subsistence strategy that includes thirteen major vegetable foods. During the rainy season, *Bauhinia macrantha* is available and becomes an important food source. This single species of bean constitutes the main element in the diet when standing water is available. *Bauhinia macrantha* is rich in protein and fat and displaces all other foods for a period of four months. When it dries in May, the Kade San turn to water-storing melons. As the dry season lengthens, these water sources become scarce and the San turn increasingly to underground tubers which are dug up approximately seventy centimeters from the surface.

Game meat is important and provides 20 to 50 percent of the diet by weight, depending on the season and the number of active hunters. Techniques for stalking are varied and effective in this sparse region: bow and poisoned arrow, hunting dogs, snares, and probing in underground burrows are all used. Probing in underground burrows is particularly rewarding since it involves less pursuit and the animals tend to be fatter. Animal fat, a concentrated caloric source, is a scarce element in the San diet and is highly prized. Small burrowing animals are the most often obtained. Larger ungulates are also captured, but with less frequency. This is generally true of desert areas. The inhabitants of the Great Basin hunted jack rabbits (*Lepus* spp.) in seasonal communal hunts (Steward 1938: 33–35). Small game do not require the long chases that larger animals do, and they reproduce faster, thereby providing a more secure source of protein. It is possible that small animals may also be hunted to prevent their excessive competition for plant food sources.

The !Kung prefer to make camp where a mix of resources is readily available, but if news of game arrives, they may be willing to risk a longer excursion away from their waterhole. The !Kung usually locate their camp near a mongongo nut grove and an accessible water source so that they may be able to rest, regain their water losses, and have abundant food. They also tend to select newer sites in the same general area, but in previously uninhabited locations, which are freer of insects. In addition, resources closest to the camp are not as likely to be overexploited. Such a pattern facilitates the productivity of the groves over time.

Effects of Social and Cultural Practices   The availability of plants, animals, and surface water would be rapidly depleted in the absence of controls on the density of the human population. Nomadic hunter/gatherers, such as the !Kung, must keep their numbers low if the resources upon which they rely are to be naturally renewed. Research by Knodel (1977) suggests that prolonged nursing practices, under certain conditions, may

Figure 7.9   **San Mother Nursing Child**
Photograph from Anthro-Photo by Mel Konner.

be responsible for reducing the fertility of women. Lactation seems to pro-
long the period of postpartum amenorrhea (that is, the time before menstruation begins after pregnancy). In addition, fertility may be reduced by
the cultural practice of intercourse taboos during lactation. Frisch and
McArthur (1974) believe that the crucial factor may be nutritional. They
assume that a minimum level of stored energy is required for the maintenance of regular ovulation. The newborn can consume about one thousand kcals per day from its mother, and so prevent her from regaining the
body fat required to accommodate a growing fetus. Thus, !Kung women
by prolonging lactation not only assure that their children are adequately
nourished, but also delay the possibility of pregnancy for up to four years
(see figure 7.9).
    The diet of the !Kung appears to be rich in animal and plant proteins,
but low in fat and starchy carbohydrates. This diet tends to reduce the

191

ratio of body fat to body weight. This results, in turn, in delayed menarche (that is, the onset of menstruation) and delayed return of ovulation (that is, postpartum amenorrhea). Nancy Howell notes that the maximum number of live births per woman among the Dobe !Kung was seven and that the mean was five (1976). The effectiveness of delayed menarche and postpartum amenorrhea is evidenced by the slow rate of population growth among the !Kung—0.5 percent per year. The rate is all the more remarkable in the absence of infanticide, famine, and war. An important factor also appears to be mortality. Life expectancy among the Dobe !Kung is 32.5 years (see table 7.3).

!Kung camps are noncorporate, bilateral groupings of people with a flexible social structure. This social strategy provides a sensible adjustment to the drier periods in the Kalahari. Central to this social adaptation are a seasonal pattern of concentration and dispersion and a set of rules and practices for allowing reciprocal access to, and joint exploitation of, key resources (Lee 1976:91). The seasonal pattern provides flexibility in adjusting **population pressure** on resources in both the short and the long term.[3] The set of rules and practices provides the mechanism for maintaining relations that may be crucial to the survival of the group over the long run, but the mechanism must also be used in the short run if it is to be readily available in the social system. Dietary practices, cultural patterns associated with lactation, and the energy costs of nomadic movement effectively limit population growth. !Kung who have become sedentary farmers have been noted to have a faster rate of population growth than their nomadic counterparts.

Irrigation

Where water is a limiting factor, some societies have sought to divert water concentrated at the surface or located underground to planted crops. In the simplest and most productive forms of irrigation, water is diverted from major rivers. Although the development of irrigation is associated with the development of agriculture and the growing complexity of social systems, it is still unclear whether irrigation preceded or followed urbanization (see Adams 1966; Steward 1955b; Downing and Gibson 1974). However, whether large-scale irrigation created "the State" or was created by an already developed state is academic—as Steward notes, "neither could exist without the other in extremely arid areas" (1977:91).

Studies of irrigation are still in an underdeveloped stage because of the great variability in environmental conditions that they present and the

---

[3]Similar patterns of organizational flexibility have been noted among desert pastoral nomads. The Al Murrah congregate during dry periods in large groupings near a well. At such times the maximal lineage forms the basis for settlement. During the wetter season, the lineages segment into smaller groups so they can exploit the grazing areas (Cole 1975:41).

Table 7.3   Retrospective Estimates of Mortality Among the !Kung: Deaths of the Children Born to Interviewed Women

Exact Age	No. of persons					Life table functions			
	Entering interval (1)	Still in interval (2)	Subtotal (3)	Deaths (4)	Survived interval (5)	q_x (6)	l_x (7)	d_x (8)	
Birth to 1 yr.	500	25	475	96	379	.202	100,000	20,200	
1 yr. to 5 yrs.	379	42	337	59	278	.175	79,800	13,965	
5 yrs. to 10 yrs.	278	46	232	17	215	.073	65,835	4,806	
10 yrs. to 15 yrs.	215	32	183	8	175	.043	61,029	2,624	
							58,405		

q_x = probability of death from age x to x + 1. Calculated as col (4) divided by col (3).
l_x = number of survivors (of a birth cohort of 100,000) to the beginning of the age interval. Calculated as $l_x = l_{x-1}$ minus d_{x-1}.
d_x = number of deaths in age interval, out of the birth cohort of 100,000. Calculated as l_x times q_x.
Source: Nancy Howell. 1976. The Population of the Dobe Area. In Kalahari Hunter-Gatherers. R. B. Lee and I. DeVore, eds. Cambridge, Ma.: Harvard University Press. © 1976 Harvard University Press.

inadequate handling of many complex components. A recent collection of papers examined these problems and concluded that an increased knowledge of hydrology will be required of investigators before adequate generalizations can emerge (Downing and Gibson 1974). Three important aspects of any irrigation or runoff control scheme are worthy of attention: the distribution of water, the relative accessibility to water by the individual user, and the scale of technology employed (Spooner 1974). After a brief consideration of these factors, we will proceed to a diachronic examination of Nile River irrigation.

Water Distribution   There are many irrigation methods by which water can be moved from its source to the fields. Human and animal power have been used in the past, and powerful pumps facilitate such work in our time. Water wheels and well sweeps are still common in many underdeveloped nations. (A well sweep is a counterpoised lever enabling a man to lift water from a lower lying source and tip it into an irrigation channel.) Canals and dams increase the ability to harness water, enlarge the area that can benefit from irrigation, and provide access to water on a year-round basis. The labor required to establish an irrigation system is justified both by the scarcity of water and by the existence of areas with relatively permanent agricultural potential. Riverine alluvium has ready supplies of soluble minerals needed by plants, which are renewed annually by flood deposition. Reliable yields are thereby possible—if only water can be assured (Aschmann 1962:8).

Since water in arid areas is the fundamental factor limiting production, control over its distribution is a certain form of wealth and power. One would expect that the greater the dependence upon water to achieve production, the greater would be the role of water in the society. Wittfogel (1957) believed that large-scale irrigation led to centralization of political power and to despotic centralized states. Opposite views have been presented by other authors (Steward 1955b; Wheatley 1971; Adams 1966; Butzer 1976; Wolf and Palerm 1955).

Much of the irrigation literature since Wittfogel has focused on how irrigation systems did not automatically lead to complex, centralized, and highly bureaucratized political systems. On the contrary, many of the best-known irrigation schemes began as small, locally controlled systems characterized by ease of maintenance and inherent conflict over water distribution (Millon 1962; Lees 1976). Fernea (1970), suggesting that less centralized political organization might serve a population better, cites the traditional ways in which populations in southern Iraq coped with the threat of salinization. These peoples shifted fields often and because of this shifting, tribal controls were more likely to function effectively than rigid state administration. Most irrigation systems in prehistoric times were on a scale too small to demand complex coercive institutions (see Geertz 1972; Leach 1961; Netting 1974b). However, centralized control may be required when the scope of the project is too great to be dealt with by local associations or when water scarcity threatens the social order.

Access to Water   Access to water is not purely a function of distribution. It also depends on the distribution of other forms of wealth (for example, land or animals) or on periodic changes in land productivity. Wittfogel (1957) argued that precise water control for specific crops grown in arid conditions was a crucial requirement of political systems. Central authorities were required to assure accurate timing in irrigation and to provide accumulated knowledge about astronomy, agriculture, and climate. However, such centralized political units, while possessing greater knowledge, may have lacked insight into local crop needs and special hydrologic conditions.

Whether large or small, irrigation systems require cooperative effort in their construction and maintenance. Specific engineering problems, existing political structures, domesticants used, and technological limitations are but a few of the factors that may cause social and environmental variations (Steward 1977:95). Although overall production may serve the needs of a state, control of local irrigation water use was often based on local decisions in what were otherwise areally extensive systems.

Leach has argued that small-scale irrigation systems present the advantages not only of reduced planning and resource costs, but they may be more stable systems as well (1961:165). Such systems may utilize a minimum of formal cooperation and function instead through intricate, informal water-sharing agreements based on crop requirements. Normal maintenance work and access to water are mutually agreed upon by local farmers, and self-regulation is assured by the personal interest of the individuals involved (Netting 1974b). When the water source is outside the territorial control of the local group, it may be necessary to have a military force that can control the providing source of water.

As small irrigation systems attempt to expand in size, they appear to become increasingly inefficient. Conflict over water and land rights increases, and the need for centralized control grows. Under conditions of population pressure, water shortages require central policing to resolve the conflicts arising over competition for such scarce resources. The complex design of irrigation canals, therefore, may make local skills inadequate to the tasks of maintenance, and centrally organized work forces may be necessary to keep the system in operation (Hunt and Hunt 1974). Moreover, numerous cases suggest that increased centralized control over the water supply is accompanied by increased instability and possible breakdown in agricultural production.

The most common causes of irrigation failure are waterlogging, salinization, and alkalinization of the irrigated soil as a result of seepage from canals or from overirrigation. The dangers are all the more problematic in that the effects may not be visible for years, at which time correction may

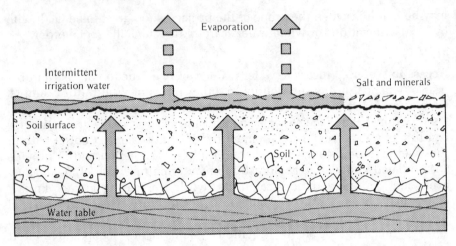

Figure 7.10   **Salinization Process**   Process is result of capillary ascent (continuous arrows) of the groundwater (horizontal dashes) and evaporation of water from the soil surface.

be too costly. Waterlogging refers to the rise of the water table as a result of deep percolation losses and the waterlogging of the crop root zone. To prevent this, a network of wells is required to monitor the location of the watertable. Effective drainage, which helps in the prevention of waterlogging, is a sine qua non of a successful irrigation system. The concentration of salt in the soil increases as water is removed by evaporation. To prevent salinity and alkalinity from reaching a level damaging to plants, frequent irrigations are necessary. In extreme cases, flushing the area to leach out the salts has proven a successful strategy (see figure 7.10).

The first irrigated areas of the world were probably natural river valleys and deltas, which possessed alluvial and nonsaline soils. Only later did populations attempt to put the salt deserts into production. These areas are the primary focus of much of the current technical work on irrigation.

Investments in Irrigation   Investments in irrigation vary from place to place and in levels of complexity. Size alone may not explain the costs of the system. Irrigating a small surface area may be costlier than irrigating a large one because of the intensive forms of channel construction that may be needed. These costs are reckoned in terms of time, labor, capital, and the social organization required. On the other hand, a more extensive system, controlled by small local units, may require a smaller investment of labor per capita and less centralization for its functional operation (Downing and Gibson 1974:ix-x). Such costs may be even smaller if the system develops slowly over time, in a piecemeal fashion.

It is important to remember that once labor has been invested in establishing irrigation works, it acts as productive capital to subsequent generations. Although later generations may choose to invest more labor to expand the system, they may also choose to carry out only routine maintenance and thereby reduce the costs of the system over time (Aschmann 1962:9). Like all large-scale public works, an irrigation system may represent huge initial costs, but over the lifetime of the system, it represents only a small cost per user and per unit of output. A major difference exists between humid tropical irrigation (where water serves mainly as a nutrient carrier) and irrigation in arid lands (where water is the chief constraint). Irrigation probably has a much more significant impact on the latter than on the former.

Nile River Irrigation   One of the best-known irrigation strategies is that of ancient Egypt. Agriculture was brought to Egypt by Asian invaders in 6000 BC, but it did not replace the existing hunting/gathering economy for another millenium (Butzer 1976:7). Explanations for this "conservative" behavior vary, but the effectiveness of hunting/gathering in the Nile Valley probably slowed the adoption of agriculture by the pre-Neolithic occupants of this region. Hassan (1972) has suggested that some exceptionally wet years or "high floods" may also have discouraged the trend towards sedentariness and agriculture near river banks. The earliest evidence of Neolithic adaptations suggest that the subsistence patterns were ecologically oriented toward riverine, lacustrine, and spring oases' faunal-rich resources (Butzer 1976:11). Hunting/gathering and fishing continued as important subsidiary activities to farming.

The Nile Valley is seasonally inundated and accumulates silts and clays primarily through bank overflow (Ibid.: 15). This seasonal inundation represented the dominant factor in promoting plant growth. Early farmers continued to live on the upper reaches of levees while they planted crops in the alluvial basin. This phase has been called one of "natural irrigation"—no drainage was practiced and low population densities were supported.

By the year 3100 BC, there is evidence that Egyptian water management had moved from "natural" to "artificial" irrigation forms in which natural features of the drainage system were extended and maintained by human action. Artificial irrigation included annual dredging of natural overflow channels in the levee, digging short ditches at low points in natural levees, blocking off streams by earthen dams, and using levered buckets to raise water from residual ponds or natural channels to fields (Ibid.:20). These improvements increased the area that could benefit from the annual floods, kept water in the basin longer during brief floodings, and permitted two or three harvests yearly rather than just one.

Shifts in climate, particularly rainfall patterns, have influenced changes in this irrigation system. After 2900 BC rainfall became increasingly rare throughout most of Egypt, and the impact of "low floods" was deeply felt throughout the region. The trend toward lower floods led to modifications of channels, levees, and flood basins. Technological changes were geared primarily toward subdividing the flood basins by dams into manageable, special-purpose units (Ibid.:47). The major limiting factor was the lack of suitable mechanical water-lifting devices. Manual lifting then available was only practicable for small-scale, horticultural activities and could not effectively reach the lower water levels during drier years. During the Dynastic Period, irrigation efforts were geared to "wet years" of high flood, rather than to the "low flood" years. In essence, the system was geared to coping with the more difficult control of the high floods that caused crop loss and disaster. However, local efforts to improve the efficiency of artificial irrigation threatened the efficiency of the total irrigation system during cyclical reversals to lower floods (Ibid.:41).

Subsistence at this time was based on cereal grains, especially wheat and barley; on vegetables such as beans and chick peas; and on flax, which was planted as a textile material. If enough irrigation permitted a second crop sequence, onions, lentils, and fodder crops were planted. Near the natural levees, date palms, sugar cane, cotton, and sorghum were cultivated. Thus, land use in Egypt during the Dynastic Period (2700–332 BC) consisted of flood basin agriculture that was locally controlled by headmen rather than directed by royal or central authorities. In time, repeated technological failure to adjust irrigation to the variation in flood levels introduced the social and political unrest that characterized the later sequences of Egyptian dynastic history (Ibid.:56).

Population expansion after 1800 BC was associated with modest increases in cultivated land and the introduction of devices that permitted irrigation agriculture even in times of low Nile floods. Figure 7.11 shows the progressive intensification of irrigation and associated population changes. The progressive expansion of population also reflects the gradual abandonment of hunting/gathering and pastoralist activities in the floodplain itself. The population seems to have peaked during the first century AD—possibly in response to Roman colonial domination and Roman demands for food. Civil and religious wars, mismanagement of waterworks, and disease were responsible for declines in population over the following six centuries (Ibid.:85-92).

Foreign domination of Egypt did not have much effect upon the traditional irrigation system until the late nineteenth century. The construction of the Suez Canal, completed in 1869, made Egypt an important connecting link between Britain and the rest of her empire. British interest in Egypt was reflected in efforts to improve health conditions, to change subsistence agriculture into commercial production, and to improve control of the Nile floods (James 1966:67). The first Aswan Dam was completed in 1902, as a result of which annual basin flood irrigation

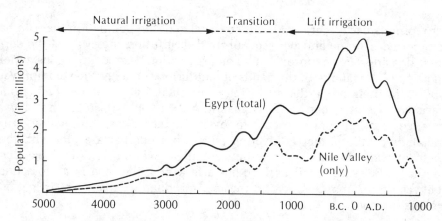

Figure 7.11 **Hypothetical Demographic Development of Egypt and Types of Irrigation Used between 5000 BC and 1000 AD**

Source: Adapted from Karl Butzer. 1976. Early Hydraulic Civilization in Egypt: A Study in Cultural Ecology. Chicago: University of Chicago Press. © 1976 University of Chicago Press.

was abandoned in favor of perpetual irrigation. Under this system, water could be directed to fields at any time of the year, and three harvests per year became commonplace.

The changes introduced by the British completely reoriented traditional land/people relationships. The power of the Egyptian elite increased, while the role of local groups in irrigation innovations was restricted. New commercial and subsistence crops were introduced, soil conditions deteriorated, and population densities began to increase rapidly. Today the Nile has population densities averaging eighteen hundred to three thousand people per square mile—a figure exceeded only by a few rural areas of China (James 1966:69).

The Aswan Dam prevents the annual floods from depositing their renewing sediments of nutrient-rich alluvium in the lower river. Since 1902 Egyptian agriculture has had to depend on the importation of fertilizers. Increases in food production have not matched population growth: per capita food supplies have steadily lagged behind. The construction of a new High Dam by independent Egypt in the 1960s again altered the system of irrigation, but did not ameliorate the problem of supplying enough food for a rapidly growing population. The loss of nutrient-rich sediments has harmed not only agriculture, but fishing as well. The Nile delta fisheries have been all but ruined. Catches of sardines in the delta declined from eighteen thousand tons in 1964 to five hundred tons in 1969 (Cloudsley-Thompson 1977:163).

The potential of irrigation for solving the problems of arid lands is limited by the total areas that can be adequately irrigated. Today only 2.5 percent of the total land area of Egypt is irrigated. Even when multiple-

199

cropping is used, there are limits to the size of the population that can be supported. Famine and widespread rural destitution suggest that the current densities are inappropriate to an arid region. Moreover, a substantial portion of the land is in the hands of landlords who do not make improvements in their properties to increase productivity but extract rent from farmers (Heintzelman and Highsmith 1973:168). Despite the many changes in Egyptian agriculture over the centuries, production still depends on the farmer cultivating crops on a one hectare plot with the help of water buffalo, pole-and-bucket lift irrigation, hoe, and wooden plow. In Egypt, as well as in other arid lands, the race is a close one between rising population and the food-producing capacity of irrigation intensification.

Harnessing Runoff for Agriculture   In arid areas where there are no large rivers like the Nile, agriculture is possible only by collection of surface water runoff or by the exploitation of underground sources. Runoff agriculture is possible only under specialized conditions. Rainfall must come in relatively light showers, wet soils must form an impermeable crust on a sloping terrain, and the terrain must have gentle inclines feeding into small catchment areas, or wadis. Utilization of runoff for cultivation of streambed alluvial fans has been observed among the North American Hopi and the Negev dwellers of the Mideast. The control of runoff was noted to be particularly sophisticated in the Negev Desert.

The Negev is a desert with rainfall of sixty to one hundred millimeters, low relative humidity (40 to 60 percent), and high potential evapotranspiration (seventeen hundred to twenty-seven hundred millimeters per year). There is an average of sixteen rainy days per year with over 80 percent of the rainfall occurring in light showers of less than ten millimeters. When these occur, they do not penetrate the ground where they fall, but rush down the hillsides into gullies and wadis in the form of short-lived flash floods. Ancient desert dwellers observed the floods created by runoff from the hillsides and learned how to harness these waters for their own benefit. Figure 7.12 illustrates what happens to rainfall in the desert. Retention of water in the soil depends on soil type. What does not evaporate from the surface or is retained at the wadis quickly disappears to replenish the ground waters.

Various populations in different historical periods have settled in the Negev. The golden period seems to have started near the end of the third century BC with the rule of the Nabateans. They appear to have been a tribe from southern Arabia who specialized in trade, transporting luxury articles, such as Indian and Arabian spices and Chinese silks. For a long time they seemed to have enjoyed a thriving trading monopoly. Such a profitable trade had to be protected, and the Nabateans built towns and fortresses along their trade routes. At its peak, the kingdom covered most of the Negev area. The rise of Rome led to the decline of the Nabatean

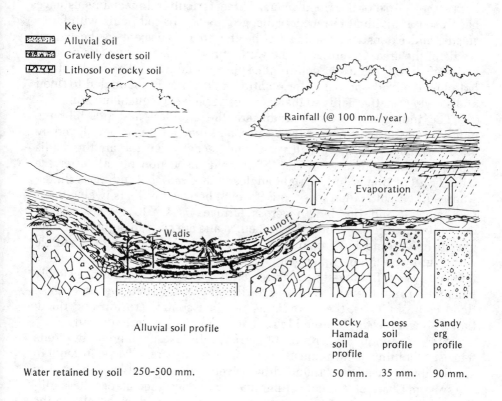

Key
Alluvial soil
Gravelly desert soil
Lithosol or rocky soil

Rainfall (@ 100 mm./year)

Evaporation

Wadis

Runoff

Alluvial soil profile		Rocky Hamada soil profile	Loess soil profile	Sandy erg profile
Water retained by soil	250–500 mm.	50 mm.	35 mm.	90 mm.

Figure 7.12   **Schematic Diagram of the Fate of Rainfall in Arid Regions**   Slope and soil type are major variables in determining how much water is retained by soils before evaporation takes up a portion of the moisture precipitated. Valley bottoms benefit not only from the precipitation, but also from watershed runoff.

kingdom, which was conquered in 106 AD, but the settlements continued, now serving as frontier outposts for the Roman Empire. When the Roman Empire was divided between East and West in 392 AD, the Negev fell under the jurisdiction of Constantinople, and a flourishing period of trade began again. Pilgrimages to Palestine contributed to the support of the Negev communities during the Christian period. After the Islamic victory over Byzantium, the area was abandoned. The new rulers had neither religious nor military motives for maintaining the costly outposts of the Negev (Evenari et al. 1971:18–27). In the past decade, populations have again tried to settle and farm the area.

Since the time of the Nabateans, Negev populations have sought to control the rushing flash floods by constructing terrace walls running across the course of the floodwaters. Three agricultural mechanisms have been used: individual terraced wadis, groups of terraced fields with farmsteads, and extensive terracing on the floodplain adjacent to the largest wadis of the area. Openings in the walls direct the slowed waters down a series of steps that further control the speed of the water. The wadis at the bottom are already prepared for planting, and water is channeled to flood and slowly soak the fields so that crops can receive adequate moisture.

The individual terraced wadis are the simplest and possibly the oldest Negev systems of floodwater use, and they have been employed by all the peoples who have cultivated the Negev. From the air the wadis look like rows and rows of steps, but field inspection reveals a terrace with a wall of stones built at right angles to the wadi. Behind the wall, the wadi is filled with silted loess soil. Spacing between walls is twelve to fifteen meters, and the length across terraces is six to twenty meters, depending on the slope of the wadi bed. Walls are sixty to eighty centimeters in height and built of five to seven layers of stones. Low inedible shrubs grow on the periphery and aid in stabilization of the area. In these terraced wadis, floodwater cascades gently from terrace to terrace slowly penetrating into the soil. (Figure 7.13 illustrates one such system of flash flood control.) Thus, these wadis do not just control erosion and flood; they also wet the soil thoroughly so that it can be used agriculturally.

More common are groups of terraced fields surrounded by stone fences, adjoining a farmhouse. Such farm units are always located in small tributary wadis surrounded by barren hillsides that are essential to the system. Channels for collecting runoff were designed across these hillsides and led the runoff to a catchment area below and eventually to the terraced fields. In one case studied by Evenari et al. (1971), the water channels drained an area of about seventeen and a half hectares (about forty-three and a half acres) and channeled a remarkable amount of water across a special opening in a fence with well-built gates or "drop-structures" (that is stone steps). These steps broke the impact of the rushing waters and allowed easier control for runoff irrigation.

Since the amount of runoff is a function of the size of the hillside catchment area, each farm unit extended its water resources by building special water conduits to storage areas adjacent to farms. Every hectare of catchment supplies an average of one-hundred to two-hundred cubic meters of runoff water. (that is, one millimeter of rainfall equals ten cubic meters of water per hectare). Since the ratio of catchment area to cultivated area in the Negev was 20:1, each hectare of cultivated land received runoff from twenty hectares of slopes, or two thousand to four-thousand cubic meters of water. Thus the cultivated area received the equivalent of three hundred to five-hundred millimeters of rainfall, although total annual precipitation is only one-hundred millimeters in the area. The conduits drained relatively small areas (that is, one-tenth to three-tenths

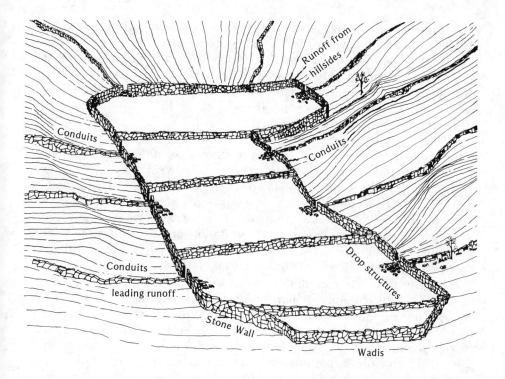

Figure 7.13   **Aerial View of a Runoff Agricultural Structure in Individually Terraced Wadis**

Source: Based on Michael Evenari, et al. 1971. The Negev. Cambridge, Mass.: Harvard University Press.

of a hectare) and divided runoff into small streams of water, thus venting flash floods. The drop structures, ditches, and spillways gave farmers control over water's action and minimized wasted water. The overall design permitted allocation of water in accordance with plant requirements.

This type of runoff agriculture is an ideal adaptation to the Negev Desert. The loess soils that characterize the region form an impermeable crust when wet, which makes even light rains run off and turn into flash floods. It is this same impermeable crust, however, that allows for technological control and runoff farming (Evenari et al. 1971).

The third type of mechanism for water control is the most complex as it requires large, intricate structures. It is also the least common since it required the diversion of large flash floods from the larger wadis. The fields supplied were large, often extending for hundreds of hectares. Despite the added complexity, however, the total water yield per unit area was low when compared with that of small watersheds. Less than 2 percent of the annual rainfall made its way to the farms studied, as compared with 10 to 20 percent net yield from small watersheds. This runoff system did not suddenly develop, but appears to have evolved through three stages of experimentation and continued difficulty in mastering the greater flash floods in the large wadis. The most marked characteristic of this systems is the repeated raising of restraining wall height. Walls often reached six meters in height along the wadis, and this suggests that deposition of silt was a continuous problem.

The Negev systems of narrow terraced wadis and of farm units with small watersheds are rational uses of technology in the desert. They prevent erosion and since they involve merely the control and slowing down of rushing flash floods, they create no threat of salinization. The danger of overirrigation, so often the case in irrigation situations, did not occur because of the limited water resources available. Most desert plant forms live on runoff, and irrigation, in its imitation of nature, has been both profitable and enduring. Israel is now employing the same imitative devices in an effort to make its desert areas productive.

Despite their success, the ancient dwellers of the Negev also made mistakes as, for example, when they harnessed the flashfloods in large wadis. The temporary success of this venture ultimately proved too costly in terms of erosion, silting of the walls, and even destruction of fields. Having overextended their exploitation of natural forces, they abandoned this costly and unprofitable system to resume their exploitation of the area in smaller watersheds, using the two alternative systems. The "overcontrol" of natural forces has seldom seemed to benefit human populations in the long run.

Runoff agriculture, as practiced in the Negev, is an important water-use strategy. It is also a costly one. In the absence of major rivers, such as the Nile, a population will maintain an extensive network of towns in a desert only under certain conditions: if it must protect its border areas; if valuable resources are present; if the desert serves important cultural purposes; or if all cultivable land has been occupied and population pressure persists. On each occasion of sedentariness in the Negev, one or more of these conditions existed.

"Protection of borders" has often been invoked in the occupation of "marginal lands," and the force of such geopolitical arguments is one that cannot be ignored. Resources change over time, and contemporary resource depletion in prime areas is likely to lead modern populations to exploit desert resources with increased frequency. The Middle East oil boom of the 1970s is an example of such exploitation. The desert, because of its starkness, has had important religious value on most continents. Its usefulness for "revitalization" of the spirit is not likely to end in our secular age. The last condition for maintaining a network of towns in the desert is, for some nations at least, the most important. Israel, for one, has 60 percent of its territory in the Negev, and it is crucial that it find ways to extract food, fiber, and drink from it. Egypt and numerous Middle Eastern and African nations also face the need to exploit such desert resources.

Summary

To survive in any ecosystem, populations must take into account the existing constraints to life.

In arid lands the challenge to human inhabitants lies in determining how much control to exercise over water resources and how to make optimal use of the water obtained. Most commonly, groups have scattered widely over these areas, thus keeping the densities per unit area down. Kalahari hunter/gatherers even today maintain effective population controls through dietary, social, and cultural adjustments.

Cyclical changes in aridity necessitate flexible forms of social organization, a nomadic way of life, or modifications in the technology of water use. We can expect that when severe drought strikes in frequent cycles, (for example, every ten years), the population will adjust their lifestyles to the driest periods of the cycle. This has been clearly the case among the populations of the Kalahari. When the driest episodes are infrequent or unpredictable, however, populations will adjust to normal years and experience serious stress during dry periods (see Slovic, Kunreuther, and White 1974; Heijnen and Kates 1974; Lovett 1973). For example, the high and low flood trends of the Nile followed cycles varying from decades to centuries. The population adjusted to short-term fluctuations and reduced uncertainty by ignoring the probability of counter-cyclical trends.

Individual survival must also be assured by behaviors that conserve water and at the same time permit constant cooling evaporation through effective sweating. Acclimatory adjustments through diminished pulse rates, reduced salt concentration in sweat, and intensified rates of insensible perspiration increase comfort. Most of the adjustments, however, are social and cultural. Clothing and shelter reduce the heat load of the body by providing insulation and promoting heat loss. Activity schedules are designed to avoid exposure to strong sun and drying winds and at the same time conserve energy and fluids. These adjustments to the requirements of the thermoregulatory system prevent dehydration, heat stroke, and possible death.

All human groups in desert ecosystems must develop management systems to exploit water and other resources. Some deserts limit the options available to an extreme degree, while other areas can be exploited by both simple *and* complex management approaches. One management option is to exploit numerous surface water resources through group migratory behavior. This strategy, which is common among hunter/gatherers and pastoralists, is seldom possible for cultivators. Hunter/gatherers focus their adaptation on the exploitation of plant resources, few of which escape their attention. Mobility also enhances their social adjustments to the area by providing a rhythmic cycle of aggregation and dispersal that reflects adjustments to water availablility. Similar adjustments are found among pastoralists—except that their focus is on herd animals and on trade with cultivators. In the Sahara the living standards of nomads are higher than those of the sedentary population (Darling and Farvar 1972:671). Herding in extremely arid areas is feasible only in combination with nomadism. Stock losses of up to 80 percent were noted in Iran after the population had become sedentary.

Increased control over an area's resources is possible when technology is applied to the exploitation of groundwater, the harnessing of surface runoff, and the diversion of water from rivers to agricultural fields. Generally these forms of increased water control are accompanied by a shift from migratory to sedentary settlement patterns, although trade relations with nomads may continue. Increased control opens the opportunity to support greater population densities, but it also opens the system to great oscillations when the normal rainfall patterns do not match expectations. Some studies (Birdsell 1953; Wynne-Edwards 1965) suggest that desert hunter/gatherers adjust the size of their populations to the periodic drought years, a conservative adaptation to the poorest condition. This sort of measure is necessary because severe drought can mean famine and death for any and all "excess" population. More technologically advanced groups, on the other hand, rely very heavily on their water control systems and adjust their populations and technology to conditions found in "good" years. Evidence from prehistoric Egypt attests to the severe consequences of allowing population loads to exceed subcritical levels for drought periods (Butzer 1976:41).

Water use in the Nile River Basin progressed from natural irrigation to increasing control of seasonal flooding. Until this century, most of the irrigation works were locally managed. Studies have suggested that such decentralization may introduce a much needed element of stability to irrigation. However, the most important modifications in Nile irrigation were the results of colonial control by Britain. British colonial policies simultaneously encouraged population growth, agricultural intensification, and permanent irrigation based upon the impoundment of the floodwaters behind the Aswam Dam.

Other forms of irrigation used surface runoff and groundwater. Both could best be handled by local labor and local political institutions. However, the costs of building and maintenance were so high that it usually took a politically centralized power to create stable communities in such areas. One of the great challenges to modern expansion into desert areas is the evaluation of the costs of making these arid lands productive. Intensified control over desert areas seems to be judged worthwhile only when the areas are crucial for territorial defense, for the exploitation of valued resources, for the access they provide to an area of symbolic value (that is, a "cradle of religion"), and for the provision of food and fiber needs when other agricultural areas are lacking.

Further research is needed on both prehistoric and contemporary forms of coping with the limitations of water availability. In the past poor irrigation management has turned arid lands with great agricultural potential into biological deserts. Today improved ways must be found to exploit, and above all, to protect the resources of arid lands on a long-term basis. This requires a solid understanding of both short- and long-term fluctuations in water availability, of physiologically adapted plants with economic potential, and of the value and limitations of pastoral nomadism in areas of unpredictable rainfall. We must learn which population distributions will outrun a region's resources and fail to provide adequately for their well-being and survival. The extended drought in the Sahel and the scientific study of desertification present an important challenge to ecological scientists. Half the nations in the world have part of their territory in arid zones, one third of which are threatened with total loss of productive capacity.

Recommended Readings

Readers will find a useful, brief, two-part survey of desert ecosystems that includes climatic and **edaphic** considerations, as well as a discussion of modeling for desert ecosystems, in Noy-Meir (1973, 1974). A good starting point for the study of animal adaptations to desert conditions is the book by Schmidt-Nielsen (1964) or the more recent one by Ingram and Mount (1975).

Publications are produced on a continual basis by the UNESCO Arid Zone Research series. These publications have been numerous and the data of high quality. The United States IBP Desert Biome Program has carried out extensive research and much of their data complements the scheme presented in this book. None of the synthesis volumes has yet been published. David Goodall of Utah State University served as coordinator of the Desert Biome Program and will probably serve as editor of the summary volume.

Patricia Paylore has edited two useful annotated bibliographies on arid zones research (1966 and 1969). The most valuable compendium of knowledge now available on deserts is the two-volume work of G. W. Brown (1968 and 1972). The more geographically oriented volume edited by Hills (1966) is a bit dated, but may be found more amenable to social and cultural anthropologists and others in the social sciences. Studies of human physiological adjustment are dominated by the figure of D.H.K. Lee (1964, 1969) and by the still unsurpassed study by Adolph et al. (1947)

Ecological anthropological studies of desert populations are dominated by the contributions of archaeologists (Butzer 1976; Adams 1966; and the collections by Downing and Gibson 1974 and by Steward 1955b).

Studies by social and cultural anthropologists have also begun to make their appearance although their level of sophistication of hydrologic knowledge tends to be lower (Cole 1975; Fernea 1970; Barth 1961). Perhaps the most notable interdisciplinary research among a desert population is that of the Harvard Kalahari Research Group. The synthesis of their decade of studies will stand as an important contribution (Lee and DeVore 1976). Members of the team have begun to publish separate studies, and the first of these is the ethnoarchaeological contribution of Yellen (1977). Exceptions to the lack of sophistication in hydrology can be found in recent studies of locally based irrigation. This research by Lees (1974, 1976), Hunt and Hunt (1974), and Netting (1974) is not only insightful, but also demonstrates the growing competence of anthropologists in the field of irrigation research.

Human
Adaptability
to Grasslands

Grasslands constitute important and sizable areas of land that have long provided human populations with subsistence. Some grasslands are natural to a biogeographic region (for example, the North American Plains and the Russian steppes), while others are the result of human management (for example, the grasslands of Japan). Figure 8.1 illustrates the extent of grasslands today. Human adaptation to these areas has emphasized hunting of wild game, herding of domesticated livestock, or a mixed pastoral and agricultural strategy. Because grasslands have an inadequate supply of rainfall to sustain agriculture on a regular basis, herding has been the most common subsistence mode. In temperate grasslands agriculture became possible only in relatively recent times with the availability of steel plows to break the sod and the introduction of special crops and management. However, in tropical grasslands agriculture has been practiced in restricted areas since Neolithic times. Pastoralists practice agriculture in both temperate and tropical areas when the rains permit.

In this chapter we will briefly discuss the characteristics of both temperate and tropical grasslands and the various adaptability strategies found in both types of areas. The chief problems presented by grassland ecosystems center around the exploitation of water and pasture; the composition and size of herds; the establishment of workable relationships between pastoralists and agriculturalists; and the achievement of a balance between the human and the animal population under conditions of great climatic uncertainty. These form the major sections of this chapter. Because of the patchy characteristics of the environment, **nomadism** is the common means of securing an adequate supply of pasture and water. Size and composition

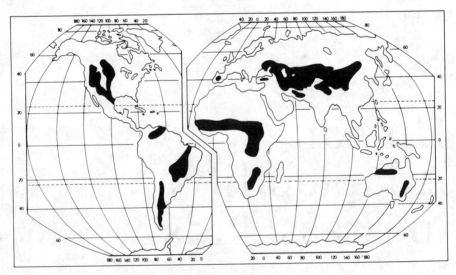

Figure 8.1   **World Distribution of Grasslands**

of herds reflect both an evaluation of the diet required to sustain the group and the need to maintain social exchanges with neighbors. Relations between pastoralists and neighboring cultivators are sometimes tense, but usually **mutualistic**—since neither can live well without the other's resources. Pastoralists inhabiting arid tropical grasslands have the same acclimatory adjustments to dry heat as populations inhabiting arid lands.

The social and cultural adjustments that characterize the occupation of temperate grasslands in North America result from various economic and ecological considerations. Subsistence on the Plains evolved from hunting/gathering through specialized cattle herding to a combination of restricted herding and seasonal agriculture. There has been great concern in recent years over the problem of desertification in both temperate and tropical grasslands. Areas where once wild and later domesticated ungulates grazed have become permanently degraded into deserts. Whether the causes of such desert expansion are climatic or the result of human management is a matter of major importance for research in semiarid grasslands.

Grassland Ecosystems

Natural grasslands occur where the level of rainfall is genererally too low to support forests, but where it is higher than the levels commonly associated with desert ecosystems. The grassland is, therefore, a transitional biome characterized by a gradient by which rainfall and humidity determine many of the characteristics of vegetation and other dependent life forms. In addition, grasslands are characterized by high rates of evapotranspiration in summer, by periodic severe droughts, and by rolling to flat terrain (R.L. Smith 1974:552). Grasslands are also found in areas with a high water table or where they are maintained by human intervention. The significance of precipitation in defining the characteristics of a natural grassland is best illustrated by a cross-sectional view of the North American Great Plains (see figure 8.2). Moisture is the crucial factor in determining ecosystem structure and function, as well as the crucial constraint in the utilization of grassland areas.

Climatic and Vegetational Features   The climate of grasslands is characterized by extremes. Rainfall is seasonal and uncertain in both time and place. Because of wide fluctuations, the average rainfall indicates very little about actual conditions faced by plants and animals in the region. Dry and wet years appear to follow each other in cycles, but until recently the climatological data have been too restricted to permit any useful quantitative manipulation that might suggest the patterns that are taking place—if any are. The major management problem presented by semiarid grasslands is that moist cycles tend to create the illusion that those conditions will last,

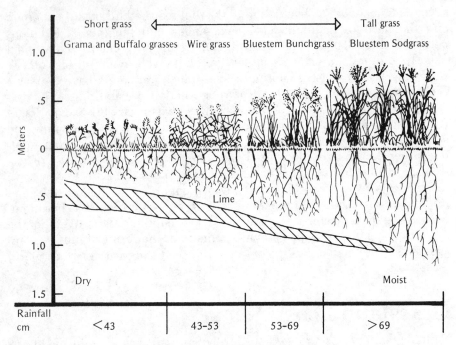

Figure 8.2   **A West-East Transect of the Great Plains**   Figure depicts the
change in plant communities in relation to changing moisture.

Source: Lynn Porter. 1969. Nitrogen in Grassland Ecosystems. *In* The Grassland
Ecosystem. R. L. Dix and R. G. Beidleman, eds. Fort Collins: Colorado State University, Range Science Department.

and when drought comes, as it always does, the population is caught
unprepared and far too numerous for the capacity of the now dessicated
environment to feed them.

In the Great Plains the five hundred millimeter rainfall line (that is, the
area between the 98° and 100° meridian) marks the difference between the
short grass and high grass plains (see figure 8.3) This area is, therefore, a
transitional zone (Ottoson et al. 1966:4). The rainfall pattern here can shift by
as much as two hundred miles to the east or west (Wedel 1961:453). These
shifts are of variable duration and intensity, do not occur in regular succession, and cannot to this day be accurately forecast (Ibid.). When drought
episodes occur, the temperatures can go to 37.8° C. or more, causing damage
to both wild and domesticated crops. At either end of the humidity spectrum
are different species of grasses, but in this transitional area a combination of
species adjusts phenotypically to aridity. It is a mixed-prairie zone wherein
short or tall grasses dominate depending on the degree of moisture. In the
short grass regions, much of the vegetation dies and dust bowl conditions
occur during drought (R.L. Smith 1974:536).

Tropical grasslands, or savannas, are found in tropical regions with five hundred to twelve hundred and fifty millimeters of rainfall, but with higher rates of evapotranspiration than temperate grasslands. In East Africa the distribution of rainfall is bimodal—that is, it is distributed in two short wet seasons. Each season by itself is inadequate to support agriculture, but bimodal rainfall distribution is helpful in the maintenance of a quality rangeland (Pratt and Gwynne 1977:16).

The savanna, as a transitional ecosystem between desert and forest, manifests a steady gradation and variety of climatic and vegetational characteristics. The humid savanna is able to support a sizable tree population, while the more arid portions of savannas resemble desert ecosystems. Although a clear delineation of the worldwide characteristics of tropical savannas is difficult, a number of features seem to be always present. Savannas are dominated by xerophytic vegetation, of which grasses are the chief components. They occur at elevations between sea level and two-thousand meters on low nutrient soils. The water cycle follows a wet/dry rhythm both annually and in the long term. Most scientists agree that the savanna is a **fire-managed** ecosystem where burning of the vegetation occurs as often as once a year. A great deal of the vegetation is fire-adapted (Hills 1965). The morphology of many grasses is adapted to withstand fires and even to thrive on them.

Explanations for the origins of savannas differ a great deal. Some pos-

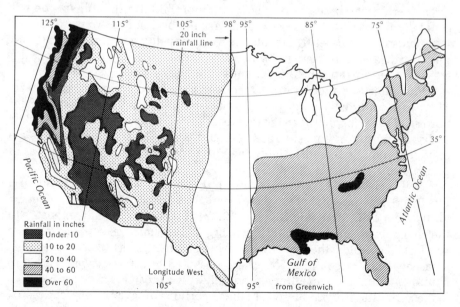

Figure 8.3   **Average Annual Precipitation of the United States along the 98°–100° Meridian, the Dividing Line between the Short and Tall Grass Prairies**

215

tulate the importance of alternating wet/dry seasons; others focus on the lack of soil fertility and the soils' deficient drainage; and still others stress the importance of fire in maintaining the grass **climax community**. It is most likely that different savannas arose as a result of one or more of these factors, but it is unlikely that any one factor could explain the existence of all savannas.

Soil Conditions   Although they can occur on a wide range of soils (Duffey et al. 1974:82), temperate grasslands have been in existence long enough to have developed a distinctive soil type (James 1966:282). Temperate grasslands have given rise to chernozem or mollisol soils. A map of the mollisols (see figure 8.4) clearly shows how closely they are associated with the major temperate grassland areas of the world: the North American prairies, the Argentinian pampas, and the Eurasian steppes.

Mollisol soils have a surface horizon that retains its soft character even during dry periods and has high base saturation. The soil humus tends to be distributed throughout the profile. In contrast to humus formation in forests, which occurs primarily by leaf fall and soil surface decomposition of soil fauna, humus in grasslands is formed primarily by the decomposition of the root network of the plants. Grasses produce both an organic mat at the surface and a dense underground root system that decomposes steadily through time (Steila 1976:113). Since grasses require greater amounts of mineral nutrients than do trees, the organic materials decomposed in grass areas are richer in bases, particularly calcium (Ibid.: 114). Mollisols do not generally derive from hard rocks like granite, but, rather, from calcareous sediments rich in bases. Mollisols are today considered prime agricultural soils because of the ease with which they can be tilled, the flatness of the grassland terrain, and the deep humus layer.

Phosphorus is often a limiting factor in grasslands where animals graze. There is a continual loss of phosphorus from range soils, because a major portion of the phosphorus in the forage is deposited throughout the animal's body—primarily in bones, hair, wool, and horns. Thus, when animals are marketed outside the area, the rangeland experiences a permanent loss of phosphorus (Humphrey 1962).

Soils in tropical savannas, while highly variable, are generally said to be low in fertility, except those that are of volcanic origin or that are enriched by alluvial deposits (Pratt and Gwynne 1977:11). Their year-round exposure to the elements has made the soils low in organic and mineral content. Because of a lack of colloids, they respond poorly to inorganic fertilizers. In savanna areas nearest the boundary between grassland and forest, water is more abundant and plant and animal productivity are greater. These areas can be made agriculturally productive. In those portions of savanna nearer deserts, aridity prevents the regular cultivation of soils, and grazing is the only effective way to utilize the area—unless irrigation is introduced. However, even here the use of organic fertilizer is required because of the low colloid

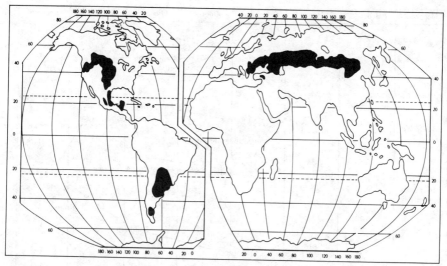

Figure 8.4   World Distribution of Mollisols

of the soils. Specialists have observed that in these areas wild ungulates outproduce domestic livestock and have suggested that these regions could be more effectively utilized by "harvesting" the wild species. Eland, oryx, and addax are three African savanna species able to occupy and exploit areas far from permanent water sources where domestic livestock cannot survive.

Formation and Development of Grasslands   Most grassland biomes developed from previously existing ecosystems as a result of changing climatic, geological, and anthropogenic factors interacting through time (Lewis 1970:1). Figure 8.5 illustrates the evolution of contemporary grasslands over time. By Miocene times, twenty million years ago, grasses were probably assuming an important place in the earth's vegetation (Barnard and Frankel 1966:1). It is now generally agreed that grasslands are not exclusively a climatic formation, but that they require the periodic occurrence of fire or steady grazing pressure for growth and maintenance. Although some of these fires are naturally caused by lightning igniting the dry grassland, some grasslands are believed to have been consciously created by hunters seeking to drive herds towards a narrow point where fellow hunters were concentrated, or by pastoralists seeking to encourage the growth of nutritious young shoots for their herds. It has been frequently noted that in the absence of fire, many grasslands turn to shrub or tree communities (Moore 1966:201).

The growing importance of grasslands as terrestrial ecosystems is associated with the rise of two great ungulate orders of herbivorous mammals in early Tertiary times: perisodactyls (for example, horses, rhinos, tapirs) and

217

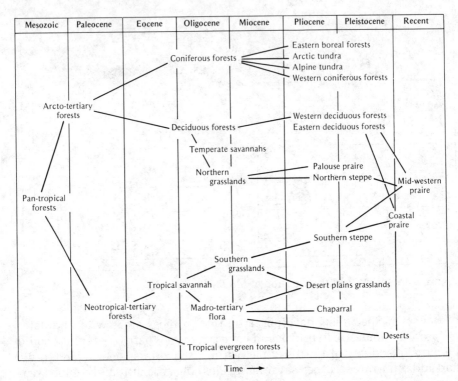

Mesozoic	Paleocene	Eocene	Oligocene	Miocene	Pliocene	Pleistocene	Recent

Coniferous forests

Eastern boreal forests
Arctic tundra
Alpine tundra
Western coniferous forests

Arcto-tertiary forests

Deciduous forests

Western deciduous forests
Eastern deciduous forests

Temperate savannahs

Northern grasslands

Palouse praire
Northern steppe

Mid-western praire

Pan-tropical forests

Coastal praire

Southern steppe

Southern grasslands

Tropical savannah

Desert plains grasslands

Neotropical-tertiary forests

Madro-tertiary flora

Chaparral

Deserts

Tropical evergreen forests

Time →

Figure 8.5 **Approximate Time Relationships between the Major Vegetational Units of North America, with Special Reference to the North American Grassland**

Source: James K. Lewis. 1970. Primary Producers in Grassland Ecosystems. In The Grassland Ecosystem: A Supplement. R. L. Dix and R. G. Beidleman, eds. Fort Collins: Colorado State University, Range Science Department.

artiodactyls. The latter order includes both nonruminant (for example, pigs, camels, hippos, peccaries) and ruminant types (for example, cattle, buffalo, sheep, goats, deer, and antelopes). The biomass of wild ungulates in East Africa has been known to be as high as thirty-five thousand kilograms per square kilometer (Pratt and Gwynne 1977:30).[1]

The great diversity of animal species exercises an important selective role upon the natural vegetation that encourages grasses at the expense of trees (Ibid.:33). A grazing herd has three main effects on a grassland: grass defoliation, nutrient redistribution, and plant trampling. Studies put cattle consumption of net primary production at between 10 and 17 percent, depending on the cattle variety. Cattle are among the least efficient herbi-

[1]A more average figure is twelve-thousand to seventeen-thousand kilograms per square kilometer for the biomass of wild ungulates. When domestic livestock graze in conjunction with the wild species, the biomass carried declines to about six-thousand kilograms per square kilometer (Little and Morren 1976:55).

vores and convert only one-twentieth of the grass ingested into meat (Strickon 1965:233). Two-thirds of the herbage is rejected as feces. Such rejection plays an important role in nutrient redistribution. Cattle and other herd animals have favorite dunging sites within a restricted pasture. Such areas contain concentrations of phosphorous and potassium. The more even distribution of urine results in the redistribution of nitrogen and potassium (Duffey et al. 1974:181).

The relationship of grazing animals to grasslands is a systematic one. Differences in animal growth patterns, in biomass production, and in behavior reflect environmental constraints, rather than mere differences between the various species. In areas where systems of cattle ranching are market oriented, biomass production per unit of consumption exceeds, by up to eight times, the ratio in areas where systems are geared at biomass stability or subsistence. In the latter areas, forage is often of lower quality, and great distances may have to be traveled to acquire it—at great energy cost. Table 8.1 compares the utilization of net primary production by cattle and by two species of wild East African ungulates. Indian cattle appear to be highly efficient—probably because of the intensive demands of the human population and conscious selection. Animal biomass production in India is 3.6 percent of net primary production. North American Pawnee and East African Karimojong conversion rates are 0.47 percent and 0.043 respectively. These efficiencies reflect the efforts made by the cattle managers to fit their animals to the requirements of their respective systems (Ellis and Jennings, 1975).

Fire Management   The need for fire management of grasslands can best be understood by looking at the two major types of temperate grasses: sod and bunch grasses. Sod grasses form a solid mat over the ground, while bunch grasses grow, as their name suggests, in clumps. Some grasses exhibit both growth patterns, depending on the local environment (R.L. Smith 1974:552). Unless mowed, burned, or grazed, grasslands accumulate a thick layer of **mulch** at the ground level that may take three years or more to decompose completely. The thicker the accumulation, the longer decomposition may take. The costs and benefits of this mulch accumulation are still a subject of scholarly debate. Some argue that mulch accumulation increases soil moisture available to the live vegetation, decreases runoff, stabilizes soil temperatures, and improves soil conditions (R.L. Smith 1974:554). Others maintain that accumulation of mulch from one species can have a toxic effect on the germination and development of other species, or that it can facilitate the invasion of a grassland by a woody species. Some range ecologists believe that heavy mulch accumulations lead to decreased forage production, smaller root biomass, and a lower caloric value to the living shoots (Ibid.: 555). From the point of view of the hunter or pastoralist, food value, elimination of woody growth, and prevention of toxic conditions

Table 8.1   **Energy Flow Parameters for Large Grazing Herbivores**

	Estimated NPP (Kcal/m²/yr)	Herbivore biomass (g/m² dry weight)	Consumption (Kcal/m²/yr)	Secondary production (Kcal/m²/yr)
Cattle				
Pawnee (U.S.)	729[a]	1.95	124.6[b]	6.85[b]
Singur (India)	>2500[c]	24.50	1327.0	90.50
Karimojong (E. Africa)	2000[d]	1.62	215.0	0.85
Wild Ungulates				
Uganda kob	747	0.72	74.1	0.81
Elephant	747	1.57	71.6	0.34

[a] Net Primary Production (NPP).
[b] Pawnee data are for six months.
[c] Estimate.
[d] Estimate from H. T. Odum 1971.
Source: James E. Ellis and Calvin Jennings. 1975. A Comparison of Energy Flow Among the Grazing Animals of Different Societies. In TIE, A Guide to Energy Flow Studies. Manuscript mimeo. Available from Institute of Ecology, Indianapolis, Ind.

were probably the most important considerations. Fire is an obvious way to reduce the natural accumulation of mulch.[2]

The literature on man's use of fire to modify the earth's vegetation is vast (cf., Heizer 1955; Hills and Randall 1968; Iizumi and Iwanami 1975; Stewart 1956; Sauer 1958). Although it is by no means a cure-all, fire can be a useful means of controlling undesirable species, eliminating excess litter, suppressing insects, preparing the seedbed, facilitating livestock movement, and fertilizing the soil. Periodic firing is useful, too, because by eliminating excess litter, it prevents the devastations of too hot or too extensive a natural fire (E. Odum 1971:150). These recurrent fires maintain woody species in a juvenile, nonfruiting stage and at the same time permit perennial grasses to put out new growth. Grasses are morphologically better adapted than shrubs to withstand fires: a large proportion of grass biomass is below ground where it is protected. In addition, because their seed heads are designed to easily broadcast their contents, grasses are effective colonizers of terrestrial ecosystems (Tivy 1971:298). Fire increases the supply of nutrients available at the soil surface, raises soil pH, and significantly expands the supply of phosphorus and potassium (Valentine 1975:164). Some authors point out a few undesirable effects of burning grassland areas: substantial amounts of nitrogen are lost during the fire; fire can spread to nearby forested areas; and if too hot or improperly timed, burning can harm desirable species of grass.

Herd Management

A major difference between herders in East Africa and herders in many temperate grasslands lies in the objectives of their economic activities. Cattle raising on the American Plains is clearly market oriented—although the lifestyle of ranching there has romantic overtones and elicits sentimental attachment by the grassland population (Bennett 1969:172). A market orientation leads to a different set of management strategies by herders. If the goal is to maximize milk or meat production for sale, the objective is to have a herding operation that will give the best returns with a minimum investment of labor. The biomass output of beef cattle in table 8.1 (p. 220) reflects these different orientations. When cattle is raised for subsistence and constitutes the essential life support of a population in a semiarid environment, the results are quite different. (Dyson-Hudson and Dyson-Hudson, 1969:2).

---

[2]Less **litter** accumulation has been noted in semiarid savannas, but fire's beneficial effects in releasing nutrients, encouraging the growth of young shoots, and suppressing insects are equally important in temperate and tropical grasslands.

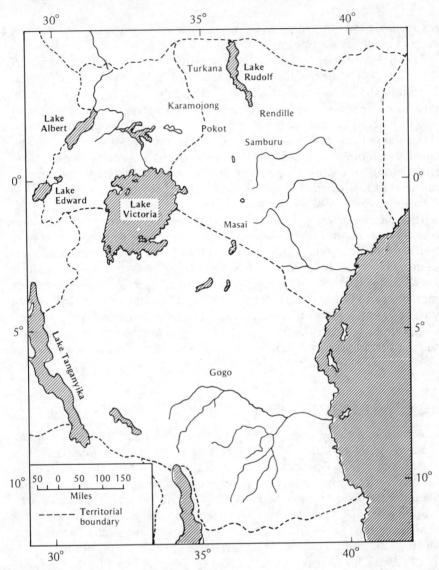

Figure 8.6   **Tribal Groups of East Africa**

Gaining Access to Water and Pasture   East African pastoralists resort to seasonal nomadism to gain access to both water and savanna pastures. Each occasion for nomadic movement involves obtaining information, assessing its reliability, forming a personal opinion, and making a decision. No single or best choice is likely to exist; pastoralists must instead deal with a set of better/worse options. Pastoral economics in semiarid tropical grasslands involves a no-win situation: if the population adapts to the normal bad years, it would leave large areas of territory unexploited; if it adjusts to good years,

222

it would find itself overextended and facing famine and death. Information is seldom complete and is usually of doubtful reliability. Yet, the population must act. Edgerton described the decision process in this manner:

The care of livestock involves the husbandman in a constant pattern of decision making. His seasonal round of activities is not routinized; he must decide each day where to take his animals, and he may have to include many diverse factors in his computation—the potential quality of the grass, the availability of water, the probability of predators, the competitive action of other herders, and so on. The cumulative quality of such decisions will determine whether the herd prospers or not. The pastoralist must be constantly aware of the condition of each animal and meet its needs. While African pastoralists do not maintain genetic records, the good husbandman does recognize that some animals should be culled, and when the opportunity arises, it is these animals that are slaughtered, exchanged, or, nowadays, sold. This matter of exchanging and selling animals is of particular importance; the herdsman is engaged in recurrent economic transactions with his neighbors, and the cogency of his decisions and the capacity to arrive at satisfactory bargains are vital to the furtherance of his welfare. (1971:281)

Most of the time, the East African pastoralist has a range of choices. Only at the end of the dry season, when few places are left with water and pasture, is choice so narrowly constrained that the direction of nomadic movement is clear and unambiguous. Figure 8.6 shows the location of the various tribes that will be discussed in the rest of the chapter.

The Karamojong of Uganda provide a good example of East African pastoralist strategies. Figure 8.7 illustrates the wanderings of two cattle herds in this area. In this case, the size of the herding family played a major role in how the cattle were moved. The family with the larger number of herders could afford to send its animals to areas as far as fifty-five miles from camp where it could find the best pastures and still not be in fear of losing the animals to raiders. The second family, constrained by its numbers of males, moved its cattle within a radius of only twelve miles. On bad years such a strategy can have serious consequences, with the family losing all its animals because of inadequate forage and water. The size of herding families is directly related to management strategy: the more people, the greater the dispersion, the more abundant the forage and water, and the larger the herd (Dyson-Hudson and Dyson-Hudson 1969:9).

Social considerations, as well as information about the location of water and pasture, influence decisions on moving the herds. According to Gulliver (1975), herders do not necessarily follow kinship lines in choosing partners for their treks. A herder may be aware of several watering places within a reasonable distance. One place may be richer in certain grasses, but poorer in water sources. Another may be near good watering

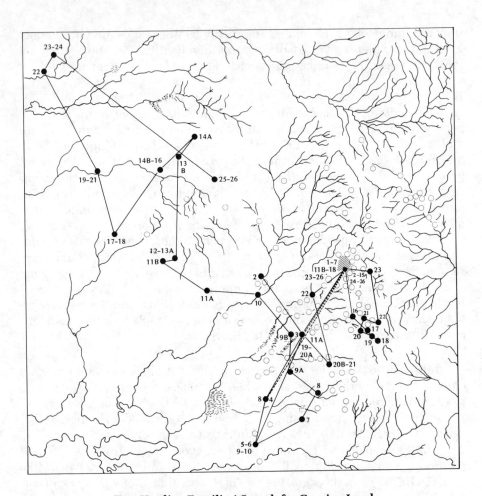

Figure 8.7   Two Herding Families' Search for Grazing Land

Source: From "Subsistence Herding in Uganda" by Rada and Neville Dyson-Hudson. Copyright © 1969 by Scientific American, Inc. All rights reserved.

holes, but involve crossing rough terrain that can exhaust the cattle and the herder. Good spots may be known to other herdsmen, for which reason the herder might anticipate resource depletion and not go there. The herder may also avoid favored grazing areas because of possible confrontations with other herders who have claim upon his property.

Herd movement may be constrained by other activities of the population, such as the seasonal practice of agriculture. This activity can place important limitations on movement. During the wet periods, women engage in agriculture, and the herd must be kept within a reasonable distance of the camp to provide the female cultivators with the necessary milk and blood that are a crucial part of the diet (Dyson-Hudson and Dyson-Hudson 1969:10). During the dry season when pasture land is reduced, movement is not so restricted, and the whole camp may travel together.

The limited possibilities of the East Africa savanna environment were convincingly outlined in 1940 by Evans-Pritchard. He described an environment intimately known by the Nuer whose subsistence activities and social life are conditioned by the environment. As is the case for so many pastoralist populations, agriculture is uncertain and the growing season short before the dry season returns. The Nuer therefore place a high cultural value upon cattle herding. Cattle can be moved to where resources are available. Furthermore, the species the Nuer use have proved their hardiness and adaptability and are able to turn from grazing to browsing when grass is unavailable. Browsing animals are those that eat twigs and shoots from trees, shrubs and vines. Movement follows a rhythm between social aggregation (in the moist winter) and far-flung migrations by small groups (in the dry season). In turn, as the dry season progresses, the groups congregate once again around the limited number of permanent water sources.

Gulliver's comparison of the Jie and the Turkana further confirms the notion that pastoralist movements in East Africa reflect adjustments to microenvironmental conditions (1955). The Jie have a mixed economy of farming and transhumant cattle pastoralism; the Turkana are nomadic herders who rarely practice any agriculture. Jieland is richer in grasslands, and the moisture is adequate for the cultivation of sorghum. The population is sedentary, but engages in seasonal movement (**transhumance**). The Turkana inhabit poorer grasslands, and therefore cannot rely on farming, but must instead depend almost totally on their herds for their needs. The necessity of movement eliminates the possibility of stable residence (Ibid.:44).

Herd Size and Composition. East African pastoralists understand the minimum size needed for an efficient herd. The Pokot consider a man with one hundred cows rich, one with ten poor, and one with none to be dead (Schneider 1959). As the herd grows, so do the problems of management. A man with too many animals will be sought after by those less fortunate and be required to lend a portion of his herd. A herd of three hundred cattle cannot be effectively managed by a single homestead: watering takes too long, and fodder per locality may be too quickly depleted. In addition, a herd of this size requires constant movement because of its rapid defoliation of a given area.

The Samburu deal with the problem of maximum herd size by dividing the herd among the male head's wives and their families (Spencer 1965). Another strategy for reducing the size of herds is trusteeship. Among the Gogo when a herd gets too large for the owner to handle, he divides the herd among associates, or trustees, who will be able to use the milk from the cows, but who promise to give the rightful owner all the offspring produced (Rigby 1969). In this manner the pastoralist is able to achieve a modicum of wealth during good times and, by dividing his herd among a variety of managers, enhance his chances that during drought periods some of his cows may be thriving. In the case of large-scale losses in his own region, this strategy permits the herder to collect his scattered animals and resume pastoral activities instead of being forced out of business.

Pastoralists may also distribute their herds over a vast territory through complex forms of lending and borrowing (Deshler 1965; Gulliver 1955). An individual pastoralist may give some of his animals to another pastoralist who temporarily needs a greater number of animals. It is understood that the owner will be paid back with an equivalent animal at a later date.

It surely did not pass unnoticed among pastoralists that their most important resource could supply them with renewable fluid resources in a semiarid environment. Milk is the major item in the diet of many East African pastoralists (for example, the Samburu, Ariaal Rendille, and the Turkana). During the wet period it is drunk whole, and during the dry period it is mixed with the blood of the animals. East African pastoralists take blood from their animals by piercing the animals' jugular veins and collecting four to eight pints of blood from each at intervals of three to five months (Dyson-Hudson and Dyson-Hudson 1969:5–6). Figure 8.8 illustrates this process. Blood mixed with milk is an important element in the diet.

By providing milk and blood, the animal can continue to sustain the population without signifying a loss of productive capital. If East African pastoralists began to rely more on beef cattle for their calories, instead of on grain obtained by sale of cattle, they could not sustain the population densities they now have. In other words, they would move to the top of the food pyramid and experience a reduction in total calories available.

The strategy of pastoralists in trying to maximize the size of their herds is related to their dietary requirements and to the cyclical droughts that decimate the herds. Among the Ariaal Rendille, milk constitutes up to 70 percent of the calories consumed by the population for a substantial portion of the year. This proportion declines during the dry season. Among the Turkana, milk constitutes the main goal of cattle production. When the milk supply goes down in the dry season, the frequency of bleeding the animals increases. The frequency of such bleeding varies with the type of stock and the relative wealth of the owner. Poorer herders with less stock bleed their animals more often than wealthier herders. This pattern of shifting from a milk-based diet to one that mixes milk and blood during the dry season has also been noted among the Masai.

Small stock, primarily sheep and goats, are kept by most pastoralists and provide most of the meat consumed. Small stock have turnover rates five times higher than those of cattle and are less a part of the social obli-

Figure 8.8   **Masai Bleed Cow**
Photograph from Anthro-Photo by Steve Washburn.

gations of meat sharing. Where the only method of preserving meat is sun-drying, small stock have the advantage of providing a smaller amount of meat to be preserved and consumed at one time. A family of eight would have to kill six steers per year to meet its subsistence needs. However, preservation would be difficult, most of the meat would have to be redistributed, and the productive capital would be reduced. Moreover, the value of cattle as an item of trade is greater than its value as meat. Two steers sold per year supply a family of eight with all their grain needs for one year (Pratt and Gwynne 1977:36–39).

Large herds are required to produce even the modest amounts of milk and blood obtained from the animals. East African cattle have been noted to be hardy, but the limitations of the environment delay their maturation (up to seven years) and lower their calving rate (that is their reproductive rate). According to a recent study, a pastoralist family of eight must keep a minimum of twenty animals averaging four hundred and fifty kilograms each to subsist in the savanna. An equivalent weight of small animals can be equally satisfactory. These many animals require approximately one hundred hectares of usable pasture at density of one stock unit per five hectares (Ibid.: 37–38). These conditions are seldom present. Most of the time pastoralist households have fewer than this ideal number of animals, and human population density is more than the eight persons per square

227

kilometer that are suggested by Pratt and Gwynne. This implies greater demand on resources and less of an available supply.

The pastoral economy of East Africa puts a prime on female animals. Most of the studies that have dealt with this question suggest that the reason for this preference is the reliance of the population on milk (Ibid.: 36; Brown 1971). It is not uncommon to find as much as 50 or 60 percent of a herd made up of breeding females—as opposed to only 20 or 25 percent in temperate grassland ranches. Although there is little doubt that such a strategy promotes nutrition, it is just as possible that the population chooses this strategy because it allows herd numbers to recover following epidemics, drought, and other devastations in herd size. Maximization of females increases the recuperative powers of the herd.

Disease The human and the livestock populations of East Africa have periodically suffered devastating losses. A terrible sleeping sickness epidemic in which 200,000 to 300,000 animals died struck Uganda between 1901 and 1908. A rinderpest epidemic destroyed 95 percent of the herds between 1890 and 1910, and it took over 40 years for herd sizes to return to 1890 levels (Ford 1977:148). East Coast fever, blackleg, and trypanosomiasis (that is, sleeping sickness) are still serious threats to the health of the cattle herds (Schneider 1970:32).

The threat of trypanosomiasis is still very much present. Tsetse flies (*Glossina spp*) transmit sleeping sickness, which affects both humans and cattle. The interactions between tsetse, wild fauna, and domesticated livestock are complex. The rinderpest epidemic of 1890 stopped the spread of tsetse because of the reduced population of host animals (that is, cattle), but it resumed once again in the 1940s. A major reason for this spread has been the reduction in the density of elephants as a result of game hunting (Ford 1977:159). Elephants modify the environment by trampling and thus discourage development of the tsetse habitat. The areas most free of tsetse flies are those with substantial elephant populations or those where elephants and domesticated stock coexist. This important ecological relationship has suffered from big game hunting.

In areas where the environment does not provide adequate pasture and water for their animals, herders may take their chances and enter tsetse infested regions. Thus the Fulani of West Africa take their cattle into the fly infested areas of Guinea. Although there are losses from trypanosomiasis, the cattle seem to have acquired some tolerance for the disease and appear to be better off than if they remained in the drought areas (Ibid.:160). In addition to being potentially lethal, trypanosomiasis also reduces calving rate. Nevertheless, the evidence in this century points to the steady increase of both human and cattle populations, despite exposure to the disease agents. The increases have been explosive in some areas—thereby making migrations increasingly difficult and putting unusual grazing pressure on the grasses. Although the cattle population

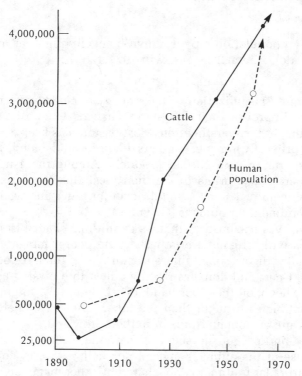

Figure 8.9   **Growth Trends of Cattle and Indigenous Populations of Rhodesia since 1890**

Source: Adapted from *The Careless Technology* by M. Taghi Farver and John P. Milton. Copyright © 1969, 1972 by The Conservation Foundation and the Center for the Biology of Natural Systems, Washington University. Reprinted by permission of Doubleday & Company, Inc.

of Rhodesia was reduced between 1890 and 1910 from 500,000 animals to a mere 25,000, the trends since that time have been clearly exponential (see figure 8.9). Many of the mechanisms that in the past served to control the growth of people and herds have been reduced in effectiveness: drought has been overcome to some degree by boring deep wells; warfare has been reduced; diseases have been controlled by public health and modern veterinary and medical sciences (West 1972:715).

Although demographic data on African nomadic pastoralists is inadequate, Swift suggests that their rate of natural increase is lower than the rates of nearby cultivators (1977). The low rate of increase may result from a combination of low birth rates, high rates of female sterility, and high ratios of men to women—at least in the Sahelian region. If this is so, it suggests that pastoralist populations have a slower reproductive rate than was previously thought.

Sato (1977) presents evidence that Rendille camel herders adjust their own growth rate to that of their herds, which results in very slow population growth. Cultural preferences encourage late marriages and bridewealth may operate as a demographic regulator. High brideprices theoretically could keep population growth down by excluding poor men from marriage and by delaying marriages (Swift 1977:470).

Diversification and Specialization   One strategy pursued by East African pastoralists that improves their long-term chances to subsist in their savanna environment is **diversification**. Most pastoralists keep a variety of animals: some primarily for meat, others for milk and blood, and still others for transportation and special products. Among the Turkana, for example, sheep are raised primarily for their meat and fatty tails. The fat is used in dressing animal skins, as a lubricant for hides and wooden vessels, and as an ointment for humans (Gwynne 1977).

A variety of livestock ensures that, as conditions change from wet to dry, the animals will differentially adjust to the poorer forage available. Table 8.2 illustrates the seasonal differences in diet of the livestock raised by the Turkana. Goats and donkeys rapidly adjust to browsing as grasses become scarce. Sheep, on the other hand, continue to rely on grasses and are more susceptible to drought than the other animals. Camels require water less often and can obtain fluids from their browsing.

In the drier portions of the semiarid savanna, camel pastoralism is practiced because of the animal's special adaptation to arid conditions. Although no particular trait that is not shared by other mammals has been identified in the camel, it does have a few quantitatively changed and developed characteristics that enhance its adaptation to life in the desert. No storage of water has been detected in the camel's body; when deprived of water, the camel loses weight, but, unlike other mammals, it can sustain dehydration of 27 percent of its body water without damage. It can regain this loss in a matter of minutes, thanks to an incredible drinking capacity. The camel also has a specialized kidney mechanism that concentrates urine. In addition, it is able to excrete dry feces. These and other characteristics, including its ability to go long distances between waterings, make it a remarkable desert dweller.[3]

For a population to utilize camels effectively, it needs to synchronize its social life with the needs of its herds. Otherwise, camels could not adequately supply the growing demand of the human population. The Rendille of North Kenya reflect a remarkable social adjustment to their camels. Age-sets are formed every fourteen years in Rendille society, a figure that approximates the generational span of a camel (that is, 13.87 years). These age-sets serve to create a close generational association between Rendille and their camels. Increases in human population match almost exactly the increases in camel herd size. Because camels have slow reproductive rates, the population institutes a variety of social mechanisms to slow down human population increases. Celibacy for males

---

[3] The best source on the remarkable physiological adaptations of camels is Schmidt-Nielsen (1964).

Table 8.2   **Seasonal Differences in the Diet of Turkana Livestock**[a]

	Wet season		Dry season	
	% Graze	% Browse	% Graze	% Browse
Cattle	71	19	43	57
Camel	16	84	—	100
Sheep	98	2	81	19
Goat	93	7	8	92
Donkey	94	6	10	90

[a] Based on stomach analyses uncorrected for differential digestion effects and retention times.
Source: M. D. Gwynne. 1977. Land Use by the Southern Turkana. Paper presented at Seminar on Pastoral Societies of Kenya. Mimeo. Ethnographic Museum of Japan.

between ages twelve and thirty-one is required and only 50 percent of these males will be able to afford the brideprice that must be paid in the form of camels (Sato 1977). Their enforced celibacy is probably the most important population control mechanism among the Rendille.

Resource Partitioning   In some fascinating cases, resource partitioning between populations is a factor in the management of herd size and composition. The Samburu and the Rendille inhabit adjacent, though different, environments (Spencer 1973). The Rendille rely primarily on camel herds as they exploit the dry lowland shrub vegetation. The Samburu herd mainly cattle in the more humid highlands and plateau zones of the district. Over the years they have acted as allies, fought common enemies, and intermarried despite differences in language and culture. A third group, the Ariaal Rendille, inhabit the region that is transitional between the Rendille lowland and the Samburu highlands. The Ariaal keep both camels and cattle in high numbers, in addition to sizable herds of small stock. They have succeeded in establishing alliances with both the Samburu and the Rendille through intermarriage, descent, and friendship. Thus Ariaal have gained access to both territories. The Ariaal are almost fully bilingual. Ties to the Rendille are primarily by marriage—fully 50 percent of the Ariaal wives are recruited from the Rendille. Cooperation is enforced through shared myths that foretell misfortune if "brother" does violence to "brother" (Fratkin 1977). Through this system of alliance the Ariaal have been able to overcome the limitations of their environment and to thrive as a herding population. The narrow strip that is their territory proper could only sustain a tiny fraction of their present herds. As it is, their share of animals is high at 3.5 cattle and 1.85 camels per capita.

    The alliances between the Samburu, the Ariaal, and the Rendille were probably not typical in the distant past. Raiding was a common way of rebuilding and redistributing both cattle and camel herds (Sweet 1969;

Dyson-Hudson and Dyson-Hudson 1969; Stenning 1960). Among the Jie and the Turkana, raiding was an established way of increasing herd size until the British colonial government put an end to this practice (Gulliver 1955). The success of the British was, however, highly variable. Dyson-Hudson (1966:247–249) recorded numerous raids by the Karamojong. Raiding is a response not only to herd depletion resulting from drought and disease, but also an integral part of the social and political organization of pastoralists. Through raiding young men acquire wealth for marriage, political alliances, and the formation of new sections (see also Evans-Pritchard 1940). The Karamojong have been noted to have formed herds of as many as one thousand animals, partly as a result of their raiding successes. The motivation for the raiding may have been the potential danger posed by decline in herd sizes.

When the size of a herd drops below a certain point, the herder must seek another subsistence style. A herder with declining animal population may seek to borrow animals from a wealthier individual; or if he has daughters, he may try to marry them off in exchange for cattle. A man with few cattle and many sons will see to it that they become herdsmen for others, but eventually the sons will find themselves unable to find wives and leading celibate existences. Thus, success in cattle herding is linked with large families, which are able to enrich the family through bridal price and through improved control over the herd, wider distribution of animals, and decreased susceptibility to environmental fluctuations.

In summary, the size and composition of herds is dictated by a management strategy that aims at maximizing the number of animals, especially female, and at diversifiying the livestock population so that it can most effectively exploit the environment and provide useful products. Because the reproductive rates of cattle and camel are slow, because the environmental conditions have in the past brought about rapid herd depopulation, and because of the importance of cattle and camels as means of exchange, the strategy of maximization is a sensible one. The major question before ecological scientists is the extent to which a radical change has taken place in East Africa. This change—cessation of raiding, control over drought and epidemics—seems to have created conditions of herd and human population growth that threaten a way of life that has been finely tuned to local conditions. The mechanisms of redistribution of herds still operate and may prove to be the most important factor in averting desertification.

Relations with Cultivators

The strategy of nomadic pastoralists is a complex mixture of productive specialization and dependence upon the nearby farming population. The development of this interdependence appears to be associated with the highly restricted areas wherein agriculture is possible and the vast expanses where only grazing animals can be productive. It may also be a result of social and technological structural commitments (for example, social organization required by irrigation) that preempt the possibility of effectively moving herds over grasslands (Lees and Bates 1977:826).

Pastoralists manifest a wide diversity of specialization. As we have seen earlier, some herd primarily one type of animal, others own very diverse stock. The factors that prompt such varied forms of specialization are both environmental and economic. From our preceding discussion, it is evident that the location of the territory, the size of the herding family, and access to water and pasture play major roles in deciding which herding strategy is chosen. Rates of exchange are no less important in the development of social relations between cultivators and herders.

Pastoralists can obtain needed grain in a variety of ways. They may diversify production within their own household or tribal group; engage in trade with other pastoral tribes; resort to raiding and other forms of appropriation; or provide services in exchange for agricultural products (Ibid.:827). Pastoralists with access to patches of land where agriculture is seasonally possible may establish an internal division of labor by which women cultivate crops and men tend the herds. This strategy seems to have provided a reliable solution for many pastoral populations, including the East African Karamojong and Jie.

A further refinement of this labor division strategy involves specialization of subgroups within a tribe. The East African Pokot gain access to resources through the idiom of kinship relations. Certain portions of the tribe carry out agriculture and transhumant pastoralism, while others are more nomadic (Schneider 1959). A similar division of labor aimed at securing resources may occur among groups that differ in language, culture, and territory. The intimate trade and alliance relations of the Samburu, Ariaal, and Rendille involve the creation of exchange partnerships guaranteed through friendship, marriage, and favorable rates of exchange.

The role of raiding and taxation in securing resources needs no elaboration. Raiding of farming communities appears to have been associated with the establishment of unfavorable exchange rates by farmers (Sweet 1965) or with poor environmental conditions. The mobility of pastoral nomads provided a vehicle for trade and communication. The latter was sometimes exchanged for agricultural products. Other pastoralists exchanged their cattle for land, which they then rented out (Barth 1961).

These various ways of obtaining nonpastoral produce are not specific solutions for a pastoralist population, but alternatives to varying conditions. A population may shift between these strategies in response to changes in rates of exchange, local agricultural possibilities, and social and political relations with neighbors.

Changes in the productivity of agriculture have a direct effect upon the management strategies chosen by pastoralists. The growth of cities may funnel farm production away from the rural sector and restrict access to grain by pastoralists—or make it available at prices unfavorable to herders. New technological input in both farm and herd sectors probably raise costs and result in changes in exchange. Politically enforced limitations upon the routes of migration open to herders bring about changes in the management of herds and affect their productivity (Lees and Bates 1977:829).

The relations between pastoralists and cultivators are characterized by cyclical oscillations. These oscillations reflect adjustments to changing ecological, social, and economic conditions. Such adjustments tend to take the form of negative feedback whereby an effort is made to return the system to its perceived level of what is normal (for example, the system tries to return to a level of flour, grain, and other products comparable to previous levels). If the adjustment fails, new forms of subsistence may be sought through established channels (for example, a shift from pastoralism to wage labor on farms). When, and if, conditions return to a state that permits resumption of the old form of subsistence, the individual or population will abandon its farm strategy or seek a more stable mixed strategy either within the household or the tribe (Lees and Bates 1977:839).

Adaptive Strategies in the Northern Plains

The constraints under which East Africans and Canadian ranchers operate are similar: uncertain rainfall, seasonally impoverished range, and livestock behavior that at desired densities can overgraze and destroy available grassland. Both populations must adjust to these potential problems, and their respective adjustments are significantly affected by the relationship of the herder to the market and by the presence of farmers in ever increasing numbers. The data base on the human ecology of the temperate grasslands is far more limited than that available on tropical grasslands. In this section we will briefly survey the historical development of subsistence strategies in the North American Plains and then focus on a region of the Canadian Plains that has been the subject of cultural ecological study (Bennett 1969).

Exploitation of Wild Flora and Fauna Hunting/gathering populations occupied the High Plains between five thousand and ten thousand years ago (Wedel 1961:458). Before the introduction of the horse into North America in the 1500s the hunter/gathers of the Plains relied on a wide variety of wild food sources. The Missouri valley populations utilized over two hundred species of plants, one-third as food and the rest as medicine, decoration, and raw material for other uses (Clements and Chaney 1936:32).

Adaptive Strategies in the Northern Plains

At the time of contact with Europeans, the inhabitants of the short grass prairies were dog-using, herd-following bison hunters (Wedel 1975:16). They followed the buffalo from spring to fall, all the while drying meat for winter consumption. Winter was spent in sheltered spots, near water, wood, and forage (Wedel 1961:453). Buffalo hunting did not require migrations across the whole Plains region. It is estimated that the buffalo of the North American prairies migrated within a relatively small territory and occurred at normal densities of one buffalo per twenty acres (that is eight hectares).

Buffalo, the wild ungulate of the Plains, was the central resource of the hunter/gatherers: it was the source of skin for shelters and of fur for blankets, a main source of food, clothing material, and footwear. The buffalo constituted the symbolic core of the religious life of the human population (Kraenzel 1955:75). The relationship can only be described as symbiotic—human movements were governed by the movements of the buffalo between spring and fall. Hunter/gathers engaged in trade relations with the cultivators of the moister parts of the Plains. Wild fruits, nuts, berries, roots, and meat were probably traded for corn and other agricultural products.

The human population of the short and tall grass plains grew more homogeneous after the introduction of the horse by the Spaniards. Plains Indian culture, as described by ethnographers, was a comparatively recent response to various stimuli, among which the horse was the most important innovation (Levy 1961). Among hunter/gatherers, the horse replaced the dog as the beast of burden and expanded the areas that bison hunters could effectively exploit (Wedel 1975:17). Some groups who had been farmers living in sizable villages (such as the Crow and the Cheyenne) became nomadic hunters as a result of the economic advantages of hunting bison from horses (Netting, personal communication). The introduction of the horse led to a change in the social structure of the Plains Indians. From a relatively classless society, the tribes developed into societies of three distinct classes, with membership in the two upper classes determined largely by degree of horse ownership (Oliver 1962:12).

Although the Plains Indians continued the specialized exploitation of the buffalo and adjusted their own movements to the buffalo migratory cycle as had earlier hunter/gatherers, the horse led to increased sedentariness among the Plains population. Since the buffalo had a migratory cycle of two hundred to four hundred miles, the distances that could be traveled on horse no longer required that the whole tribe move, but only the mounted horsemen. Women, children, and the elderly stayed behind and cultivated crops in areas where this was possible (Secoy 1953:88). The large scale exploitation of the bison by horsemen demanded a large number of hunters and encouraged concentration of larger populations in relatively permanent camps (Ibid.:44). Oliver (1962) notes major oscillations in the size of groups. Winter camps were probably small and highly variable in composition during the periods of relative scarcity of buffalo (Netting, personal communication). Thus the typical profile of Plains Indian culture grew out of the annual cycle of environmental exploitation that combined nomadic bison hunting with sedentary agriculture and divided labor along sexual and/or class lines (Oliver 1962:89).

Farming versus Ranching   As the Euro-American population moved west, it encountered the now mounted Indian population, and a lengthy period of struggle ensued. By the time it ended, the population of nomadic mounted hunters had been overrun by a humid zone agricultural population, and farming strategies unadapted to the plains had been introduced (Kraenzel 1955:vii). Corn, oats, barley, rye, and soft wheat were brought by the homesteaders. "Humid zone strategies" managed to exist only by the constant provision of subsidies from outside the region.

The earliest homesteaders came to the Great Plains with their own ideas about farming, and it took them many years and repeated crop failures to adjust to their new habitat. Size of properties evolved from the small, largely self-sufficient farms of the Homestead Act era (circa 1862) to increasingly large landholdings. Management practices were conservative during the transitional period, and the farmers who were able to survive did so by virtue of frugality of lifestyle, patience in deciding whether to increase acreage planted or to increase the size of the herd, and large families who could respond rapidly when opportunities arose to farm an area of their property.

Farmers were slow to appreciate the great variability of soils on the Plains. Continued cultivation of even the rich mollisols leads to declines in fertility, and not all farming has the same effect on soil fertility. Figure 8.10 illustrates the effects of various farming strategies. Corn cultivation depletes the soil the most rapidly, while crop rotations combined with mulching tend to slow the rate of nutrient loss. Bennett notes that Northern Plains farmers in Saskatchewan resisted adopting artificial fertilization and the rotational sowing of legumes to replenish the soil (1969:236). In the more commercial operations of the Central Plains, the highly mechanized agricultural operations rely heavily upon fertilization to maintain the high yields that characterize the so-called corn and wheat belts of the United States.

For a while, the Plains were at the verge of adopting a strategy derived from Mexico, known as the "Texas model of land use." In this system, part of the land sold to homesteaders bordered a stream and part of it was grazing land away from the stream. The land units were relatively large—as indeed they should be in semiarid areas, such as the Plains, where farmers lack the opportunities to apply variable input to enhance yields and depend on the accumulation of reserves during good years to weather the adverse years. However, the humid zone pattern of small landholdings, encouraged by the Homestead Act, led to the establishment

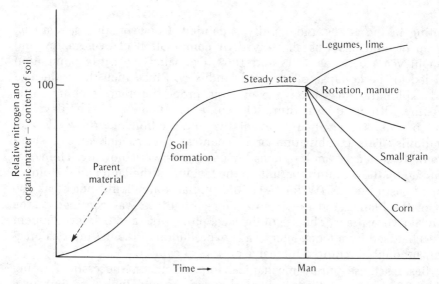

Figure 8.10   **A Hypothetical Illustration of Nature's Build-Up of Soil Fertility and Its Subsequent Modification by Humans**

Source: Lynn Porter. 1969. Nitrogen in Grassland Ecosystems. *In* The Grassland Ecosystem. R. L. Dix and R. G. Beidleman, eds. Fort Collins: Colorado State University, Range Science Department.

of production units that were too small to be economical and that sometimes lacked access to a water source (Webb 1931:227–235). Farmers competed for the well-watered lands and reduced open ranges by fencing their farms. Conflict between homesteaders and ranchers became commonplace as the homesteaders pushed cattle herders to the more arid short grass plains. The use of barbed wire fencing after 1874 put an end to open range cattle. Webb (1931:239) quotes an old herder's feelings about the fencing of the plains:

In those days [1874] there was no fencing along the trails to the North, and we had lots of range to graze on. Now there is so much land taken up and fenced that the trail for most of the way is little better than a crooked lane, and we have a hard time to find enough range to feed on. These fellows from Ohio, Indiana and other northern and western states—"the bone and sinew of the country" as politicans call them—have made farms, enclosed pastures, and fenced in water holes until you can't rest; and I say, d–n such bone and sinew! They are the ruin of the country, and have everlastingly, eternally, now and forever, destroyed the best grazing land in the world.

In the early stages of occupation of the short grass prairies, farming was not seriously considered. Surface runoff is inadequate for irrigating the Plains, and underground artesian sources are few in number and can supply only limited amounts of water. Cattle ranching replaced bison hunting in the 1870s and rapidly expanded. However, this specialized system of land use was short-lived. A combination of overgrazing and drought years between 1885 and 1887 decimated the cattle population and led to the collapse of the cattle industry. Since then the pattern of land exploitation has been one of large properties that combine cattle ranching with grain agriculture (Ottoson et al. 1966:42–43). The development of this strategy had to await the introduction of drill wells and windmills. This combination of mechanical devices delivered a small amount of water day and night as long as winds were blowing. The water supplied by the windmill permitted the fencing of the land and the reduction of pasture areas (Webb 1931:336). Indian tools could not break the turf of the Plains, and as a result their agriculture was confined to the alluvial river valleys. The use of the steel plow, first, and the development of mechanized farm tools, later, made exploitation of the flat prairies practical, although it required intensive outlays of capital.

Besides these purely mechanical improvements, successful farming of the Plains required managerial changes as well, including improvements in choice of crops grown and in tillage, fallow, and mulching practices. Drought-resistant hard wheat and other cereal varieties, which were brought to North America by Russian Mennonite immigrants, lessened the susceptibility of crops to drought. Red Fife hard spring wheat came from Russia, winter wheats from the Crimean region of Eurasia, and sorghums from Africa. These plants from dry regions have made agriculture possible where rainfall is inadequate and irrigation impossible.

The development of the management system known as "dry farming" was also instrumental in extending the cultivation of the Plains. In dry farming, the land is allowed to go fallow every other year, and mulching is accomplished by leaving the chaff of harvested crops on the ground to facilitate the accumulation and retention of moisture and to keep soil from blowing. The field can then be replanted with adapted wheat varieties (Steila 1976:118). Tillage of the prairies should only loosen the soil somewhat, rather than plow deeply. This helps to conserve moisture and provides better weed control. These four practices, in combination, were major breakthroughs (Kraenzel 1955:308–316).

To understand the nature of grazing, one must look at the relationship between the cattle and the pasture. Usually this relationship is expressed in terms of the number of acres of land necessary to support one head of livestock per year. In the Northern Plains this is said to be about twenty acres (eight hectares) per head (Strickon 1965:234). However, how a pasture is grazed is primarily a function, in North American society, of the prices in the livestock market.[4] When prices decline, ranchers

---

[4]As we have already noted, the rate of exchange in East Africa also influences management decisions. However, subsistence needs there probably play a more important role than in North America where economic cushions are provided by a modern market economy.

tend to keep their cattle longer, and this, if sufficiently prolonged, may lead to serious overgrazing problems no matter what the ratio may be. Thus, whether land is overgrazed or not is not purely a matter of management, but is also a result of market conditions and other factors.

The emergence of ranching on the Plains was a response to the high prices offered in the growing industrial centers of the eastern seaboard (Ibid.:236). A similar phenomenon took place in Australia and in Argentina's grasslands, but full-scale development there had to await the development of canning and refrigeration because of the distances between grazing land and markets.

Farming with Ranching   The routine practices by the Canadian Plains ranchers of Jasper who were studied by Bennett reflects the needs of livestock and the seasonality of the area (1969). Wintertime is similar for all ranchers: constantly inspecting and feeding the herd with stored hay, assuring that the water sources stay open and running, and sheltering the herd during inclement weather. Springtime is calving season, and summer is the time to wean, brand, and fatten the cattle with summer grass. In the fall, ranchers sell spring calves, culled cows, and other animals. Hay must be stored for winter, and social life becomes busy before the relative isolation brought on by winter (Ibid.:185). Because on the Northern Plains one herdsman can handle one hundred head of cattle over a territory of more than two thousand acres (that is, one head per eight hectares), there is no pressure for constant innovation. Once a productive operation is established, ranchers tend to operate with a minimum of experimentation (Ibid.:181).

Pastures become specific units of resources, and individuals operate through a combination of accumulated experience and adjustment to new market conditions (Ibid.:194). Ranchers note that cattle tend to concentrate their grazing in areas near water sources and salt and that such areas tend to become overgrazed. Thus, several of their management practices center around preventing the herd from following its own tendencies: (1) cattle are concentrated on high fields in summer because of the high protein values of such grasses; (2) salt is placed away from immediate watering places; (3) fences are built at higher altitudes if cattle use the grasses there during the summer; and (4) either cattle are allowed to graze one area intensively, which is then rested for a year or they are allowed to graze all fields evenly.

These management practices affect the land tenure preferences of ranchers since they require possession of both high and low fields (Ibid.:185). Unlike the open range herding of earlier years or the contemporary herding of East African pastoralists, ranching on the Canadian High Plains involves a fixed range. This means that water must be provided by special devices (that is, windmills); grass must be nurtured and special varieties encouraged for various livestock goals; and hay or alfalfa must be grown to feed the animals during the long winters (Ibid.:197).

The yearly cycle of a Plains farmer resembles or differs from that of a rancher depending on the farmer's degree of reliance on grain crops (Ibid.:226). Planting of grain occurs in April and May in the Canadian High Plains, and work extends through the summer and ends in September with the harvest. During late fall and winter, time is spent repairing tools and buildings. An increasing number of farmers have learned that total reliance on crops may result in economic instability. They have therefore undertaken the raising of cattle on portions of their land. During dry years when crops are unsuccessful, the cattle can add to the income of farmers. Such a mixed operation changes the lifestyle of the farmer so that it begins to resemble that of the rancher—as a result of the year-round attention required by the animals.

There are probably no better examples of the adaptiveness of such a mixed strategy for the exploitation of the Plains than the operations of the Hutterites and the Amish. The Hutterites of Jasper have a communal organization, live frugally, control large expanses of land, and have adopted modern technology to increase their yields. Among the Hutterites, diversification is a cultural ideal. It is also an ideal that enabled the group to succeed in the Plains. Capital expenditures that normally drain the individual farming household, such as a vehicle, are shared by up to thirteen nuclear Hutterite families—at a substantial saving to all thirteen of them. The Hutterites invest the capital thus saved in productive or innovative activities. Austerity of life and reliance on prayer means that capital is not spent on recreation—whereas one Jasper farming family in one year spent $2,500 on recreation, a colony of seventy-four Hutterites spent a mere $1,500. For recreation they turn to crafts and the manufacture of useful items and simple tools. Hutterites make most of their own clothes, shoes, furniture, houses, buildings, and other necessities. Their farming practices are also more conservation-minded than those of other Jasper farmers. Because of the large scale of their operations, they can take poor land out of operation, improve water resources, and improve forage crop production (Ibid.:267–268).

The Amish are even more conservative and less dependent on technology than the Hutterites. The Amish view farming as the optimal setting for the good life and see nature as God's work and their role as that of stewards. Their technology is simple: their homes lack electricity, and they use horses for plowing and buggies for transportation. Their technology must constantly adjust to provide jobs for their families and sufficient profits to make the purchase of land possible for succeeding generations of Amish young people.

Despite their efforts at adjustment, the Amish lose a substantial portion of their population—possibly as much as a third. The Amish who leave their settlements join neighboring Mennonite communities where modern technology is used. Amish technology probably could not sustain the population without this steady out-migration. The Hutterites, on the other hand, keep most of their population (Bennett, personal communication, 1978).

Although the Amish will consult with agricultural advisers, they will not accept subsidies from agricultural support agencies. However, much differentiation has occured among them, and many groups have adopted a degree of mechanization. Despite this, their productive system is basically unsuited to economic exploitation of the Great Plains, for which reason most Amish have chosen not to move there. Characteristically, the Amish engage in labor-intensive, small farming operations that rely on the proximity of markets to sell the high quality products of their gardens, barnyards, and farmhouses (Johnson et al. 1977:374). Thus, the economic exploitation of the plains region would almost surely mean an abandonment of their cultural traditions—a task that the communal Hutterites have dealt with effectively. The Amish style of agriculture would have to become like the Hutterites' to effectively exploit the Plains—just as the Hutterites would have to rely less on heavy machinery in the rolling country of Pennsylvania and southwestern Wisconsin where the Amish thrive (Ibid.:378).

Summary

Grasslands, whether temperate or tropical, present problems to their human inhabitants. Chief of these is lack of sufficient year-round moisture to sustain agriculture on a regular basis. As a result of this lack, xerophytic plants thrive and nomadic herds must be constantly moved to use the widely spaced resources.

Like the East African population, the Great Plains population relied first on the hunting of wild ungulates and later on the herding of domesticated stock. Both areas are characterized by erratic rainfall and cyclical drought. Human adjustments have been remarkably similar—except those regarding herd size and composition. The reason for this difference lies in the goals of each group and in their exchange opportunities.

The East African herd is large in number, but relatively poor in quality (that is, it has low weight per animal and a low calving rate). Nevertheless, their management is a rational adjustment to a no-win situation: whether to adjust to the drought periods and underexploit resources during the good years or whether to make full use of good years and risk the consequences of drought periods. The nomadic pastoralist responds in a variety of ways. The herd is exploited, without diminishing its numbers, through personal consumption. Small stock provide meat, while cattle are exploited for their milk and blood production. Because of this reliance on blood and milk, the number of females is maximized. Such an approach to herd composition may also permit rapid recovery after episodes of drought and disease. When

241

disaster does not strike, herds grow too large and become unmanageable. Social mechanisms serve to divide up the herd, improve the giver's long-term well-being and status, and provide short-term opportunity to less successful herders.

The rancher of the Great Plains orients his herding more to market demand than to subsistence production. Because of this, his strategy involves less emphasis on female animals and a greater emphasis on weight gains by individual animals. The rancher adjusts the size of the herd to the prevalent market price for beef and to the capacity of the pasture to provide desired weight gains. Grass feeding has in recent times been supplemented by grain feeding before slaughter. Although such a process is energetically inefficient, it has been justified by market conditions.

In both the grasslands of North America and East Africa, utilization of water and pasture has depended on mobility. During the last century the invasion of North American grasslands by farmers led to the fencing of the prairies and to a change in cattle management. The area available to the cattle rancher became restricted, and more intensive forms of management evolved—intensive both in terms of capital and area. In some cases the intensification took the form of mixed farming, which combined ranching with the growing of cereals. In East Africa, agriculture is more areally restricted because of higher rates of evaporation that preclude the practice of "dry farming" in many areas. Although there has been no fencing of the savanna for agricultural purposes, movement of herds has been restricted for political reasons. Sedentariness has been more highly valued than nomad-ism, and deep wells have been drilled to restrict the grazing range of herds. Overgrazing has been a problem near such wells and near the communities where nomads have been encouraged to settle.

Relations between cultivators and herders have been tense in both temperate and tropical grasslands whenever their respective production goals have taken contradictory paths. The herder wants a favorable rate of exchange for his animals and easy access to free pastures. The cultivator also wants a favorable rate and, in addition, wishes to limit the movement of herds. It is not unlikely that the experience of the Great Plains will be repeated in the East African savanna: the increased sedentariness of the population leads to the fencing off of land near water sources, which is followed by social confrontation. This eventually leads to the emergence of a mixed strategy that combines restrictive herding and grain cultivation. The rapid increase in the population of East Africa in this century almost cer-tainly guarantees the intensification of grassland use.

Human adaptatability to grasslands primarily takes the form of social and cultural regulatory adjustments. These adjustments facilitate access to pasture and water, help adjust the size and composition of herds to prevalent socioeconomic and ecological conditions, and provide a workable idiom between cultivators and herders. Specialization in herding, to the neglect of agriculture, occurs where cultivation is highly uncertain or where relatively

242

permanent economic cooperation has been assured through the idiom of kinship.

Because of the need to provide an adequate supply of water and pasture, land tenure systems in grasslands evolve toward larger expanses of land per household than they do in more humid areas. When such systems are instituted, a mixed strategy tends to emerge. Such a strategy reduces conflict between farmer and herder, provides access to water and pasture, and reduces the uncertainty of exchange. Households can thus emphasize herd growth or grain cultivation in accordance with expected economic or ecological conditions. However, on the marginal edges of grassland which border desert areas, nomadic pastoralism may be the only workable long-term strategy.

Research on adaptations to grasslands has still not adequately dealt with the systemic interactions between short-term and long-term strategies. The trend has clearly been in the direction of converting grasslands to farmland. The energetic efficiency, the long-term stability, and the short-term profits of the farming system present conflicting goals and solutions. Their consequences for the human and nonhuman parts of the system remain unexplored

Recommended Readings

Grassland biomes were the focus of research by the International Biological Program (IBP). Most of the research published to date is from the United States component, but is scattered in journals. The head of the project is George M. Van Dyne, Natural Resources Ecology Laboratory, Colorado State University. A current list of publications should be available from his office. Several volumes have appeared from the Japanese/IBP research group (Numata 1975). (Unlike the North American grasslands, the Japanese grasslands consist of secondary growth vegetation maintained by the use of fire, mowing, and grazing.) The volume from Dix and Beidleman (1969, 1970) is a preliminary synthesis from the United States component of the IBP. The studies by Humphreys (1962) and Vallentine (1971) are classics in the field of range ecology.

The ecology of tropical savannas has been studied by many scientists and disciplines. Hills and Randall (1968) review the research on the boundary zone between savanna and forest. The earlier synthesis by Hills (1965) compared what was known at the time it was written. The most recent review is that of Bourliere and Hadley (1970). None of these studies adequately deals with the impact of human populations on the environment or with human adaptations to environmental constraints.

Unlike the IBP research on arctic and high altitude populations, the IBP grassland studies did not include a human adaptability component. Fortunately, a number of useful studies have been carried out over the years on the human ecology of the Plains and the savanna. Wedel (1961) studied the prehistory of the Plains and tied the analysis to the characteristics of the grassland environment. Webb (1931) dealt with the historical occupation of the Northern Plains and with the impact of the introduction of the horse and gun on the adaptations of the population. Oliver (1962) studied the cultural ecology of the Plains Indians and related features of their social organization to the environment. Kraenzel (1955) presented a regional analysis of the Plains and evaluated the adaptiveness of many of the management practices and institutional forms imported from the East. Bennett (1969, 1973) analyzed the differential adaptations of various human populations to the same region of the Canadian Plains and found strategies that represented the adjustment of people to resources and to each other.

Studies of East African savannas are numerous, although few have been carried out with a conscious ecological approach. (An exception is the work of Dyson-Hudson [1966, 1969].) However, the intimate relations of pastoral nomads with their environment have been topics of interest to many researchers and have generated useful data on their adjustments. Among the earliest is the study of the Nuer by Evans-Pritchard (1940) which was followed by Gulliver's comparison of the Jie and the Turkana (1955). Since then the amount of work has rapidly escalated (for example, Schneider 1959, 1970; Spencer 1965, 1973; Rigby 1969; Pratt and Gwynne 1977). A particularly valuable recent work is the attempt to quantify the fluctuations in herd size by Dahl and Hjort (1976).

Human
Adaptability
in the
Humid Tropics

The tropical rain forest is one of the world's most extensive biomes. Evidence from Malaya suggests that it has existed continuously since the Cretaceous period, which ended more than sixty million years ago (Richards 1973:3). Human populations have long occupied these humid tropical areas, adapted to their constraints, and benefitted from their opportunities.[1]

Our discussion of human adaptations to these areas will begin with a consideration of the structure and function of the ecosystem—emphasizing its diversity and complexity. Ecosystem diversity and vigorous **secondary growth** or succession are both constraints and opportunities. Diversity in the humid tropics means an abundance of weeds and pests. Human populations manage these problems through slash-and-burn agricultural techniques, multistoried intercropping of fields (which mimics the system's complexity), and wide separation of fields. The productivity of the ecosystem hinges upon the prevention of erosion and on the availability of soil nutrients after forest clearance. The techniques applied to managing weeds and pests are also effective conservation measures, as are population controls and the practice of lengthy fallows. Variations in population density throughout the rain forests provide an interesting opportunity to observe the relationship of density to subsistence strategy and to labor returns. High humidity and high ambient temperatures present a problem to which human populations have responded by regulatory adjustments: thermal sweating, minimal use of clothing, location of settlements on a rise of ground, and scheduling activities.

This chapter will focus on the tropical forest populations of South and Middle America, Melanesia, and Africa. The study of human adaptations to these areas is of more than passing interest. Tropical rain forests are the last cultivable frontiers on earth.[2] In a world that is coming to realize that fossil fuels are limited in supply, the solar energy available in these areas provides an important energy source that is rich and renewable. The humid tropics receive solar radiation year-round, and their complex flora converts this radiation into a lush, green landscape.

As other areas have felt the pressure of growing population, governments have seen fit to build roads that cut across these hitherto undeveloped regions (Moran 1975, 1976; Smith 1976). The construction of roads has been followed in many instances by a great influx of humanity, not always knowledgeable of the ecosystem it has come to exploit. Massing (1976) has shown that if the current rate of lumbering continues in West Africa, the forests there will not last another decade. Mining, ranching, and modern

---

[1]Throughout this chapter, we will use the term *rain forests* interchangeably with *humid tropical regions*. The concept of the humid tropics is a strictly climatic one. UNESCO specialists, gathered to map and delimit the humid tropics, had to turn to vegetational criteria (Fosberg et al. 1961).

[2]The other great frontiers are the arctic and subarctic regions, but farming is not a foreseeable possibility in these heat-limited regions. Current development in arctic regions is based on the exploitation of nonrenewable resources.

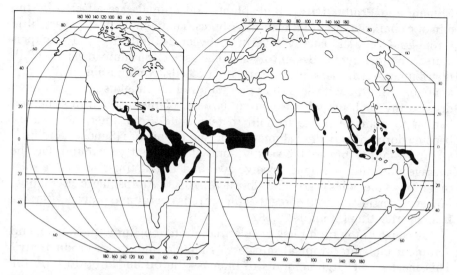

Figure 9.1   **Distribution of Tropical Rain Forests**

agricultural populations are also penetrating the previously forbidden jungles, and ecologically oriented scientists have expressed concern for the impending demise of the unique evolutionary accomplishment that tropical rain forests represent (Denevan 1973; Gomez-Pompa 1972; Dickinson 1972; Meggers 1971). To learn how some populations have adapted to life in this biome is not only of scientific interest, but of immediate significance to the well-being of all.

Tropical Rain Forest Ecosystems

Areas covered by tropical rain forest form a belt around the globe, with most of the area lying to the north of the equator. Three major tropical rain forests have been identified: South American, African, and Indo-Malayan. The largest of these is the South America rain forest, which covers most of the Amazon Basin and extends into the drainage areas of the La Plata and Orinoco rivers. Isolated areas also exist in southern Mexico and Central America, primarily along the Caribbean coast. The African rain forest, extensive in the past, has been much reduced by human activities (Bates 1960:102). It still covers large areas of the Congo Basin and areas along the Gulf of Guinea to Liberia. The Indo-Malayan forests are largely insular and cover an estimated 25 to 30 percent of the islands of Sumatra, Borneo, Celebes, New Guinea, and the Philippines. The coast of Indochina and a portion of the Australian coast are also covered in rain forest (see figure 9.1).

249

Climate and Productivity Both plants and animals are affected by the climatic characteristics of the humid tropics. Temperature means vary little throughout the year, usually hovering between 24° and 26° C. Daily temperatures, on the other hand, can vary as much as 9° C. on sunny days. Rainfall, distributed in two "seasons," commonly exceeds two thousand millimeters annually. Months with less than one hundred millimeters are considered dry. During such periods of relative dryness, plants respond in a manner similar to plant response to cold in temperate areas: they shed leaves, become dormant and close stomata to preserve moisture (Sanchez and Buol 1975). Humidity hovers between 75 and 100 percent year-round. On the average, the humid tropics receive two and a half times as much solar radiation as the poles (Barry and Chorley 1970:33). Atmospheric circulation, however, carries away 80 percent of the surplus energy and prevents the area from overheating (Steila 1976:152).

Because of the high rates of solar radiation, long growing season, and abundant moisture, tropical rain forests have a high gross productivity.[3] This means that large amounts of biomass die off and drop to form the ground litter. Such litter is quickly mineralized and nutrients are rapidly absorbed again by roots. Despite the high rainfall, there is no appreciable loss of nutrients due to leaching. Research in the Brazilian Amazon found that the feeding rootlets of trees possess, at a depth of only two to 15 centimeters, mycorrhiza (that is, root fungi). Through this fungi, trees are directly connected with the litter layer. The trees can thus exploit the fungi to obtain their inorganic nutrients directly from the litter. Stark (1969) estimated that 5.4 grams per square meter per day are mineralized, a figure that approaches the gross primary production of 6.0 grams per square meter per day.

Soils of the Humid Tropics Perhaps the most misunderstood aspect of tropical environment is the presence of **laterite** in the soils. Among soil scientists, the term *laterite* is being abandoned because of its lack of clarity in the literature. The term *plinthite* has replaced it—to refer to the iron-rich, humus-poor soil material that irreversibly hardens after repeated wetting and drying once it is exposed to air. It has been recently estimated that plinthite occurs in only 7 percent of the tropical world (Sanchez and Buol 1975). Plinthite can be a useful resource: in Thailand it is poured into large blocks before it has time to harden and used in construction. Some of the most ancient Thai temples are made from this material.

Tropical soils are said to be old, leached, acidic, lacking in horizons, poor in nutrients, and able to be cultivated for only a couple of years. Recent

---

[3]Annual total net primary productivity averages 23.9 metric tons per hectare per year. The rate for temperate forests is only 13 metric tons per hectare per year (Farnworth and Golley 1974:81–82). In a Puerto Rican rainforest, gross production equalled energetic costs of respiration—permitting rapid litter turnover and high levels of transpiration (Lugo and Snedacker 1971:113).

250

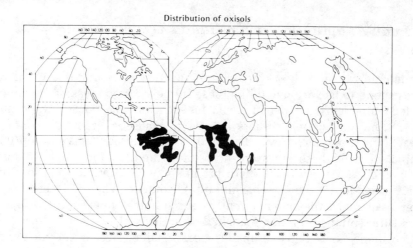

Distribution of oxisols

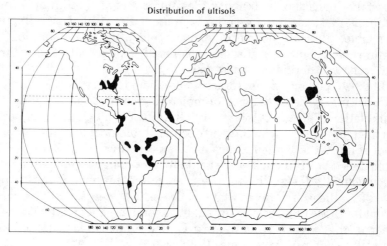

Distribution of ultisols

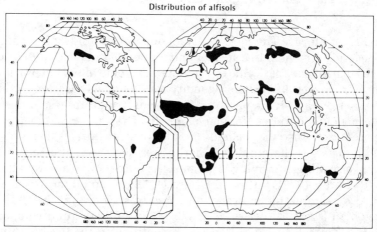

Distribution of alfisols

Figure 9.2   **Soils Most Commonly Found in the Humid Tropics**   Note that they are found elsewhere as well, and it is not only weather but also parent material that affects the presence of soil types in a biome.

251

agronomic research, however, is showing that soils under tropical rain forests tend to be very much like those in the forested areas of the nonglaciated temperate zone. (See figure 9.2 for a map of the major soil types found in wet, humid regions.) Where the parent materials are acidic, the soils closely correspond to those of the southeastern United States and southeast China. Both of these areas are now under highly productive, intensive cultivation. These soils all share problems of low **cation** retention, high acidity, and high exchangeable aluminum content. Where soils are derived from basic rocks, they are frequently neutral in reaction (Ibid.: 1975).

Three soil types predominate in the humid tropics: oxisols, alfisols, and ultisols. The most extensive are the oxisols, characterized by an oxic horizon (that is, they consist of hydrated oxides of iron and/or aluminum). When the conditions that create the oxic horizon are accompanied by a fluctuating water table, plinthite develops. Alfisols and ultisols are soils of humid moisture areas, but they are less weathered than oxisols and commonly result from weathering of basic rocks.

In the 78 percent of the tropics where there is a pronounced dry season of at least ninety days, the lack of moisture greatly reduces organic matter accumulation. This effect is similar to the effect of low winter temperatures in temperate regions, which greatly reduce biological activity. A comparison of soils in the United States and soils in Brazil and Zaire led to the conclusion that differences in organic matter content were agronomically and statistically insignificant. The average organic matter in the top one meter of southeastern United States soils was 1.11 percent while it was 1.05 percent for those of Zaire and Brazil. In general, organic matter content was higher in the tropical soils than in United States soils with comparable temperature and rainfall regimes (Ibid.: 1975).

Rain Forest Flora   The most conspicuous features of tropical rain forests are the large number of tree species and the small number of individuals of a species in a given area. Table 9.1 summarizes some of the botanical work in tropical rain forests. The heterogeneity of rain forests has been explained as resulting from herbivore pressure. The seeds, fruits, and seedlings of trees are the major food sources for many animals. The pressure is greatest close to the parent tree since the predator population concentrates its numbers near it. With distance, the number of herbivores decreases, and thus the likelihood of a seedling surviving is greatest the farther one goes from the parent tree (Richards 1973). Cain and Castro (1959:61) note that in some stands studied by sample plots, every third tree was a new species. In a central Amazonian forest, Klinge et al. (1975:119) found six hundred species per hectare, of which five hundred were identified in the 0.2 hectare sample plot.

The rain forest biome has the largest known standing crop biomass, due to the high levels of solar radiation, generally favorable environment, and a twelve-month growing season (see table 4.2). Not only is there a greater

Table 9.1   Number of Tree Species Ten Centimeters in Diameter and Over on Sample Plots in Tropical Rain Forests at Various Locations

Vegetation	Place	Plot size (Hectares)	Species	Author
Mora rain forest	British Guiana	1.5	60	Davis & Richards
Morabukea rain forest	British Guiana	1.5	71	Davis & Richards
Mixed rain forest	British Guiana	1.5	91	Davis & Richards
Greenheart rain forest	British Guiana	1.5	95	Davis & Richards
Wallaba rain forest	British Guiana	1.5	74	Davis & Richards
Mixed rain forest	Sarawak, Borneo	1.5	98	Richards
Mixed rain forest	Ivory Coast	1.4	74	Aubreville
Mixed rain forest	Nigeria	1.5	70	Richards
Mixed rain forest	Mauritius	1.0	52	Vaughn & Wiehe
Terra firme rain forest	Para, Brazil	1.0	87	Black, Dobzhansky and Pavan
Igapo rain forest	Para, Brazil	1.0	60	Black, Dobzhansky and Pavan
Terra firme rain forest	Amazonas, Brazil	1.0	79	Black, Dobzhansky and Pavan
Terra firme rain forest	Para, Brazil	3.5	179	Pires, Dobzhansky and Black
Terra firme rain forest	Para, Brazil	2.0	173	Cain, et al.

Source: Table 5 (p. 60) in *Manual of Vegetation Analysis* by Stanley A. Cain and G. M. de Oliveira Castro. Copyright © 1959 by Stanley A. Cain and G. M. de Oliveira Castro. By permission of Harper & Row, Publishers, Inc.

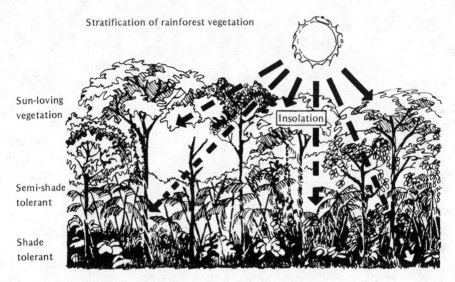

Stratification of rainforest vegetation

Sun-loving vegetation

Insolation

Semi-shade tolerant

Shade tolerant

Figure 9.3   Structure of a Mature Tropical Rain Forest

accumulation of biomass, but it reaches a steady state in a shorter time (Farnworth and Golley 1974:76). Tropical forests approach maximum biomass value in about eight to ten years (Sanchez 1976:351), while temperate forests reach steady state in from fifty to one hundred years (Farnworth and Golley 1974:76). This means that the tropical forest ecosystem has incredible recuperative powers, and that secondary succession can occur with surprising vigor. However, large variations between sample plots at a given age have been noted and reflect differences in biota and other environmental factors (Farnworth and Golley 1974:123). The maintenance of the climax vegetation is important in the cycling of nutrients that sustain both forest and dependent animal life.

Trees in the tropical forest can reach a height of ninety meters, but such instances are rare. Some ecologists hold that three strata are recognizable (see figure 9.3). The highest stratum is not compact, but consists of solitary giants with umbrella-shaped crowns that reach far above the other trees. Observers flying over the tropical rain forest have noted that the middle stratum gives the appearance of uniformity. The lower stratum is made up of mosses, ferns, palms, and epiphytes that receive little light. The trunks of rain forest trees are usually slender and have thin barks. The crowns begin high up and are relatively small as a result of crowding. It is difficult to judge the age of the trees since annual rings are not present, but they are estimated to be two hundred to two hundred fifty years old. Much of the vegetation lacks deep roots, and the trees achieve support by developing plank buttresses that reach as high as nine meters up the tree (See figure 9.4). The presence of these buttresses has led to the nearly universal use among

Figure 9.4   **Buttresses of a Rain Forest Tree**
Photograph from Anthro-Photo by Irven Devore

indigenous peoples of platforms from which to cut the giant trees above the planks.

Both growth and flowering are periodic, but fairly independent of any particular season since external conditions are relatively constant. In some tree species, leaf fall occurs before the new leaves begin to form, and a tree may even be bare for a short period. Individuals of the same species may bloom at different times or the branches of the same tree species may bloom at different times. These are all manifestations of an autonomous periodicity that is not bound to a twelve-month cycle. This means that a rain forest has no definite flowering season, but that there is always a variety of trees in bloom. This presents a particular problem for tropical animals and humans,

255

who depend on forest resources for survival. They are forced to resort to nomadism to take advantage of this continuous, but dispersed, resource base.[4]

Rain Forest Fauna   In the rain forest, plants have evolved effective ways of repelling and controlling the herbivore population. For example, in Barro Colorado, Panama, animal population growth is restricted by alternating seasons of fruit abudance and shortage. During a season of shortage, mass starvation can occur (Leigh, Jr. 1975:82). In rain forests some trees reproduce by means of large, hard nuts. The hard endocarp protects the nuts from predators, but the mesocarp tends to be rewarding and some species of animals function as dispersal agents (Smith 1974a). Animals play important roles in processes such as pollination, fruiting, flowering, litter decomposition, consumption of green plants, and mineral cycling (Fittkau and Klinge 1973). Animal consumption of plant tissue and consequent excretion of feces represent a shortcut in nutrient cycling.[5]

The richness of speciation is as true for animals as it is for plants. For example, in a six square mile area on Barro Colorado in Panama, there are twenty thousand identified insect species, as compared with a mere few hundred in all of France. Numerous archaic types of both animals and plants survive in the many niches of the rain forest. Many scientists feel that the rate of evolution in the rain forest is particularly rapid and that many of the species presently occupying northern temperate environments evolved in tropical environments[6] (Bates 1960:109–110).

Animals represent a small fraction of the ecosystem's total biomass and are largely unobtrusive. Fittkau and Klinge (1973) calculated that the living plant biomass was nine-hundred metric tons per hectare, while that of animals was only one-fifth of a ton. A number of biogeographers and ecologists have indicated that the low net productivity of the rain forest biome provides little food for forest animals, and for this reason animal biomass per unit area is quite small. Although this argument is sound, it overlooks the large area utilized by most indigenous populations and the lack of adequate quantitative data. A much more useful study of animal biomass is that of Eisenberg and Thorington (1973) in Barro Colorado. They estimated 4,431 kilograms per square kilometer of nonvolant terrestrial mammals of which 72.3 percent is entirely arboreal. The hunting ter-

---

[4]Nomadism is found in most environments and is not a response peculiar to the humid tropics. It is a rather universal adjustment to scattered or seasonally available resources and, in modern times, to economic marginality.

[5]The collected articles in Meggers et al (1973) have an excellent compilation of data on floral and faunal aspects of tropical rain forest ecosystems of Africa and South America. Numerous articles in the journal *Biotropica* treat plant and animal interactions.

[6]Baker (1970) reviews the theories that attempt to explain richness of species in the tropics.

ritory of human groups varies with population size and settlement pattern. In a quantitative study of hunting among the Siona-Secoya in lowland Ecuador, Vickers (1976) showed that the population harvested 9.8 percent of the potential 337,000 kilograms of animal biomass of interest to hunters—a not insignificant amount of meat for a population of 132 persons.

A much larger proportion of animals live in the upper layers of vegetation of tropical forests than is the case in temperate forests. Thirty-one of fifty-nine species of mammals in Guyana are arboreal, five are amphibious, and only twenty-three are ground dwellers. The larger predators are ground dwellers, and it comes as no surprise to find that much of the ground animal life is nocturnal.

Some mammals adopt a more or less uniform distribution of individuals, each defending a home range; others pursue a continuous nomadism over a wider area in search of fruiting trees. These two strategies are not necessarily exclusive. Most nonarboreal rain forest mammals are solitary and have a dispersed form of social organization. Among arboreal rain forest mammals, two major trends are also discernible: small troops scattered over the habitat range of the species and a more fluid type of social organization where the age and sex groups join and separate according to prevalent food distribution. Without their mammal components, tropical rain forests would not be self-perpetuating. Bats and marsupials contribute to the dispersal of many species, primarily through ingestion and transportation of seeds without loss of germinative potential. Through predation they help to scatter, rather than concentrate, numbers of individuals in a given area (Meggers et al. 1973:279).

Coping With Ecosystem Complexity

Several strategies may be noted in human adaptations to tropical rainforests, each of which reflects efforts to deal with the diversity and complexity of the habitat. Hunting requires a finely tuned knowledge of the sounds of animals, their food preferences, and migratory behavior. Such human adjustments are closely tied to complex systems of belief that clearly define the relationship of the hunter to the game. The gathering of food is less clearly defined in belief systems, but forms an important element in the diet of many tropical populations. Given the periodicities of tropical trees, seasonal nomadism is required for adequate exploitation of the fruits and nuts of the forest.

Fishing and animal husbandry are practised by more sedentary populations. Because these two subsistence strategies generate a considerable amount of protein, population concentrations are greater, and warfare with groups aspiring to possess those resources is not uncommon. Such warfare may serve to redistribute populations and prevent depletion of a region's resources.

Farming requires identification of appropriate soils and location of fields in ways that both decrease labor costs and prevent pest damage. It also requires an adequate fallow to ensure the continued fertility of the system. Such a fallow is guaranteed by ritual regulation, by automatic field abandonment after one or two years, or by other means.

The integrity of shifting agricultural systems is predicated on a careful balance between population and resources. Infanticide, sexual abstention, and other means of population control are used to maintain such a balance. Human populations are relatively low in most of the humid tropics. Densities of 0.6 to 1.0 persons per square kilometer are still common in South America, but they are higher in Africa (7 to 10 persons per square kilometer) and Asia (20 plus persons per square kilometer).

Hunting and Gathering Strategies Human populations dependent on a hunting technology exploit tropical forest resources in variable ways that reflect local habitat characteristics, periodicity, seasonability, and previous patterns of exploitation in the territory. The technology of hunting in the tropical rain forest consisted primarily of the use of bows and arrows, lances, and blowguns. Characteristics of these weapons vary across continents, and no analysis has adequately explained the benefits of one type vis-à-vis another. Hunting has been a male-dominated occupation, and observers have noted that it is viewed as half work and half sport (Vickers 1976:96). The use of blowguns with poisoned tips is a delicate art and allows hunters to shoot repeatedly' without frightening their prey, thereby increasing the chances of a multiple kill. Blowguns are used primarily against arboreal fauna, while lances are used mainly in hunting the larger land mammals, which usually involves open pursuit. Tapirs, boars, and other group animals are pursued by several hunters who foresee in a good kill a chance of several days rest from hunting work. Wherever bows and arrows are used, they usually preempt use of the blowgun.

Hunters have various hunting goals that reflect adjustments to resources and that affect the methods used. Linares (1976) has noted that hunting in the vicinity of planted gardens may have partially eliminated seasonality and scheduling problems, increased the biomass of selected animals that live at the edge of the forest (for example, armadillos, rodents and small deer raid gardens looking for food to eat and are caught in so doing) and served as a substitute for animal domestication. "Garden hunting" is still practiced among many inland South American groups, such as the Guaymi and the Cuna.

Some hunts occur in daytime only and may involve just a single hunter. If the lone hunter identifies the presence of a band of animals, a group hunting effort may emerge. Perhaps most common of all are group hunts that involve two or three hunters who carry out this work as part of their kinship obligations to provide for their families.

Hunters must rely not only on an appropriate hunting technology, but also on intimate knowledge of the forest and the animals. Tropical rain forest hunters are capable of imitating the calls and sounds of most animals they hunt, as well as recognize their telltale footsteps. Knowledge of the animals' diet is particularly useful. As hunters move through the forest, they note the location of the trees that are flowering or fruiting and use the knowledge in their next hunting expedition. Table 9.2 identifies the trees used by hunters, in an area of the Lower Xingú in the Amazon Basin, to choose hunting sites. Since trees of a given species do not flower simultaneously, hunters must pay constant attention to these details. They may have to cover a wide range of hunting territory in a given period to find trees that are attractive to game. Anthropologists have often noted that one of the major reasons for the lack of sedentary villages in many tropical forest areas is the necessity of relocating to maintain productive hunting (Carneiro 1970:243).

Yields from hunting are extremely variable, as table 9.3 indicates. Gross (1975) suggests that hunting productivity limits the size and permanence of settlements in the Amazon. Such single-factor explanations have been questioned recently. Vickers (1975, 1976) demonstrates that the amount of game obtained is surprisingly large in both new and old settlements. Most statements on the lack of meat among native South Americans are based not on personal observation and careful gathering of data on game hunted and eaten, but on the acceptance of the natives' point of view (that is, folk categories). Indeed, among tropical forest peoples, "hunger for meat" is a constant concern (Holmberg 1969; Siskind 1973). However, that ethnoecological concern may not be based on a real dietary lack. Ruddle (1973) has noted that the consumption of insects by native South Americans helps compensate for protein deficiencies. Among the Yukpa, twenty-two genera of insects were regularly consumed and contributed significant amounts of fat and protein to the diet.

Among the Siona-Secoya it was found that even the least successful hunter managed a mean of 13.08 kilograms of butchered meat per hunt—with the average for all hunters being 21.35 kilograms. Even in an area continuously inhabited for thirty-two years, the mean kill was 5.67 kilograms per hunt per hunter. Over the whole year, the Siona-Secoya hunted the equivalent of 255 kilograms of meat for each of the 132 persons in the village. This translated into 65 grams of animal protein per person per day. However, in view of the nocturnal habits of much of the game, the high canopy habits of most of the birds and monkeys, and the aggressiveness of the peccaries, it is not surprising that a great deal of cultural attention is given to hunter/animal relations. Religion and ritual are filled with taboos for hunters that clearly define the behavior of one for the other and

259

Table 9.2   Trees Used in Waiting for Game in Night Hunting

Common name[a]	Scientific name	Flower and fruit consumed by most species
Matamatá	Eschweilera spp.	Yes
Sapucaia	Lecythis paraensis Hub.	Except armadillos and birds
Jarana	Eschweilera jarana Ducke	Yes
Castanha do Pará	Bertholetia excelsis	Only cutias eat the fruit
Jaracatiá	Unidentified	Yes
Tamburí	Enterolobium maximum Ducke	Yes
Piquizeiro	Caryocar spp.	Yes
Cupuaçú	Theobroma grandiflorum Spring	Only dear, paca and tapir eat the fruit
Babaçú	Orbignya martiana	Only deer and pacas eat the fruit after cutias open the hard shell
Bacaba	Oenocarpus bacaba Mart.	Yes
Açai Entrepeoleraceae Mart		Yes
Frutão	Lucuma spp. and Pouteria spp.	Yes
Ninharé	Unidentified	Yes
Toari	Couratari spp.	Yes

[a] This is a composite list of all trees mentioned by the five hunters interviewed. None of the hunters included all of the above, but all regular hunters had a minimum of ten trees that they used to seek a point of waiting. It is important to move each night, especially if a hunter has killed an animal at a given spot. A number of farmers were occasional hunters whose knowledge of the forest was very restricted.

Table 9.3 Estimated Rates of Animal Protein Capture for Nine Tropical South and Central American Societies

Society	Location	Habitat type	Firearms present?	Principal food staple	Animal protein per capita per day (g)	Length of study (days)	Average size of pop. unit
Campa	E. Peru	interfluve forest	+	manioc (72%)	15-20	3	5-15
Bayano Cuna	Panama	riverine forest	+	bananas (89%)	18	14	170
Miskito	Eastern Nicaragua	tropical forest (coastal)	+	manioc	20	365	997
Kaingáng	Southern Brazil	subtropical forest	–	pine nuts	19	38	106
Sirionó	Eastern Bolivia	interfluve forest	–	maize and manioc	44	92	60-154
Wayaná	Guyana-Brazil	riverine forest	–	manioc	31	365	16
Sharanahua	E. Peru	riverine forest	+	manioc	63	28	90
Shipibo	E. Peru	riverine forest	+	plantains	48	365	107
Waiwai	Guyana-Brazil	riverine forest	–	manioc	54	varies	77
				mean =	35 g		

Source: Daniel Gross. 1975. Protein Capture and Cultural Development in the Amazon Basin. Reproduced by permission of the American Anthropological Association from the American Anthropologist 77:531, 1975.

the dangers of such encounters. Of all the subsistence activities, hunting is the least secure.

In numerous aboriginal societies, symbolic systems define hunter behavior and control depletion of wild game. These symbolic systems reflect culturally sanctioned adjustments of populations to resources. According to Reichel-Dolmatoff (1971, 1976), the Tukano of the Vaupés River in the Colombian northwest Amazon see human society and the fauna of their habitat as sharing the same pool of reproductive energy. The fertility of both men and animals has a fixed limit, rather than being an infinite or unrestricted resource. It is therefore important for the Tukano to seek an equilibrium in human sexual activity so that the animals of the forest can reproduce and, in turn, serve as nourishment for the human population. Cultural rules place strict controls over the recognized tendency of people to exploit the environment to the limits of their technological capacity.

Within this system of controls, sexual repression of the hunter plays a major role. Since this repression could have highly undesirable psychological effects, the Tukano have filled the relationship between hunter and prey with erotic content.[7] The hunter dreams and hallucinates about sexual contact with the animals, which he fertilizes and which multiply for his benefit. At times, the animals ravish the hunter in dreams. The hunt is part courtship and part sexual act, filled with care, respect and ritual. The verb to hunt is *vai-mera gametarari*, which means literally "to make love to the animals." Courtship behavior manifests the idea of sexually attracting the game so it can be killed, and the kill has a strong element of sexual domination. Before the hunt, as well as after, the hunter abstains from sexual contact. None of the women in the big house (*maloca*) must be menstruating, nor should the hunter allow erotic dreams before a hunt.

Such a system, in fact, limits both the sexual activity of the hunter, as well as the frequency of hunting. A child is gradually indoctrinated into this complex set of beliefs and before puberty already knows that he should never mock a dead animal or treat animals carelessly. He also knows that not all animals can be hunted, but only some of them, and those only under stringent conditions. Noncompliance leads to fear of death, since the spirits of the animals can lure the hunters away from familiar terrain and kill them.

There is cultural hostility among the Tukano toward families with numerous children. Their lack of sexual abstinence robs the animals of their energy for reproduction. Furthermore, these families demand more meat to feed their excessive number of children. The animals are believed to grow jealous and refuse to serve as prey—an idea that reflects lower

[7]Heider notes however, that among the Dani of western Irian, there was, despite imposed sexual repression, very little interest in sex and no apparent consequent tension (1970).

hunting yields under conditions of population growth.

Systems of belief such as those of the Tukano operate well under aboriginal conditions, but are quickly disrupted by contact with outside groups. This is particularly the case if the cultural contact is associated with the spread of diseases to which the population has not built immunities. In a comparison of two South American tribes, Wagley showed that the one with the stricter ideology that encouraged small families was threatened with extinction following exposure to European diseases (1969). The other one, which actually encouraged large families, was able to withstand depopulation more successfully.

Like hunting, the gathering of forest products is subject to the peculiar periodicities and seasonality of the tropical forest. Forest populations have traditionally engaged in concentrated gathering efforts during the dry season, not only because of product availability, but also because of the greater ease of traveling during that time. Forest plant products make important contributions to the diet and are gathered by men, women, and children. Table 9.4 documents the yields by a household of Ecuadorian Siona-Secoya (Vickers 1976:117). Gathering is nutritionally significant not so much for the total calories it provides as for its mineral, vitamin, and micronutrient content. In hunting, the men do not overlook the presence of plant resources and may collect or consume them on the spot. A wide variety of products is gathered, but major contributors, by volume, are few in number. For ecological analysis, however, careful note should be taken of even small amounts, since they may provide crucial trace elements. Brazil nuts *(Bertholletia excelsa)*, for example, are crucial because they contain large amounts of the amino acid *methionine*, which Gross (1975:534) cites as perhaps the most limiting nutritional element in Amazonian diets.

To date, there has been no documented systematic measurement of the consumption by South American aboriginal or peasant populations of the Brazil nut or most other wild plant products. This is partly the result of a tendency by many populations to gather and eat, on the spot, any edible products they come across. Accounts tend to mention only the plants that return to camp (Lyon 1974:70). Part of the problem has also been that many observers have lacked botanical knowledge. The diversity of the tropical rain forest flora presents major problems to the ecologically oriented scientist, even when properly trained. Sampling techniques largely developed in temperate areas give variable results in the tropical rain forest and require special adjustments.

Fishing Strategies Populations inhabiting coastal or riverine habitats find it easier to become sedentary than seminomadic hunters. Large rivers and coastal areas offer tremendous resources that encourage both sedentariness and increased dependence on horticulture. Examples of river-adapted populations are the Kalapalo and the Kuikuru of Central Brazil

Table 9.4   Annual Collecting Yields for a Household of Four in Lowland
                 Ecuador

Food	kg	% Edible portion kg	Edible portion kg	kcal kg E.P.[a]	Total kcal
Flora					
Palm fruit (*Mauritia vinifera*)	27.22	38	10.34	1,430	14,786
Palm nut (*Astrocaryum tucuma*)	22.68	28	6.35	990[b]	6,286
Heart of palm (various spp.)	.45	100	.45	260	117
Nut (*Caryodendron orinocense*)	18.14	37	6.71	6,960[c]	46,702
Wild sapote (*Matisia cordata*)	10.89	26	2.83	480	1,358
/yahi/ (unidentified berry)	.60	75[d]	.45	810[e]	364
Wild cacao (*Herrania* sp.)	1.56	37	.58	710[f]	412
Groundcherry (*Physalis angulata*)	.45	90[d]	.40	730[g]	292
Wild guaba (*Inga* spp.)	4.54	20	.91	600	545
Pokeweed (*Phytolacca* sp.)	2.72	85[d]	2.31	300[h]	693
Tree grape (*Pourouma aspera*)	1.00	50[d]	.50	570[i]	285
/sayaro/ (unidentified fruit)	1.36	40[d]	.54	480[j]	259
Dwarf banana (*Musa* sp.)[k]	500.76	78	390.59	970	378,875
Fauna					
turtle eggs	7.36	83	6.11	1,150	7,026
honey	1.36	100	1.36	3,060	4,162
grubs	.40	100	.40	2,150[l]	860
Total					463,022

[a] INCAP
[b] Data for *Astrocaryum standleyanum* used as analogue.
[c] Data for *Carya illinoensis* used as analogue.
[d] Estimated.
[e] Data for *Prunus capuli* used as analogue.
[f] Data for *Theobroma bicolor* used as analogue.
[g] Data for *Physalis peruviana* used as analogue.
[h] Data for *Spinacea oleracea* used as analogue.
[i] Data for *Vitis tiliifolia* used as analogue.
[j] Data for *Matisia cordata* used as analogue.
[k] Higher than most years due to immaturity of plantains in gardens. (This is a self-propagating variety of dwarf banana).
[l] Data for "*mortadela*" sausage used as analogue.
Source: William T. Vickers, 1976. Human Adaptation to Amazonian Habitats: The Siona-Secoya of Eastern Ecuador. Ann Arbor, Mich.: University Microfilms (Ph.D. dissertation, University of Florida).

(Basso 1973; Carneiro 1957). Observers have noted that these two riverine groups show little interest in wild game and even surround its exploitation with taboos—cultural prohibitions that emphasize the poor return of labor invested on hunting (vis-à-vis fishing) in a riverine environment (Ross 1978).

The rich variety of species found in rivers cutting through tropical rain forest regions has only begun to be carefully studied. Junk notes that 1,300 to 2,000 fish species have been identified in the Amazon rivers, and that yearly harvests of 633,000 metric tons are theoretically possible on a sustained basis (1975:109). However, such potential has never been realized, and the intensive utilization of the larger aquatic resources has led, in our day, to the clear danger of species extinction—for example, of the giant Amazon river turtle, caymans, and the giant manatee.

Before the adoption of the hook and line, tropical forest populations used a variety of harpoons, bows and arrows, traps, and poisons to capture fish. These are specific techniques used in particular times and places to catch specific species of fish (Vickers 1976:105). Spears and harpoons are used against larger prey, such as cayman and manatee. Fishing with poisons can be practices only in small streams and requires a large group effort. The plants used as poisons are wild, but because of their importance, have become semidomesticates. A barrier must be built in the stream to keep the fish from escaping, and the plants usually have to be beaten to release the poisonous substance. The fish are stupefied, their breathing is impaired by the substance, and they float to the surface where they are caught. These communal fishing efforts occur during the dry season and are of restricted occurrence (Ibid.:111). Bow and arrow fishing is widely practiced in tropical areas. It is usually done early in the day and involves standing on a canoe or near the river bank and waiting for a fish to pass underneath.

Vickers (Ibid.:124), while studying the Siona-Secoya of Ecuador, estimated the energetic efficiency of fishing at 2.99:1, less than that of hunting in a new village settlement (9.33:1), but more than the return for the labor of hunting in an old village (2.48:1). Among the Machiguenga of the Upper Amazon in southeastern Peru, energy efficiencies differ from those just cited. The Machiguenga live in smaller groups (that is, seven to twenty-five members) in an upland habitat where game and fish are less abundant than in the lowlands. The forest offers a low rate of return on labor: the region is mountainous, trails are steep, and resources scattered. Hunting provides .16 kcals for each kcal spent, gathering yields .68 kcals for each kcal spent, and fishing averages 1.95 kcals (Johnson 1977). Nietschmann (1971) notes that among the Miskito of Central America the return on labor from fishing green turtles was 5.5:1. This figure is lower than the efficiency he noted for hunting, but the protein return was higher for fishing.

Game depletion is a problem of greater immediacy than fish depletion in aboriginal situations. Game relies on the relatively low net productivity of the forest, whereas fish can draw from nutrients carried by the river from distant areas. As a result, populations probably preferred riverine to inland locations, where they would have to rely on hunting to supply the bulk of the protein. Some researchers have attributed the chronic state of warfare and raiding in tropical rain forest regions before contact, and since then, to a constant struggle for control of riverine sites where subsistence efforts, particularly in terms of securing protein, were more rewarding (see review in Gross, 1975).

A study by Nietschmann (1973) of a coastal Miskito population in Nicaragua is an excellent data source on fishing adaptations to coastal

Figure 9.5 **Miskitos Hauling in a Turtle**
Photograph courtesy of Bernard Nietschmann.

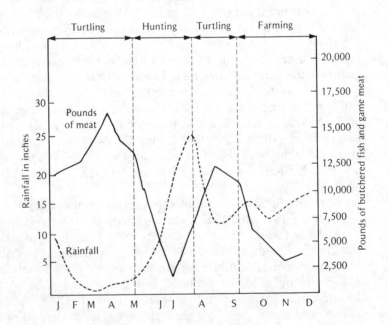

Figure 9.6 **The Seasonal Rhythms of a Miskito Community** The rhythms reflect the spatial and temporal availability of green turtles.

Source: Adapted from p. 50 of B. Nietschmann, 1972, "Hunting and Fishing Focus Among the Miskito Indians, E. Nicaragua," *Human Ecology* 1, (1) 41–67.

resources. The Miskito have long depended on the green turtle as a dietary staple and as an item of trade (see figure 9.5). However, the introduction of a cash economy and the presence of two factories that process turtle meat for pet food have resulted in overfishing that threatens this way of life. The Miskito have responded to contemporary cash incentives and have abandoned the diversified subsistence economy that sustained them in the past. The young Miskito have begun to turn away from horticulture—which in the past supplied the bulk of their calories—and from seasonal hunting. The net result has been a decline in the protein available to the Miskito, a steady breakdown in the system of reciprocity, and a decline in the yields of turtles per unit of effort spent on fishing them.

In exploiting the large green turtles, the Miskito must adjust their subsistence technology, lifestyles, and economic patterns to the temporal and spatial occurrence of the turtles (see figure 9.6). Relatively little attention is paid to wild game. Choices between hunting and fishing are made according to the information feedback that reflects evaluations of the dependability and productivity of each strategy. Turtlemen were found to have a larger percentage of successful trips than hunters (73 percent and 54 percent respectively), and this is a more important consideration for the Miskito than the effort expended. Hunting provided more kcals per hour invested (1,270 as compared to 962 for fishing), but calories are not in limited supply in this environment (Nietschmann 1972:59). As a result, in the past as now, the majority of the Miskito choose to specialize in turtling (see table 9.5).

Farming Strategies   Shifting cultivation can be defined as an agricultural system in which fields are cropped for fewer years than they are allowed to remain fallow. It is a dominant land preparation technique in 30 percent of the world's cultivable soils, especially in those covered by tropical rain forest. It is a common misconception that shifting (also known as slash-and-burn or swidden) cultivation is practiced by primitive farmers on inferior soils (Kellogg, 1959). Popenoe's study in Central America (1960) refuted this notion with evidence of tropical soils cultivated by slash-and-burn methods that had high levels of organic matter, low bulk densities, high cation exchange capacities, and high potassium content.

Because it is a practical procedure, shifting cultivation is practiced by over 250 million people worldwide. (Spencer 1966, Sanchez 1976:346). It is, in a sense, a pioneering system utilized today by peoples lacking capital resources and economic privilege. In this approach to cultivation, the nutrients accumulated in the forest biomass are made available to crops on a periodic basis. It is a conservative measure that, when practiced according to tradition, preserves forest complexity and provides sustained yields.

In swidden cultivation, an area of land is cleared by cutting the standing vegetation and then burning it, after it has had time to dry. Burn-

Table 9.5   Time and Yield Data for Hunting and Turtle Fishing, Tasbapauni, October 1968 through September 1969[a]

	Pounds of meat (share)	Total hours	Hours traveling	Hours hunting and fishing
Hunter	875	533	305	228
Turtleman	812	455	241	214

	Pounds of meat: hour	Calories	Protein (g)	Fat (g)
Hunter	1.64:1	677,044	73,317	41,496
Turtleman	1.78:1	437,500	78,750	7,875

	Calories per hour	Grams of protein per hour	Grams of fat per hour
Hunter	1270	138	78
Turtleman	962	173	17

	Number of trips	Number of successful trips	Percentage of successful trips
Hunter	26	14	54
Turtleman	15	11	73

[a] Composition of turtle, deer, and white-lipped peccary meats was adjusted from Wu Leung (1961) to allow for Miskito consumption of "mixed meat" and fat.
Source: From p. 58 of B. Nietschmann, 1972 "Hunting and Fishing Focus Among the Miskito Indians, E. Nicaragua," *Human Ecology* 1, (1) 41–67.

ing brings about numerous changes in the physical properties of soils. It kills parasites, insects, fungi, nematodes, and pathogenic bacteria that interfere with crop productivity. The effect of the burn on soil physical properties is highly dependent on the soils themselves. In soils high in oxides, such as the oxisols, the structural changes are actually beneficial. In areas with shrinking clays, the effect may be detrimental.

With the burn, all nutrients are deposited as ash except nitrogen and sulphur, which are lost as gases. There is great variability on how many nutrients are deposited as ash. The amounts depend on the success of the burn, how humid the environment is, and how dense the vegetation is. The deposition of ashes decreases soil acidity as shown by an increase in soil pH (see figure 9.7). The effect is most marked in the top 10 centimeters of soil, but studies have noted changes in pH to a depth of 40 centimeters. The presence of basic cations in the ashes brings about a favorable increase in exchangeable calcium, magnesium, and potassium that improves crop growth conditions. In acid soils the effect of burning is to

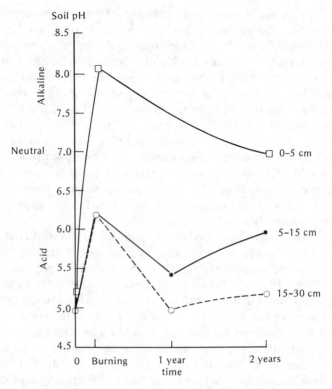

Figure 9.7 **Changes in pH at Different Soil Depths in Kade, Ghana** The beneficial effect of the ashes on soil pH is most dramatic in the top five centimeters of the soil. The neutralization of acidity by the ashes is also accompanied by an increase in nutrients found in the ash.

Source: Adapted from P. H. Nye and D. J. Greenland. 1964. Changes in the Soil after Clearing a Tropical Forest. Plant and Soil 21:101–112.

decrease exchangeable aluminum and thereby decrease the danger of aluminum toxicity in some plants. These positive effects usually remain for only one or two years. The ash layer responsible for many of these changes is leached, washed down through the soil, or the nutrients taken up by plants (Sanchez 1976:364–368)

Burning does not have much effect on soil organic matter. Soil temperatures during burning of forest are not commonly high enough to destroy soil organic matter. In fact, several studies have even noted small increases in soil organic carbon and total nitrogen after burning (Nye and Greenland 1964). The positive effect of burning on pH and on organic matter brings about an increase in cation exchange capacity (CEC) of soils and, therefore, in overall fertility. One of the most significant changes brought about is a dramatic increase in available phosphorus from the ash layer. The increases range from seven to twenty-five kilograms per hectare (Nye and Greenland, 1960). Many of the soils in areas where shifting cultivation is used have been noted to be deficient in phosphorus, and burning is important in making such soils productive for agriculture.

In studies in Africa, Nye and Greenland observed that when the forest is cleared and burned, the heating of the soil leads to increased fertility, largely as a result of the change in the state of nitrogen mineralization, or **nitrification** (Ibid.:72). When properly timed to occur before the beginning of the rainy season, the moisture brings about a rapid increase in the amount of nitrogen available to plants. The heating up of the soil also has a favorable effect on the soil microbial population. Anaerobic nitrogen-fixing bacteria, such as *Clostridium* spp., increase their activity. Aerobic bacteria, such as *Beijerinkia*, are killed but they appear to recolonize within a relatively short time (Baldanzi 1959).

Burning eradicates seeds and vegetative material that can lead to a large crop of weeds. It also destroys or drives out animal and insect pests. Eradication of weeds and pests is beneficial in any effort to cultivate crops. Weed invasion limits crop production not only by its natural competition for soil nutrients, but also through the accompanying increase in the rodent population. During the early stages of weed invasion, rodent populations undergo accelerated growth. The damage caused by rodents to young plants can be very severe (Popenoe 1960:59–62).

In a series of Brazilian experiments, burned areas produced 30 percent more than those that were cleared mechanically and cultivated with a plow (Baldanzi 1959). In studies carried out in Peru, Sanchez et al. (1974) found that yields using traditional slash-and-burn methods were 50 to 60 percent higher than yields from areas cleared by bulldozer. Sanchez and his colleagues attributed the lower mechanized yields to reduced infiltration of water resulting from soil compaction, the lack of nutrients from the ash layer, and the loss of the humic horizon by bulldozer scraping (see table 9.6)

The practice of slash-and-burn agriculture is not only economically sensible, but is also ecologically sound. Given the vigor of secondary succession, efforts to establish simplified (that is, monocrop) agricultural systems are likely to run into serious problems, such as pest infestation, weed invasion, and nutrient loss as a result of runoff. The intercropped fields of swidden horticulturalists are an imitation of the natural ecosystem: generalized and diverse, multistoried, and providing good soil protection from both direct solar radiation and precipitation (Geertz 1963:16–25). Floyd (1969:181) has given an excellent description of one such field in Nigeria:

The impression gained is one of multi-tiered systems of farming with several levels of crops being maintained on the same few square yards of soil: an ingenious technique of mixed and sequential cropping. Lowly

Table 9.6   **Effects of Land-Clearing Methods and Fertilization on Crop Production on an Ultisol from Yurimaguas, Peru (tons/ha)**

| Land-clearing method | Fertility treatment | Continuous upland rice | | | Cassava | Soybeans | Guinea grass (annual production) |
		2nd year	3rd year	4th year			
Slash-and-burn	None	1.93	1.36	0.77	22.5	0.72	9.9
	Complete[a]	3.20	3.53	2.00	34.2	2.34	24.1
Bulldozer clearing	None	1.09	0.92	0.20	10.1	0.12	8.3
	Complete	2.52	3.19	1.42	32.0	1.31	18.4

Source: North Carolina State University (1973, 1974); Reprinted in Pedro Sanchez. 1976. Properties and Management of Soils in the Tropics. New York: Wiley-Interscience.

ground creeping plants such as the cucurbits are shaded by the foliage of root crops, which in turn are found growing within the shade of the smaller "economic" trees such as banana, plantain, orange, mango, breadfruit, native pear, cashew, castor bean and kola; the ubiquitous oil palms grow taller, varying in height from some 30 to 60 feet, and are only eclipsed by scattered specimens of forest giants from the original rain-forest, especially cottonwood trees. In sum, as many as a dozen food-yielding, beneficial plants may be struggling for survival and fruition in hard proximity.

Swidden horticulture thus protects the complexity natural to the eco-system. In addition, it preserves natural controls by avoiding concentration of food sources for anthropod pests, protecting the soil from leaching and erosion, and providing intense shade that discourages the colonization of sun-loving weeds. It also thereby reduces expenditures for fertilizers and pesticides. The new forest that it helps to create provides a higher net yield for humans. Such a system requires numerous controls to assure its integrity (Conklin 1957).[8] It can break down by population increases, which lead to shortening of the fallow period; by insufficient attention to its intercropped, multistoried characteristics, which leads to erosion; and by extension of the system to less humid areas where grasslands may quickly replace the primary forest vegetation.

Studies in African rain forests have indicated that 90 percent of the maximum biomass is attained within eight years after a field has been abandoned (Sanchez 1976:351). Figure 9.8 illustrates how the biomass plateau is reached on an ultisol in Zaire. Presumably regrowth may be even faster on soils with higher fertility. Seedlings and regrowth from the previous forest form a quick, low canopy which reduces soil temperatures and erosion potential. Growth is rapid, and litter is decomposed so rapidly that a nearly closed nutrient cycle is established (Nye and Greenland 1960). However, it is well established that if cropping is extended too long, forest regrowth will not occur and coarse grasses will take its place (Sanchez 1976:354).

A number of the practices of swidden cultivators assure the renewal of the forest. These planting practices mimic, in a simplified fashion, the process of secondary succession. The first crops planted tend to be those most demanding of nutrients (for example, corn, rice, millet). They are intercropped with root crops and plantains that take longer to develop, provide better shade, and are in some cases taller. By the time the grains are harvested, the other crops are well established and provide both yield and protection. Numerous cultivators seem to also plant leguminous trees

---

[8]The most common reasons for decline in yields that lead to fallowing are: lower soil nutrient availability, deterioration of soil structure, erosion of topsoil, increased density of weeds, pests and diseases, and greater labor costs (Nye and Greenland 1966:75). The little weeding that has been observed favors forest regrowth (Gomez-Pompa et al. 1972).

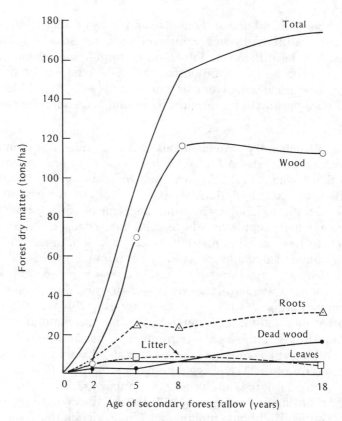

Figure 9.8   **Increases of Biomass of Forest Components with Age of Second-ary Forest Growth in Yangambi, Zaire**

Source: Adapted from W. Bartholomew, et al. 1953. Mineral Nutrient Immobiliza-tion under Forest and Grass Fallow in the Yangambi (Belgian Congo) Region. Insti-tut National pour L'Etude Agronomique du Congo. Série 57:1–27.

and shrubs. Brookfield and Brown (1963:166) have noted such practices in southern Nigeria, Indonesia, and New Guinea. The Ibo of Nigeria plant *Acior barteri* and *Macrolobium macrophyllum* to help restores soil fertil-ity when woody plants do not return spontaneously (Netting 1978). The practice of having small, multiple, scattered plots in the forest — instead of single, large clearings — facilitates forest succession by providing seeds that can recolonize the cultivated land when it is abandoned (Clarke 1976:250).

The productivity of swidden cultivation has been a topic of contro-versy. Because of research undertaken since the late 1950s, we now have an excellent data base from which to judge this system's merits. Rappa-port (1968) found that the Tsembaga in New Guinea obtained 15.9 kcals per calorie spent on swidden cultivation. Even higher caloric returns have been obtained in Mexico, Ecuador, and Brazil under comparable techno-logical conditions. However, energetic efficiencies do not tell the whole story. Are the differences the result of population pressure, soil quality, higher labor costs, or other factors? The complexity of the problem becomes evident when one is confronted with a swidden system that acquires a portion of its agricultural output from domesticated animals.

Animal Husbandry Mechanisms that encourage abandonment of fields at regular intervals so that forest can take over are crucial to long-term swidden systems. In the Amazon, where land has traditionally not been in limited supply, populations shifted in response to decreased farm yields, lower returns to labor in hunting, and fear of sorcery and raids. In New Guinea, where populations have been much denser, there has been a ten-dency to have continuous cultivation in prime areas. This can lead to environmental degradation, and some populations have, in fact, turned their montane rain forest into low quality grassland. The Kundegai and the Fore have wrought large-scale and irreversible changes on their envi-ronment to the detriment of their own well-being (Harris 1974b:72). Another population, the Tsembaga Maring, has maintained a more stable relationship with the local environment. It has accomplished this through the workings of a complex homeostat that "effectively adjusts the size and distribution of the Tsembaga's human and animal population to conform to available resources and production opportunities" (Ibid.:48).

According to Rappaport (1968, 1971b), the cyclical pig festivals of the New Guinea Highlands function as a logic switch that leads to the invest-ment of the pig herd in alliance formation and at the same time eases the stress of pig population numbers. The alliances that take place at the pig festivals are a prelude to warfare. In these intertribal conflicts, people/land ratios are altered and prime garden lands are allowed to become fallow.[9] The ten to fifteen year cycles establish a range of time within which eval-uations of labor and resource use must be made. If pig husbandry suc-ceeds to the point that pigs become "too much of a good thing," the stress is felt by the laborers, and this is translated into a cybernetic signal that is made operational by the tribal leaders.

The ritual cycle regulates the human and the pig population. In fig-ure 9.9 the nearly vertical portion (or A to B path) represents the drastic reduction in the pig population. This is followed by warfare, represented in path B to C, which causes a slight decrease in the human population. Both populations then increase for a number of years until a new festival initiates the cycle again (Shantzis and Behrens 1973:276). A festival is induced by an increase in labor costs of pig husbandry beyond an accept-able threshold and by growing danger of land degradation as larger areas

---

[9] Without these intertribal conflicts, overcultivation and repeated burnings would lead to soil compaction, weed invasion, and environmental degradation.

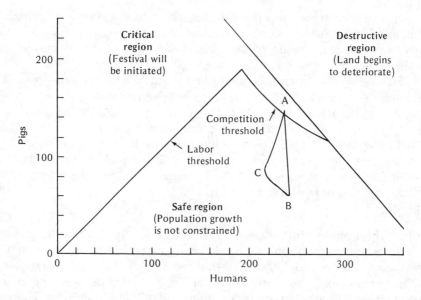

Figure 9.9   A Ritual Cycle with Behavior Regions Indicated

Source: S. D. Shantzis and W. W. Behrens 1974:277, fig. 9–14. Population Control Mechanisms in a Primitive Agricultural Society. Reprinted from *Towards Global Equilibrium* by D. H. Meadows by permission of The MIT Press, Cambridge, Massachusetts. © 1974 by The MIT Press.

must be cultivated. These factors are also plotted in figure 9.9. As the system moves from the safe region and enters the critical region, it must order the ritual cycle or else it enters the destructive region—wherein the land's productivity is threatened. The regulatory role of the pig rituals is predicated upon the status value attached to pigs. Without this value, the pig herd would not receive the attention necessary for it to function as an information indicator or signal. (Ibid.).

Bennett views the process not as that of a cybernetic signal, but as a problem of livestock management (1976). The cost of raising swine in unconfined environments periodically exceeds the gain, and Melanesian men make economic decisions when the cost (that is, of fence mending, distance to fields, fear of raids) gets too high. Ritual provides an effective cultural mechanism for maintaining a sustained-yield system, but other mechanisms could work equally well (Ibid.:178–186).

Friedman (1974) argues that the ritual cycle's occurrence is best understood by focusing on the strain felt by women, who carry out most of the agricultural work and pig husbandry. They complain, they nag their husbands, and they snap at their children, and it is these social facts that trigger the pig festivals and warfare cycle. According to Friedman, it is social relations that determine the composition and quantity of labor that goes into pig raising. In a recent reply to Friedman, Rappaport argues that at low densities of pig populations the crucial factor may indeed be women's labor returns, but at higher densities the depredation caused by pigs (for example, tearing of fences and invasion of fields) may be all-important in triggering a ritual cycle (1977:159).

These cases of farming behavior and regulation of pig herds raise the question of how can such systems operate in the absence of ritually operated cybernetic controls? Most studies have not noted equivalent structures in other tropical forest populations. Traditional populations relied on various forms of population control, the most important being warfare, infanticide, and village fissioning. By reducing the size of their populations, other groups maintained less pressure on their land, and ritualized shifting of land was not necessary.

Village Fissioning, Infanticide, and Warfare Adaptation to lowland rain forests under aboriginal conditions involves a broad spectrum of practices that may be related to the characteristics of a diverse ecosystem. Whenever possible, low population densities are maintained by practices that include warfare, female infanticide, and village fissioning. The ease and frequency of village fissioning in South American tribes is striking. Carneiro (1961) believes that villages rarely reach carrying capacity, but fission (that is, split up) well before they reach the point of overshooting their resources. As population increases, stresses and strains increase with it, and weak chieftainship and a lack of internal political controls do nothing to discourage a village faction from splitting off from its parent community (Carneiro 1974:78). In addition, there are no ecological deterrents to village fissioning. Suitable land is easily found and the vast network of streams and rivers facilitates travel. In other words, in the absence of both internal and external deterrents, tropical forest tribes follow the path of least resistance and seek avoidance of the stresses that come with increased population density.[10]

The situation is quite different in Asia, Melanesia, and Africa. Clarke (1966) notes that with increased population in New Guinea, there is a shift from extensive to intensive shifting cultivation. This is manifested in shortened fallows, lower productivity per unit of land and per unit of labor, but a higher total production as a result of higher labor input and more sedentary settlement patterns. Boserup (1965) notes a similar relationship in Africa between increased population and the intensification of agriculture.

Eder (1977) has studied a typically Boserupian scenario in the Philippines. As man/land ratios have declined, farmers have progressively shortened fallow periods. Returns to labor have decreased, since increased weeding has been necessary. As a substitute for swidden cultivation, the farmers have turned to vegetable gardening, which gives a

[10] Chagnon explains village fissioning in terms of tribal politics (1968).

poor caloric return to labor, but has a high economic value in nearby markets. Gardens, however, can also absorb ten times more labor input per unit of land than swiddening and provide the most intensive forms of cultivation in rain forests today.

Female infanticide, abortion, long periods of sexual abstinence after childbirth, warfare, and a strong male fear of too frequent sexual contact with women are characteristic of many of the world's peoples, including rain forest dwellers. Among some populations, intercourse between husband and wife is forbidden from the onset of pregnancy until the child is weaned—often not until between ages three and five. Sexual continence is commonly required prior to ceremonies, raids, and hunting. The number of prohibitions that are practiced varies a great deal and may be related to other forms of population control (Meggers 1974:104). All these practices have had the net effect of controlling the size of aboriginal populations throughout the humid tropics.

Harris (1977) has recently argued that primitive warfare puts a premium on raising warriors and that this has an important influence on population growth. Although women do contribute the bulk of calories among both hunters/gatherers (Lee 1968) and agriculturalists (Rappaport 1968), "recurring intergroup combat places a premium upon rearing males rather than female infants." (Harris 1977:40–43). The more numerous the adult males, the more likely the group is to hold on to its territory and, when needed, to increase it.

Many hunting/gathering and horticultural societies practice both overt and covert female infanticide. This practice seems to result from reproductive pressure, as well as from high adult male mortality associated with warfare, feuding, and accidental deaths. Female infanticide reduces the number of reproductive females, thereby lowering the rate of population growth. In the long run, it evens out the average sex ratios and thus may have encouraged the warfare complex (Chagnon 1968; Harris 1977).

War, in itself, does not significantly control population (Livingstone 1968:8). Casualties are seldom so large that a group cannot regain its previous size within a couple of generations. The practice of female infanticide aids in reducing the number of persons capable of bearing children and increases the number of persons capable of hunting (that is, males). Thus, it also ensures higher protein per capita for the group. Warfare is the cultural price that must be paid to keep these mechanisms of population control operative. As an adaptive strategy it is more effective than abortion or contraception. The latter, until the invention of the condom, was seldom effective. Abortion could be effective, but it had the undesirable effect of killing mothers only slightly less frequently than the embryo (Harris 1974b).

Vayda outlined the possible functions of warfare in an elaborate hypothesis:

*1) A diminishing per capita food supply and increasing intra-group com-
petition for resources generate intense domestic frustrations and other in-
group tensions; 2) when these tensions reach a certain level, release is
sought in warfare with an enemy group; 3) a result of the warfare is
reduction of the pressure of people upon the land, either because of
heavy battle mortality or because of the victorious groups' taking its
defeated and dispersed enemy's territory; 4) the reduced pressure on the
land means the diminution of per capita food supply and the increase of
intra-group competition over resources are arrested and that domestic
frustrations and in-group tensions can be kept within tolerable limits
(1968:89).*

This suggests that adaptable human populations must have a variety of
mechanisms that adjust the magnitude of the response to the magnitude
of the perturbation (Vayda 1976). The ecological role of aggressive, or
agonistic, behavior has not been adequately demonstrated, and King
(1973:133) suggests that the problem here lies in the difficulty of controlling relevant variables under "natural conditions."

Adaptability to Humid Heat

In addition to the adjustments that we have already discussed, which
center on human strategies for coping with ecosystem complexity, rain
forest populations must manage the potential stress and discomfort of
high humidity combined with high temperatures. Most of these adjustments to humid heat are cultural, rather than physiological. Unlike the
dry tropics, which are generally characterized by low humidity and lack
of water, the humid tropics have abundant water resources. However,
high humidity and high temperatures in combination impede the effective evaporation of sweat that cools the human body. Human adaptation
to humid heat is still little understood. Most of the data is from Africa
(Ladell 1964) and only one field study is available from South America
(Baker 1966; Hanna and Baker 1974).

Cultural adaptations to humid heat are similar throughout the world,
and they are relatively few in number. Settlements are located on a rise of
ground near a water source. No perfect solution for housing is available.
Houses are characterized either by open design (to provide maximum
daytime cooling) or by designs aimed at the conservation of heat to provide warmth during the relatively chilly nights (see figure 9.10). Minimal
use of clothing minimizes the body's heat load (Ladell 1964:650–1) and
provides maximum surface area for sweat evaporation. Daily tasks are
adjusted to the pattern of solar insolation: the population bathes frequently, starts work early, remains relatively sedentary at midday, and
follows a moderate pace in work. Physiologists have noted that tropical

278

a

b

Figure 9.10   The Two Basic Housing Approaches in the Humid Tropics: *a.*
Open Design for Daytime Cooling; *b.* Closed Design for Nighttime Warmth (Xingú maloca in central Brazil).

peoples "move more efficiently" and do not allow themselves to become
overheated (Ibid.:652). After thermal midday (2 PM) most tropical peoples
avoid heavy work and engage in relatively unstrenuous activity in shaded
areas.

279

The main physiological adaptation of indigenous tropical peoples is the combination of cutaneous vasodilation and a ready onset of sweating (Ibid.:626). On the other hand, because of the high humidity, there is a fairly low limit to the cooling that is possible through evaporation. Cross-cultural comparisons of sweat rates do not indicate any conclusive adaptations by tropical peoples (Lowenstein 1973:294). This may be associated with the low salt intakes of tropical populations, which are dictated by appetite, custom, and the limited availability of salt. At moderate levels of activity, tropical peoples sweat less and have slightly lower body temperatures than unacclimatized people. In addition, their heart rates increase less with rises in body temperatures. Nontropical peoples during acclimatization overadapt to heat by uneconomical high sweat rates and steep increases in heart rate with rise in body temperature. This leads to fatigue, dehydration, and serious salt losses.

Other biological adaptations of value to rain forest dwellers are relative reduction of mass with respect to surface area (Newman 1960; Ladell 1964:647; Baker 1966:296); highly tannable skin; insensible sweat evaporation, which insures maximum evaporation with a minimum loss of electrolytes (Lowenstein 1968; Ladell 1964:652); and reduced heart rates at moderate levels of activity (Hanna and Baker 1974). A study that compared Shipibo Indians with acclimatized *mestizo* workers in South America found that, although neither group was seriously stressed by heat and radiation loads during moderate exercise, the pulse rate was significantly lower among the native population. This advantage was lost when the level of activity was increased (Ibid.). Table 9.7 gives the results of the tests used in this study.

Lowenstein concluded that tropical indigenous populations do not show any remarkable adaptations to heat stress, but enjoy comfortable lives in humid heat because of moderate levels of activity and sensible, low sodium diets (1968:394). However, much more research on adaptations to humid heat is needed before any really conclusive statement can be made.

Contemporary Alternatives for Production and Conservation

The recent flow of publications expressing concern over the impending demise of rain forest ecosystems suggests that the traditional isolation of these regions is rapidly coming to an end (Richards 1973; Gomez-Pompa et al. 1974; Denevan 1973; Meggers 1974; Fosberg 1973). In the preceding sections we have discussed some of the human adjustments for coping with the problems of diversity and complexity in the humid tropics. Any contemporary system of production or conservation should give serious

Table 9.7   **Physiological Reponses of Shipibo Indians
and Peruvian Mestizos to Heat Exposure**

	Group	Final rectal temp. (°C)	Pulse rate (per min.)	Sweat loss (g/hour)
Moderate level	Shipibos walking at 5 km/hr	37.78	93.55	673
	Mestizos walking at 5 km/hr	37.83	102.73	618
Increased level	Shipibos walking at 8.3 km/hr	38.24	133.33	970
	Mestizos walking at 8.3 km/h4	38.24	129.92	913

Source: Paul Baker. 1966. Ecological and Physiological Adaptations in Indigenous S. Americans. In The Biology of Human Adaptability. P. Baker and J. S. Weiner, eds. Oxford: Clarendon Press.

consideration to these practices before discarding them as unsuitable for the modern world.

The Corridor System   Agronomic institutions worldwide have begun to acknowledge the advantages of slash-and-burn agriculture and have tried to systematize it. One such effort is the corridor system (Jurion and Henry 1969), which was developed by the Belgians in the Congo (now Zaire). This system organizes the somewhat random shift of fields into a rotational system that assures each field an adequate fallow period (see figure 9.11). By clearing corridors, forest regeneration is facilitated, erosion is checked, and forest germ-plasm is protected.

In one variation of this system, each annual field or "corridor" runs east to west and is 100 meters wide.

The east-west alignment ensures maximum light for the strip under cultivation, while proximity of forest guarantees quick recovery of cleared areas. The 100 meter corridor is a compromise: a narrower one would mean lack of light to crops, but a wider one would take longer to return to forest. The length of the corridor can be adjusted to the needs of the population. The cultivation cycle is three years of cropping and three years of fallow. The principle works by setting aside fifteen corridors with boundaries drawn perpendicular to a north-south baseline. Forest fields with

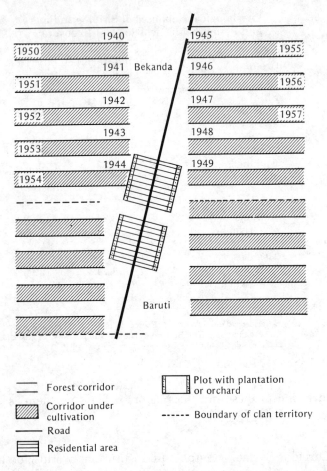

Forest corridor

Plot with plantation or orchard

Corridor under cultivation

Road

Boundary of clan territory

Residential area

Figure 9.11   **The Arrangement of a Corridor System in the Belgian Congo**

Source: F. Jurion and J. Henry. 1969. Can Primitive Farming Be Modernized? London: Agra–Europe.

even numbers are cleared first and then those with uneven numbers are cleared, so that each field has forest of at least ten years regeneration surrounding it. (Secondary succession in rain forests reaches 90 percent maximum biomass within nine years.)

This system is particularly effective in level areas. Where mountains and other topographical variations occur, the corridors must adjust to these conditions (that is, slopes should be planted in perennial tree crops, such as fruit and nut-bearing trees, to protect the soil from erosion). The chief problem with the corridor system is that is requires a great deal of control and conservation. Except in the colonial situation in which it developed, the tendency has been to clear new areas, as long as unoccupied lands are available. (When the Congo became independent Zaire, the corridor system was abandoned [Ruthenberg 1971].) Nevertheless, this alternative should be seriously considered, for it can offer rain forest populations a highly productive system of cultivation. In addition, populations living in corridors are able to harvest game to improve their protein intake.

Crop Selection Yields can be increased without altering the shifting cultivation cycle. One realistic solution is to plant new varieties that reduce labor input and that are also disease-resistant but do not sacrifice yield. (In the Peruvian Amazon, yields were increased 76 percent by using special varieties of rice planted in reduced spacing [Sanchez 1976:38].) In addition, since only eight to ten years are needed for fallows to reach almost maximum biomass levels, it may be possible to shorten the fallow period without reducing nutrient availability for crops.

Special deficiencies in given areas may be overcome and the land improved by selecting trees for the successional cycle that accumulate certain nutrients at faster rates than the mixed successional species. The capacity of *Heliconia* and *Gynerium* spp. to accumulate phosphorus can be important in areas where that element is in short supply. *Acioa barteri* was found to accumulate calcium and magnesium at rapid rates in Nigeria, while *Cassuarina* fixes nitrogen symbiotically (Ibid.:384–385). However, few of the combinations that have been tried thus far have proved superior to the natural mixed fallows.

Other Methods of Cultivation Ruthenberg (1971) describes the existence in Africa of semipermanent cultivation that occurs in a continuum between permanent and shifting cultivation. Permanent orchards, made possible by the use of manure and weeding, are located near the village. Beyond this area the steady continuum to less permanent cultivation begins. Staples are planted in the semipermanent areas, and beyond that one finds grass fallows and, on the edge of the forest, shifting agricultural fields for root crops, bananas, and yams. Figure 9.12 illustrates this diverse exploitative system.

Increase in population densities in tropical areas and in migration of peoples to these areas make it increasingly difficult to maintain the integrity of shifting agriculture. More continuous cultivation of rain forest soils seems almost inevitable, but this need not spell the creation of deserts (Goodland and Irwin 1975), nor an end to hope for populations seeking new lives in the lowland tropics (see Moran 1975, 1976; Smith 1976; Nelson 1973). The change from shifting to permanent cultivation invariably involves the use of either organic or inorganic fertilization; a move from communal to private land ownership; and higher labor input, particularly into weeding. Figure 9.13 illustrates the importance of combined fertilization and weeding on an alfisol of Nigeria. Without fertilization and with-

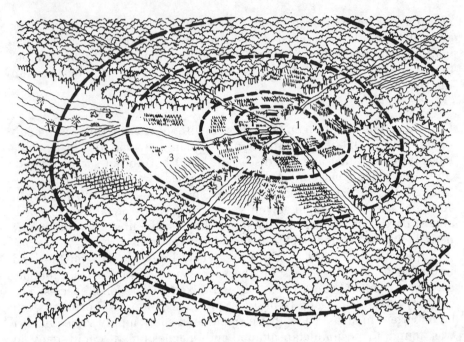

Figure 9.12   **Spatial Arrangement of Continous, Semipermanent, and Shifting Cultivation Systems around a Village in Senegal** (1) Houses and gardens, (2) continuous cultivation, (3) semipermanent cultivation, (4) shifting cultivation.

out weeding, yields declined to less than 30 percent by the second year; with weeding alone, the decline was less pronounced. With fertilization but no weeding, yields declined by the third year, but with weeding included, yields actually increased substantially. The benefits of such input probably compensate and justify the costs involved (Sanchez 1976:398).[11]

It has been suggested that "tree agriculture" might be an alternative means both of protecting the soil from leaching and of providing a profitable, sustained-yield system. Planning permanent tree crops offers the advantage of establishing an ecosystem with its own nearly closed nutrient cycle. Moreover, the areas can be cultivated with food crops while the trees grow. Tropical tree crops—such as cocoa, rubber, *Robusta* coffee, coconuts, oil palms, Brazil nuts, guaraná, bananas, plantains, and a wide variety of exotic fruits—could be cultivated in mixed stands rather

[11]The costs of inorganic fertilizers make their use impractical in isolated rain forest areas and in areas with low amounts of colloids to hold the fertilizer. Animal manures and crop rotation using legumes offer a workable alternative in the intensification of temperate zone agriculture (Grigg 1974). In one area of Zaire, small, three-hectare pastures produced enough manure to fertilize one hectare of crops for an indefinite period (Sanchez 1976:400).

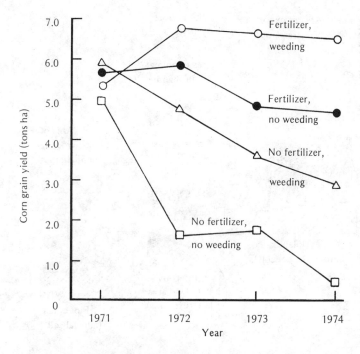

Figure 9.13 **Effects of Fertilization and Weeding on Rainy Season Corn Yields in a Continuously Cropped Experiment on an Alfisol near Ibadan, Nigeria** Forest was cleared in 1970 and subjected to a uniformity trial with corn. Fertilization consisted of application of 120 kilograms of nitrogen per hectare, 40 kilograms of phosphorus per hectare, and 50 kilograms of potassium per hectare per crop.

Source: International Institute for Tropical Agriculture (IITA). 1974 Annual Report, Farming Systems Program. Ibadan, Nigeria: IITA.

than in **monocultures** on plantations. (The disaster of Henry Ford's rubber plantations in Brazil is a witness to the danger of monoculture in an environment favorable to living things, including fungi, pests, and other plant pathogens.) Such mixed stands would provide both ecosystem diversity and profitable incomes. Sioli (1973) presents such a scheme in which forest or tree agriculture on poorer soils is combined with dairying, poultry, and swine husbandry—all of which yield organic fertilizer for intensively cultivated gardens. Such a mixed system (see figure 9.14) can yield stable income and maintain agricultural productivity almost indefinitely without costly input.

In Asia, large leguminous trees are planted in association with other tree crops. This system involves forest clearing and the subsequent selection of successional species that yield both profit and food for the human population. Some timber species can be mixed with a view both to diver-

285

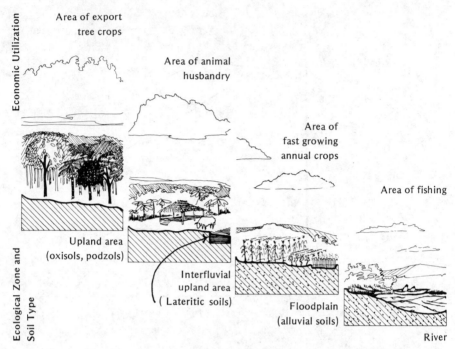

Figure 9.14   **Scheme for Diversified Use of Amazonian Environments**   The seasonally enriched floodplain produces annual crops, while the interfluvial area is used for animal husbandry. Part of the animal manure is sent to the floodplain to further enrich the soils or to the upland area to enrich the area of tree crops. Among the crops with export potential are rubber, cocoa, hardwoods, Brazil nuts, oil palms, and coconuts. The trees help protect the upland soils from leaching and erosion.

sity and profit. Like tree agriculture, this production system attempts to replicate succession in a given area of land.

A mulching approach to tropical agriculture has been tried in both Java and southern Brazil. In this system, vigorous tropical **legumes** are planted and are then plowed under before food crops are cultivated. The legumes fix nitrogen in the soil, and the green manure adds organic matter to the soil. Among these legumes are *Centrosema pubescens*, *Theprosia candida*, *Pueraria javanica*, *Crotalaria* spp., and *Mimosa invisa*. The soil is continuously covered and noxious grasses such as *Imperata* are choked and suppressed. In addition, species are selected for specific location conditions. (For example, in Brazil *Theprosia candida* gives excellent results, while in Indonesia this is nearly impossible because of the presence of the *Theprosia* beetle.) Reports of nitrogen fixation in excess of two hundred kilograms of elemental nitrogen per hectare have been recorded (Mott and Popenoe 1975:30). Mulching and minimum tillage

286

(that is, tilling the row only and mulching the rest) can be integral parts of tropical agriculture since they decrease soil temperature, conserve moisture, prevent erosion, and add nutrients to the soil.

Intensive multiple cropping is a modern adaptation of aboriginal practices. Effective multiple cropping minimizes the number of days that land is idle. To date, much of the research on this method has taken place at the International Rice Research Institute (IRRI) in the Philippines, but other Rockefeller Foundation centers (for example, Centro Internacional de Agricultura Tropical (CIAT) in Colombia, International Institue of Tropical Agriculture (IITA) in Nigeria, and Instituto Interamericano de Agricultura Tropical (IIAT) in Costa Rica) are now following suit. The Philippines studies are designed around rice, given its importance in Asia, while those in Colombia are centered on manioc, corn, and beans. In the Philippines, rice is planted first during the wet season and is followed by sweet potatoes, soybeans, corn, and green soybeans. In experimental situations, twenty-two thousand kilograms per hectare of food have been produced in twelve months, a feat not possible in temperate zones where plant growth is interrupted by cold weather.

Intercropping, which is a variation of multiple cropping, is also derived from traditional systems of cultivation. Intercropping usually involves planting a tall-growing crop and one or more shorter crops. Such crop combinations can increase land productivity from 30 to 60 percent over monoculture cropping (IRRI 1973:2). Intercropping has a number of advantages: higher total light interception, better weed control, and minimal leaching. In addition, pests have a less ideal environment for major crop damage. A diverse combination of legumes, grains, and root crops presents a higher potential for both food and income productivity (IRRI 1973:15).

Another alternative management system is the development of tropical grasslands on which livestock can graze and high quality protein can be produced. Most indigenous legumes and grasses are very tolerant of the acid soils, low levels of fertility, high aluminum and manganese levels, and moisture stress that characterize many areas of the humid tropics (Mott and Popenoe 1975). Some tropical grasses seem to utilize the carbon 4 pathway of photosynthesis on the order of two to three times that of temperate grasses and tropical legumes, both of which utilize the carbon 3 pathway. Carbon 4 grasses have the facility to convert up to 5 or 6 percent of incoming solar radiation at relatively high temperatures. Yields of over fifty thousand kilograms of dry matter per hectare have been reported from such grasses as *Pennisetum purpureum* and *Panicum maximum* (Ibid.: 11). By contrast, tropical legumes and temperate grasses are in the range of twelve thousand to sixteen thousand kilograms per hectare. Carbon 4 grasses also use water much more efficiently than carbon 3 plants. Some organisms associated with grasses fix nitrogen. Dobereiner in Brazil has described such associations in *Paspalum nota-*

tum, *Pennisetum purpureum*, maize, and sugarcane. A mixture of nutritious tropical legumes and productive tropical grasses offers both soil protection and sustained yields in areas not optimal for agriculture.

All these contemporary alternatives, and many others that we lack space to discuss, are modern approaches that do not do violence to the rain forest environment, but increase its yield for man. Much research in this still relatively unknown environment is needed—particularly research of an integrated nature that combines cultural ecological studies of native systems with the scientific knowledge of forestry, agronomy, terrestrial and marine biology, and other disciplines (Janzen 1975). Such research may help to assure that we do not destroy the variety and potential of ecosystems in our efforts to feed a growing population. The hope of the present and the future lies in equal emphasis on production and conservation.

Summary

The characteristics of tropical rain forests have influenced the adaptation patterns of human populations. The climatic characteristics of the humid tropics encourage biological productivity and richness of speciation. Much of the gross primary production goes into maintenance of the complex ecosystem rather than into net production. Moreover, flowering and fruiting follow species-specific cycles that make location of food resources a difficult task without recourse to nomadism. Soils are highly variable in quality and require specialized knowledge for identification of those appropriate for intensive agriculture.

Near major rivers or along the coast, settlements have tended to be larger because of the concentration of protein resources in the aquatic environment and the relatively high returns to labor in fishing. In forested areas, away from riverine or coastal resources, nomadic hunting and gathering or swidden agriculture, combined with animal husbandry and/or hunting, have been more common. The cycle of nomadism is regulated by the relative difficulty of movement during the rainy season and by the location of culturally identified resources. Although it is possible to find groups that rely almost solely on hunting/gathering in tropical rain forests, proximity to horticultural groups and the ease of growing plants in this ecosystem have led most populations to become at least part-time cultivators.

Human populations have been relatively low, but the influence of missionaries (Nietschmann 1973), the decline in ritual practices embodying cybernetic controls over people/environment relations, improvements in health care, and the abandonment of infanticide have led to increasingly larger populations. Length of fallow and degree of intensification appear to be clearly tied to population density (Boserup 1965; Clarke 1966). Swidden agricultural technologies have been highly productive, but demographic shifts demand more intensive forms of cultivation.

In the humid tropics emphasis has been given to root crops—manioc and sweet potatoes in the Neotropics, yams in Africa, and taro in Asia. These crops yield a high output per unit of labor and per unit of land. In addition, they are pest-resistant and can be left in the ground until needed. Intensification of agriculture may proceed by converting land growing cereal to these crops; by promotion of tree agriculture, by multiple cropping, and by greater use of technological input.

Work capacity is not constrained by humid heat, but moderate and steady levels of activity enhance comfort and well-being. Avoidance of thermal midday provides rest, prevents overheating, and is socially beneficial.

The challenge of the tropical forest to human populations lies in how to make it yield more for our purposes without destroying its rich diversity. The tropical rain forest's rich pool of life forms is a biological treasure that short-term gain should not entice us into destroying. The farming systems of native rain forest populations have much to teach us about how to accomplish the dual goal of long-term sustained yields and short-term needs.

Recommended Readings

For a long time the humid tropics were neglected by nearly everyone except writers of purple prose. Their tendency to deal with the humid tropics in dramatic, and often negative, terms encouraged Marston Bates to write a book exposing the reasons for the difficulties encountered by outsiders moving to the tropics (1952). Since that time, a slow but steady flow of serious research on the humid tropics has been published. The first and still indispensable overview is that of Richards (1952, 1964).

In the 1970s interest in the humid tropics has increased dramatically and is producing a body of knowledge that is of high quality and that seriously questions long-held assumptions. The volume by Meggers (1971) stimulated much controversy by reviving the specter of environmental limits to cultural development in the humid tropics. Similar views have been voiced more recently by Goodland and Irwin (1975).

Among the less pessimistic works produced in recent years, one can cite the review of knowledge on the New World tropics by Farnworth and Golley (1974). In addition to reviewing the current state of knowledge, they explore the potential of the area for development along a variety of lines. Such development must be carefully carried out, as Denevan (1973), Gomez-Pompa (1972), and Dickinson (1972) remind us. The collection of papers in Meggers, Ayensu, and Ducksworth (1973) is an excellent compendium on ecosystem components in the tropical rain forests of South America and Africa. A more integrated coverage, but with a heavy emphasis on Africa, is the volume edited by Garlick and Keay (1977). The Asian area is still the most neglected area of the humid tropics.

The monumental series of papers in the volume by Odum and Pigeon (1970), which was generated from a long-term study on the effects of gamma radiation on the tropical forest, is an unusual work. The study was carried out in Puerto Rico and contains the most thorough collection of ecological data ever assembled on the humid tropics ecosystem. Unfortunately, this study's neglect of people makes it seen disembodied. More attuned to this subject are the studies on the effect of shifting cultivation on natural vegetation by Popenoe (1960), Nye and Greenland (1960), Moran (1975), and Smith (1976).

The complexity of the tropical rain forest ecosystem has led scientists wishing to study the human ecology of such areas to concentrate on specific problems or subsistence modes. Rappaport (1967) emphasized the role of ritual in the maintenance of a stable relationship between the people and their environment. Conklin (1957) focused on the finely tuned environmental knowledge of a Philippine population and contrasted it with the more predatory agricultural practices of migrant populations. Nietschmann (1973) discussed the advantages of a zone between land and water, focusing on the diversified subsistence that was possible. Moran (1975;1976) and Smith (1976) studied an area suddenly opened to an onrush of migrants and tried to measure both the constraints and the success or failure of the migrants as they adjusted to a totally different environment.

An important debate in the literature has been over the availability of animal protein in the forest. Meggers (1971) argued that the low densities of populations that prehistorically inhabited the uplands suggested that animal protein was limited. Chagnon (1968) seemed to agree with this conclusion. A synthesis article by Gross (1975) gathered the studies available and postulated that shortage of animal protein might have been more significant than any other factor in determining the settlement pattern of lowland South America. Vickers (1976) questioned this hypothesis by showing how a lowland Ecuador population was successful in hunting and postulated that the problem may be more a lack of adequate data than any major difference in substance.

The humid tropics are still a fertile area for investigators. The complex factors that are involved have not begun to be penetrated, and many geographical areas have not even been discovered by investigators. The ecological effect of forest simplification by modern cultivators is one of the many ecological processes that merit serious and immediate attention from researchers. Knowledge of the epidemiological and nutritional aspects of such change is urgently needed.

Part

3

Past Problems
and New
Directions

New Directions
in Human
Adaptability
Research

The preceding pages have presented a view of ecological study that identifies critical problems to permanent human habitation in various ecosystems and focuses on the nongenetic means of human adaptability. Such an approach, we believe, puts the focus where it belongs—on human beings solving problems. It also suggests a methodology that simulates the way most humans cope with their surroundings—that is, one first becomes aware of a constraint posed by the surrounding physical environment on the well-being of the human population. One then suggests hypotheses about the causes of the stress. Strategies are tested based on (1) their congruence with current practices, (2) their perceived costs, (3) their expected benefits, and (4) the social pressures that may be brought to bear in favor of one or another solution.

The true focus of human ecology is to understand and explain the strategies of human populations in ecosystems—how they are affected by the environment and how, in turn, they shape it and change it. Obviously this becomes a never-ending task. As soon as a population interacts with its physical environment, it brings about modifications that will make the physical environment just that much different for all other users. It is a dynamic process and, as such, poses a particular challenge to any modeling or predictive effort. A model, in summarizing the relationship between variables, may become a static construct. In ecological modeling, one must be particularly careful to include factors that explain changes in rates of flow in the system, as well as changes in relationships between system parts.

Increasingly, the biomes under scrutiny will not be pristine, but will instead consist of radically modified ecosystems; and their inhabitants will not be isolated populations finely attuned to their local habitat, but a mixed population aware of, and affected by, national and international affairs. Issues such as how our species evolved from a hunting/gathering to an agricultural way of life will continue to be the focus of ecological study. More researchers, however, will begin to deal with the contemporary adaptation of people to their surroundings, with human adaptation to stresses posed by natural hazards, and with the adjustment of populations to modified habitats—as in the case of populations in urban and developing areas.

One conclusion that should be evident to the reader of this book is that human adaptability research is optimally a task for team effort. Dual competence, at least, should be achieved to facilitate dialogue within a team and a multidisciplinary systems approach. Such dual competence might take the form of expertise in, for example, cultural geography and soil science or in social anthropology and epidemiology. The preceding chapters serve as an introduction to the multidisciplinary approach to human adaptability research, although many relevant fields could not be included because of the limitations of space and the author's own disciplinary limitations.

The most important task of ecological scientists in the years ahead will be to seek greater integration. Among the exceptions to the single scientist tradition of research are the studies of the Harvard Kalahari group (Lee and DeVore 1976) and of the United States IBP human adaptability teams (see Baker and Little 1976; Jamison, Zegura, and Milan 1978). For most ecosystems there is still need of a great deal of basic data. Therefore, in this chapter we will try to point out some of the important questions that call for immediate and long-term research efforts. The discussion follows the order of preceding chapters, beginning with the one in methods. A brief discussion of urban ecology surveys past research efforts and suggests the research potential of urban ecosystems.

New Directions in Research Methods

The toolbox of the human ecologist varies with the biome and the problem to be researched. The IBP program facilitated the international acceptance of standardized research methods and procedures for human biology so that research results could be compared most effectively (Weiner and Lourie 1969; and Yoshimura and Weiner 1966). Similar efforts should be attempted in other areas. Scientists studying agricultural societies might try to standardize their soil sampling procedures and laboratory analyses. Acceptance of an international system of soil classification would also enhance comparability of data across nations, although the lack of success of soil scientists in agreeing on an international soil taxonomy should forewarn us of the difficulties of the task. An organization, such as a "society for the anthropological study of agrarian societies," might promote standardization by organizing symposia for this purpose. Demographically oriented ecologists might seek comparable standardization of techniques without abandoning the search for more innovative approaches.

Increased communication between ecologically minded scientists is necessary if more sophisticated and complete models of people/environment interactions are to be produced. Efforts at modeling whole ecosystems, including the human population, are relatively recent. Most of the work has consisted of fitting data to the classical models of Elton (1927) and Lindeman (1942)—that is, to solar-driven systems made up of producers, herbivores, carnivores, and decomposers (Crawley 1973:134). Even the best efforts have consisted largely of either qualitative models or nonsimulated quantitative ones (for example, Rappaport 1971a; Kemp 1971; Waddell 1972; Nietschmann 1973). The reason is clear: the task of modeling a whole ecosystem is gargantuan and its payoffs uncertain. For the model to be *complete*, in any sense of the term, each process must be studied and rate equations developed to describe the interaction of each component with every other (Crawley 1973:135).

Most researchers choose to simplify by selecting the most sensitive aspects of the system. This can best be done by selecting small systems that can later be synthesized into larger efforts—but it must be clear from the start that this is the strategy and that synthesis will be attempted at a later date. Such a small system is best defined by a particular question about the relationships in an ecosystem, which results in an emphasis on processes, such as rate of photosynthesis or nutrient cycling. More emphasis is placed on the distances between parts and control mechanisms, rather than on the classical four compartments and macrolevel flows between them. This question-oriented approach to modeling permits a greater degree of sophistication and may further our knowledge of system properties (that is, stability, diversity, and hierarchical structures) beyond that provided by earlier efforts using too broad a "macroscope."

An example of how an ecologically oriented team proceeds in studying human response to drought might help in understanding the methodology of human adaptability research. The literature on drought is fairly extensive and would need to be consulted at the outset. Most of this literature deals with climatic and definitional problems of what constitutes drought. Some geographical research has been carried out on human perception of, and responses to, drought. A few references are available from sociology on community-level responses and institutional assistance to drought-affected populations. Anthropological literature on people inhabiting dry areas is extensive, although it does not focus on drought responses.

From this search for a broad set of considerations, researchers might generate a question or a set of questions about human adaptability: (1) Do individuals join or leave the group as dry conditions grow into drought? (2) Which features of social life or of cultural information enhance the adaptiveness of individuals or the group? (3) Do changes in social structure during drought lead to permanent changes in group structure or does the traditional structure return once drought conditions end? (4) How do individuals and groups respond to various magnitudes, durations, and types of stress?

From each of the above questions one can generate a subsystem model and postulate the probable dominant relationships (or driving functions). For example, from the first question, which is actually based on the general problem of fission/fusion responses to stress, one can include considerations of aridity, group evaluation of arid conditions, family-level responses to prevalent climatic and economic conditions, community-wide responses, resort to institutional or external assistance, migratory or trade responses, changes in management practices, rate of emigration as a function of aridity and so forth.

For each of these considerations various categories of data must be found or collected. The nature of the problem and the specific questions that it entails help define the sort of team that must be assembled to research and analyze it. The type of team that is assembled will cause further modifications in the model and in the sorts of data that will be sought to elucidate the question and provide valid answers. Throughout this process one seeks to make increasingly realistic and more useful assumptions about the relevant aspects of the model so that the resulting theoretical explanation will account for a large variety of facts and permit more precise predictions.

While the ultimate goal of most science is the development of grand theory, the greatest need we have is for "middle-range theory"—i.e., theory that attempts to explain particular kinds of phenomena with clear sets of interrelated hypotheses able to account for apparently diverse phenomena. The simple associations generated by general or broad theory are in themselves insufficient. They require the specificity of middle-range theory to adequately explain the particular characteristics of observable phenomena. That human adaptability to stress follows a stepwise response gradient constitutes a general theoretical pronouncement, but it tells us little about human responses. The specific responses to cold stress, heat stress, crowding stress, and altitude stress must be elucidated and middle-range theories generated. An example of such specific elucidation and theory is the finding that human adaptability to cold stress relies more heavily on the physiological response of peripheral blood flow than on cultural means to protect the extremities.

Human adaptability research has so far walked a fine line between pure and applied research. Because this type of research is concerned with problems in human coping, applications are usually found for research findings. Problems that do not lend themselves to applications must also be clarified since they are important in understanding the systemic nature of human responses.

New Directions in Arctic Research

In chapter 5 we noted that the crucial problems for arctic populations are coping with extreme and prolonged cold, low productivity of the land, extremes of light and darkness, and snow cover for two-thirds of the year. It also was noted that arctic Eskimos or Inuit adapt primarily by social and cultural strategies—with a relatively minor dependence on physiological responses. Housing and shelter create inner environments of relative comfort. Socially the Inuit rely on sharing strategies enforced by cultural norms. They compensate for the low productivity of the land by exploiting sea mammals, fish, and migrating animals. A great deal of the socialization effort centers on educating the child in the art of observation—how to note differences in ice and snow, to interpret winds and other climatic indicators, and to learn the behavior of the animals on which life has depended.

Physiologically, nonshivering thermogenesis protects the body core temperature; high rate of peripheral blood flow to the extremities prevents injury and enhances manual dexterity; and high core to shell conductance complements a slightly higher BMR in protecting the body. Problems such as arctic hysteria, or *pibloktok*, during winter months are still not well understood, but appear to be tied to calcium homeostasis failure as a result of the light and dark pattern of the arctic and a low calcium, high phosphorus diet.

Despite the high quality of recent human ecological research, the data available is limited to a few geographic locations in the arctic. Efforts comparable to those carried out by the International Biological Program in northwest Alaska are needed in the Aleutians and similar intertidal areas—given the contrast in life expectancy and age structure that emerges from some demographic studies (Laughlin 1972).

Simulations using energy flow measurements would fail at the outset without improved measurements of the amount of energy fixed by plants and the amount of energy and nutrients making their way into the arctic environment through upwelling. It is necessary to have a better understanding of how the timing and functions of religious practices are tied to ecological and cybernetic functions. We need to establish whether religion still functions as a conservationist force through myth and folklore, and, if lost, whether it is possible and desirable to bring this to the attention of the Inuit as an important priority in Inuit cultural revival efforts.

The Inuit, and some scientists as well, would argue that the Inuit way of life is intimately tied to the hunt. As hunting and perhaps even whaling decline, it is crucial to monitor the direction of social and cultural change. In areas where pipeline activities decline or disappear, it will be important to study the readjustment of the Inuit. Can they survive without the subsidies to which they grew accustomed? Do they leave the area and follow the pipeline? Burch (1975) mentions the revival of kinship networks through the use of technology in the arctic. Further research on this phenomenon is needed to establish what the functions of the new networks are and whether they are implicated in Inuit out-migration to continental cities or whether they will enhance the survival of the Inuit as an arctic population.

In chapter 5, it was argued that most of the effects of these changes on human adaptability are for the worse, but we also noted a decline in tuberculosis and other respiratory ailments. If the provision of subsidies from outside and the Inuit use of watches and non-native schools have minimized the biological effects of the arctic light and dark pattern, does this mean that there has been a decline in arctic hysteria? Has there been an overall decline in mental stress and insecurity as a result of outside subsidies or has there been an increase as a result of cultural disorganization, loss of dignity, and changing patterns of family relationships? To what extent is middle ear disease implicated in the learning disabilities of Inuit schoolchildren? How do the Inuit perceive opportunities in the arctic today? These are all important questions for research.

The serious problem of old age bone loss may slowly disappear if the diet is less reliant on animal protein and more reliant on enriched flour, sugars, and vegetables. Many beneficial changes clearly result from the availability of imported foods. However, in the more isolated areas of the arctic where such imports are not available, it is important to continue studying the effect of population growth on the ability of the environment to sustain larger numbers of people. As in the case of the Lapps, increased market involvement may lead to a rapid decline in the animal population and to the inability of the environment to sustain dense human population.

Many of the gaps identified by Laughlin (1966) and Hildes (1966) have been filled by the recent synthesis from the IBP (Jamison, Zegura, and Milan, 1978). However, the social and cultural aspects of human adaptability have not been adequately researched, and more work following up on the baseline studies of Spencer (1959), Nelson (1969), and Birket-Smith (1959) is sorely needed.

New Directions in High Altitude Research

Research on human adaptation to high altitudes is among the most advanced, given the length of time the problem has been studied and the team effort that this type of research has always pursued. In chapter 6 we noted that the crucial problem for populations inhabiting high altitude zones is hypoxia. Other problems associated with high altitude are cold stress, aridity, low biological productivity, pulmonary disease, reduced reproductive success, and a high level of solar radiation.

As in the arctic, researchers have found little evidence of genetic adaptation. Most of the mechanisms for coping with the biological stress of low oxygen pressure are physiological: increased pulmonary ventilation, decreased alveolar-arterial oxygen gradient, polycythemia, enlargement of the capillary bed, and chemical-enzymatic changes related to internal respiration. Cold stress is handled by use of warm clothing and shelter, by scheduling of activities to allow maximum time out in the sun, and by the physiological adjustments of nonshivering thermogenesis and increased blood flow to the extremities when these are exposed. The Andean population copes with the low productivity of its environment by complex intrazonal trade along an altitude gradient, by seasonal migration, and by prescriptions of zonal intermarriage. To increase the efficiency of energy usage, children are assigned many tasks given to adults in other cultures. Preservation techniques, such as freeze-drying potatoes, allow the population to store food for lean times.

Further research should clarify the functions of village exogamy and regional endogamy: the spacing and distributing of kinsmen over a broader ecosystem need to be carefully analyzed. How are spacing and distribution tied to the exploitation of "islands of resources" and to intra-zonal exchange networks? How are children socialized into recognizing the importance of these intrazonal trade networks? Perhaps most important of all is the need for more data on human adaptation to high altitude zones other than the Andes, where most of the research has taken place. Research on the Himalayan Sherpas has been slow in becoming available. Useful data on Himalayan responses can be found in Ward (1975), but most of the volume deals with Western mountain climbers' responses.

High altitude populations have been of special interest to investigators because of the relative isolation from national institutions possible in the valleys and peaks of mountains. That isolation, however, has never been complete and it is increasingly being broken down. In most cases, the impact is felt primarily among the high altitude dwellers who migrate to the lowlands, but national school systems, health services, and other institutions are making their presence felt and may lead to the same abandonment of adaptive practices noted in the arctic. For example, the work of Brooke Thomas on energy flow in the Andes has convincingly shown that the assignment of pastoral activities to children saves a family nearly one hundred thousand kcals per year (1973). The participation of children in the regular school hours of the Peruvian educational system will remove them from such work and their labor will have to be assumed by adults. This will cost families not only an added one hundred thousand kcals, but also the value of books, uniforms, and other school requirements. Whether the sparse environment can yield those extra calories is questionable at this point.

The migration of highlanders to the lowlands may be partially explained in terms of the perception of greater potential yields at lower altitudes. The work of Winterhalder and Thomas (1974) might be expanded into a more complete accounting of the vertical transfer of dung, crops, coca, and other crucial crops necessary for a productive system. The work of Thomas (1973; 1976) has laid a solid basis for more sophisticated mathematical modeling and simulation efforts capable of predicting ecosystem processes and of fostering improved management of mountain zones.

Further work is also necessary on the biology of human adaptability to altitude. We need studies to better explain how natives hyperventilate without an associated rise in BMR; to establish whether there is a critical age at which migration must occur if one is to achieve maximum aerobic capacity (as has been suggested by work to date); to illuminate the effects of a high carbohydrate diet on work endurance at high altitude and the effects of changes in diet on that endurance; and to test Burchard's thesis that coca chewing helps overcome problems of carbohydrate malabsorption. Much of the research in the past has focused on single stresses. To further our contemporary understanding, research should focus on multiple stresses since adaptation to one stress may influence positively or negatively one's ability to respond to another stress factor.

New Directions in Arid Lands Research

The key constraints to habitation in arid lands are unpredictable and infrequent precipitation, high daytime temperatures, and the need to conserve available water despite high rates of evaporation. Human adaptation to these areas centers on how to find water, how to schedule activities to minimize the body's heat load and water losses, and how to organize as social units to exploit a scarce and seasonally spaced resource. Human strategies have concentrated on the management of surface and underground water resources. Individual survival is assured by acclimatory adjustments such as diminished pulse rate, reduced salt concentration in sweat, and increased rates of insensible perspiration. The shift from migratory to sedentary settlement of arid lands is accompanied by increased use of technology to exploit groundwater, to harness runoff, or to divert water from rivers to agricultural fields.

Arid lands are currently the focus of attention because of the Sahelian crisis that brought death to so many people and their herds. Many of the semiarid lands of the world are becoming increasingly arid, and the danger of desertification makes research efforts of more than passing significance. A major portion of the lands of the earth are arid or semiarid, and management of these areas is increasingly important. Much of the current management effort tends to neglect the prehistoric and contemporary forms of coping with limited water supplies by peoples native to these areas. Future research must try to test the accuracy of past strategies and determine the point at which past systems broke down. There is evidence that irrigation systems and runoff systems ran into trouble when they tried to control too large a watershed or to irrigate areas too large to permit careful monitoring of the water table. Contemporary efforts to manage arid lands seem to share this technological optimism.

The thrust of research from a human adaptability perspective must be on management of population density that is in accord with the availability of resources. Predicting at what points given densities of population will cause irreparable damage to an ecosystem and endanger the survival of the population should be an important goal. Both limitations of capital and the comparative advantages of various systems must be considered if we are to arrive at sensible approaches to the future use of arid lands.

303

Migration together with long-distance trading has always been an important strategy of populations in areas with widely scattered resources. How these systems operate and how they facilitate the adaptation of the desert populations is still inadequately understood. Among the questions that call for immediate answer are: How many nodes in a trade network are required to assure long-term survival? How are decisions made concerning the distance to be traveled and how are costs, benefits, and obligations weighed in such decisions? How are transactions timed in terms of the prevalent climatic conditions?

Since Wittfogel's initial study, research on irrigation systems has raised the question of the relative merits of centralized versus decentralized controls over irrigation works. Although decisions on these matters may be viewed as beyond the hands of those involved, in fact they are not. Firmer evidence is needed to establish the conditions under which centralized control is counterproductive and the conditions under which it is the best solution possible.

New Directions in Grasslands Research

Human populations in grasslands have had to cope with problems in the location of water and pasture, the establishment of workable relationships with agriculturalists, and the balancing of herd size and composition with the size and composition of their own population. Until recent pressure on land forced more intensive efforts at improving pastures, nomadism was the most common means of obtaining an adequate supply of water and pasture. Size and composition of herds reflect the food needs of the herding population and their requisities for trade with neighbors. Relationships between herder and farmer fluctuate between tension and mutualism. Each side needs the other's resources, but each vies for gains in the exchange rates and in the expansion of territory under its direct control.

Research on both tropical and temperate grasslands is heir to the compartmentalized aspects of disciplinary research. There is excellent data on types of range grasses, on social groups in grasslands, on herding ideology, and on alliance systems. However, there is very little that truly integrates all these aspects and that provides hard facts to support the conclusions.

Grasslands, particularly those in the tropics, currently face increased pressure from people and their livestock. This pressure is the result of improved health services, restriction of warfare, and international aid. Human adaptability research needs to follow the interaction between these variables and their systemic impact upon the capacity of the environment to sustain the increasingly larger population. The end of famine, war, and disease as factors in population control means that some other mechanism must replace them or that new methods of making these semiarid areas productive must be found. These are issues that affect vast numbers of people and they demand immediate attention.

The temperate grasslands have become increasingly productive, but only because of an intensive capital and energy cost. The value of the product (that is, meat) has justified such expenditures, and cheap sources have made it possible. With the increased price of energy inputs and the reevaluation of the dietary value of beef in human nutrition, these intensive paths may be less popular, in which case new alternatives to the use of these lands will have to be found.

More so than other ecosystems, the grasslands have long been sensitive to the fluctuations of the market. Greater attention needs to be given to the cues used in determining the appropriate times for selling animals; the process of deciding how many females or males to have in a herd; the conditions under which populations eat their animals or withhold them from market; and to the conditions under which populations shift to farming.

Most research tends to have a very limited time depth. This results from the conditions of research funding and the inadequacy of data collected with objectives other than resource management and adaptability. However, for several regions of the globe there are now over one hundred years of good climatic data and good historical accounts. What is lacking is an analysis of the changes in grassland management over time. The alternative uses of grassland are relatively few in number, and such work might help to determine the thresholds for different human choices and the willingness to pay the costs of overcoming impending stress.

New Directions in Humid Tropic Research

In chapter 9 we noted that the greatest constraint to the human use of humid tropical areas is the diversity and complexity of the biome. Other important constraints are the high levels of precipitation, humidity, and ambient temperature; lack of seasonality; and the vigor of secondary succession. Little research on physiological responses to the humid tropics has been carried out, but results thus far suggest that insensible sweat evaporation and reduced heart rates at moderate levels of activity are useful. Most of the adaptations to heat are social and cultural: open design in housing, usually located on a bluff overlooking a river or the sea; minimal use of clothing; low sodium diets; and tasks adjusted to the pattern of solar insolation.

Near major rivers, the population copes with diversity by specializing in a limited number of abundant resources—fish rather than game—and by cutting and burning the forest to plant crops. To cope with the diversity of pests, weeds, and high levels of sunlight and rain, fields are planted in a variety of crops often of different heights. This planting pattern prompted Geertz (1963) to describe it as an imitation of the natural forest. Populations away from major streams may also cultivate crops, but their dependence on game makes the size of settlements generally smaller and more subject to fissioning. Fissioning serves to distribute people over the forest and to prevent overexploitation of wild plants and game.

The great challenge to human ecological research in the humid tropics lies in discovering how to disturb the natural ecosystem for the benefit of the human population without jeopardizing the complex set of life forms that are found there. Numerous countries are encouraging both human settlement of the rain forest and large-scale exploitation by multinational enterprises. Most of the African rain forest is gone and irrecoverable, but large areas of the Malayan and South American forests remain intact. The complexity of the biome is scarcely known, much less understood. The simple notions that we had in the past about tropical soils and laterite have given way to an appreciation of the great variety of soils present and of the site-specific research that will be required to manage this vast biome (National Academy of Science 1972; Sanchez 1976). A volume appeared in 1974 summarizing existing knowledge of and providing research priorities for the Neotropics (Farnworth and Golley 1974). Similar recapitulations are needed for the Asian and African tropics.

The complex systems of rivers in rain forests teem with fish that can play an important role in regional development. Commercial fishing should be controlled so that the rich bounty of tropical rivers can enhance the diets of local populations, rather than exit to markets where abundant protein is already available and where these important resources may be wasted as pet foods and other such superfluous luxuries. Research should be an integral part of the development of fisheries so that the most productive approach to the exploitation of these valuable resources can be taken.

Research on new domesticants should continue. We seem content with the animals domesticated long ago, without investing effort in breeding new animals with a potential for high yields and with local adaptations that might minimize veterinarian cost and special diets. Research on domesticated capybara (*Hydrochoerus hydrochoeris*) in Brazil has produced evidence that such breeding is possible (SUDAM 1971). In addition, river turtles have been successfully raised in captivity in Brazil (Smith 1974b). Research on the potential of the manatee as a domesticated or managed species also shows some promise.

Another fruitful avenue for research and development lies in the field of food engineering. Many tropical crops can be commercialized so that they not only feed local populations, but also compete successfully with less productive crops. Manioc, which has been known to replace barley in England when barley prices have risen, is an example of such a crop. Tapioca, a by-product of manioc, has long been an important mild dessert. Aroids (*Xanthossoma* spp. and *Colocassia* spp.) are known to have the most easily digestible starch and could become important foods in temperate regions, among an increasingly nervous and ulcerous population of post-Industrial times. These root crops produce, without fertilizer input, yields of eight to fifteen tons per hectare. The production of cashews and Brazil nuts, already favorite items on the cocktail circuit, could be increased and marketed more effectively. Tropical fruits could add natural flavors to our growing taste for ice creams and natural food drinks. Drinks and brandies made from exotic fruits could induce development of the kind of tree agriculture that makes use of the less fertile soils of the tropics. Richer soils could be intensively cultivated with multicropping and intercropping methods, using plants that have natural adaptations to the local conditions.

Studies of aboriginal societies in the tropical rain forest have yielded interesting insights into the productivity of traditional agroecosystems, and ways must be found to achieve comparable stability and yields over larger areas. Numerous wild plants and animals might be domesticated and made more productive in their familiar habitat. The size of forest biological reserves needs to be studied so that maximum protection may be attained. The impact of river basin development upon the life forms currently present and the impact of human use on these areas need to be further assessed. The inaccessibility of many humid tropical areas has prevented the collection of climatological data. Aiding in the establishment of collection for this data should be a research priority as this knowledge is essential to the understanding and prediction of ecological processes. Assessments are needed on the impact of the construction of roads and other transportation networks, of mining, tourism, and other types of land use. The impact of urbanization and industrialization merits special attention because of the scale of damage that could result. The Brazilian Amazon merits particularly close study because of the scale of development underway there.

Few of the studies carried out in South America in the past have included the painstaking collection of ecological knowledge possesed by the native peoples. The case has not been much different in Africa and Asia. Studies usually chose to concentrate on the major crops and animals and neglected to record, or to present in much detail, the utilization of the less important, but possibly crucial plants used for medicinal and other nonfood purposes. Many of the foods native to the tropics are unusually productive and nutritious, as a recent National Academy of Science publication made clear (NAS 1976). Exploration of the utilization of these plants, as opposed to non-native plants, will require careful experimentation under field conditions.

Except for malaria and yellow fever, which at one time affected temperate regions, most health problems of tropical populations are restricted to the tropics and have therefore failed to interest medical researchers in areas with greater research funds. Even those tropical diseases that have received attention are still not adequately understood, and new vectors are found whenever studies go beyond what is already known. Many of the health problems of the humid tropics are related to people creating habitats for the disease vectors——for example, standing water near roads, exposed trash and sewage, and defecation near water sources.

If necessary research tasks are to be carried out, the researcher will need improved training in botany, zoology, and in tropical ecology. Seminars exploring the advantages and disadvantages of various sampling techniques when applied to the tropical rain forest would be particularly valuable. Time spent at the Organization of Tropical Studies in Costa Rica and Panama——or similar institutes elsewhere that are dedicated to the study of lowland tropical regions——would also be very useful. The diversity of the tropical rain forest calls for a sizable team of experts from a variety of fields who are prepared to discuss the problems on a continuous basis.

Much of the impetus in the development of tropical rain forests comes from nationalistic governments wanting to make a claim to these territories that often hold significant reserves of raw materials. Any ecological effort in humid tropics will have to take into account these political forces and include them in the simulations of ecosystem management. Leaders of such nations will need clear proof that there are alternatives to the ways in which they are carrying out their development of the lowland tropics.

Urban Ecology

Urban populations are not currently an important focus of human adaptability research. This situation reflects the traditional preoccupation of ecological scientists with "natural systems" and the avoidance of what is correctly perceived as a system too complex for precise analysis. The study of human adaptability to urban areas thus represents yet another new direction for ecological and anthropological research. The field of urban ecology has attracted mainly sociologists, architects, environmental engineers, geographers, and psychologists. As one might expect, these disciplines have concentrated on problems best handled by their respective tools: the social structure of urban populations, the physical design of urban structures, the handling of urban material flows, the design of urban transportation networks, and the psychological effects of crowding on small groups and individuals. What has been lacking is a broader and more holistic attempt at dealing with the interaction of cities with their supporting natural environment.

The City as Consumer Cities are human-created ecosystems that have a tendency to consume power produced by natural ecosystems and to allocate power from a self-serving point of view (Michelson 1976:50). Urban growth has been so spectacular in this century that urban areas are rapidly becoming the dominant settlement pattern throughout the earth (McLoughlin 1969:15). Cities concentrate power and increase the rate at which energy is consumed, as reflected in the per capita energy consumption of modern cities vis-a-vis the rates estimated for earlier stages of cultural evolution.

Any society depends on two kinds of energy sources: somatic and extrasomatic. Somatic energy comes to human populations via the food chain. Extrasomatic energy, on the other hand, comes from harnessing the energy found in fossil fuels, wood, wind, water, tides, radioactive materials, and heat from the sun and the earth's core (Man and the Biosphere/UNESCO 1973:14). Preindustrial cities relied primarily on somatic energy and the limited power that could be obtained from wind, water, and animals. This has radically changed in recent years and the industrial cities of our time rely on enormous inputs of extrasomatic energy to subsidize their growth in size and in complexity.

The development of urban society is clearly associated in the archaeological record with the introduction of food production as recently as five thousand years ago (Sjoberg 1965). Before cities became political and economic centers of power controlled by elites, the provisioning of urban needs probably took place through interzonal exchange and redistributing mechanisms supported by patterns of marriage and kinship. These did not differ much from the patterns of exchange of rural Andean populations discussed in chapter 6. The earliest cities seem to have been more like nodes in regional networks than control centers (Adams 1968:42–48).

In studying cities one must keep in mind a number of ecologically significant characteristics that recur time and again. One characteristic is the illusion of self-sufficiency. From the earliest city to the largest megalopolis, urban dwellers have acted as if their existence were not dependent on the rural environments that provided them with somatic energy sources. This was sometimes translated into demands that could not be fulfilled without seriously threatening the natural environment. In numerous cases the results were soil exhaustion or overirrigation—the latter leading to soil salinization and a breakdown in the food production system (Ibid.: 54).

The utilization of extrasomatic energy sources is another urban characteristic and can lead to an even greater oversight. Because they import their food and energy needs from distant areas, urbanites fail to see the environmental consequences of their demands. Until very recently, cities have relied on the surrounding natural areas for the disposal of urban wastes. It is only the scale of urbanization and of the communications revolution that has led to a reconsideration of this policy. Although causal relationships have not been clearly established, the dimensions of modern industrial cities appear to be associated with a variety of forms of system disorganization, crowding pathologies, and pollution levels that threaten their existence. Part of the problem is the very complexity of urban ecosystems.

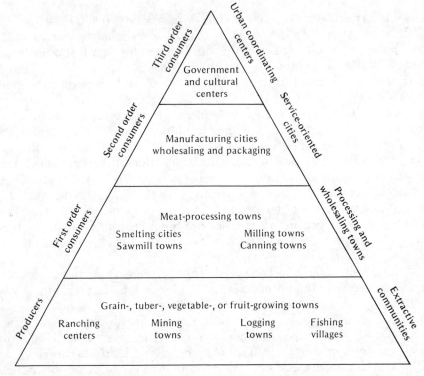

Figure 10.1   **Urban Trophic Levels**

Source: Reprinted with permission of Macmillan Publishing Co., Inc. from The *Urban Organism* by Spencer Havlick. Copyright © 1974 Spencer W. Havlick.

Urban regions participate in food webs that reflect the upward flow of energy and materials from "producer communities" controlling cultural and administrative centers, or "third-order consumers." Figure 10.1 illustrates these trophic levels and reminds us of the danger of having consumer cities continually encroaching on the productive lands that support the whole urban ecosystem. The utility of this approach to urban analysis has not been fully demonstrated, but any effort at quantifying the flow of energy through urban ecosystems can benefit from this kind of trophic level approach (Havlick 1974:27).

Industrial urban settlements can also be viewed as a "climax" stage of human succession, similar in characteristics to the later stages of forest development (R. L. Smith 1974:284). The urban settlement begins as a small village or central core and grows outward—just as a forest invades abandoned fields. Over time, the city undergoes a process of segregation of both social and functional units. In this segregation process, zones with specialized functions or dominant social groups are developed. The central core deteriorates in the middle stage and becomes less desirable, while the younger outer zones become more attractive, expensive, and exclusive. The central area, if sufficiently deteriorated, must be ravaged by fire or "wrecking ball" to bring it to a younger, more productive stage of succession, similar to the positive effect of fire in a natural community (Ibid.: 285). Most ecology books deal with urban areas in terms of this "climax" stage approach and are based on the concepts of the Chicago human ecologists.

The Chicago Urban Ecology Approach   The earliest systematic effort at formulating an urban ecology came from University of Chicago sociologists Robert Park and Roderick McKenzie. Although there had been earlier efforts that sought correlations between social variables and spatial distributions, the Chicago sociologists were the first to approach the topic with a systematic theory. The theory was borrowed from biology—particularly the notion of competitive cooperation. According to Park the subject of human ecological research consisted of *biotic* relationships: competition for space leading to the formation of cooperative bonds or symbiotic relationships (Park et al. 1925). As these change over time and space, successional forces come into play, dominance changes, and groups invade either unoccupied or deteriorated areas. Park saw the other aspect of human society, the *cultural*, as a superstructure resting on the biotic forces. This superstructure included the various symbols and meanings used in human communication to achieve consensus. Only the biotic level was seen as the proper object of study for human ecology (Theodorson 1961:4). Thus Park believed that the biological concepts of competition, dominance, invasion, and succession were applicable to human organization and behavior in cities.[1] These concepts seem to define real forces that govern and make sense of natural areas or territories in the American city (Michelson 1976:8).

Perhaps the best known of the spatial models is associated with Burgess of the Chicago ecologist school. His "concentric zones" model was an attempt at describing urban structure and development in North America. The model emphasized the dominance of the central business district (that is, the oldest section) and the gradual filtering outward of populations as they improved their status, income, and level of assimilation (Herbert 1972:70). The model is exemplified in Burgess's explanation of the concentration of vice and gambling just outside of urban central business districts. Burgess showed how the central business district has the highest urban land values and how speculators purchase properties on the periphery of the district in the hopes of the city expanding. In the meantime, the speculators do not improve the buildings and this dilapidated housing becomes the home of recent migrants and deviants who cannot afford homes elsewhere (Michelson 1976:9). Although Burgess's concentric zones model tends to be

---

[1]The best account of the foundation of the Chicago approach to human ecology is in Burgess and Bogue (1964:2-14). Useful, too, are the summaries by Robson (1969) and Quinn (1940).

overly general, it is still a useful point of reference for testing hypotheses and for developing new models—particularly those that attempt to find spatial variation among interrelated social variables (Theodorson 1961:7).

Michelson (1976:17) has noted that the human ecologists had an incomplete conceptualization of the environment—that is, they viewed it as a *social* medium rather than as a variable. Because the urban ecologists were fixed on the use of aggregate data, they treated urban dwellers as undifferentiated masses ruled by economic forces. Again because of their need for aggregate data, they often turned to economic data for the development of indicators, which resulted in an all too frequent *economic* explanation of urban phenomena.[2] The concentration of the Chicago group on the arrangement of social aggregates in space as a result of competition led to the erection of interdisciplinary barriers between these sociologists and biology and ecology that ultimately isolated them from the biological theories that had given birth to their approach.

An Ecosystem Approach to Urban Ecology The need for a holistic approach to urban ecology can hardly be argued, but some authors doubt whether such an approach can be applied to larger, more complex urban areas. (Stearns and Montag 1974:28). Forrester has pointed out that there are limits to the human capacity to manage complex systems. Complex systems, he says, are *counterintuitive*—that is, the evident control centers may not be the true ones, and efforts at control are likely to elicit ineffective, or even adverse, actions (1969:9). Simple systems rely on first-order negative feedback loops (see figure 1.1). Such loops usually have only one important variable, and cause and effect relations are immediate in time and space. However, in complex systems cause and effect are not closely related in time and space. Instead, a multiplicity of interacting positive and negative feedback loops are involved, and rates of flow are usually nonlinear functions.

Some urban analysts believe that simulation models can overcome the difficulties of applying a holistic approach to a complex system (Lapatra 1973; Stearns and Montag 1974), but Schwartz and Foin (1972) point out that some modeling approaches err in viewing human beings as rational—that is, as seeking and using all available information to achieve desired states. How often does a city council take into account all possible consequences of an industrial permit before granting it? More often than not, the decision is a simple matter of weighing the contribution of the industry to the city in terms of jobs, taxes, and political support, with some limited verbal assurances that the industry will try to comply with environmental prescriptions.

Despite the evidence of a growth crisis, few humans see the seriousness

[2]Firey (1945) showed how historical, cultural, symbolic, and sentimental aspects associated with Boston's Beacon Hill district invalidated the mechanistic evolution of the central business district and the primacy of economic considerations in urban development.

of the threat. Human adaptation to the environment traditionally has been a slow process. Yet, in the last fifty years human populations have consumed most of the petroleum that took millions of years to create and generated a previously unknown volume of waste products. It is for this reason that Harrison and Gibson (1976) speak of the danger of cities as being based on the uncontrolled *pace* of change. Population has increased so rapidly that we do not yet understand how it happened nor what we can realistically do to reverse the trend.

Dubos (1968a:235) reminds us that human adaptation is frequently shortsighted. Inhabitants of industrialized urban areas have been able to adapt, even cheerfully, to the polluted air. We know that the body adapts to these pollutants by increased mucous secretion and other inflammatory responses that protect the organism; but the constant exposure to the irritating substances leads to chronic pathological states, such as emphysema, fibrosis, and other "aging" phenomena (Ibid.: 236). In short, adaptation masks the seriousness of the problem, isolates the individual from seeking a solution to the problem, and lowers the long-term healthfulness of the individual.

Urban Health Stresses   The change from a rural to an urban existence is accompanied by changes in eating habits, activity patterns, and increased probability of exposure to contagious diseases. Studies of the complex biomedical interactions that impinge upon the well-being of urban populations have been made, but only occasionally have they had an ecological framework (Man and the Biosphere/UNESCO 1973:38). Because of the complexity of the factors that may be implicated, evidence has been slow in demonstrating that urban living involves biological and physiological hazards. Urbanization has been with us long enough to make one think of some pathologies as normal. The increase of blood pressure with age noted in Europe and North America was thought to be normal until it was shown that in other societies with different lifestyles, this did not occur (Harrison and Gibson 1976:3). Because the urban environment is so new and changes occur so rapidly, it is likely to impose unusually high levels of physiological, biochemical, and psychosocial stress.

Significant changes in the nutritional status of a population occur with urbanization or with exposure to an urban lifestyle. Diseases such as diabetes, obesity, coronary heart disease, and dental caries increase with adoption of urban lifestyles (Durnin 1976:129). A worldwide pattern, originally noticed in the United Kingdom, seems to be that with rising income and urbanization, an increased proportion of the total food energy budget of individuals is derived from oils, fats, dairy products, and sugars. At the same time there is a steady decline in the use of grain products and other carbohydrates. Although no significant changes have been noted in total protein intake, the proportion of animal proteins is increased (Ibid.: 130).

These changes in diet are partly the result of work routines in which less time is spent on the buying, preparation, and eating of food than on its production. Consequently there is increased reliance on snacks, ready-processed foods, and alcohol for one's calories. The brief lunches and breakfasts that result from participation in industrial labor and urban education routines lead to a pattern of one major meal per day, which is noted to lead to increased consumption of fattening items during that meal. When these eating patterns are combined with reliance on motor transportation and sedentary activities such as television watching, the urban individual shows a marked predisposition for obesity and heart diseases.

Obesity is one of the major disabilities connected with modern urban life. Unfortunately, we have very little knowledge of the varying distribution of body fat at different sites of the body. Research has also overlooked the alterations in body fat that accompany aging and the differing body fat of different physique types. Although diet may have much to do with obesity, the whole context within which it occurs is virtually unknown: the role of social factors, psychological influences, eating and activity patterns, and economic circumstances (Ibid.:139).

The City and the Natural Ecosystem   Urban systems share many important basic characteristics with natural ecosystems. Both are composed of interacting flows of energy, matter, and information. However, the differences between these systems are just as important as the similarities. Natural ecosystems are strongly influenced by the stabilizing role of negative feedback. On the other hand, urban systems are controlled by the human population (Stearns and Montag 1974:29-31). In the urban system natural controls such as starvation and disease, are replaced by human controls whose effectiveness has been uneven—for example, human controls have resulted in the reduction of contagious diseases, but in an increase in the incidence of chronic and pollution-related illnesses. An understanding of urban ecosystems requires an understanding of the natural limits of the environment, as well as of how values are formed, how goals are formulated, and how actions are implemented (Ibid.:62).

Greenwood and Edwards (1973:226) have said that "from a strictly ecological point of view, the modern industrial city is a parasite upon the natural environment, taking resources from it and returning nothing but harmful refuse."[3] A look at a simplified model of the in and out flows of energy and matter suggests that such an evaluation may be largely correct (see figure 10.2). Today's cities often rely on distant areas for their fuel and food needs. Primary production within cities is largely aimed at pro-

[3]The increasing volume of residuals (waste) makes it possible to postulate that their accumulation will be an important limiting factor to growth in the future (Man and the Biosphere/UNESCO 1973:74).

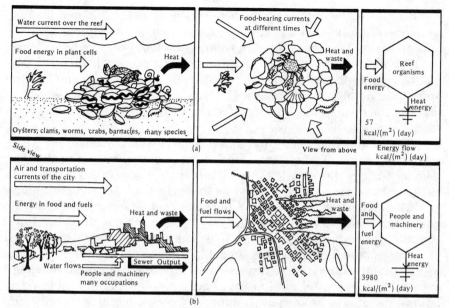

Figure 10.2   **Comparison of Two Consumers: An Oyster Reef and a City**   Both rely on concentrated inputs of energy. Figure (a) shows a reef of oysters in an estuary, and (b) an urban-industrial center.

Source: H. T. Odum. 1971. Environment, Power and Society. New York: Wiley-Interscience.

viding aesthetic areas of greenery, not at providing food and fiber for its inhabitants.[4] Thus, the contemporary city is best seen as a consumer organism. Figure 10.2 also illustrates the essential similarity between a living organism and a city.

The relations of cities to their surroundings have changed as the locus of political power and population has shifted from rural to urban areas. Power is today concentrated in a limited number of cities not only in the form of energy-demanding industrial parks, but also in growing population densities and in the concentration of nodal institutions. The net result has been that urban choices about resource utilization are increasingly based on a need to satisfy urban masses and institutional priorities rather than on an understanding of the regional basis of urban ecosystems. Wolman (1965), in a classic article on the metabolism of cities, found that urban energy requirements were high and that their waste outputs put a serious burden on the surrounding habitat (see figure 10.2).

[4]Other roles of vegetation in cities are (1) to ameliorate the "heat island" conditions; (2) to remove gaseous and particulate pollutants; (3) to baffle noise; and (4) to provide a habitat for small and migratory wildlife (Detwyler and Marcus 1972).

315

Because of the complex trade networks of modern cities and the ineffectiveness of local habitat resistance, cities have grown without interruption or inhibition. The more cities grow, the more they seem to attract industry and rural populations rather than to discourage them. Rural populations come to cities with hopes of higher wage and employment opportunities, of better standards of living, better health facilities, or as a result of the displacement of small farmers by the large, mechanized operators (Turner 1976).

The relations between rural and urban areas are systemic in nature. Improved communications make the city attractively visible to the rural dweller (that is, the "pull factor"). Per capita wages in Mexico City in 1970, for example, were $1,824, while they were only $622 in the country as a whole. In nearly any corner of the globe, public services are of higher quality and more accessible in the city than in the countryside. Health facilities, infrastructure, public utilities, entertainment, and schools tend to be concentrated in cities. Investment in rural areas, when it does occur, leads to further migration because the resulting education heightens expectations. Improved rural health conditions also tend to lead to populations too large to be adequately supported by the traditional agriculture available to small farmers (that is, the "push factors"). Roads also facilitate the migrants' access to cities. Their dreams are seldom realizable. There are not enough jobs, schools, health facilities, and so forth to accommodate the onrush of migrants. These migrations also mean a shift of political influence from the countryside to the city and a homogenization of the rural population into urban ways.

The landscape, too, is changed. What were once prime lands for cultivation now are covered with suburban developments (for example, the Santa Clara Valley) or by the sprawl of separate urban centers into a megalopolis such as is seen in the Boston-Washington area (Borgstrom 1973:82). In 1949, 70 percent of the farmland in Santa Clara County was classified as prime agricultural land, but as the city of San Mateo grew, it saw the flat, deep soils of the Santa Clara Valley as ideal for reducing the costs of urban development. Price for land went high enough that farmers were induced to sell their land. This pattern has been repeated elsewhere in the United States where one-half of the best croplands have been urbanized (Wagner 1974:412).

The adaptability of our species to life in an increasingly urban world should indeed be a topic of research. The physiological adjustments required for coping with air pollution are no less complex than those observed in adapting to cold or altitude. Crowded and overstimulating life in cities elicits complex behavioral and cultural adjustments that have important long-term significance for our lives as social animals and generators of symbols and meaning. The complexity of urban analysis has so far discouraged ecological scientists. This neglect must end, if for no other reason than the rapid disappearance of pristine situations and the incorporation of the whole earth under the influence of urban controls and priorities.

Epilogue

The study of human adaptability is shared by many disciplines, each with specific interests and capabilities. This has proved to be both an asset and a liability. It has been an asset insofar as new insights and interconnections are always being generated by any one of a host of fields—among them anthropology, biology, geography, medicine, and physiology. The multidisciplinary nature of human adaptability research is a liability in that sometimes little common theoretical or methodological ground is shared by these disciplines, making communications among researchers difficult and the advance of the field slow. It is hoped that each discipline is making increasing use of findings in other fields and searching for better explanatory models and improved research methods.

The historical development of studies dealing with people/environment interactions has followed a trajectory that began with deterministic or single-cause explanations that were based, in turn, on climatic, geographic, racial, cultural, and environmental factors. Julian Steward's emphasis on a limited set of variables, defined by their relevance to subsistence, avoided single causes, but gave a priori primacy to economic considerations. Neglect of other considerations generated alternative approaches, some with an ecological systems emphasis, others with a structural orientation emphasizing cultural categorization of perceived phenomena.

With each change, the field increasingly opened itself to new approaches and to more disciplines. At the same time, the objectives of research became better defined and the shared knowledge across disciplines was enhanced. The current status of human adaptability research is an exciting one. The ecological viewpoint today permeates both the biological and the social sciences. The widespread adoption of a systems approach to research has facilitated multidisciplinary dialogue. Reseachers have achieved increased communication through newsletters and multidisciplinary journals like *Science, Human Biology, Biotropica,* and *Human Ecology.*

The exchange of ideas across disciplines has generated new methodological and theoretical approaches. Much of the research used in this book was produced by the historical and comparative approaches traditional to the social sciences. The main contribution of this approach to ecological study has been to demonstrate the interconnections between human behavior, cultural traditions, population, and the physical environment. This approach is still in use and continues to generate useful data and insights into human ecology.

Epilogue

In the past two decades, a few social scientists have begun to adopt the theoretical and methodological tools of the ecological sciences in an effort to broaden the scope of their analyses. Although not always successful, and many times more analogic than precise, such experimental use of biological approaches has spawned stimulating studies. Perhaps the most useful crossover has been the coming together of social scientists and human biologists as they have sought to understand the adaptive responses of people to stressful conditions. This convergence of research interests has produced more comprehensive explanations of human responses to specific environmental problems. It has also provided us with the framework for this book.

The problems or constraints presented in chapters 5 to 9 do not represent a final compilation. They are, rather, a preliminary list of the major constraints faced by populations in five types of ecosystems. Many other ecosystems still await treatment in this manner, and problems specific to particular habitats within the larger biomes require singular treatment.

The emphasis on problems perceived and faced by human populations is a major step forward. Human beings are engaged in a constant process of dynamic interaction with their surroundings. As a species, we deal with problems of varying complexity. At times one stress will be dominant, while at other times we must adjust to several very different constraints. Responses rarely represent "best" choices, but instead express compromises among the various demands made upon the organism. Any analysis must include a wide set of variables and deal with the fact that human adaptability occurs at various levels: the individual, the familial or household, and the populational.

One of the ever-present problems in human adaptability research, and in much of ecology, is the fragmentary knowledge we have of population-level patterns, such as complexity and stability. A comprehensive description and analysis of the interactions between a population and its environment have been provided in very few cases. Clearly, we must describe ecological patterns much more thoroughly before we can advance theory beyond its present state.

One reason for the lack of holistic descriptions is the difficulty in adopting a generally acceptable "common currency" or language. The only efforts at bridging this gap have come from systems ecologists and others advocating a systems approach. Modeling provides a guideline to research in which one summarizes current understandings and data and projects the relationships hypothesized to be "driving functions" or crucial variables. Modeling, which was discussed in chapter 4, is descriptive of process and aids in the search for explanation. Models help us summarize available knowledge, identify gaps in the literature, generate hypotheses, and decide what variables must be tested and in what units the data can best be handled thereafter.

Modeling, however, is no panacea or cure-all. It has inherent limitations in that the only complete model of a natural system is the system itself.

320

Efforts to duplicate the real system in block diagrams or computer programs may fail to realize the inherent limitations of modeling and systems analysis. The best we can do is to elucidate the general properties of systems or explain the dynamics of a small portion of a natural system.

Most of the systems models used to date have an intrinsic weakness. They are deductive models, and the behavior of such models can only be predicted for the conditions for which the model was constructed. The models, therefore, tend to be static in that they can predict neither changes in the structural relations of system parts nor new interconnections. Further constraints to modeling have been the high costs of time and labor needed to simulate complex ecological systems and the lack of knowledge of most system modelers about the complexities of social systems. The use of deductive models in ecology appears to be practical, at present, only in dealing with restricted situations or parts of complex systems.

Major challenges to the modeling of human ecosystems are the multiple levels that characterize these systems and the crucial effect of human decisions on systems behavior. In dealing with these problems the comparative approach may have more explanatory power than the deductive models often used. One of the recurring strategies of populations studied in earlier chapters involved some form of *resource diversification*. Human populations have sought to overcome potential system instability by localized diversification approaching self-sufficiency; by seasonal mobility to deal with periodic scarcities; or by complex trade and exchange networks that facilitate access to a wider resource base than could be practically controlled by a given population.

Many social and cultural practices appear to support and assure the functioning of this quintessential adaptive strategy. Among these, kinship structures and marriage practices serve to localize or disperse a population. Information networks embodied in fictive kin, quasi-kin, and informal associations provide information and evaluation of resources available. Socialization patterns serve to introduce the growing child to the resources around him or isolate him from them.

As a population moves from diversification to a specialized trading strategy, the change usually spells the reorganization of the whole social and cultural life of the group, and the survival of the population depends on a successful transition. In the case of the Miskito, discussed in chapter 9, the change has meant a neglect of slash-and-burn cultivation and a decline in nutritional status as a result of overfishing the green turtle and the consequent decline in yields. Belief systems have changed, and the adoption of new beliefs has encouraged a rapid rise in population. This makes a return to the traditional system increasingly difficult because of the higher subsistence demands of the growing population. Relations between young and old are in process of redefinition, and the system of reciprocity has been undermined by the introduction of cash and the declining yields from fishing and reduced activities in farming. Thus, a change from diversification to specialized trading usually spells a total restructuring, not just a change in rates of flow. Deductive models could not have aided us in explaining the thorough changes that have taken place in Miskito society; nor could they have explained the changes in the subsistence ecology of this population.

In chapters 5 through 9 we reviewed evidence of human adaptability to a variety of constraints posed by different biomes. In every case, it was noted that in recent years the nature of the interaction between the human population and the environment had changed. The usual reason for the radical change has been the incorporation of those previously isolated regions into national development schemes. Such development brings about a radical change in how humans look at environmental constraints and how they deal with them. To a large extent, our species has escaped the restrictive world of natural selection—at least in the short run. Human purposive acts have complex motives and seldom result from careful evaluation of long-term effects. Decision-making studies tend to emphasize the selectivity of information that goes into human decisions. Such selectivity means that we do not interact with whole systems, but with highly selected aspects of systems. In this simplification of "reality" human culture plays a crucial role.

The role of human culture in human adaptability is ambiguous. On the one hand, cultural knowledge embodies information that has proved useful in human survival. Much of our success as a species derives from our ability to learn from our elders the accumulated wisdom of the past and to add through our own life experiences to that pool of knowledge. On the other hand, cultural knowledge also includes much that is no longer useful or accurate for enhancing our survival. Cultural knowledge is full of contradictions out of which individuals must extract the knowledge that will be applied to new situations.

When the rate of change quickens, the gap between environmental change and cultural change tends to widen. As the gap widens, the likelihood of making decisions that inadequately perceive the problem at hand is increased. One of the crucial questions for our time is how to protect the pool of past knowledge and at the same time bridge the gap between cultural and environmental change. It is important to remember that the rapid pace of change in environment is a direct result of human activities and "choices." However, most of these choices are being made with relatively limited objectives or awareness of consequences or costs.

The world inhabited by most of the world's peoples today is a very different one from that traditionally chosen by human ecologists for research. The studies discussed in this book are representative of the traditional choices—the Alaskan Inuit, Andean Quechuas, !Kung San, East African pastoralists, and Amazon Basin aborigenes. These choices reflect a desire to study inadequately understood populations, an effort to obtain important knowledge of native populations before such knowledge is lost through acculturation, and a desire to have a limited number of variables to deal with in the course of study. The findings of these studies have been extremely significant, and in fact most of the insights presented throughout this book derive from such work. Nevertheless, it is notable that each biome chapter ended with a discussion of how all these native peoples are adopting energy-intensive technologies acquired from industrial societies and how such adoptions are rapidly modifying native habitats and in some cases lowering overall adaptability.

We might be tempted to think that such change is a totally new phenomenon. That is indeed not the case. For millenia populations have been engaged in a process of change that has changed us and the face of the earth. Any change has its costs. However, the price for "stability" paid by some of the populations discussed in this book has included infanticide, short life spans, high infant mortality, susceptibility to disease, and a marginal or insecure food supply. These factors, rather than conscious decision, were responsible for maintaining a stable relationship between population and food supply. Today, technology has reduced the force of many of these factors that once effectively limited population growth. This change has had serious costs—overpopulation, pollution, loss of natural ecosystems, increase in degenerative diseases, and rapid resource depletion.

We must doubt whether any human being ever chooses between these two alternatives of stability (which implies famine, a short life span, and so forth) and instability (which implies pollution and an increase in degenerative disease). In fact, most of our choices are very limited in their scope and fail to recognize the long-term, or systemic, implications of such choices. The limited evidence available suggests that the stability of traditional systems must be attributed more to isolation and lack of alternatives than to a recognition of how a perfect balance between people and natural resources is achieved. This is a sobering thought and makes further research on the process of human adaptability all the more necessary and relevant.

If human ecosystems are counterintuitive (that is, too complex to be correctly understood by the human mind) and if as a result our minds simplify the complexity and draw from a pool of knowledge that contains both accurate and inaccurate information about the state of the world—then the task of human adaptability and survival is indeed an awesome one. Given all that can go wrong, it might perhaps be more pertinent in future research efforts to look less at how stable and adaptable we have been and more at how often we have failed to succeed as communities—but yet succeeded as a species.

The ultimate goal of human adaptability studies is to discover generally applicable systemic properties and to understand the processes of human coping behavior. By focusing on system-wide strategies, such as diversification vis-à-vis specialization in resource use, we get a framework both for study and for explaining long-term social, cultural, and ecosystemic change. One cannot arrive at an understanding of these systemic processes unless one deals with specific problems and the multiple responses that people bring to bear on them. Ecological studies will need to integrate, even more in the future than they have to date, the physiological, behavioral, and ideo-

Epilogue

logical aspects of human resource use if more adequate theoretical explanations are to be generated. The task of human adaptability research is of more than passing significance: we are studying how we have coped in the past and how we will survive in the future.

Glossary

Adaptation, Genetic or Evolutionary: Changes at the level of the population due to changes in gene frequencies that confer reproductive advantage to the population in a particular environment.

Adaptive Strategy: Refers to conscious or unconscious, explicit or implicit plans of action carried out by a population in response to either external or internal conditions.

Adjustment, Acclimatory: Modest, reversible physiological adjustments to an environmental change or stress.

Adjustment, Cultural: The learned knowledge that people acquire as members of a society. It is their most important means of coping as a species. Cultural adjustments permit the human species to respond quickly to changes in the environment.

Adjustment, Developmental: Nonreversible physiological and morphological changes resulting from organismic adaptation to environmental conditions during the individual's growth and development.

Adjustment, Regulatory: An organism's relatively rapid physiological and behavioral responses to changes in its environment.

Adobe: Building material formed from natural clays, sun-dried, and used in construction.

Affinal Relations: Kinship relations created by marriage.

Age-Area Concept: A notion developed by C. Wissler to arrive at the relative age of a cultural trait from its spatial distribution. Traits found at the edge of an area would be the oldest since they had diffused farthest from their origin.

Age Distribution: The proportion of a population found in each age class.

Albedo: Reflection of solar light from a surface of the earth.

Alfisols: *See* Soils.

Allele: Abbreviation for allelomorph. Refers to any one of the alternative forms of a gene.

Alluvial Fans: Deposits of sandy, loamy, or other light soils carried from their point of origin by water runoff and deposited in lower level, flat fans as the water is slowed down.

Amino Acid: Building units from which proteins are constructed. Twenty-two amino acids have been conclusively demonstrated to be constituents of plant proteins.

Anemia: A blood condition characterized by a decrease in the number of circulating red blood cells, hemoglobin, or both. Anemias may result from a variety of causes: deficient iron intakes in the diet, hemorrhage, lack of vitamin B_{12}, or intestinal diseases.

Aquifer: A stratum of rock able to hold water in its mass (for example, chalk, limestone, and sandstone). Aquifers get charged with water by exposure at some point to the ground surface——near a range of hills, for example.

Glossary

Aridisols: *See* Soils.

Arterial (Blood) Pressure: A measurement of the force of the blood on the arterial walls as it leaves the heart. May be increased by movement to higher altitudes, reduction of arterial dimensions by deposits of fatty materials, or changes in the viscosity of the blood itself.

Basal Metabolic Rate (BMR): The amount of energy needed to maintain body functions when a person is at digestive, physical, and emotional rest. BMR is expressed as calories per square meter of body surface per hour.

Bergmann's Rule: Describes body size increase in mammals, as environmental temperature decreases. Based on the relation between body volume and surface area.

Bilateral Descent: Reckoning descent through both mother and father.

Biomass: Total mass of living organisms present at a given moment in a population or area. It may be expressed in terms of kilocalories or in weight units per unit area. It may also refer to a portion of the total biomass, as in plant biomass, domestic livestock biomass, etc.

Biome: A broad ecological unit, characterized by a set of climatic parameters and types of floral and faunal associations. The term is sometimes used to refer to distinctive life zones.

Biota: The flora and fauna of a region or ecosystem.

Biotic Community: The biological components in a given ecosystem, which are mutually interdependent and sustaining and which transfer, utilize, and give off energy.

Birth Rate: Number of births per 1,000 persons per year.

Body Core, Body Shell: Terms used in studies of human thermoregulation. The core is the internal part of the body and consists of the brain, lungs, heart, liver, and the viscera. The shell is said to be the skin, muscles, subcutaneous fat, and extremities. Core temperature is measured rectally, while shell temperature is measured at the skin.

Brown Adipose Tissue: The primary tissue responsible for chemical heat production or nonshivering thermogenesis. It is found only in mammals and primarily in the cervical, interscapular, axillary, and abdominal regions.

Capillary: One of the microscopic blood vessels that join the arterial to the venous blood supply.

Carbohydrate: Compounds of carbon, hydrogen, and oxygen that form one of the three major groups of organic substances of which living matter is composed. (The others are proteins and fats.)

Carnivore: Meat-eating animals. Sometimes they are referred to as second or third order consumers.

Carrying Capacity: The number of individuals that a habitat can support. *See* Population Pressure.

Cation Exchange Capacity: The sum total of exchangeable cations that a soil can absorb. Cation absorption refers to the adhesion of substances to the surfaces of solids (especially colloids). It may be referred to also as *total exchange capacity* or *base-exchange capacity*. It is expressed in milliequivalents per 100 grams of soil. *See also* Ion.

Circadian Rhythm: Daily rhythm that characterizes a species. The rhythm is set by environmental synchronizers among which light is the most important.

Circannual Rhythm: Yearly biological rhythm that reflects seasonal changes in the environment. Light, temperature, social interaction, and other factors may be implicated in these annual biological fluctuations in an organism.

Climax Community: The plant community that is at the end of secondary succession. The dominant plants of the climax bring about no further modifications in the physical environment and are said to be in equilibrium with prevailing conditions.

Closed System: One that is bounded for heuristic reasons and treated as if it were not affected by forces outside the system. A closed system is maintained by internal cycling and negative feedback.

Colloid: Refers to both organic and inorganic matter characterized by small particle size and large surface/mass ratio.

Comparative Approach: An approach to the study of human societies in which a sample of societies or features of each are compared. It is evolutionist in its objectives and, through the use of the Human Relation Area Files, increasingly quantitative.

Consanguineal Relations: Relations based on common biological descent only, as in parental or sibling relationships.

Constraints: Intervening variables, present in the environment, that may alter the effects of a process, flow, or state. The effect may be positive or negative, but it is commonly used synonomously with *limiting factors*.

Consumers: Organisms that eat plants (for example, herbivores) and other animals (for example, carnivores) to survive. Consumers are dependents on producers to convert dispersed solar energy into biomass energy.

Correlation: The degree to which statistical variables vary together. It is measured by the correlation coefficient, which has a value from zero (that is, no correlation between the variables) to plus or minus one (that is, perfect positive or negative correlation between the variables).

Cultivators: Populations who rely on agriculture for subsistence.

Cultural Ecology: The study of how human adaptation to the environment takes place by way of cultural mechanisms.

Culture: Learned knowledge, used to interpret experience and to generate behavior. It is the primary means of adaptation for *Homo sapiens*.

Cushion Plants: Plant forms common in cold, dry, or frost-prone areas. Plants are low and compact, with growth organs below or near ground level. This form minimizes exposure, maintains internal warmth, and preserves moisture.

Cybernetic System: A system that maintains control and adaptability by the process of information feedback.

Death Rate: Number of deaths per 1,000 persons per year.

Glossary

Decomposers: Microscopic fungi and bacteria that reduce dead organic material to its elemental forms, thus making possible the cycling of matter.

Decomposition: Metabolic breakdown of organic materials. The result is heat energy and both simple organic and inorganic compounds.

Desert: Areas of less than 100 millimeters of rainfall per year, which usually lie in latitudes exposed to drying trade winds, subtropical high pressure belts, on lee side of mountains, or near cold ocean currents. Their primary productivity is low; they have little ground cover and high surface evaporation

Determinism: A theoretical stance that is reductionist in its approach and seeks basic causes for phenomena. Environmental or geographic determinism was an important intellectual tradition up to and into the twentieth century. Current efforts at explanation opt for a more probabilistic (as opposed to an absolute) approach.

Diachronic: Refer to studies with a historical or evolutionary time dimension.

Diapause: Temporary interruption of growth associated with a period of dormancy.

Diffusion, Cultural: Refers to the tendency of human groups to share their cultural knowledge with others whom they encounter.

Diversification: One form of adaptive strategy, whereby risk is minimized through the use of multiple resources.

Dormant: Being in a period of reduced biological activity——for example, hibernation or estivation.

Drought: A general condition of water shortage. Commonly a drought is so defined only when the shortage has an economic impact on populations.

Ecological Anthropology: The multidisciplinary study of how human populations cope with problems in their environments.

Ecology: The study of the interaction between living and nonliving components of the environment. See also Cultural Ecology, Ecological Anthropology, and Ethnoecology.

Ecosystem: The assemblage of living and nonliving components in an environment together with their interrelations. As a unit of study, it may be defined broadly or narrowly, according to how the research problem is defined by the investigator.

Ecotone: A transitional zone between two distinct biomes; an "edge" habitat in which species from both biomes are found in a gradation from one biome to another.

Edaphic: The factors or features that deal with the influence of soils on living things, especially on plants.

Efficiency, Energetic: The maximization of output per unit of energy input.

Electrolytes: A chemical compound that in solution dissociates by releasing ions (this is known as the process of ionization). See also Ion.

Endemic: Restricted in distribution to a certain region or area.

Endogamy: Marriage practice in which individuals within a single kin group, community, or region tend to marry others included in this delimited population. See also Exogamy.

Energy: The capacity to do work (and carry information). May be chemical, nuclear, radiant, electrical, or mechanical in form. It is neither created nor destroyed, but may be changed from one form to another. *See also* Thermodynamics.

Energy Flow: The changes in energy form and its rate in a system as it moves from one component of a system to another. Also a manner of modeling systems.

Entropy: Increased disorder in a system due to loss of potential energy (that is, degradation).

Environmental Degradation: A loosely defined concept used to convey the notion of lowered soil quality, which in turn lowers floral and faunal productivity and diversity; a state wherein an ecosystem cannot reach it climax stage. Precipitating factors may be overgrazing, salinization, overcropping without replacement of the lost soil nutrients, erosion, or, in general, mismanagement.

Epiphyte: A plant growing upon another living plant without taking anything from it (that is, it is not parasitic).

Equilibrium, Dynamic: The maintenance of those properties essential to the continued existence of the system. Many ecological factors can influence the position of the equilibrium: evolutionary rates, barriers to dispersal, productivity levels, habitat heterogeneity, predation, and feedback processes. Dynamic equilibrium takes into account both negative and positive feedback processes.

Equilibrium, Static: Deals only with the processes of negative feedback that help maintain the system at a given level of existence.

Estivation: The reduction of biological activity by an organism, particularly during hot/dry periods.

Ethnoecology: The study of the ecological folk knowledge of a population.

Ethnology: The comparative study of human societies.

Ethology: The study of animal behavior, especially in its natural habitat. Ethologists try to understand why an animal behaves the way it does and what selective pressures have influenced the development of observed patterns.

Eutrophication: Process of nutrient concentration in an ecosystem. This accelerated enrichment may be the result of agricultural, urban waste, mining, or industrial activities. Eutrophication of aquatic ecosystems leads to changes in species composition and, in its extreme forms, to the death of most of the species valued by the human population.

Evapotranspiration: The total water loss from a plant surface by the processes of evaporation and plant transpiration (that is, respiration). Since it is difficult to separate these two aspects of water loss, the term *evapotranspiration* is used to more accurately describe this double water loss.

Evolution, Biological: The changes in the hereditary makeup of populations over time as a result of the interaction of populations with their environments.

Exchange Network: A system of trading, gift exchange, or barter, regulated by systems of mutual obligation. Such networks may provide for transfer of needed goods from one population to another or between regions having different sets of resources or it may help to maintain networks of mutual assistance.

Exogamy: A marriage practice in which individuals must marry outside of their own group. This may be defined as a kin group (for example, lineage), a community, a caste, or a region. It seems to be associated with social organizational features that aim at expanding the network of social cooperation.

Glossary

Extractivism: Refers to a system of management that relies on the periodic exploitation of removable natural resources without efforts at reinvestment in the region to assure its long-term productivity or development. Extractive economic systems are found most often in frontier and colonial situations.

Family, Extended: A unit to which members other than those of the nuclear group are added. These may include affinal, consanguineal, or fictive kin, who tend to reside in the same immediate surroundings or dwelling and who cooperate economically and socially.

Family, Nuclear: Group composed of male and female mates and their children, who tend to occupy the same dwelling and in which group the offspring are reared. Also referred to as *family of origin, orientation, or procreation.*

Feedback: A flow of information (energy) from one component to another in a system, which allows for its return to previous equilibrium state (negative feedback) or a readjusting and reorganization of the system along new lines (positive feedback).

Fertility Rate: The number of births per 1,000 females of child-bearing age (fifteen to forty-five years old).

Fictive Kin: See Quasi-Kin.

Fire Management: The conscious or unconscious use of fire to bring about desired changes in vegetational cover. Use of fire eliminates litter and speeds its conversion into usable nutrients in forests, eliminates woody growth in grasslands, and encourages young grass growth preferred by grazing animals.

Fitness: Refer to reproductive success of a population. The more fit a species the greater will be its ability to reproduce in a given territory.

Functionalism: A type of analysis used in the sciences that attempts to explain phenomena in terms of the functions they perform in the system.

Gene: General name given to a unit of heredity. Genes are located within the cell nucleus of chromosomes. Changes in genes (that is, mutations) occur with a very low frequency and give rise to different forms of the same gene (that is, alleles). Genes control the formation of the enzyme systems that determine the structure and function of organisms.

Gene Flow: Exchange of genetic traits between populations.

Genetic Plasticity: The ability of an organism to find expression for its genotypic qualities in a variety of physical expressions, all of which may represent various levels of adaptability to different forms of environmental stress. The more specific a genetic adaptation is to an environment, the less generalized the species and the less its genetic plasticity.

Genotype: The genetic contribution of an organism or its hereditary potential. Together with the environment, they produce the phenotype. The genotype may mask traits, as in the suppression of a recessive gene, or its potential may be unexpressed due to environmental conditions.

Grassland: A transitional biome between arid and humid zones. It is characterized by ten to thirty millimeters of rainfall per year and is dominated by *Graminae* vegetation (grasses). Grasslands are characterized by rolling to flat terrain, periodic droughts, and high evapotranspiration in summer. They often occur in areas with a high water table. *See also* Savannah.

Groundwater: Water flowing or stored underground. It is a product of local or

330

extraregional sources of water and may be stored below the surface in water-bearing rocks, aquifers, or other storage areas.

Group Fissioning: The splitting up of villages or kin groups and their reestablishment in smaller, independent units. Used as a strategy to lower population pressure and reduce interpersonal conflict.

Habitat: Place where a plant or animal lives. It is often characterized by either dominant plant forms or physical characteristics (for example, grasslands habitat).

Hardpan: A hardened soil layer resulting from the cementation of soil particles with organic matter, silica oxides, calcium carbonate, and so forth.

Hectare: A metric unit of surface area. It is equal to 10,000 square meters or to 2.471 acres.

Herbivore: Any plant-eating animal.

Heterozygous: An individual that has inherited two different alleles at one or more corresponding gene loci in a pair of chromosomes. As a result it does not breed true to character.

Histisols: See Soil.

Historical Possibilism: An approach to the study of human society in which historical circumstances are given a predominant role is shaping observable phenomena. Associated with the work of Franz Boas and his followers.

Homeostasis: The maintenance of constant internal conditions in the face of varying environment.

Homozygous: An individual that has inherited two identical, rather than different, alleles at one or more corresponding gene loci. It breeds true for a particular character.

Horizon, Soil: A layer of soil with distinctive characteristics resulting from processes of soil formation.

Humus: Product of decomposition of organic matter, found in soils, usually dark in color. In many soils, the top layer is known as the "humic horizon," a zone of great importance for most domesticated plants.

Hunter/Gatherers: A human group characterized by the exploitation of wild food sources. Hunter/gatherers live in small bands or camps, are fairly mobile, and exploit relatively extensive territory with rather simple tools. They tend to maintain a mode of subsistence whereby males exploit local animal resources and females gather wild vegetative and other materials, which are shared by members of the group. Groups tend to be egalitarian, highly fissionable, and possess few items of personal property.

Hydromorphic Soils: Soils formed under conditions of poor drainage in marshes, swamps, or flat zones.

Hyperventilation: Excessively high and rapid intake of oxygen, following work stress or low oxygen (that is, hypoxic) conditions of high altitude areas. Excessive hyperventilation results in low carbon dioxide levels in the blood, or hypocapnia.

Hypothermia: A state of lowered body temperature. As the core temperature approaches 33°C. there is increased danger of malfunction in the thermoregulatory system.

Glossary

Hypothesis: A statement of a causal or correlational relationship between two variables, X and Y; usually stated in a declaratory form. The magnitude and the direction of the relation are also indicated in a form that can be tested.

Hypoxia: Condition of low oxygen pressure, either in the atmosphere (at high altitudes) or in the bloodstream (for example, as a result of demanding exercise by an athlete).

Inceptisols: See Soils.

Information: Knowledge that is transferred. There is evidence that an evolutionary trend toward increased frequency of and dependence on the communication of information exists. The transmission of information is particularly sophisticated in *Homo sapiens*.

Intercropping: The practice of planting several crop species on one field simultaneously or of multilevel planting of species of varying heights. Provides cover for erosion prevention and protection of more tender crops. Minimizes risk of crop loss and increases land productivity.

Interfluve: An area of land between two rivers or water courses.

International Biological Program (IBP): A multinational research venture that was launched in 1964 and ended in 1974. Its goal was to study the biological basis of productivity and human welfare.

Ion: A molecular constituent of one or more atoms that is free in a solution. An ion may carry a positive (that is, cation) or a negative (that is, anion) charge.

Kilocalorie: The amount of heat required to raise one gram of water one degree centigrade. The energy content of matter is measured by igniting a material in the presence of oxygen in a bomb calorimeter.

Lactase Deficiency: The hereditary inability to produce the intestinal enzyme lactase, which breaks down the milk sugar, lactose. The ingestion of lactose-containing milk by persons so affected creates symptoms of gastrointestinal cramps, flatulence, and diarrhea. It is most common in populations without long dairying histories, such as the Inuit. Using acidified milk or yogurts (nonlactose) prevents these symptoms.

Laterite: A general term to refer to reddishbrown, iron, and aluminum oxide-rich soils. When exposed to air, the layer may turn to hardpan irreversibly. Because the term has been used too loosely to refer to tropical soils of reddish coloration, the term *plinthite* has now replaced *laterite* in the soil science literature.

Leaching: The removal of soluble mineral salts from the upper layers of a soil by the movement of water through the horizons.

Lee Side: The protected side of a mountain or island away from the direction of prevailing winds. Opposite of "windward" side.

Legume: Members of the *Leguminosae* family. They have the property of fixing atmospheric nitrogen in the soil.

Levirate: A marriage custom wherein a man is expected to marry his deceased brother's widow.

Lineage, Segmentary: A lineage characterized by internal divisions or sections that may result in the emergence of new and separate descent groups. It is a flexible form of organization particularly appropriate to pastoral nomadic populations.

Litter: Fallen organic (plant) matter that accumulates on the surfaces of the soil. It forms first a natural mulch and, if decomposed, humus. Litterfall is often used as a measure of productivity in forest ecosystems.

Management: Refers to the plan of action, whether conscious or not, of a population in its utilization of social and environmental resources. Used synonymously with strategy, behavioral adjustment.

Matter: Anything that has the properties of mass (weight) and occupies space. May be in solid, liquid, or gaseous states.

Matter, Cycles of: The cyclical movements of all physical elements from complex organic to inorganic forms and back again. Examples include oxygen cycle, water cycle, and nutrient cycle.

Microclimate: The climatic condition, especially the temperature, nearest to an individual (for example, inside a dwelling or inside of clothing). Refers to the creation of environmental conditions different from those in the general area.

Migration: A short-term mechanism for dispersion of people or animals. May mean a permanent relocation, but is distinguished from cyclical nomadism. *Seasonal migration* is subsumed under *transhumance.* May be considered an adaptive strategy of populations.

Model: A simplified representation of the interactions and components of a system. May elicit speculations about the processes that would explain or produce the observed facts of the system.

Mollisols: *See* Soils.

Monoculture (Monocropping): Cultivation of a single crop species in large fields, usually as an export commodity with market value. Often associated with plantation systems or intensive forms of food production requiring major inputs of energy and technology.

Mulching: Process of organic matter accumulation for maintaining soil moisture (and secondarily, nutrients) by covering the surface of the soil with live or decomposing plant material. Mulching helps prevent erosion, soil heating by solar radiation, and reduces evaporation from the soil surface.

Mutualistic: A symbiotic relationship wherein both species benefit from their intimate association.

Niche: All the components of the environment with which the organism or population interacts.

Nitrification: The biochemical oxidation of ammonium to nitrate. The process is essential to the provisioning of usable nutrients by plants.

Nomadism: An adaptation of cyclical human mobility to the scattered (and diverse) resources of a region, resulting in a lack of permanent settlements.

Open Systems: One that requires constant input from outside the system for self-maintenance. It includes considerations of positive feedback.

Glossary

Oxisols: *See* Soils.

Parent Material (Bedrock): The underlying hard rock material under any soil profile, from which the soil horizons have originated. May be referred to as the C horizon.

Pastoralists: Persons who subsist by the herding of large groups of domesticated animals, opportunistic agriculture, and trade with more sedentary peoples. The pastoralist mode of production tends to be utilized in biomes that are marginal to agriculture and where pastures are scattered.

Pathogen: A bacterium, virus, or other disease-causing agent.

Peripheral Blood Flow: A physiological adjustment found in populations habitually exposed to cold in the extremities. It refers to the spontaneous rewarming of fingers and toes during cold exposure in a cyclical pattern of vasoconstriction and dilation. It is also known as *cold-induced vasodilation*.

pH: The scale along which acidity and alkalinity of a solution is measured. Acid solutions have a smaller pH and alkaline solutions a greater pH within a range from zero to fourteen.

Phenotype: The physical manifestation of the hereditary potential of an organism. The visible phenotype may express genetic traits most appropriate to the current environmental conditions.

Photosynthesis: The conversion of light energy into chemical energy in green plant cells.

Plinthite: *See* Laterite.

Population: A group of individuals of the same species that occupy a given area and interbreed with one another.

Population Pressure: The demands of a population on the resources of its ecosystem. Refers to the relationship between population size and the ability of the ecosystem to sustain it.

Primary Production: Refers to either the assimilation of energy and nutrients by green plants (gross *primary production*) or to its accumulation and transformation into biomass (net *primary production*).

Producers: Ecological term that refers to organisms capable of converting solar energy into biomass. The most notable are green plants and blue green algae.

Quasi-Kin or Fictive Kin: The treatment of others who are not related by consanguineal or affinal ties as if they indeed were so connected. Often associated with adaptive forms of exchange, protection, and cooperation and established by ritual actions and the use of "kin-like" terms of address.

Recovery, Rate of: Refers to regeneration of plant or animal species following a period of biological degradation of an ecosystem.

Regression Coefficient: The rate of change of a dependent variable with respect to an independent variable.

Reproductive Success: The essential concept of the theory of natural selection. Helps explain how species have evolved, become extinct, or become dominant. The more "adapted" a species is in its environment, the greater the opportunity for individuals of the population to survive and reproduce and thus to occupy the territory. Also known as the *theory of natural selection.*

Resource Base: An environment's group of organic and inorganic resources upon which a population habitually depends for its subsistence.

Respiration: The metabolic process by which oxygen is assimilated and combined with nutrients and water to produce energy (calories) for body maintenance and work. By this same process the waste products of metabolism are returned to the environment.

Rhizobium: A soil bacterium able to utilize atmospheric nitrogen to build organic compounds (that is, nitrogen fixation). These bacteria are often found in special structures of legumes and other plants and aid plants in their nutrition. In turn, the rhizobia obtain sugars from the plant.

Savanna: A tropical grassland environment.

Secondary Growth: The process of vegetational succession in an ecosystem.

Semiarid Areas: Regions varying from 150–250 to 250–500 millimeters of rainfall per year. Dry land farming in diffuse areas is possible, but not always reliable. Pastoral nomadism and forms of oasis agriculture are often found in these areas.

Simulation: A technique of solving and studying problems by following the changes over time of a dynamic model of a system. A simulation model is built from a series of sections whose relationship to one another can be stated mathematically, but which permits their simultaneous solution.

Slash-and-Burn: See Swidden Agriculture.

Social Organization: Distinguished by Firth from social structure as that aspect of a social system which refers to the systematic ordering of social relations. The existing forms of social organization are guided by precedents and rules set in the social structure. These rules delimit a range of socially "possible" or acceptable behavior and imply the role of the social group in coordinating individual behaviors.

Social Structure: Principles according to which social features are organized. Includes kinship relation patterns, technoeconomic organization, belief systems, and political structure.

Socialization: The process of learning a culture through a lifelong process of internalizing. May also be termed *enculturation.* Includes both institutional and informal learning processes.

Soil Profile: A cross-section that includes all the layers or horizons in a soil. A sample that expresses the type of processes experienced by the soil. Also used to determine its present characteristics and future potential.

Soil Structure: The arrangement of soil particles, such as granular, blocky, or columnar forms. Types of soil structure are characterized by differences in size and shape, and by degree of distinctness.

Soil Texture: Determined by the proportion of different sizes of soil particles, such as sand, gravel, silt, and clay. Soil texture is an important criterion in the classification of soils and is used by populations in evaluating the potential uses of a land area.

Soils: The portions of the earth's surface resulting from the weathering of rock and which support plant life. Soils can be categorized according to their current characteristics into ten orders: (1) *alfisols* are soils with argillic subsurface horizons, good supply of bases, and with adequate moisture for plant growth; (2) *aridisols* are soils usually dry in all horizons and never moist for ninety consecutive days; (3) *entisols* lack horizon development; (4) *histisols* are soils characterized by high levels of organic matter, for example, bog soils, muck soils; (5) *inceptisols* are soils with one or more diagnostic horizons that are believed to form quickly, but not as a result of leaching or weathering; (6) *mollisols* are soils characterized by a thick, dark mineral surface horizon and are associated with soils of grassland regions; (7) *oxisols* are soils of the tropics and subtropics characterized by the presence of an oxic horizon (that is, a horizon from which most of the silica has been removed by weathering, leaving oxides of iron and aluminum); (8) *spodisols* are soils with accumulation of amorphous materials in subsurface horizons; (9) *ultisols* are soils with argillic subsurface horizons and low supply of bases; (10) *vertisols* are soils with swelling clays that develop deep, wide cracks during dry periods.

Sororate: A marriage custom wherein a man is expected to marry the sister of his deceased wife.

State Variables: Refers to the components of a system (for example, producers, consumers, and so forth).

Stoma: Tiny leaf pores that allow for carbon dioxide/oxygen exchange in the respiratory/photosynthetic processes of green plants.

Strategy: An adjustment by an organism or population to environmental or social conditions. Strategies may involve physiological or behavioral change.

Stress: A force or extreme situation in the environment of an organism or population that produces a deviation from homeostasis. Unless positive feedback responses can head the system away from the stress, death or disruption will tend to occur.

Subsistence: A broad term that includes the study of a form of production (that is, production for use); it may also mean the essential for survival (that is, the food supply). Subsistence production characterizes many populations where the units of production are small, where a variety of food sources are grown or captured, and where reciprocity is utilized as a chief mechanism of exchange.

Succession: The process by which plant communities sequentially succeed one another as they proceed to a stable or climax community.

Sucrase Deficiency: Lack of the intestinal disaccharide sucrase. It may produce a variety of gastrointestinal problems due to inability to digest the sugar sucrose.

Swidden Agriculture: Also known as *shifting agriculture, slash-and-burn, milpa, and citemene.* A system in which fields are cropped for fewer years than they are allowed to remain fallow. Often characterized by regrowth of the secondary species during fallow and by reliance on the slash-and-burn method of clearing fallow fields in preparation for planting.

Synchronic: Refers to studies at one point in time.

Systems Theory, General: Refers to a body of systematic theoretical constructs that deal with the general relationships in the empirical world. It attempts to develop theories with applicability to more than one discipline. Also can be used as a framework for developing theory.

Taiga: Zone of subarctic boreal coniferous forests.

Taxonomy: Systems of classification (by any group) that are predicated on the notion of distinctive features, which are used to separate distinct items into categories of "like" items. A way of ordering knowledge, which then provides a standard by which to interpret and categorize new phenomena.

Thermodynamics, Laws of: First law: energy is neither created nor destroyed, Second law: part of energy used in work is lost as heat, leading to degradation of energy and increase in entropy or disorder.

Thermogenesis: Refers to the types of mechanisms that initiate heat production in the body. For example, nonshivering thermogenesis is a chemical form associated with the presence of brown adipose tissue.

Thermo-neutral Temperature: When environmental temperatures are between 25° to 27° C., humans are said to be in thermal equilibrium.

Transhumance: Seasonal migration of domesticated livestock and herders in order to exploit the semiarid grasslands.

Trophic Levels: Levels of feeding relationships from primary plant consumers to the most distant and complex member of the "food chain." The trophic level defines the species' position in the food chain depending on the number of energy transfers associated with feeding habits. At the bottom are the food producers, then herbivores, followed by consumers.

Tropical Rain Forest: One of the oldest existing ecosystems, which is characterized by high ambient humidity and temperature and by diversity and complexity of life forms.

Tundra: The northernmost frontier of vegetation, which is treeless and alpine-like. A transitional ecotone between the tree line and permanent snow areas. Subvarieties include *bush, grass, and desert* tundras.

Upwelling: Vertical movements of water currents near coasts that bring nutrients from the ocean bottom to the surface. Rich fish and sea mammal populations are found in these coastal areas.

Vapor Pressure: Gaseous molecules, constantly in random motion, that at an equilibrium point between condensation and evaporation exert pressure. The magnitude of this vapor pressure depends on the bonding nature of the liquid and its temperature. Water, with strong internal bonding forces, has a low vapor pressure at room temperature. At higher ambient temperatures, vapor pressure is increased, and warm air can hold greater quantities of water, or humidity. Warm and dry air causes rapid liquid gas exchange, or evaporation.

Vasoconstriction and Vasodilation: Process of opening and narrowing of capillaries to restrict or permit greater blood flow to the shell.

Vegetative Reproduction: Plant reproduction by grafts, cuttings, leaf sections, and so forth, rather than by production of seeds.

Wadi: A dried-up desert watercourse, except after rains when it may become a roaring torrent or flashflood.

Work (or Aerobic) Capacity: Refers to the ability of the body to deliver oxygen to the tissues per unit of ventilatory or heart rate.

Glossary

World View: Body of beliefs about the nature, structure, and parts of the world shared by members of a society. Such views may be expressed in myths, ceremonies, social interactional patterns, and attitudes toward nature.

Xerophytic Vegetation: Plants able to grow in extremely dry regions. They are characterized by physical features that minimize loss of water and leaf exposure to drying air and that make more effective use of water.

Bibliography

Abelson, Philip, ed.
1975 Food: Politics, Economics, Nutrition and Research. Washington, D.C.: American Association for the Advancement of Science.

Abu-Lughod, J.L.
1969 Testing the Theory of Social Area Analysis: The Ecology of Cairo, Egypt. American Sociological Review 34:198–212.

Adams, Richard N.
1973 Energy and Structure. Austin: University of Texas Press.

1974 The Implications of Energy Flow Studies on Human Populations for the Social Sciences. In Energy Flow in Human Communities. Proceedings of a Workshop. Paul L. Jamison and S. M. Friedman, eds. University Park, Pa.: US/International Biological Program (IBP) and Social Science Research Council (SSRC).

Adams, Robert McC.
1966 The Evolution of Urban Society. Chicago: Aldine.

1968 The Natural History of Urbanism. In The Fitness of Man's Environment. Washington, D.C.: Smithsonian Institution Press.

Adolph, E. F. et al.
1947 Physiology of Man in the Desert. London: Interscience Publications.

Alavi, S. M. Ziauddin
1965 Arab Geography in the Ninth and Tenth Centuries. Aligarh (India): Aligarh Muslim University, Department of Geography.

Allan, William
1965 The African Husbandman. Edinburgh: Oliver and Boyd.

Alland, Alexander
1969 Ecology and Adaptation to Parasitic Diseases. In Environment and Cultural Behavior. Andrew P. Vayda, ed. Garden City, N.Y.: Natural History Press.

1970 Adaptation in Cultural Evolution: An Approach to Medical Anthropology. New York: Columbia University Press.

1973 Evolution and Human Behavior. Second ed. Garden City, N.Y.: Doubleday-Anchor Books.

1975 Adaptation. Annual Review of Anthropology 4:59–73.

Alland, Alexander and B. McCay
1973 The Concept of Adaptation in Biological and Cultural Evolution. In Handbook of Social and Cultural Anthropology. John Honigmann, ed. Chicago: Rand McNally.

Bibliography

Anderson, E.
1972 Some Chinese Methods of Dealing with Crowding. Urban Anthropology 1(2):141–150.

Anderson, H. D. and W. C. Eells.
1935 Alaska Natives. Stanford, Cal.: Stanford University Press.

Anderson, J. N.
1974 Ecological Anthropology and Anthropological Ecology. In Handbook of Social and Cultural Anthropology. John Honigmann, ed. Chicago: Rand McNally.

Anderson, J. R. and J. B. Hardaker
1973 Management Decisions and Drought. In The Environmental, Economic and Social Significance of Drought. J.V. Lovett, ed. Sydney: Angus and Robertson.

Anthropological Society of Washington (ASW) and Organization of American States
1957 Studies in Human Ecology. Washington. D.C.: ASW and OAS.

Antonini, Gustavo et al.
1975 Population and Energy. Gainesville: University of Florida Press.

Aoki, Masana
1967 Optimization of Stochastic Systems. New York: Academic Press.

Arima, Eugene
1975 A Contextual Study of the Caribou Eskimo Kayak. Ottawa: National Museum of Man.

Arnott, Margaret, ed.
1976 Gastronomy: The Anthropology of Food and Food Habits. The Hague: Mouton.

Aschmann, Homer
1962 Evaluations of Dry Land Environments by Societies at Various Levels of Technical Competence. In Civilizations in Desert Lands. Richard Woodbury, ed. Salt Lake City: University of Utah Press.

Ayres, S. M. and M. E. Buchler
1970 The Effects of Urban Air Pollution On Health. Clinical Pharmacology Therapeutics 11:337–371.

Bajema, C. J.
1971 Natural Selection in Human Populations. New York: John Wiley.

Baker, Herbert
1970 Evolution in the Tropics. Biotropica 2(2): 101–111.

Baker, Paul T.
1958 The Biological Adaptation of Man to Hot Deserts. American Naturalist 92:237–257.

———

1966 Ecological and Physiological Adaptations in Indigenous South Americans. In The Biology of Human Adaptability. Paul T. Baker and J. S. Weiner, eds. Oxford: Clarendon Press.

———

1968 Human Adaptation to High Altitude. In High Altitude Adaptation in a

340

Peruvian Community. P. T. Baker et al., eds. University Park: Occasional Papers in Anthropology, No. 1, Pennsylvania State University.

_____

1969 Human Adaptation to High Altitude. Science 163:1149–1156.

_____

1976a Evolution of a Project: Theory, Method, and Sampling. *In* Man in the Andes. Paul T. Baker and M. Little, eds. Stroudsburg, Pa.: Dowden, Hutchinson and Ross.

_____

1976b Work Performance of Highland Natives. *In* Man in the Andes. Paul T. Baker and M. Little, eds. Stroudsburg, Pa: Dowden, Hutchinson and Ross.

Baker, Paul T. et al.
1968 High Altitude Adaptation in a Peruvian Community. University Park: Occasional Papers in Anthropology, No.1, Pennsylvania State University.

Baker, Paul T. and J. S. Dutt
1972 Demographic Variables as Measures of Biological Adaptation: A Study of High Altitude Human Populations. *In* The Structure of Human Populations. G. A. Harrison and A. J. Boyce, eds. Oxford: Clarendon Press.

Baker, Paul T. and W. T. Sanders
1972 Demographic Studies in Anthropology. Annual Review of Anthropology 1:151–178.

Baker, Paul T. and J. S. Weiner, eds.
1966 The Biology of Human Adaptability. Oxford: Clarendon Press.

Baker, Paul T. and M. Little, eds.
1976 Man in the Andes. Stroudsburg, Pa: Dowden, Hutchinson and Ross. US/IBP Synthesis Series, No.1.

Baker, Paul T. ed.
1978 The Biology of High Altitude Populations. Cambridge: Cambridge University Press.

Baker, Thelma
1976 Child Care, Child Training and Environment. *In* Man in the Andes. Paul T. Baker and M. Little, eds. Stroudsburg, Pa.: Dowden, Hutchinson and Ross.

Baldanzi, Giampiero
1959 Efeitos da Queimada sobre a Fertilidade do Solo. Pelotas, Rio Grande do Sul (Brazil): Instituto Agronómico do Sul.

Balikci, Asen
1968 The Netsilik Eskimos: Adaptive Processes. *In* Man the Hunter. Richard B. Lee and I. DeVore, eds. Chicago: Aldine.

_____

1970 The Netsilik Eskimo. Garden City, N.Y.: Natural History Press.

Bandi, H. G.
1969 Eskimo Prehistory. London: Methuen.

Barclay, George
1958 Techniques of Population Analysis. New York: John Wiley.

341

Bibliography

Barlett, Peggy
1977 The Structure of Decision-Making in Paso. American Ethnologist 4(2):285–308.

Barnard, C. and O. H. Frankel
1966 Grass, Grazing Animals and Man in Historic Perspective. In Grasses and Grasslands. C. Barnard, ed. New York: St. Martin's Press.

Barnard, C., ed.
1966 Grasses and Grasslands. New York: St. Martin's Press.

Barry, R. G. and R. J. Chorley
1970 Atmosphere, Weather and Climate. New York: Holt, Rinehart and Winston.

Barth, Fredrik
1956 Ecologic Relationships of Ethnic Groups in Swat, North Pakistan. American Anthropologist 58:1079–1089.

———

1961 Nomads of South Persia. Boston: Little, Brown.

———

1972 Ethnic Processes on the Pathan-Baluch Boundary. In Directions in Sociolinguistics. J. Gumperz and D. Hymes, eds. New York: Holt, Rinehart and Winston.

Bartholomew, W., et al.
1953 Mineral Nutrient Immobilization under Forest and Grass Fallow in the Yangambi (Belgian Congo) Region. Institut National pour L'Etude Agronomique du Congo Série 57:1–27.

Basso, Ellen
1973 The Kalapalo Indians of Central Brazil. New York: Holt, Rinehart and Winston.

Bates, Marston
1952 Where Winter Never Comes. New York: Scribners.

———

1953 Human Ecology. In Anthropology Today. Alfred L. Kroeber, ed. Chicago: University of Chicago Press.

———

1960 The Forest and the Sea. New York: Vintage Books.

Bateson, Gregory
1963 The Role of Somatic Change in Evolution. Evolution 17:529–539.

———

1972 Steps to an Ecology of Mind. New York: Ballantine Books.

Bell, R. R. and C. A. Heller
1978 Nutrition Studies: An Appraisal of the North Alaskan Eskimo Diet. In The Eskimo of Northwestern Alaska: A Biological Perspective. P. L. Jamison, S. L. Zegura, and F. A. Milan, eds. Stroudsburg, Pa.: Dowden, Hutchinson and Ross.

Bell, R. R., H. H. Draper, and J. G. Bergan
1978 Nutritional Studies: Lactose and Sucrose Tolerance. In The Eskimo of Northwestern Alaska: A Biological Perspective. P. L. Jamison, S. L. Zegura, and F. A. Milan, eds. Stroudsburg, Pa.: Dowden, Hutchinson and Ross.

342

Bennett, John
1967 Social Adaptation in a Northern Plains Region: A Saskatchewan Study. *In* Symposium in the Great Plains of North America. C. C. Zimmerman and S. Russel, eds. Fargo: North Dakota Institute for Regional Studies.

——
1969 Northern Plainsmen. Chicago: Aldine.

——
1972 The Significance of the Concept of Adaptation for Contemporary Socio-Cultural Anthropology. *In* Proceedings of the Eighth Congress of Anthropological and Ethnological Sciences, S–7:237–241.

——
1973 Adaptive Strategy in the Canadian Plains. Canadian Plains Studies 1:181–199.

——
1976 The Ecological Transition. London: Pergamon Press.

Berg, Gosta, ed.
1969 Circumpolar Problems: Habitat, Economy and Social Relations in the Arctic. London: Pergamon Press.

Bertalanffy, Ludwig von
1968 General Systems Theory. Revised ed. New York: Braziller.

Bicchieri, M.G., ed.
1972 Hunters and Gatherers Today: A Socio-Economic Study of Eleven Such Cultures in the Twentieth Century. New York: Holt, Rinehart and Winston.

Billings, W. D.
1974 Arctic and Alpine Vegetation: Plant Adaptations to Cold Summer Climates. *In* Arctic and Alpine Environments. J. D. Ives and R. G. Barry, eds. London: Methuen.

Birdsell, J. B.
1953 Some Environmental and Cultural Factors Influencing the Structure of Australian Aboriginal Populations. American Naturalist 87:171–207.

——
1968 Population Control Factors: Infanticide, Disease, Nutrition and Food Supply. *In* Man the Hunter. Richard B. Lee and I. DeVore, eds. Chicago: Aldine.

——
1976 Realities and Transformations: The Tribes of the Western Desert of Australia. *In* Tribes and Boundaries in Australia. N. Petersen, ed. Canberra: Australian Institute of Aboriginal Studies.

Birket-Smith, Kaj
1959 The Eskimos. London: Methuen.

Bishop, C. A.
1970 The Emergence of Hunting Territories among the Northern Ojibwa. Ethnology 9:1–15.

Bledsoe, L. J. and D. A. Jameson
1969 Model Structure for a Grassland Ecosystem. *In* The Grassland Ecosystem. R. Dix and R. G. Beidleman, eds. Fort Collins: Colorado State University.

343

Bibliography

Bliss, L. C.
1975 Devon Island, Canada. *In* Structure and Function of Tundra Ecosystems. T. Rosswall and O. W. Heal, eds. Stockholm: Swedish Natural Science Research Council.

Bliss, L. C., et al.
1973 Arctic Tundra Ecosystems. Annual Review of Ecology and Systematics 4:359–399.

Blurton-Jones, N. and M. Konner
1976 !Kung Knowledge of Animal Behavior. *In* Kalahari Hunter-Gatherers. Richard B. Lee and I. DeVore, eds. Cambridge, Mass.: Harvard University Press.

Boas, Franz
1896 The Limitations of the Comparative Method of Anthropology. Science (New Series) 4:901–908.

———
1964 The Central Eskimo. Lincoln: University of Nebraska Press. Originally published in 1888 by the Smithsonian Institution Press.

Bogue, Donald
1969 Principles of Demography. New York: John Wiley.

Bohlen, J., F. Milan and F. Halberg
1970 Circumpolar Chronobiology. Proceedings of the Ninth International Congress of Anatomists, Leningrad.

Bolton, Ralph
1973 Aggression and Hypoglycemia Among the Qolla: A Study in Psychological Anthropology. Ethnology 12:227–257.

Borgstrom, Georg
1973 The Food and People Dilemma. North Scituate, Mass.: Duxbury Press.

Boserup, Ester
1965 The Conditions of Agricultural Growth. Chicago: Aldine.

Boulding, Kenneth
1968 General Systems Theory: The Skeleton of Science. *In* Modern Systems Research for the Behavioral Scientist. Walter Buckley, ed. Chicago: Aldine.

Boyden, Stephen
1972 Ecology in Relation to Urban Population Structure. *In* The Structure of Human Populations. G. A. Harrison and A. J. Boyce, eds. Oxford: Clarendon Press.

———
1974 Modeling Energy Requirements in Human Communities. *In* Energy Flow in Human Communities. Paul L. Jamison and S. M. Friedman, eds. University Park, Pa.: US/IBP and SSRC.

Branch, E. D.
1929 The Hunting of the Buffalo. New York: Appleton.

Briggs, L. Cabot
1975 Environment and Human Adaptation in the Sahara. *In* Physiological Anthropology. Albert Damon, ed. New York: Oxford University Press.

Bronson, B.
1972 Farm Labor and the Evolution of Food Production. *In* Population

Growth: Anthropological Implications. Brian Spooner, ed. Cambridge, Mass.: MIT Press.

—— 1975 The Earliest Farming: Demography as Cause and Consequence. *In* Population, Ecology and Social Evolution. Steven Polgar, ed. The Hague: Mouton.

Brookfield, H. C.
1968 New Directions in the Study of Agricultural Systems in Tropical Areas. *In* Evolution and Environment. E. T. Drake, ed. New Haven, Conn.: Yale University Press.

Brookfield, H. C. and P. Brown
1963 Struggle for Land: Agriculture and Group Territories among the Chimbu of the New Guinea Highlands. Melbourne: Oxford University Press.

Brooks, Reuben and D. G. Colley
1973 Which Comes First, the Snail or the Egg?: The Problem of Schistosomiasis Diffusion in Brazil. Nashville, Tenn.: Vanderbilt University, mimeo manuscript.

Brown, G. W., ed.
1968 and 1972 Desert Biology. 2 vols. New York: Academic Press.

Brown, Leslie
1971 The Biology of Pastoral Man as a Factor in Conservation. Biological Conservation 3(2):93–100.

Brown, P. and A. Podolefsky
1976 Population Density, Agricultural Intensity, Land Tenure and Group Size in the New Guinea Highlands. Ethnology 15:211–238.

Bruemmer, F.
1971 Seasons of the Eskimo. Greenwich, Conn.: New York Graphic Society.

Brush, Stephen
1976 Man's Use of an Andean Ecosystem. Human Ecology 4(2):128–132; 147–166.

—— 1977 Mountain, Field and Family: The Economy and Human Ecology of an Andean Valley. Philadelphia: University of Pennsylvania Press.

Buckley, Walter
1967 Sociology and Modern Systems Theory. Englewood Cliffs, N.J.: Prentice-Hall.

Buckley, Walter, ed.
1968 Modern Systems Research for the Behavioral Scientist. Chicago: Aldine.

Buckman, Harry and N. Brady
1969 The Nature and Properties of Soils. Seventh ed. New York: Macmillan.

Budd, G. M.
1974 Physiological Research at Australian Stations in the Antarctic and the Subantarctic. *In* Human Adaptability to Antarctic Conditions. E. K. E. Gunderson, ed. Washington, D. C.: American Geophysical Union.

Bullard, R. W.
1972 Vertebrates at Altitudes. *In* Physiological Adaptations: Desert and Mountain. R. W. Bullard et al., eds. New York: Academic Press.

345

Bibliography

Bunnell, F. L., S. F. MacLean, and J. Brown
1975 Barrow, Alaska, U.S.A. In Structure and Function of Tundra Ecosystems. T. Rosswall and O. W. Heal, eds. Stockholm: Swedish Natural Science Research Council.

Burch, Ernest
1975 Eskimo Kinsmen: Changing Family Relationships in Northwest Alaska. New York: West Publishing Company. American Ethnological Society Monograph, No. 59.

Burch, Ernest S and T. C. Correll
1972 Alliance and Conflict: Inter-regional Relations in Northern Alaska. In Alliance in Eskimo Society. L. Guemple, ed. Seattle: University of Washington Press.

Burchard, Roderick
1976 Myths of the Sacred Leaf: Ecological Perspectives on Coca and Peasant Biocultural Adaptation in Peru. Ph.D dissertation, Department of Anthropology, Indiana University.

Bureau of Indian Affairs (B.I.A.)
1971 A Study of the Impact of the Proposed Trans-Alaska Pipeline on the Alaska Native Population. Arlington, Va.: Educational Systems Resources Corporation.

Burgess, E. W. and D. J. Bogue, eds.
1964 Contributions to Urban Sociology. Chicago: University of Chicago Press.

Burling, R.
1964 Cognition and Componential Analysis: God's Truth or Hocus-Pocus? American Anthropologist 66:20–28.

Burton, A. C. and O. G. Edholm
1955 Man in a Cold Environment. London: Edward Arnold Ltd.

Burton, I.
1969 The Quality of the Environment. In Vegetation, Soils and Wildlife. J. G. Nelson and M. J. Chambers, eds. Toronto: Methuen.

Buskirk, Ellsworth
1976 Work Performance of Newcomers to the Peruvian Highlands. In Man in the Andes. Paul T. Baker and M. Little, eds. Stroudsburg, Pa.: Dowden, Hutchinson and Ross.

Butzer, Karl
1976 Early Hydraulic Civilization in Egypt: A Study in Cultural Ecology. Chicago: University of Chicago Press.

Cain, Stanley and G. M. de Oliveira Castro
1959 Manual of Vegetation Analysis. New York: Hafner Publishing Co.

Calhoun, J. B.
1962 Population Density and Social Pathology. Scientific American 32:139–146.

———
1963 The Ecology and Sociology of the Norway Rat. Washington, D. C.: U.S. Public Health Service, Publication No. 1008.

Cammer, P. and K. Philipson
1973 Urban Factor and Tracheobronchial Clearance. Archives of Environmental Health 27:81–84.

Campbell, J.M.
1968 Territoriality among Ancient Hunters: Interpretations from Ethnography and Nature. *In* Archeology in the Americas. Washington, D. C.: Anthropological Society of Washington.

Cancian, Frank
1972 Change and Uncertainty in a Peasant Economy. Stanford, Cal.: Stanford University Press.

Cantor, Leonard
1970 A World Geography of Irrigation. Second ed. Edinburgh: Oliver and Boyd.

Carlson, L. D. and A. C. L. Hsieh
1965 Cold. *In* The Physiology of Human Survival. O. G. Edholm and A. L. Bacharach, eds. London: Academic Press.

Carneiro, Robert L.
1957 Subsistence and Social Structure: An Ecological Study of the Kuikuru. Ph.D. dissertation, University of Michigan, Department of Anthropology.

———
1961 Slash-and-Burn Agriculture: A Closer Look at its Implications for Settlement Patterns. *In* Man and Culture. Anthony F. Wallace, ed. Fifth International Congress of Anthropological and Ethnological Sciences.

———
1970 The Transition from Hunting to Horticulture in the Amazon Basin. *In* Eighth Congress of Anthropological and Ethnological Sciences 3:243–251.

———
1974 Slash-and-Burn Cultivation among the Kuikuru and Its Implications for Cultural Development in the Amazon Basin. *In* Native South Americans. Patricia Lyon, ed. Boston: Little, Brown.

Carter, William E.
1969 New Lands and Old Traditions. Gainesville: University of Florida Press.

Castaglioni, Arturo
1958 A History of Medicine. Second ed. New York: Alfred A. Knopf.

Catanese, Anthony
1972 Scientific Methods of Urban Analysis. Urbana: University of Illinois Press.

Chagnon, Napoleon
1968 Yanomamo: The Fierce People. New York: Holt, Rinehart and Winston.

Chance, N. A.
1966 The Eskimo of North Alaska. New York: Holt, Rinehart and Winston.

Chandler, T. J.
1976 Human Settlements in the Atmospheric Environment. *In* Man in Urban Environments. G. A. Harrison and J. B. Gibson, eds. Oxford: Oxford University Press.

347

Bibliography

Chapple, Eliot
1970 Culture and Biological Man. New York: Holt, Rinehart and Winston.

Chernigovsky, V. N., ed.
1969 Problems of Space Biology: Adaptation to Hypoxia and the Resistance of an Organism. Washington, D.C.: NASA.

Childe, V. Gordon
1951 Man Makes Himself. New York: New American Library.

Chorley, R. J.
1973 Geography as Human Ecology. In Directions in Geography. R. J. Chorley, ed. London: Methuen.

Clark, Andrew
1956 The Impact of Exotic Invasion on the Remaining New World Mid-Latitude Grasslands. In Man's Role in Changing the Face of the Earth. William L. Thomas, ed. Chicago: University of Chicago Press.

Clarke, William
1966 From Extensive to Intensive Shifting Cultivation: A Succession from New Guinea. Ethnology 5:347–359.

———
1971 Place and People. Berkeley: University of California Press.

———
1976 Maintenance of Agriculture and Human Habitats within the Tropical Forest Ecosystem. Human Ecology 4(3):247–259.

Cleland, C.B.
1966 Do we Need a Sociology of Arid Regions? In Social Research in North American Moisture-Deficient Regions. John W. Bennett, ed. Las Cruces, New Mexico: American Association for the Advancement of Science.

Clements, F. E. and R. W. Chaney
1936 Environment and Life in the Great Plains. Washington, D. C.: Carnegie Institution of Washington.

Cloudsley-Thompson, J.L.
1964 Desert Life. Oxford: Pergamon Press.

———
1977 Man and the Biology of Arid Zones. London: Edward Arnold Publishing Ltd.

Cody, M. L.
1974 Competition and Community Structure. Princeton, N.J.: Princeton University Press.

Cohen, Abner
1965 Arab Border Villages in Israel. Manchester, England: University Press.

Cohen, Yehudi, ed.
1968 Man in Adaptation: The Cultural Present. Chicago: Aldine.

Cole, Donald P.
1975 Nomads of the Nomads. Chicago: Aldine.

Cole, J. W.
1970 Inheritance Processes and their Social Consequences: A Case Study from Northern Italy. Sociologica: Rivista di Study Sociali 4(N.S.): 133–146.

Collier, John
1973 Alaskan Eskimo Education. New York: Holt, Rinehart and Winston.

Colson, Elizabeth
1971 The Social Consequences of Resettlement. Manchester, England: University Press.

Conklin, Harold C.
1954 An Ethnoecological Approach to Shifting Agriculture. Transactions of the New York Academy of Sciences 17(2): 133–142.

——
1957 Hanunóo Agriculture. Rome: Food and Agricultural Organization.

——
1961 The Study of Shifting Cultivation. Current Anthropology 2:27–61.

——
1963 The Study of Shifting Cultivation. Washington, D.C.: Pan American Union.

——
1969 An Ethnoecological Approach to Shifting Agriculture. In Environment and Cultural Behavior. Andrew P. Vayda, ed. New York: Natural History Press.

Cottrell, Fred
1955 Energy and Society: The Relation between Energy, Social Change, and Economic Development. New York: McGraw-Hill.

Crawley, M. J.
1973 Modeling and the Synthesis of Ecological Systems. In Ecological Energetics of Homeotherms. J. A. Gessaman, ed. Logan: Utah State University Press.

Crist, Raymond
1964 Andean America: Some Aspects of Human Migration and Settlement. Nashville, Tenn.: Center for Latin American Studies, Vanderbilt University.

Culver, W. E.
1959 Effects of Cold on Man: An Annotated Bibliography, 1938–1951. Physiological Reviews, Vol. 39, Supplement 3.

Cyert, R. M. and J. G. March
1963 A Behavioral Theory of the Firm. Englewood Cliffs, N. J.: Prentice-Hall.

Dahl, Gudrum and A. Hjort
1976 Having Herds: Pastoral Herd Growth and Household Economy. Stockholm: Department of Social Anthropology, University of Stockholm.

Dahlberg, A. A., et al.
1978 Craniofacial Studies. In The Eskimo of Northwestern Alaska: A Biological Perspective. P. L. Jamison, S. L. Zegura, and F. A. Milan, eds. Stroudsburg, Pa.: Dowden, Hutchinson and Ross.

Dale, M.B.
1970 Systems Analysis and Ecology. Ecology 51:2–16.

Damas, David
1968 The Diversity of Eskimo Societies. In Man the Hunter. Richard B. Lee and I. DeVore, eds. Chicago: Aldine.

Bibliography

———
1969a Environment, History, and Central Eskimo Society. In Contributions to Anthropology: Ecological Essays. David Damas, ed. Ottawa: National Museums of Canada.

Damas, David, ed.
1969b Contributions to Anthropology: Ecological Essays. Ottawa: National Museums of Canada.

Darling, F. F. and M. A. Farvar
1972 Ecological Consequences of Sedentarization of Nomads. In The Careless Technology. M. T. Farvar and J. P. Milton, eds. Garden City, N.Y.: Natural History Press.

Darnell, Rezneat
1973 Ecology and Man. Dubuque, Iowa: William C. Brown.

Davis, Kingsley
1965 The Urbanization of the Human Population. Scientific American 213:41–53.

Dawson, C. A. and E. R. Young
1940 Pioneering in the Prairie Provinces. Toronto: Macmillan.

DeJong, Gordon
1968 Demography and Research with High Altitude Populations. In High Altitude Adaptation in a Peruvian Community. Paul Baker et al., eds. University Park: Pennsylvania State University, Department of Anthropology. Occasional Papers in Anthropology, No. 1.

Denevan, William
1973 Development and the Imminent Demise of the Amazon Rain Forest. Professional Geographer 25(2):130–135.

———
1974 Campa Subsistence in the Gran Pajonal. In Native South Americans. Patricia Lyon, ed. Boston: Little, Brown.

Dettwyler, Steven
1977 The Effects of Verticalization on Adaptation in New Guinea. Unpublished manuscript, Indiana University, Department of Anthropology.

Detwyler, Thomas R. and M. G. Marcus
1972 Urbanization and Environment. North Scituate, Mass.: Duxbury Press.

Detwyler, Thomas, ed.
1971 Man's Impact on Environment. New York: McGraw-Hill.

Deutsch, K. W.
1968 Toward a Cybernetic Model of Man and Society. In Modern Systems Research for the Behavioral Scientist. Walter Buckley, ed. Chicago: Aldine.

di Castri, Francesco
1976 International, Interdisciplinary Research in Ecology: Some Problems of Organization and Execution, the Case of the Man and the Biosphere Program. Human Ecology. 4(3):235–246.

Dice, Lee
1955 Man's Nature and Nature's Man. Ann Arbor: University of Michigan Press.

Dickinson, Joshua
1972 Alternatives to Monoculture in the Humid Tropics of Latin America. The Professional Geographer 24(3):217–222.

Dickinson, Robert
1970 Regional Ecology: The Study of Man's Environment. New York: John Wiley.

Dix, R. and R. G. Beidleman, eds.
1969 The Grassland Ecosystem: A Preliminary Synthesis. Fort Collins: Colorado State University, Range Science Department.

Dorney, R. S.
1973 Role of Ecologists as Consultants in Urban Planning and Design. Human Ecology 1(3):183–199.

Doughty, Paul
1968 Huaylas: An Andean District in Search of Progress. Ithaca, N.Y.: Cornell University Press.

Downing, Theodore and M. Gibson, eds.
1974 Irrigation's Impact on Society. Tucson: University of Arizona Press. Anthropological Papers, No. 25.

Downs, J. and R. Ekvall
1965 Animals and Social Types in the Exploitation of the Tibetan Plateau. In Man, Culture and Animals. Anthony Leeds and Andrew Vayda, eds. Washington, D.C.: American Association for the Advancement of Science.

Doxiadis, Constantinos
1968 Ekistics: An Introduction to the Science of Human Settlements. New York: Oxford University Press.

———
1972 Ekistics: The Science of Human Settlements. In Systems Approach and the City. M. D. Mesarovic and A. Reisman, eds. Amsterdam: North-Holland Publishing Co.

Draper, H. H.
1977 The Aboriginal Eskimo Diet. American Anthropologist 79:309–316.

———
1978 The Aboriginal Eskimo Diet: A Modern Perspective. In The Eskimo of Northwestern Alaska: A Biological Perspective. P. L. Jamison, S. L. Zegura, and F. A. Milan, eds. Stroudsburg, Pa.: Dowden, Hutchinson and Ross.

Dubos, Rene
1968a Man and his Environment: Adaptations and Interactions. In The Fitness of Man's Environment. Washington, D.C.: Smithsonian Institution Press.

———
1968b So Human An Animal. New York: Scribners.

Duffey, E., et al.
1974 Grassland Ecology and Wildlife Management. London: Chapman and Hall.

Duhl, Leonard, ed.
1963 The Urban Condition. New York: Basic Books.

Bibliography

Duncan, Otis D.
1969 The Ecosystem Concept and the Problem of Air Pollution. *In* Environment and Cultural Behavior. Andrew P. Vayda, ed. Garden City, N.Y.: Natural History Press.

Duncan, Otis D. and L. F. Schnore
1959 Cultural, Behavioral and Ecological Perspectives in the Study of Social Organization. American Journal of Sociology 65:132–146.

Durham, William
1976 The Adaptive Significance of Cultural Behavior. Human Ecology 4(2):89–121.

Durnin, J. V. G. A.
1976 Nutrition. *In* Man in Urban Environments. G. A. Harrison and J. B. Gibson, eds. Oxford: Oxford University Press.

——
1975 Energy Expenditure in Humans. *In* Institute of Ecology (TIE) A Manual of Energy Flow Studies. Manuscript mimeo. Available from Institute of Ecology, Indianapolis, Ind.

Durnin, J.V.G.A. and A. Passmore
1955 Human Energy Expenditure. Physiological Reviews 35:801–839.

Dyson-Hudson, Neville
1966 Karimojong Politics. Oxford: Clarendon Press.

Dyson-Hudson, Rada and N. Dyson-Hudson
1969 Subsistence Herding in Uganda. Scientific American 220:76–89.

Eames, E. and J. G. Goode
1977 Anthropology of the City. Englewood Cliffs, N.J.: Prentice-Hall.

Eder, James
1977 Agricultural Intensification and the Returns to Labour in the Phillippine Swidden System. Pacific Viewpoint 19:1–21.

Edgerton, Robert
1965 Cultural vs. Ecological Factors in the Expression of Values, Attitudes and Personality Characteristics. American Anthropologist 67:442–447.

——
1971 The Individual in Cultural Adaptation. Berkeley: University of California Press.

Edholm, O.G.
1967 The Biology of Work. New York: McGraw-Hill.

Edholm, O. G. and H. E. Lewis
1964 Terrestrial Animals in Cold: Man in Polar Regions. *In* Handbook of Physiology: Adaptation to the Environment. D. B. Dill, ed. Washington, D. C.: American Physiological Society.

Edholm, O. G. and A. L. Bacharach, eds.
1965 The Physiology of Human Survival. London: Academic Press.

Eisenberg, J. F. and R. W. Thorington
1973 A Preliminary Analysis of a Neotropical Mammal Fauna. Biotropica 5(3):150–161.

Ekblaw, W.E.
1927 The Material Response of the Polar Eskimo to their Far Arctic Environment. Annals of the Association of American Geographers 27(4):147–198.

Ellis, James E. and Calvin Jennings
1975 A Comparison of Energy Flow Among the Grazing Animals of Different Societies. *In* TIE, A Manual of Energy Flow Studies. Manuscript mimeo. Available from Institute of Ecology, Indianapolis, Ind.

Elton, Charles
1927 Animal Ecology. London: Sedgwick and Jackson.

Emlen, J.M.
1973 Ecology: An Evolutionary Approach. Reading, Mass.: Addison-Wesley.

Emmel, Thomas
1973 An Introduction to Ecology and Population Biology. New York: Norton.

Escobar, Gabriel M.
1976 Social and Political Structure of Nuñoa. *In* Man in the Andes. Paul T. Baker and M. Little, eds. Stroudsburg, Pa.: Dowden, Hutchinson, and Ross.

Evans, Clifford
1955 New Archaeological Interpretations in Northeastern South America. *In* Aboriginal Culture History. Washington, D.C.:Anthropological Society of Washington.

Evans-Pritchard, E.E.
1940 The Nuer. London: Oxford Unversity Press.

Evenari, Michael, et al.
1971 The Negev. Cambridge, Mass.: Harvard University Press.

FAO/UNESCO
1973 Irrigation, Drainage and Salinity. Paris: UNESCO.

Farnworth, Edward and Frank Golley, eds.
1974 Fragile Ecosystems: Evaluation of Research and Applications in the Neotropics. New York: Springer-Verlag.

Fernea, R. A.
1970 Shaykh and Effendi. Cambridge, Mass.: Harvard University Press.

Firey, W.
1945 Sentiment and Symbolism as Ecological Variables. American Sociological Review 10:140–148.

Fischer, Claude
1976 The Urban Experience. New York: Harcourt Brace Jovanovich.

Fittkau, E.J.
1968 The Fauna of South America. *In* Biogeography and Ecology in South America. Vol. 2. E. J. Fittkau et al., eds. The Hague: Junk.

Fittkau, E. J. and H. Klinge
1973 On Biomass and Trophic Structure of the Central Amazonian Rain Forest Ecosystem. Biotropica 5(1):2–14.

Fittkau, E.J., et al., eds.
1968 Biogeography and Ecology in South America. 2 vols. The Hague: Junk.

Bibliography

Fitzhugh, William, ed.
1975 Prehistoric Maritime Adaptations of the Circumpolar Zone. The Hague: Mouton.

Flannery, Kent
1968 Archeological Systems Theory and Early Mesoamerica. In Anthropological Archeology in the Americas. Betty Meggers, ed. Washington, D.C.: Anthropological Society of Washington.

———
1976 The Cultural Evolution of Civilizations. In Human Ecology. Peter Richerson and J. McEvoy, eds. North Scituate, Mass.: Duxbury Press.

Flannery, Kent and Michael Coe
1965 Human Ecology in Southern Coastal Guatemala. Washington, D.C.: Smithsonian Institution.

Flerow, C. C.
1969 On the Origin of the Mammalian Fauna in Canada. In Vegetation, Soils and Wildlife. J. G. Nelson and M. J. Chambers, eds. Toronto: Methuen.

Floyd, B.
1969 Eastern Nigeria. New York: Praeger.

Folk, G. E., Jr.
1966 Introduction to Environmental Physiology. Philadelphia: Lea and Febiger.

Ford, J.
1977 Interactions between Human Societies and Various Trypanosome-Tsetse-Wild Fauna Complexes. In Human Ecology in the Tropics. Second ed. J. P. Garlick and R. W. J. Keay, eds. London: Taylor and Francis.

Forde, C. Darryl
1934 Habitat, Economy and Society. New York: Dutton.

———
1971 Ecology and Social Structure. Proceedings of the Royal Anthropological Institute, Huxley Memorial Lecture: 15–29.

Forrester, Jay
1961 Industrial Dynamics. Cambridge, Mass.: MIT Press.

———
1968 Principles of Systems. Cambridge, Mass.: Wright-Allen Press.

———
1969 Urban Dynamics. Cambridge, Mass.: MIT Press.

———
1971 World Dynamics. Cambridge, Mass.: Wright-Allen Press.

———
1971b Counterintuitive Behavior of Social Systems. Technological Review 73(3):1–16.

Fosberg, F. R.
1973 Temperate Zone Influence on Tropical Forest Land Use: A Plea for Sanity. In Tropical Forest Ecosystems in Africa and South America. Betty Meggers et al., eds. Washington, D.C.: Smithsonian Institution Press.

Fosberg, F. R., et al.
1961 Delimitation of the Humid Tropics. The Geographical Review 51(3):333–347.

Fosberg, F. R., ed.
1963 Man's Place in the Island Ecosystem. Honolulu: Bishop Museum Press.

Foster, George
1966 Reply to Kaplan, Saler and Bennett. American Anthropologist 68:210–214.

Foulks, Edward
1972 The Arctic Hysterias of the North Alaskan Eskimo. Washington, D.C.: American Anthropological Association.

Frake, Charles
1961 The Diagnosis of Disease among the Subanum of Mindanao. American Anthropologist 63:113–132.

———
1962 Cultural Ecology and Ethnography. American Anthropologist 64(1) Part I: 53–59.

Fratkin, Elliot
1977 The Dual Camel-Cattle Economy of the Ariaal Rendille. Paper presented at Seminar on Pastoral Societies of Kenya. Mimeo. Ethnographic Museum of Japan.

Freedman, Ronald, ed.
1964 Population: The Vital Revolution. Garden City, N.Y.: Doubleday.

Freeman, Milton
1971 A Social and Ecologic Analysis of Systematic Female Infanticide among the Netsilik Eskimo. American Anthropologist 73:1011–1018.

Friedman, Jonathan
1974 Marxism, Structuralism and Vulgar Materialism. Man 9:444–469.

Frisancho, A. Roberto
1975 Functional Adaptation to High Altitude Hypoxia. Science 187:313–319.

———
1976 Growth and Morphology at High Altitude. In Man in the Andes. Paul T. Baker and M. Little, eds. Stroudsburg, Pa.: Dowden, Hutchinson and Ross.

Frisch, Rose and J. McArthur
1974 Menstrual Cycles: Fatness as a Determinant of Minimum Weight Necessary for Their Maintenance or Onset. Science 185:949–951.

Frisow, G., ed.
1974 The Casper Site: A Hell Gap Bison Kill on the High Plains. New York: Academic Press.

Fuchs, Andrew
1978 Coca-chewing and High Altitude Stress: Possible Effects of Coca Alkaloids; on Erythropoiesis. Current Anthropology 19(2):277–291.

Gans, Herbert
1967 The Levittowners. New York: Vintage Books.

Bibliography

Garlick, J. P. and R. W. J. Keay, eds.
1977 Human Ecology in the Tropics. Second ed. London: Taylor and Francis.

Garruto, Ralph
1976 Hematology. In Man in the Andes. Paul T. Baker and M. Little, eds. Stroudsburg, Pa.: Dowden, Hutchinson and Ross.

Gaylord-Simpson, George
1964 This View of Life: The World of an Evolutionist. New York: Harcourt, Brace and World.

Geertz, Clifford
1963 Agricultural Involution. Berkeley: University of California Press.

———
1972 The Wet and the Dry: Traditional Irrigation in Bali and Morocco. Human Ecology 1:23–40.

George, C. J. and D. McKinley
1974 Urban Ecology. New York: McGraw-Hill.

Gettys, W.E.
1940 Human Ecology and Social Theory. Social Forces 18:469–476.

Giesel, James
1974 The Biology and Adaptability of Natural Populations. St. Louis, Mo.: C. V. Mosby Company.

Glacken, Clarence
1967 Traces on a Rhodian Shore. Berkeley: University of California Press.

Glantz, Michael, ed.
1977 Desertification: Environmental Degradation in and around Arid Lands. Boulder, Colo.: Westview Press.

Goldenweiser, Alexander
1937 Anthropology. New York: F. S. Crofts and Company.

Goldschmidt, Walter
1971 Independence as an Element in Pastoral Social Systems. Anthropological Quarterly 44(3):132–142.

Golley, Priscilla and Frank Golley, eds.
1972 Tropical Ecology, with an Emphasis on Organic Productivity. Athens, Ga.: International Society of Tropical Ecology.

Gómez-Pompa, A., et al.
1972 The Tropical Rain Forest: A Non-Renewable Resource. Science 177:762–765.

Goodland, R. J. and H. S. Irwin
1975 Amazon Jungle: Green Hell to Red Desert? Amsterdam: Elsevier.

Graburn, Nelson and B. S. Strong
1973 Circumpolar Peoples: An Anthropological Perspective. Pacific Palisades, Cal.: Goodyear Publishing Company.

Graves, Nancy and T. D. Graves
1974 Adaptive Strategies in Urban Migration. Annual Review of Anthropology 3:117–151.

Gray, G. M.
1973 Drugs, Malnutrition and Carbohydrate Absorption. American Journal of Clinical Nutrition 26:121–124.

Greenwood, N. and J. M. B. Edwards
1973 Human Environments and Natural Systems: A Conflict of Dominion. North Scituate, Mass.: Duxbury Press.

Gregor, Thomas
1973 Privacy and Extra-Marital Affairs in a Tropical Forest Community. *In* Peoples and Cultures of Native South America. Daniel Gross, ed. New York: Natural History Press.

Grigg, D. D.
1974 The Agricultural Systems of the World. London: Cambridge University Press.

Gross, Daniel
1975 Protein Capture and Cultural Development in the Amazon Basin. American Anthropologist 77(3):526–549.

Gross, Daniel and Barbara Underwood
1970 Technological Change and Caloric Costs. American Anthropologist 73:725–740.

Gross, Daniel, ed.
1973 Peoples and Cultures of Aboriginal South America. New York: Natural History Press.

Grossman, Larry
1977 Man-Environment Relationships in Anthropology and Geography. Annals of the Association of American Geographers 67(1):126–144.

Grover, R. F.
1974 Man Living at High Altitudes. *In* Arctic and Alpine Environments. J. D. Ives and R. G. Barry, eds. London: Methuen.

Gubser, N. J.
1965 The Nunamiut Eskimos: Hunters of Caribou. New Haven, Conn.: Yale University Press.

Guemple, Lee, ed.
1972 Alliance in Eskimo Society. Seattle: University of Washington Press. Proceedings of the American Ethnological Society.

Gulliver, P. H.
1955 The Family Herds. London: Routledge and Keagan Paul.

———
1975 Nomadic Movements: Causes and Implications. *In* Pastoralism in Tropical Africa. T. Monod, ed. London: International African Institute.

Gunderson, E. K. E., ed.
1974 Human Adaptability to Antarctic Conditions. Washington, D.C.: American Geophysical Union.

Gussow, Z.
1960 Pibloktok Hysteria Among the Polar Eskimos. *In* Psychoanalytic Study of Society. W. Muensterberger, ed. New York: International University Press.

Gwynne, M. D.
1977 Land Use by the Southern Turkana. Paper presented at Seminar on Pastoral Societies of Kenya. Mimeo. Ethnographic Museum of Japan.

Bibliography

Haas, Jere
1976 Prenatal and Infant Growth and Development. *In* Man in the Andes. Paul T. Baker and M. Little, eds. Stroudsburg, Pa.: Dowden, Hutchinson and Ross.

Hadley, G.
1967 Introduction to Probability and Statistical Decision Theory. New York: Holden-Day.

Haffer, J.
1969 Speciation in Amazonian Forest Birds. Science 165:131–137.

Hall, Edward T.
1968 Human Needs and Inhuman Cities. *In* The Fitness of Man's Environment. Washington, D.C.: Smithsonian Institution Press.

Hammel, H. T.
1964 Terrestrial Animals in Cold: Recent Studies of Primitive Man. *In* Handbook of Physiology: Adaptation to the Environment. D. B. Dill, ed. Washington, D.C.: American Physiological Society.

Hanna, Joel
1968 Cold Stress and Microclimate in the Quechua Indians of Southern Peru. *In* High Altitude Adaptation in a Peruvian Community. Paul T. Baker et al., eds. University Park: Occasional Papers in Anthropology, No. 1, Pennsylvania State University.

——— 1976 Natural Exposure to Cold. *In* Man in the Andes. Paul T. Baker and M. Little, eds. Stroudsburg, Pa.: Dowden, Hutchinson, and Ross.

Hanna, J. M. and P. T. Baker
1974 Comparative Heat Tolerance of Shipibo Indians and Peruvian Mestizos. Human Biology 46:69–80.

Harris, Larry, et al.
1975 Modelling and Systems Studies as a Tool in Understanding Human Ecology. *In* TIE, A Guide to Energy Flow Studies. Mimeo manuscript. Available from Institute of Ecology, Butler University, Indianapolis, Ind.

Harris, Marvin
1968 The Rise of Anthropological Theory. New York: Crowell.

——— 1974a Why a Perfect Knowledge of All the Rules One Must Know to Act Like a Native Cannot Lead to the Knowledge of How Natives Act. Journal of Anthropological Research 30(4):242–251.

——— 1974b Cows, Pigs, Wars and Witches. New York: Vintage Press.

——— 1977 Cannibals and Kings. New York: Random House.

Harrison, G. A., et al.
1977 Human Biology. Second Ed. Oxford: Clarendon Press.

Harrison, G. A. and A. J. Boyce, eds.
1972 The Structure of Human Populations. Oxford: Clarendon Press.

Harrison, G. A. and J. B. Gibson, eds.
1976 Man In Urban Environments. Oxford: Oxford University Press.

Hart, J. S., et al., eds.
1969 Proceedings of the International Symposium on High Altitude and Cold. Federation Proceedings 28(3):933–1321.

Hassan, F. A.
1972 Population Dynamics and the Beginnings of Domestication in the Nile Valley. Paper presented at annual meeting, American Anthropological Association.

Hatcher, J. D. and D. B. Jennings, eds.
1966 Proceedings of the International Symposium on the Cardiovascular and Respiratory Effects of Hypoxia. New York: Hafner.

Havlick, Spenser W.
1974 The Urban Organism. New York: Macmillan.

Hawley, Amos
1950 Human Ecology: A Theory of Community Structure. New York: Ronald Press.

———
1971 Urban Society: An Ecological Approach. New York: Ronald Press.

———
1973 Ecology and Population. Science 179:1196–1201.

Hawley, Amos, ed.
1968 Roderick McKenzie on Human Ecology. Chicago: University of Chicago Press.

Heer, David, ed.
1968 Readings on Population. Englewood Cliffs, N.J.: Prentice-Hall.

Hegen, E. E.
1966 Highways into the Upper Amazon. Gainesville: University of Florida Press.

Heider, Karl
1970 The Dugum Dani. Chicago: Aldine.

———
1972 Environment, Subsistence and Society. Annual Review of Anthropology 1:207–226.

Heijnen, Joop and R. W. Kates
1974 Northeast Tanzania: Comparative Observations along a Moisture Gradient. In Natural Hazards. Gilbert White, ed. New York: Oxford University Press.

Heintzelman, O. H. and R. M. Highsmith
1973 World Regional Geography. Fourth ed. Englewood Cliffs, N.J.: Prentice-Hall.

Heizer, Robert
1955 Primitive Man as an Ecologic Factor. Kroeber Anthropological Society Papers 13:1–31.

Helly, Walter
1975 Urban Systems Models. New York: Academic Press.

Helm, June
1962 The Ecological Approach in Anthropology. American Journal of Sociology 67:630–639.

Bibliography

Helms, Mary W.
1971 Asang: Adaptations to Culture Contact in a Miskito Community. Gainesville: University of Florida Press.

Herbert, David
1972 Urban Geography. London: David and Charles.

Herskovits, Melville
1926 The Cattle Complex in East Africa. American Anthropologist 28:230–272; 361–388; 494–528.

Hett, J. M. and R. V. O'Neill
1974 Systems Analysis of the Aleut Ecosystem. Arctic Anthropology 11:31–40.

Hildes, J. A.
1966 The Circumpolar People: Health and Physiological Adaptations. In The Biology of Human Adaptability. Paul T. Baker and J. S. Weiner, eds. Oxford: Clarendon Press.

Hill, E. S., ed.
1966 Arid Lands. London: Methuen.

Hills, T. L. and R. E. Randall
1968 The Ecology of the Forest/Savanna Boundary. Montreal: McGill University Savanna Research Project, Department of Geography.

Hoff, C. J. and A. E. Abelson
1976 Fertility. In Man in the Andes. Paul T. Baker and M. Little, eds. Stroudsburg, Pa.: Dowden, Hutchinson and Ross.

Holding, A. J., et al.
1974 Soil Organisms and Decomposition in Tundra. Stockholm: IBP Tundra Biome.

Holdridge, L. R.
1967 Life Zone Ecology. Revised ed. San Jose, Costa Rica: Tropical Science Center.

Holling, Crawford S.
1973 Resilience and Stability of Ecological Systems. Annual Review of Ecology and Systematics 4:1–23.

Holmberg, Allan
1969 Nomads of the Long Bow. New York: Natural History Press.

Hopkins, Brian
1974 Forest and Savanna. Second ed. London: Heinemann.

Hopkins, D. M., ed.
1967 The Bering Land Bridge. Stanford, Cal.: Stanford University Press.

Horowitz, M.
1975 Herdsman and Husbandman in Niger: Values and Strategies. In Pastoralism in Tropical Africa. T. Monod, ed. London: International African Institute.

Howell, Nancy
1976 The Population of the Dobe Area. In Kalahari Hunter-Gatherers. Richard B. Lee and I. DeVore, eds. Cambridge, Mass.: Harvard University Press.

Humphrey, Robert
1962 Range Ecology. New York: Ronald Press.

360

Hunt, E. and R. Hunt
1974 Irrigation, Conflict and Politics: A Mexican Case. *In* Irrigation's Impact on Society. T. Downing and M. Gibson, eds. Tucson: University of Arizona Press.

Huntington, Ellsworth
1915 Civilization and Climate. New Haven, Conn.: Yale University Press.

Hurtado, Alberto
1964 Animals in High Altitudes: Resident Man. *In* Handbook of Physiology: Adaptation to the Environment. D. B. Dill, ed. Washington, D.C.: American Physiological Society.

Hyder, D. N.
1969 The Impact of Domestic Animals on the Function and Structure of Grassland Ecosystems. *In* The Grassland Ecosystem. R. L. Dix and R. G. Beidleman, eds. Fort Collins: Colorado State University.

Iizumi, S. and Y. Iwanami
1975 Effects of Burning in Grasslands. *In* Ecological Studies in Japanese Grasslands. M. Numata, ed. Tokyo: University of Tokyo Press.

Ingold, Tim
1974 On Reindeer and Men. Man 9(4):523–538.

Ingram, D. L.
1977 Physiological Reactions to Heat in Man. *In* Human Ecology in the Tropics. Second ed. J. P. Garlick and R. W. J. Keay, eds. London: Taylor and Francis.

Ingram, D. L. and L. E. Mount
1975 Man and Animals in Hot Environments. New York: Springer-Verlag.

International Institute for Tropical Agriculture (IITA)
1974 Annual Report, Farming Systems Program. Ibadan, Nigeria: IITA.

International Rice Research Institute (IRRI)
1973 Annual Report. Los Baños, Philippines. Mimeo.

Irons, William
1968 The Turkmen Nomads. Natural History 77(9):44–51.

———
1971 Variation in Political Stratification among the Yomut Turkmen. Anthropological Quarterly 44(3):143–156.

———
1972 Variation in Economic Organization: A Comparison of the Pastoral Yomut and the Basseri. *In* Perspectives on Nomadism. William Irons and N. Dyson-Hudson, eds. Leiden, The Netherlands: Brill.

———
1975 The Yomut Turkmen: A Study of Social Organization among a Central Asian Turkic-Speaking Population. Ann Arbor: University of Michigan, Anthropological Papers, No. 58.

Irving, Laurence
1960 Human Adaptation to Cold. Nature 185: 572–574.

———
1972 Arctic Life of Birds and Mammals, Including Man. New York: Springer-Verlag.

Bibliography

Irving, Laurence, et al.
1960 Metabolism and Temperature of Arctic Indian Man during a Cold Night. Journal of Applied Physiology 15(4): 635–648.

Irving, W. and C. Harington
1973 Upper Pleistocene Radiocarbon-dated Artifacts from the Northern Yukon. Science 179: 335–340.

Ives, Jack D.
1974 The Impact of Motor Vehicles on the Tundra Environments. In Arctic and Alpine Environments. J. D. Ives and R. G. Barry, eds. London: Methuen.

Ives J. D. and R. G. Barry
1974 Postscript. In Arctic and Alpine Environments. J. D. Ives and R. G. Barry, eds. London: Methuen.

Jaeger, Edmund
1957 The North American Deserts. Stanford, Cal.: Stanford University Press.

Jaffe, A. J.
1951 Handbook of Statistical Methods for Demographers. Washington, D.C.: U.S. Bureau of the Census, Government Printing Office.

James, Preston
1966 A Geography of Man. Third ed. New York: John Wiley.

Jamison, Paul L.
1978 Research Area and Populations. In The Eskimo of Northwestern Alaska: A Biological Perspective. P. L. Jamison, S. L. Zegura, and F. A. Milan, eds. Stroudsburg, Pa.: Dowden, Hutchinson and Ross.

Jamison, Paul and S. Friedman, eds.
1974 Energy Flow in Human Communities. University Park, Pa.: US International Biological Program and Social Science Research Council.

Jamison, Paul L., S. L. Zegura, and F. A. Milan, eds.
1978 The Eskimo of Northwestern Alaska: A Biological Perspective. Stroudsburg, Pa.: Dowden, Hutchinson and Ross. US/IBP Synthesis, Vol. 8.

Janick, Jules, et al.
1974 Plant Science. Second ed. San Francisco: W. H. Freeman and Co.

Janzen, Daniel
1975 Tropical Agroecosystems. In Food: Politics, Economics, Nutrition and Research. Philip Abelson, ed. Washington, D.C.: American Association for the Advancement of Science.

Johnson, Allen
1971 Sharecroppers of the Sertao. Stanford, Cal.: Stanford University Press.

_____
1974 Ethnoecology and Planting Practices in a Swidden Agricultural System. American Ethnologist 1:87–101.

_____
1977 The Energy Costs of Technology in a Changing Environment: A Machiguenga Case. In Material Culture. Proceedings of the American Ethnological Society. St. Paul, Minn.: West Publishing Company.

Johnson, W., V. Stoltzfus, and P. Craumer
1977 Energy Conservation in Amish Agriculture. Science 198:373–378.

Jonassen, C. T.
1949 Cultural Variables in the Ecology of an Ethnic Group. American Sociological Review 14:32–41.

Jones, P. A.
1968 Fieldwork in Geography. London: Longmans, Green and Company.

Junk, W. J.
1975 Aquatic Wildlife of Fisheries. In The Use of Ecological Guidelines for Development in the American Humid Tropics. Morges, Switzerland: International Union for Conservation of Nature and Natural Resources.

Jurion, F. and J. Henry
1969 Can Primitive Farming Be Modernized? London: Agra-Europe.

Kallio, P.
1975 Kevo, Finland. In Structure and Function of Tundra Ecosystems. T. Rosswall and O. W. Heal, eds. Stockholm: Swedish Natural Science Research Council.

Kates, R. W.
1971 Natural Hazard in Human Ecological Perspective: Hypotheses and Models. Economic Geography 47:438–451.

Keller, Wesley
1973 Future Needs in Range Research. In The Biology and Utilization of Grasses. V. B. Youngner and C. M. McKell, eds. New York: Academic Press.

Kellogg, Charles
1959 Shifting Cultivation. Journal of Soil and Water Conservation in India. 7:35–59.

Kemp, William
1971 The Flow of Energy in a Hunting Society. Scientific American 224(3):104–115.

———
1974 Energy Flow in Inuit Communities: An Analysis of Theory, Models and Measurement. In Energy Flow in Human Communities. Paul L. Jamison and S. Friedman, eds. University Park, Pa.: US/IBP and SSRC.

Kerslake, D. McE.
1972 The Stress of Hot Environments. London: Cambridge University Press.

Keyfitz, Nathan
1968 Introduction to the Mathematics of Population. Reading, Mass.: Addison-Wesley Co.

Keyfitz, Nathan and W. Fliegler
1971 Population: Facts and Methods of Demography. San Francisco: W. H. Freeman and Co.

Kilbridge, M. D., R. P. O'Block, and P. V. Teplitz
1970 Urban Analysis. Boston: Harvard University Business School, Division of Research.

King, J. A.
1973 The Ecology of Aggressive Behavior. Annual Review of Ecology and Systematics 4:117–138.

Bibliography

Klinge, H., et al.
1975 Biomass and Structure in a Central Amazonian Rain Forest. *In* Tropical Ecological Systems. Frank B. Golley and E. Medina, eds. New York: Springer-Verlag.

Knodel, John
1977 Breast-feeding and Population Growth. Science 198:1111–1115.

Kormondy, Edward
1976 Concepts of Ecology. Second ed. Englewood Cliffs, N.J.: Prentice-Hall.

Krader, Lawrence
1961 Ecology of Central Asian Pastoralism. *In* Studies in Human Ecology. G. A. Theodorson, ed. New York: Harper & Row.

─────
1963 Peoples of Central Asia. Bloomington: Indiana University Publication.

Kraenzel, C. F.
1955 The Great Plains in Transition. Norman: University of Oklahoma Press.

Kraus, M. E.
1973 Eskimo-Aleut. *In* Linguistics in North America. Thomas A. Sebeok, ed. Current Trends in Linguistics, Vol. 10. The Hague: Mouton.

Kroeber, Alfred
1939 Cultural and Natural Areas of Native North America. Berkeley: University of California Press.

Kummer, Hans
1971 Primate Societies: Group Techniques of Ecological Adaptation. Chicago: Aldine.

Ladell, W. S. S.
1964 Terrestrial Animals in Humid Heat: Man. *In* Handbook of Physiology: Adaptation to the Environment. D. B. Dill, ed. Washington, D. C.: American Physiological Society.

Laessing, R. H., et al.
1978 Biochemical Variation: The Development of Biochemical Normal Ranges for Eskimo Populations. *In* The Eskimo of Northwestern Alaska: A Biological Perspective. Paul L. Jamison, S. L. Zegura and F. A. Milan, eds. Stroudsburg, Pa.: Dowden, Hutchinson and Ross.

Lakshmanan, T. R., L. Chatterjee, and P. Roy
1976 Housing Requirements and National Resources. Science 192:943–949.

Lambrecht, Frank
1972 The Tsetse Fly: A Blessing or a Curse? *In* The Careless Technology. M. T. Farvar and J. P. Milton, eds. Garden City, N.Y.: Natural History Press.

Landsberg, H.E.
1956 The Climate of Towns. *In* Man's Role in Changing the Face of the Earth, Vol. 2, William L. Thomas, ed. Chicago: University of Chicago Press.

Lange, K., et al.
1960 Physical Fitness of Arctic Indians. Journal of Applied Physiology 15(4):645–648.

Lantis, Margaret
1947 Alaskan Eskimo Ceremonialism. New York: J. J. Augustin. Monograph of the American Ethnological Society, No. 11.

Lapatra, Jack
1973 Applying the Systems Approach to Urban Development. Stroudsburg, Pa.: Dowden, Hutchinson and Ross.

Lasker, Gabriel
1976 Human Biological Adaptability. *In* Human Ecology. Peter Richerson and J. McEvoy, eds. North Scituate, Mass.: Duxbury Press.

Lathrap, Donald
1970 The Upper Amazon. New York: Praeger.

Laughlin, Charles D., Jr. and I. Brady, eds.
1978 Extinction and Survival in Human Populations. New York: Columbia University Press.

Laughlin, C. and E. d'Aquili
1974 Biogenetic Structuralism. New York: Columbia University Press.

Laughlin, William S.
1952 The Eskimo-Aleut Community. Anthropological Papers of the University of Alaska 1(1):25-43.

——— 1963 Eskimos and Aleuts: Their Origins and Evolution. Science 142:633–645.

——— 1966 Genetical and Anthropological Characteristics of Arctic Populations. *In* The Biology of Human Adaptability. Paul T. Baker and J. S. Weiner, eds. Oxford: Clarendon Press.

——— 1968a Hunting: An Integrating Biobehavior System and its Evolutionary Importance. *In* Man the Hunter. Richard B. Lee and I. DeVore, eds. Chicago: Aldine.

——— 1968b The Demography of Hunters: An Eskimo Example. *In* Man the Hunter. Richard B. Lee and I. DeVore, eds. Chicago: Aldine.

——— 1972 Ecology and Population Structure in the Arctic. *In* The Structure of Human Populations. G. Harrison and A. Boyce, eds. Oxford: Clarendon Press.

——— 1975 Aleuts: Ecosystem, Holocene History and Siberian Origin. Science 189:507–515.

Lave, C. and J. March
1975 An Introduction to Models in the Social Sciences. New York: Harper & Row.

Leach, E. R.
1961 Pul Eliya. Cambridge: Cambridge University Press.

Leake, Chauncey
1964 Perspectives of Adaptation: Historical Backgrounds. *In* Handbook of Physiology: Adaptation to the Environment. D. B. Dill, ed. Washington, D.C.: American Physiological Society.

Lee, D. H. K.
1964 Terrestrial Animals in Dry Heat: Man in the Desert. *In* Handbook of Physiology: Adaptation to the Environment. D. B. Dill, ed. Washington, D.C.: American Physiological Society.

365

Bibliography

——— 1968 Man in the Desert. *In* Desert Biology. G. W. Brown, ed. New York: Academic Press.

——— 1969 Variability in Human Response to Arid Environments. *In* Arid Lands in Perspective. W. McGinnies and B. Goodman, eds. Washington, D.C.: American Association for the Advancement of Science.

Lee, Richard B.
1968 What Hunters Do for a Living, or How to Make Out on Scarce Resources. *In* Man the Hunter. Richard B. Lee and I. DeVore, eds. Chicago: Aldine.

——— 1969 !Kung Bushman Subsistence: An Input-Output Analysis. *In* Contributions to Anthropology: Ecological Essays. David Damas, ed. Ottawa: National Museums of Canada.

——— 1972 !Kung Spatial Organization: An Ecological and Historical Perspective. Human Ecology 1(2):125–147.

——— 1976 !Kung Spatial Organization. *In* Kalahari Hunter-Gatherers. Richard B. Lee and I. DeVore, eds. Cambridge, Mass.: Harvard University Press.

Lee, Richard B. and I. DeVore, eds.
1968 Man the Hunter. Chicago: Aldine.

——— 1976 Kalahari Hunter-Gatherers. Cambridge, Mass.: Harvard University Press.

Leeds, Anthony
1974 The Ideology of the Yaruro Indians in Relation to Socio-Economic Organization. *In* Native South Americans. Patricia Lyon, ed. Boston: Little, Brown.

Leeds, Anthony and Andrew P. Vayda, eds.
1965 Man, Culture and Animals. Washington, D.C.: American Association for the Advancement of Science.

Lees, Susan
1974 Hydraulic Development as a Process of Response. Human Ecology 2(3):159–175.

——— 1976 Choice of Technology in Irrigated Agriculture. Paper presented at 75th Annual Meeting, American Anthropological Association.

Lees, Susan and D. Bates
1977 The Role of Exchange in Productive Specialization. American Anthropologist 79(4):824–841.

Leibenstein, H.
1976 Beyond Economic Man. Cambridge, Mass.: Harvard University Press.

Leigh, Egbert Giles, Jr.
1975 Structure and Climate in Tropical Rain Forest. Annual Review of Ecology and Systematics 6:67–86.

Leithard, C. S. and A. R. Lind
1964 Heat Stress and Heat Disorders. London: Cassell.

Levin, R. I. and C. A. Kirkpatrick
1975 Quantitative Approaches to Management. Third ed. New York: McGraw-Hill.

Levin, S. A., ed.
1974 Ecosystem Analysis and Prediction. Philadelphia: Society for Industrial and Applied Mathematics.

Levine, Norman, et al.
1975 Human Ecology. North Scituate, Mass.: Duxbury Press.

Levins, Richard
1968 Evolution in Changing Environments. Princeton, N.J.: Princeton University Press.

Levy, Jerrold
1961 Ecology of the South Plains. American Ethnological Society Proceedings. Mimeo.

Lewis, James K.
1970 Primary Producers in Grassland Ecosystems. *In* The Grassland Ecosystem: A Supplement. R. L. Dix and R. G. Beidelman, eds. Fort Collins: Colorado State University, Range Science Department.

Lewontin, R. C., ed.
1968 Population Biology and Evolution. Syracuse, N.Y.: Syracuse University Press.

Linares, Olga
1976 Garden Hunting in the American Tropics. Human Ecology 4(4):331–349.

Lindblom, Charles
1964 The Science of Muddling Through. *In* The Making of Decisions. W. J. Gore and J. W. Dyson, eds. New York: Free Press.

Lindeman, R. L.
1942 The Trophic-dynamic Aspect of Ecology. Ecology 23:399–418.

Linkola, Martti
1973 The Snowmobile in Lapland: Its Economic and Social Effects. *In* Circumpolar Problems: Habitat, Economy and Social Relations in the Arctic. G. Berg, ed. Oxford: Pergamon Press.

Little, Michael
1968 Racial and Developmental Factors in Foot Cooling: Quechua Indians and U.S. Whites. *In* High Altitude Adaptation in a Peruvian Community. Paul T. Baker et al. University Park: Occasional Papers in Anthropology, No. 1, Pennsylvania State University.

———
1976 Physiological Responses to Cold. *In* Man in the Andes. Paul T. Baker and M. Little, eds. Stroudsburg, Pa.: Dowden, Hutchinson and Ross.

Little, Michael, et al.
1971 Population Differences and Developmental Changes in Extremity Temperature Responses to Cold among Andean Indians. Human Biology 43:70–91.

Little, Michael and D. H. Hochner
1973 Human Thermoregulation, Growth and Mortality. Reading, Mass.: An Addison-Wesley Module in Anthropology, No. 36.

Bibliography

Little, Michael and Paul T. Baker
1976 Environmental Adaptations and Perspectives. *In* Man in the Andes. Paul T. Baker and M. Little, eds. Stroudsburg, Pa.: Dowden, Hutchinson and Ross.

Little, Michael and G. Morren
1976 Ecology, Energetics and Human Variability. Dubuque, Iowa: William C. Brown Publishers.

Livingstone, F. B.
1968 The Effects of Warfare on the Biology of the Human Species. *In* War: The Anthropology of Armed Conflict. Morton Fried et al., eds. New York: Doubleday.

Longman, K. A. and J. Jenix
1974 Tropical Forest and its Environment. London: Longman.

Loucks, Orie
1972 Contaminants and Recycling in Relation to Biogeochemical Cycles. *In* Challenging Biological Problems. J. A. Behnke, ed. New York: Oxford University Press.

Lovett, J. V., ed.
1973 The Environmental, Economic and Social Significance of Drought. Sydney, Australia: Angus and Robertson.

Lowenstein, Frank
1968 Some Aspects of Human Ecology in South America. *In* Biogeography and Ecology in South America. E. J. Fittkau et al., eds. The Hague: Junk.

——
1973 Some Consideration of Biological Adaptation by Aboriginal Man. *In* Tropical Forest Ecosystems in Africa and South America. Betty Meggers et al., eds. Washington, D.C.: Smithsonian Institution Press.

Lugo, Ariel and Samuel Snedaker, eds.
1971 Readings in Ecological Systems. New York: MSS Educational Publishing Company.

Lyon, Patricia, ed.
1974 Native South Americans. Boston: Little, Brown.

McGhee, Robert
1974 The Peopling of Arctic North America. *In* Arctic and Alpine Environments. J. D. Ives and R. G. Barry, eds. London: Methuen.

McKell, C. M.
1975 Shrubs: A Neglected Resource of Arid Lands. *In* Food: Politics, Economics, Nutrition and Research. Philip Abelson, ed. Washington, D.C.: American Association for the Advancement of Science.

McLoughlin, J. B.
1969 Urban and Regional Planning: A Systems Approach. New York: Praeger.

McLuhan, Marshall
1962 The Gutenberg Galaxy. New York: Signet.

MacArthur, R. H. and E. Pianka
1966 An Optimal Use of a Patchy Environment. American Naturalist 100:603–609.

368

Mackay, D. M.
1968a The Informational Analysis of Questions and Commands. *In* Modern Systems Research for the Behavioral Scientist. Walter Buckley, ed. Chicago: Aldine.

———

1968b Towards an Information-Flow Model of Human Behavior. *In* Modern Systems Research for the Behavioral Scientist. Walter Buckley, ed. Chicago: Aldine.

Mackay, J. R.
1969 Tundra and Taiga. *In* Vegetation, Soils and Wildlife. J. G. Nelson and M. J. Chambers, eds. Toronto: Methuen.

Mackintosh, W. A.
1934 Prairie Settlement. Toronto: Macmillan.

Malin, J. C.
1947 The Grassland of North America. Ann Arbor, Michigan: Edward Brothers, Inc.

Man and The Biosphere/UNESCO
1973 Ecological Effects of Energy Utilization in Urban and Industrial Systems. Paris: UNESCO. Final Report of Panel 11.

———

1974 Integrated Ecological Research and Training Needs in the Sahelian Region. Paris: UNESCO.

March, J. G. and H. A. Simon
1958 Organizations. New York: John Wiley.

Martin, Peggy
1976 Ideas for the Study of Ritual and Ecology among the Early Historic Native Peoples. Unpublished manuscript Indiana University, Department of Anthropology.

Massing, Andreas
1976 Economic Development and Its Effects on Traditional Land Use Systems in the Tropical Forests of West Africa. Paper presented at the 75th Annual Meeting, American Anthropological Association.

Matveyeva, N. V., et al.
1975 Maria Pronchitsheva Bay, USSR. *In* Structure and Function of Tundra Ecosystems. T. Rosswall and O. W. Heal, eds. Stockholm: Swedish Natural Science Research Council.

Mauss, Michael and M. H. Beuchat
1905 Essai sur les variations saisoniéres des sociétés Eskimo. Paris: L'Annee Sociologique.

Maybury-Lewis, David
1967 Akwē-Shavante Society. Oxford: Clarendon Press.

Mazess, Richard
1975 Human Adaptation to High Altitude. *In* Physiological Anthropology. Albert Damon, ed. New York: Oxford University Press.

Mazess, Richard and W. Mather
1978 Biochemical Variation: Bone Mineral Content. *In* The Eskimo of Northwestern Alaska: A Biological Perspective. Paul L. Jamison, S. L. Zegura, and F. A. Milan, eds. Stroudsburg, Pa.: Dowden, Hutchinson and Ross.

Meadows, Dennis and D. Meadows
1972 The Limits to Growth. New York: Universe Books.

Meggers, Betty
1954 Environmental Limitations on the Development of Culture. American Anthropologist 56:801–824.

_____
1957 Environment and Culture in the Amazon Basin: An Appraisal of the Theory of Environmental Determinism. In Studies in Human Ecology. Washington, D.C.: Anthropological Society of Washington/Organization of American States.

_____
1971 Amazonia. Chicago: Aldine.

_____
1974 Environment and Culture in Amazonia. In Man and the Amazon. Charles Wagley, ed. Gainesville: University of Florida Press.

_____
1975 Application of the Biological Model of Diversification to Cultural Distributions in Tropical Lowland South America. Biotropica 7(3):141–161.

Meggers, Betty, E. S. Ayensu, and W. D. Ducksworth, eds.
1973 Tropical Forest Ecosystems in Africa and South America. Washington, D.C.: Smithsonian Institution Press.

Megitt, M.
1965 The Lineage System of the Mae Enga of New Guinea. Edinburgh: Oliver and Boyd.

_____
1968 Marriage, Classes and Demography in Central Australia. In Man the Hunter. Richard B. Lee and I. DeVore, eds. Chicago: Aldine.

Meier, Richard
1976 A Stable Urban Ecosystem. Science 192:962–968.

Mesarovic, M. D. and A. Reisman, eds.
1972 Systems Approach and the City. Amsterdam: North-Holland Publishing Company.

Messerschmidt, Donald
1976 Ecological Change and Adaptation among the Gurungs of the Nepal Himalayas. Human Ecology 4(2):167–185.

Michelson, William
1976 Man and His Urban Environment: A Sociological Approach. Revised ed. Reading, Mass.: Addison-Wesley.

Milan, F. A.
1978 Multidisciplinary Research on Northwest Alaskan Eskimos. In The Eskimo of Northwestern Alaska: A Biological Perspective. P. L. Jamison, S. L. Zegura, and F. A. Milan, eds. Stroudsburg, Pa.: Dowden, Hutchinson and Ross.

Milgram, Stanley
1970 The Experience of Living in Cities. Science 167:1461–1468.

Miller, G. Tyler
1975 Living in the Environment. Belmont, Cal.: Wadsworth Publishing Company.

370

Millon, René
1962 Variations in Social Responses to the Practice of Irrigation Agriculture. *In* Civilizations in Desert Lands. R. B. Woodbury, ed. Salt Lake City: University of Utah Anthropological Papers.

Minshull, Roger
1970 The Changing Nature of Geography. London: Hutchinson University Library.

Miracle, Marvin
1973 The Congo Basin as a Habitat for Man. *In* Tropical Forest Ecosystems in Africa and South America. Betty Meggers et al., eds. Washington, D.C.: Smithsonian Institution Press.

Mitchell, R. E.
1976 Cultural and Health Influences on Building, Housing, and Community Standards: Cost Implications for the Human Habitat. Human Ecology 4(4):297–330.

Moerman, M.
1968 Agricultural Change and Peasant Choice in a Thai Village. Berkeley: University of California Press.

Moir, W. H.
1969 Energy Fixation and the Role of Primary Producers in Energy Flux of Grassland Ecosystems. *In* The Grassland Ecosystem. R. L. Dix and R. G. Beidleman, eds. Fort Collins: Colorado State University, Range Science Department.

Monge, Carlos
1948 Acclimatization in the Andes. Baltimore: Johns Hopkins University Press.

Moore, C. W. E.
1966 Distribution of Grasslands. *In* Grasses and Grasslands. C. Barnard, ed. New York: St. Martin's Press.

Moran, Emilio
1973a An Energetics Methodology for Cultural Ecology. Mimeo manuscript. Indiana University, Department of Anthropology.

———
1973b Energy Flow Analysis and *Manihot esculenta* Crantz. Acta Amazonica 3(3):28–39.

———
1975 Pioneer Farmers of the Transamazon Highway: Adaptation and Agricultural Production in the Lowland Tropics. Ph.D. dissertation, University of Florida, Department of Anthropology.

———
1976 Agricultural Development in the Transamazon Highway. Bloomington: Indiana University/Latin American Studies Working Papers.

Morgan, Lael
1977 An Ancient Eskimo Nation Takes on New Life. Alaska 43(9):34–35, 86–89.

Mott, G. O. and Hugh Popenoe
1975 The Ecophysiology of Tropical Grasslands. Gainesville: Center of Tropical Agriculture, University of Florida. Mimeo.

Bibliography

Müller-Beck, Hansjürgen
1967 On Migrations of Hunters across the Bering Land Bridge in the Upper Pleistocene. *In* The Bering Land Bridge. D. M. Hopkins, ed. Stanford, Cal.: Stanford University Press.

Müller-Wille, L.
1974 The Snowmobile, Lapps and Reindeer Herding in Finnish Lapland. *In* Arctic and Alpine Environments. J. D. Ives and R. G. Barry, eds. London: Methuen.

Mumford, Lewis
1956 The Natural History of Urbanization. *In* Man's Role in Changing the Face of the Earth, Vol. 1. William L. Thomas, ed. Chicago: University of Chicago Press.

Murchie, R. W., W. Allen and J. F. Booth
1936 Agricultural Progress on the Prairie Frontier. Toronto: Macmillan.

Murdoch, William
1971 Ecological Systems. *In* Environment: Resources, Pollution and Society. William Murdoch, ed. Stamford, Conn.: Sinauer Assoc.

Murra, John
1965 Herds and Herders in the Inca State. *In* Man, Culture and Animals. Anthony Leeds and A. P. Vayda, eds. Washington, D.C.: American Association for the Advancement of Science.

____

1972 El Control Vertical de un Máximo de Pisos Ecológicos en La Economía de las Sociedades Andinas. *In* Visita de la Provincia de León de Huanuco en 1562. John Murra, ed. Huanuco, Peru: Universidad Nacional.

Nachman, B.
1969 Fits, Suicides, Beatings and Time-Out. Anchorage, Alaska: U.S. Public Health Service, Alaska Native Service.

Nam, Charles, ed.
1968 Population and Society: A Textbook of Readings. Boston: Houghton Mifflin.

Natani, K. and J. T. Shurley
1974 Sociopsychological Aspects of a Winter Vigil at S. Pole Station. *In* Human Adaptability to Antarctic Conditions. E. K. E. Gunderson, ed. Washington, D.C.: American Geophysical Union.

National Academy of Science (NAS)
1972 Soils of the Humid Tropics. Washington, D.C.: NAS.

____

1976 Promising Plants for the Developing Tropics. Washington, D.C: NAS.

Nauta, Doede
1972 The Meaning of Information. The Hague: Mouton.

Nelms, J. D. and R. S. Soper
1962 Cold Vasodilation and Cold Acclimatization in the Hands of British Fish Filleters. Journal of Applied Physiology 17:444–448.

Nelson, Michael
1973 The Development of Tropical Lands. Baltimore: Johns Hopkins University Press.

Nelson, R. K.
1969 Hunters of the Northern Ice. Chicago: University of Chicago Press.

Netting, Robert
1968 Hill Farmers of Nigeria. Seattle: Washington University Press.

———
1969 Ecosystems in Process. *In* Contributions to Anthropology: Ecological Essays. David Damas, ed. Ottawa: National Museums of Canada.

———
1971 The Ecological Approach to Cultural Study. Reading, Mass.: Addison-Wesley Module in Anthropology.

———
1974a Agrarian Ecology. Annual Review of Anthropology 3:21–56.

———
1974b The System Nobody Knows: Village Irrigation in the Swiss Alps. *In* Irrigation's Impact on Society. T. E. Downing and M. Gibson, eds. Tucson: University of Arizona Press.

———
1976 What Alpine Peasants Have in Common: Observations on Communal Tenure in a Swiss Village. Human Ecology 4(2): 135–146.

———
1977 Cultural Ecology. Menlo Park, Cal.: Cummings.

Newman, Russell
1975 Adaptation to Heat. *In* Physiological Anthropology. Albert Damon, ed. New York: Oxford University Press.

Nickerson, N. H., et al.
1973 Native Plants in the Diet of North Alaskan Eskimos. *In* Man and His Foods. C. E. Smith, ed. Birmingham: University of Alabama Press.

Nicolaisen, Johannes
1963 Ecology and Culture of the Pastoral Tuareg. Copenhagen: The National Museum.

Nietschmann, Bernard
1971 The Study of Indigenous Food Production Systems: Mere Subsistence or Merrily Subsisting? Revista Geográfica 74:83–99.

———
1972 Hunting and Fishing Focus among the Miskito Indians, Eastern Nicaragua. Human Ecology 1(1):41–67.

———
1973 Between Land and Water. New York: Seminar Press.

Noy-Meir, Imanuel
1973 Desert Ecosystems: Environment and Producers. Annual Review of Ecology and Systematics 4:25–51.

———
1974 Desert Ecosystems: Higher Trophic Levels. Annual Review of Ecology and Systematics 5:195–214.

Numata, M., ed.
1975 Ecological Studies in Japanese Grasslands: Productivity of Terrestrial Communities. Tokyo: University of Tokyo Press. Japan IBP Synthesis Volume.

373

Bibliography

Nye, P. H. and D. J. Greenland
1960 The Soil under Shifting Cultivation. Harpenden, U. K.: Commonwealth Bureau of Soils. Technical Communication, No. 51.

_____
1964 Changes in the Soil after Clearing a Tropical Forest. Plant and Soil 21:101–112.

Odum, Eugene
1969 The Strategy of Ecosystem Development. Science 164:262–270.

_____
1971 Fundamentals of Ecology. Third ed. Philadelphia: Saunders.

Odum, Howard T.
1971 Environment, Power and Society. New York: Wiley-Interscience.

Odum, Howard T. and Elizabeth Odum
1976 Energy Basis for Man and Nature. New York: McGraw-Hill.

Odum, Howard and F. Pigeon, eds.
1970 A Tropical Rain Forest. Springfield, Virginia: U.S. Department of Commerce/Atomic Energy Commission.

Oliver, Symmes
1962 Ecology and Cultural Continuity as Contributing Factors in the Social Organization of the Plains Indians. Berkeley: University of California Publications in American Archaeology and Ethnology.

Oliver-Smith, Anthony
1977 Traditional Agriculture, Central Places and Postdisaster Urban Relocation in Peru. American Enthnologist 4 (1): 102–116.

Orlove, Benjamin
1977 Integration through Production: The Use of Zonation in Espinar. American Ethnologist 4(1):84–101.

Osburn, William, Jr.
1974 The Snowmobile in Eskimo Culture. In Arctic and Alpine Environments. J. D. Ives and R. G. Barry, eds. London: Methuen.

Oswalt, Wendell H.
1963 Mission of Change in Alaska. San Marino, Cal.: Huntington Library.

_____
1967 Alaskan Eskimos. San Francisco: Chandler.

Ottoson, H. W., et al.
1966 Land and People in the Northern Plains Transition Area. Lincoln: University of Nebraska Press.

Palen, J. J.
1975 The Urban World. New York: McGraw- Hill.

Palerm, A.
1968 The Agricultural Basis of Urban Civilization in Mesoamerica. In Man in Adaptation. Yehudi Cohen, ed. Chicago: Aldine.

Pan American Health Organization
1966 Life at High Altitudes. Washington, D.C.: Pan American Health Organization.

374

Park, Robert E., E. W. Burgess and R. D. McKenzie
1925 The City. Chicago: University of Chicago Press.

Patten, B. C., ed.
1971 Systems Analysis and Simulation in Ecology, Vol. 1. New York: Academic Press.

Paylore, Patricia, ed.
1966 Seventy-five Years of Arid Lands Research at the University of Arizona. Tucson, Ariz.: Office of Arid Lands Studies.

——— 1969 Desert Research: Selected References. Tucson, Ariz.: Office of Arid Lands Studies.

Pelto, Pertti
1973 The Snowmobile Revolution. Menlo Park, Cal.: Cummings.

Peterson, N.
1975 Hunter-Gatherer Territoriality: The Perspective from Australia. American Anthropologist 77:53–68.

Picón-Reátegui, Emilio
1976 Nutrition. *In* Man in the Andes. Paul T. Baker and M. Little, eds. Stroudsburg, Pa.: Dowden, Hutchinson and Ross.

Plattner, Stuart, ed.
1974 Formal Methods in Economic Anthropology. Washington, D.C.: American Anthropological Association.

Plog, Fred
1975 Systems Theory in Archaeological Research. Annual Review of Anthropology 4:207–224.

Popenoe, Hugh
1960 Effects of Shifting Cultivation on Natural Soil Constituents in Central America. Ph.D. dissertation, University of Florida, Department of Agronomy.

Porter, Lynn
1969 Nitrogen in Grassland Ecosystems. *In* The Grassland Ecosystem. R. L. Dix and R. G. Beidleman, eds. Fort Collins: Colorado State University, Range Science Department.

Porter, P. W.
1965 Environmental Potentials and Economic Opportunities. American Anthropologist 67:409–420.

Porter, R. and R. Knight, eds.
1971 High Altitude Physiology. Edinburgh: C. Livingstone.

Prance, G. T.
1973 Phytogeographic Support for the Theory of Pleistocene Forest Refuges in the Amazon Basin, Based on Evidence from *Dischapetalaceae* and *Lecythidaceae*. Acta Amazonica 3(3):5–28.

Pratt, D. J. and M. D. Gwynne, eds.
1977 Rangeland Management and Ecology in East Africa. London: Hodder and Stoughton.

Pugh, A. L.
1970 Dynamo 2: Users Manual. Cambridge, Mass.: MIT Press.

Bibliography

Pugh, L. G. C.
1965 High Altitudes. In The Physiology of Human Survival. O. G. Edholm and A. L. Bacharach, eds. London: Academic Press.

———
1966 A Programme for Physiological Studies of High Altitude Peoples. In The Biology of Human Adaptability. Paul T. Baker and J. S. Weiner, eds. Oxford: Clarendon Press.

Quinn, J. A.
1940 Topical Summary of Current Literature on Human Ecology. American Journal of Sociology 46:191–226.

Raiffa, Howard
1968 Decision Analysis. Reading, Mass.: Addison-Wesley.

Rapoport, Amos
1967 Yagua, or the Amazon Dwelling. Landscape 16(3):27–30.

———
1969 House Form and Culture. Englewood Cliffs, N.J.: Prentice-Hall.

Rapoport, Anatol
1968 The Promise and Pitfalls of Information Theory. In Modern Systems Research for the Behavioral Scientist. Walter Buckley, ed. Chicago: Aldine.

Rappaport, Roy
1968 Pigs for the Ancestors. New Haven, Conn.: Yale University Press.

———
1971a The Flow of Energy in an Agricultural Society. Scientific American 224(3):116–132.

———
1971b The Sacred in Human Evolution. Annual Review of Ecology and Systematics 2:23–44.

———
1977 Ecology, Adaptation and the Ills of Functionalism. Michigan Discussions in Anthropology 2:138–190.

Rawski, E. S.
1972 Agricultural Change and the Peasant Economy of South China. Cambridge, Mass.: Harvard University Press.

Reichel-Dolmatoff, G.
1971 Amazonian Cosmos. Chicago: University of Chicago Press.

———
1976 Cosmology as Ecological Analysis: A View from the Rain Forest. Man 11:307–318.

Rennie, Donald
1978 Exercise Physiology. In The Eskimo of Northwestern Alaska: A Biological Perspective. Paul L. Jamison, S. L. Zegura, and F. A. Milan, eds. Stroudsburg, Pa.: Dowden, Hutchinson and Ross.

Reynolds, Hudson
1959 Brush Control in the Southwest. In Grasslands. H. Sprague, ed. Washington, D.C.: American Association for the Advancement of Science.

Rhoades, Robert and S. Thompson
1975 Adaptive Strategies in Alpine Environments: Beyond Ecological Particularism. American Ethnologist 2(3):535–551.

Richards, Audrey
1939 Land, Labour and Diet in Northern Rhodesia. London: Oxford University Press.

Richards, Paul W.
1952 The Tropical Rain Forest. Cambridge, England: University Press.

———
1973 The Tropical Rain Forest. Scientific American 229:58–67.

Richerson, Peter
1977 Ecology and Human Ecology: A Comparison of Theories in the Biological and Social Sciences. American Ethnologist 4(1):1–26.

Richerson, Peter and James McEvoy, eds.
1976 Human Ecology: An Environmental Approach. North Scituate, Mass.: Duxbury Press.

Ricklefs, Robert
1973 Ecology. Portland, Oregon: Chiron Press.

Robinson, S., et al.
1941 Adaptation of White Men and Negroes to Prolonged Work in Humid Heat. American Journal of Tropical Medicine 21:261–287.

Robson, B. T.
1969 Urban Analysis. Cambridge: Cambridge University Press.

Robson, J. R., et al.
1972 Malnutrition: Its Causation and Control. 2 vols. New York: Breach.

Rodin, L. E., ed.
1972 Ecophysiological Foundation of Ecosystem Productivity in Arid Zones. Leningrad: NAUKA.

Roe, F. G.
1951 The North American Buffalo: A Critical Study of the Species in its Wild State. Toronto: University of Toronto Press.

———
1955 The Indian and the Horse. Norman: Oklahoma University Press.

Rogers, Carol
1977 Desertification. Science News 112:282–284.

Rose, G. A.
1976 Epidemiological Evidence for the Effects of Urban Environment. In Man in Urban Environments. G. A. Harrison and J. B. Gibson, eds. Oxford: Oxford University Press.

Rosow, Irving
1961 The Social Effects of the Physical Environment. Journal of the American Institute of Planners 27(2):127–133.

Ross, Eric
1978 Food Taboos, Diet and Hunting Strategy: The Adaptation to Animals in Amazon Cultural Ecology. Current Anthropology 19:1–36.

Bibliography

Ross, M. A.
1969 An Integrated Approach to the Ecology of Arid Australia. Proceedings of the Ecological Society of Australia 4:67–81.

Rosswall, T. and O. W. Heal, eds.
1975 Structure and Function of Tundra Ecosystems. Stockholm: Swedish Natural Science Research Council. Ecological Bulletin, No.20.

Ruddle, Kenneth
1973 The Human Use of Insects: Examples from the Yukpa. Biotropica 5(2):94–101.

Ruthenberg, Hans
1971 Farming Systems in the Tropics. London: Oxford University Press.

Sahlins, Marshall
1957 Land Use and The Extended Family in Moala Fiji. American Anthropologist 59:449–462.

___

1964 Culture and Environment: The Study of Cultural Ecology. In Horizons in Anthropology. Sol Tax, ed. Chicago: Aldine.

___

1976 Culture and Practical Reason. Chicago: University of Chicago Press.

Sanchez, Pedro
1976 Properties and Management of Soils in the Tropics. New York: Wiley-Interscience.

Sanchez, Pedro, et al.
1974 Investigaciones en Manejo de Suelos Tropicales en Yurimaguas, Selva Baja del Perú. Paper presented at Seminario de Sistemas de Agricultura Tropical (Lima, Peru: June 1–8, 1974).

Sanchez, Pedro and S. W. Buol
1975 Soils of the Tropics and the World Food Crisis. Science 188:598–603.

Sargent, Frederick, ed.
1974 Human Ecology. Amsterdam: North-Holland Publishing Company.

Sato, Shun
1977 The Camel Ecology of the Rendille. Paper presented at Seminar on Pastoral Societies of Kenya. Mimeo. Ethnographic Museum of Japan.

Sauer, Carl
1958 Man in the Ecology of Tropical America. Proceedings of the Ninth Pacific Science Congress 20:104–110.

Schlaiffer, R. O.
1967 Analysis of Decisions under Uncertainty. New York: McGraw-Hill.

Schmidt-Nielsen, K.
1964 Desert Animals: Physiological Problems of Heat and Water. New York: Oxford University Press.

Schneider, Harold K.
1957 The Subsistence Role of Cattle among the Pakot in East Africa. American Anthropologist 59:278–300.

___

1970 The Wahi Wanyaturu: Economics in an African Society. Chicago: Aldine.

—
1974a Economic Man. New York: Free Press.

—
1974b Economic Development and Economic Change. Current Anthropology 15:259–276.

Schnore, Leo F.
1961 The Myth of Human Ecology. Sociological Inquiry 31:128–139.

Schoener, T. W.
1971 Theory of Feeding Strategies. Annual Review of Ecology and Systematics 2:369–404.

Schrire, Carmel and W. L. Steiger
1974 A Matter of Life and Death: An Investigation into the Practice of Female Infanticide in the Arctic. Man 9(2):161–181.

Schultz, A. M.
1969 A Study of an Ecosystem: The Arctic Tundra. In The Ecosystem Concept in Natural Resource Management. G. Van Dyne, ed. New York: Academic Press.

Schwabe, G. H.
1968 Towards an Ecological Characterization of the South American Continent. In Biogeography and Ecology in South America. E. J. Fittkau et al., eds. The Hague: Junk.

Schwartz, S. I. and T. C. Foin
1972 A Critical Review of the Social Systems Models of Jay Forrester. Human Ecology 1(2):161–173.

Schwarzweller, H. K., J. Brown, and J. Mangalam
1971 Mountain Families in Transition. University Park: Pennsylvania State University Press.

Scudder, Thayer
1962 The Ecology of the Gwenbe Tonga. Manchester, England: Manchester University Press.

—
1973 The Human Ecology of the Big Projects: River Basin Development and Resettlement. Annual Review of Anthropology 2:45–61.

—
1975 Resettlement. In Man-Made Lakes and Human Health. N. F. Stanley, ed. London: Academic Press.

Sebeok, Thomas A.
1974 Semiotics: A Survey of the State of the Art. Current Trends in Linguistics 12:211–264.

Secoy, F. R.
1953 Changing Military Patterns on the Great Plains. Locust Valley, N.Y.: J. J. Augustin Publishers. Monographs of the American Ethnological Society, No. 21.

Shannon, Fred
1940 An Appraisal of W. P. Webb's The Great Plains. New York: Social Science Research Council.

Bibliography

Shantzis, S. D. and W. W. Behrens
1973 Population Control Mechanisms in a Primitive Agricultural Society. *In* Toward Global Equilibrium. Dennis L. Meadows and D. H. Meadows, eds. Cambridge, Mass.: Wright-Allen Press.

Shelford, Victor
1963 The Ecology of North America. Urbana: University of Illinois Press.

Shepard, R. J.
1974 Work Physiology and Activity Patterns of Circumpolar Eskimos and Ainu: A Synthesis of International Biological Program Data. Human Biology 46:263–294.

Shevky, E. and W. Bell
1955 Social Area Analysis. Stanford, Cal.: Stanford University Press.

Short, James
1969 The Social Fabric of the Metropolis. Chicago: University of Chicago Press.

Shryock, Henry et al.
1971 The Methods and Materials of Demography.2 vols. Washington, D.C.: U.S. Bureau of the Census, Government Printing Office.

Shugart, H. H. et al.
1975 Viewpoints on Energy Flow in Ecosystems. *In* TIE, A Guide to Energy Flow Studies. Mineo manuscript. Available from Institute of Ecology, Indianapolis, Indiana.

Simmons, I. G.
1974 The Ecology of Natural Resources. New York: John Wiley (Halsted Press).

Sioli, Harold
1973 Recent Human Activities in the Brazilian Amazon Region and Their Ecological Effects. *In* Tropical Forest Ecosystems in Africa and South America. Betty Meggers, E. Y. Ayensu, and W. D. Ducksworth, eds. Washington, D.C.: Smithsonian Institution Press.

Siskind, Janet
1973 To Hunt in the Morning. New York: Oxford University Press.

Sjoberg, Gideon
1965 The Origin and Evolution of Cities. Scientific American 213:55–63.

Slobodkin, L. B.
1968 Toward a Predictive Theory of Evolution. *In* Population Biology and Evolution. R. C. Lewontin, ed. Syracuse, N.Y.: Syracuse University Press.

———
1972 On the Inconstancy of Ecological Efficiency and the Form of Ecological Theories. *In* Transactions of the Connecticut Academy of Arts and Sciences 44:293–305.

———
1974 Mind, Bind and Ecology. Human Ecology 2:67–74.

Slovic, P., H. Kunreuther, and G. White
1974 Decision Processes, Rationality and Adjustment to Natural Hazards. *In* Natural Hazards. Gilbert White, ed. New York: Oxford University Press.

380

Smith, Lorne
1972 The Mechanical Dog Team: A Study of the Ski-Doo in the Canadian Arctic. Arctic Anthropology 9(1):1–9.

Smith, Nigel
1974a Agouti and Babassu. Oryx 22(5):581–582.

————

1974b Destructive Exploitation of the South American River Turtle. Yearbook of the Association of Pacific Coast Geographers 36:85–102.

————

1976 Transamazon Highway: A Cultural-Ecological Analysis of Settlement in the Lowland Tropics. Ph.D. dissertation, University of California, Berkeley, Department of Geography.

Smith Robert Leo
1974 Ecology and Field Biology. Second ed. New York: Harper & Row.

Spencer, Joseph E.
1966 Shifting Cultivation in Southeast Asia. Berkeley: University of California Press.

Spencer, Paul
1965 The Samburu. London: Routledge and Keagan Paul.

————

1973 Nomads in Alliance. London: Oxford University Press.

Spencer, Robert F.
1959 The North Alaskan Eskimo. Washington, D.C.: Smithsonian Institution. Bulletin No. 171 of the Bureau of American Ethnology.

Spiegelman, Mortimer
1968 Introduction to Demography. Cambridge, Mass.: Harvard University Press.

Spooner, Brian
1973 The Cultural Ecology of Pastoral Nomads. Reading, Mass.: Addison-Wesley Modules in Anthropology.

————

1974 Irrigation and Society: The Iranian Plateau. *In* Irrigation's Impact on Society. T. E. Downing and M. Gibson, eds. Tucson: University of Arizona Press.

Spooner, Brian, ed.
1972 Population Growth: Anthropological Implications. Cambridge, Mass.: MIT Press.

Sprague, Howard, ed.
1959 Grasslands. Washington, D C.: American Association for the Advancement of Science.

Sprout, H. and M. Sprout
1965 The Ecological Perspective on Human Affairs. Princeton, N.J.: Princeton University Press.

Stark, N.
1969 Direct Nutrient Cycling in the Amazon Basin. *In* II Simposio y Foro de Biología Tropical Amazónica. Bogotá, Columbia: Editorial Pax.

Bibliography

Stearns, F. and T. Montag, eds.
1974 The Urban Ecosystem: A Holistic Approach. Stroudsburg, Pa.: Dowden, Hutchinson and Ross.

Steegman, A. T.
1967 Frostbite of the Human Face as a Selective Force. Human Biology 39:131–144.

_____

1970 Cold Adaptation and the Human Face. American Journal of Physical Anthropology 32:243 –250.

_____

1975 Human Adaptation to Cold. In Physiological Anthropology. Albert Damon, ed. New York: Oxford University Press.

Steila, Donald
1976 The Geography of Soils. Englewood Cliffs, N.J.: Prentice-Hall.

Stenning, D. J.
1957 Transhumance, Migratory Drift, Migration: Patterns of Pastoral Fulani Nomadism. Journal of the Royal Anthropological Institute 87:57–73.

Steward, Julian
1936 The Economic and Social Basis of Primitive Bands. In Essays in Anthropology Presented to A. L. Kroeber. Robert Lowie, ed. Berkeley: University of California Press.

_____

1975 Human Adaptation to Cold. In Physiological Anthropology. Albert Damon, ed. New York: Oxford University Press.

Steila, Donald
1976 The Geography of Soils. Englewood Cliffs, N.J.: Prentice-Hall.

Stenning, D. J.
1957 Transhumance, Migratory Drift, Migration: Patterns of Pastoral Fulani Nomadism. Journal of the Royal Anthropological Institute 87:57–73.

Steward, Julian
1936 The Economic and Social Basis of Primitive Bands. In Essays in Anthropology Presented to A. L. Kroeber. Robert Lowie, ed. Berkeley: University of California Press.

_____

1938 Basin-Plateau Aboriginal Sociopolitical Groups. Washington, D.C.: Smithsonian Institution. Bulletin 120, Bureau of American Ethnology.

_____

1955a Theory of Culture Change. Urbana: University of Illinois Press.

_____

1977 Evolution and Ecology. Urbana: University of Illinois Press.

Steward, Julian, ed.
1939-1946 Handbook of South American Indians. 7 vols. Washington, D.C.: Bureau of American Ethnology, Smithsonian Institution.

_____

1955b Irrigation Civilizations: A Comparative Study. Washington, D.C.: Pan American Union, Social Science Monograph 1.

Stewart, Omer
1956 Fire as the First Great Force Employed by Man. *In* Man's Role in Changing the Face of the Earth. William L. Thomas, ed. Chicago: University of Chicago Press.

Stini, William
1975 Ecology and Human Adaptation. Dubuque, Iowa: William C. Brown Publishers.

Stoddart, D. R.
1967 Organism and Ecosystem as Geographical Models. *In* Integrated Models in Geography. R. Chorley and P. Haggett, eds. London: Methuen.

Stokols, Daniel
1972 A Social-Psychological Model of Human Crowding Phenomena. Journal of the American Institute of Planners 38(2):72–83.

Street, J.
1969 An Evaluation of the Concept of Carrying Capacity. Professional Geographer 21:104–107.

Strickon, Arnold
1965 The Euro-American Ranching Complex. *In* Man, Culture and Animals. A. Leeds and A. P. Vayda, eds. Washington, D.C. American Association for the Advancement of Science.

Sturtevant, William
1964 Studies in Ethnoscience. American Anthropologist 66(3) Part 2:99–131.

Superintendencia do Desenvolvimento da Amazônia (SUDAM)
1971 Criadouros Artificias de Animais Silvestres. Vol. I: Criadouros de Capivara. Belem (Brazil): SUDAM.

Suttles, D.
1968 The Social Order of the Slum. Chicago: University of Chicago Press.

Suttles, W.
1968 Coping with Abundance. *In* Man the Hunter. Richard B. Lee and I. DeVore, eds. Chicago: Aldine.

Sutton, Ann and Myron Sutton
1966 The Life of the Desert. New York: McGraw-Hill.

Sutton, David and N. P. Harmon
1973 Ecology. New York: John Wiley.

Sweet, Louise
1965 Camel Pastoralism in Northern Arabia and the Minimal Camping Unit. *In* Man, Culture and Animals: The Role of Animals in Human Ecological Adjustments. Anthony Leeds and A. P. Vayda, eds. Washington, D.C.: American Association for the Advancement of Science.

Swift, Jeremy
1977 Sahelian Pastoralists: Underdevelopment, Desertification, and Famine. Annual Review of Anthropology 6:457–478.

Tanaka, Jiro
1976 Subsistence Ecology of Central Kalahari San. *In* Kalahari Hunter-Gatherers. Richard B. Lee and I. DeVore, eds. Cambridge, Mass.: Harvard University Press.

Bibliography

Taylor, Griffith
1951 Geography in the Twentieth Century. London: Methuen.

Tedrow, T. C. F.
1977 Soils of the Polar Landscapes. New Brunswick, N.J.: Rutgers University Press.

Tedrow, T. C. F. and J. E. Clanton
1969 Concepts of Soil Formation and Classification in Arctic Regions. In Vegetation, Soils, and Wildlife. J. G. Nelson and M. J. Chambers, eds. Toronto: Methuen.

Theodorson, George A., ed.
1961 Studies in Human Ecology. New York: Harper & Row.

Thomas, Elizabeth Marshall
1958 The Harmless People. New York: Vintage Books.

Thomas, Franklin
1925 The Environmental Basis of Society. New York: The Century Company.

Thomas, R. B.
1973 Human Adaptation to a High Andean Energy Flow System. University Park: Pennsylvania State University, Department of Anthropology, Occasional Papers.

———
1976 Energy Flow at High Altitude. In Man in the Andes. Paul T. Baker and M. Little, eds. Stroudsburg, Pa.: Dowden, Hutchinson and Ross.

Thomas, R. B. and B. P. Winterhalder
1976 Physical and Biotic Environment of Southern Highland Peru. In Man in the Andes. Paul T. Baker and M. Little, eds. Stroudsburg, Pa.: Dowden, Hutchinson and Ross.

Tivy, Joy
1971 Biogeography. London: Oliver and Boyd.

Troll, Carl
1958 Las Culturas Superiores Andinas y el Medio Geográfico. Lima, Peru: Instituto de Geografía, Universidad Nacional de San Marcos.

Turner, J. F. C.
1966 Uncontrolled Urban Settlement: Problems and Politics. New York: United Nations Center for Housing, Building and Planning.

———
1976 The Rush to the Cities in Latin America. Science 192:955–962.

Vallentine, John
1975 Range Development and Improvements. Provo, Utah: Brigham Young University Press.

van Heerden, Pieter
1968 The Foundation of Empirical Knowledge. Wassenaar, The Netherlands: N.V. Vitgeverij Wistik.

Van Liere, E. J. and J. C. Stickney
1963 Hypoxia. Chicago: University of Chicago Press.

Van Wie, Claudia C.
1974 Physiological Responses to Cold Environments. *In* Arctic and Alpine Environments. J. D. Ives and R. G. Barry, eds. London: Methuen.

Vanzolini, G.
1970 Zoología Sistemática, Geografía e a Origem das Espécies. São Paulo: Instituto de Geografía.

Vayda, Andrew P.
1968 Hypotheses about Functions of War. *In* War: The Anthropology of Armed Conflict and Aggression. Morton Fried et al., eds. New York: Doubleday.

1974 Warfare in Ecological Perspective. Annual Review of Ecology and Systematics 5:183–193.

1976 Warfare in Ecological Perspective. New York: Plenum.

Vayda, Andrew P. and B. McCay
1975 New Directions in Ecology and Ecological Anthropology. Annual Review of Anthropology 4:293–406.

Vayda, A. P. and Roy Rappaport
1976 Ecology, Cultural and Noncultural. *In* Human Ecology. Peter Richerson and J. McEvoy, eds. North Scituate, Mass.: Duxbury Press.

Vayda, Andrew P., ed.
1969 Environment and Cultural Behavior. Garden City, N.Y.: Natural History Press.

Velásquez, Tulio
1976 Pulmonary Function and Oxygen Transport. *In* Man in the Andes. Paul T. Baker and M. Little, eds. Stroudsburg, Pa.: Dowden, Hutchinson and Ross.

Vickers, William
1975 Meat is Meat: The Siona-Secoya and the Hunting Prowess-Sexual Reward Hypothesis. Latinamericanist 11(1):1–5. University of Florida Center for Latin American Studies.

1976 Cultural Adaptation to Amazonian Habitats: The Siona-Secoya of Eastern Ecuador. Ph. D. dissertation, University of Florida, Department of Anthropology.

Voget, Fred
1975 A History of Ethnology. New York: Holt, Rinehart and Winston.

Waddell, Eric
1972 The Mound-Builders. Seattle: University of Washington Press.

Wagley, Charles
1941 Economics of a Guatemalan Village. Washington, D.C.,: American Anthropological Association Memoirs, No. 58.

1951 The Brazilian Amazon: The Case of an Underdeveloped Area. *In* Four Papers Presented in the Institute for Brazilian Studies. Nashville, Tenn.: Vanderbilt University Press.

Bibliography

———

1953 Amazon Town. New York: Macmillan.

———

1969 Cultural Influences on Population: A Comparison of Two Tupi Tribes. *In* Environment and Cultural Behavior. Andrew P. Vayda, ed. New York: Natural History Press.

———

1977 Welcome of Tears: The Tapirapé Indians of Central Brazil. New York: Oxford University Press.

Wagner, Richard
1974 Environment and Man. Second ed. New York: Norton.

Wallace, Anthony F. C.
1956 Revitalization Movements. American Anthropologist 58(2):264–281.

———

1960 An Interdisciplinary Approach to Mental Disorders among the Polar Eskimos of Northwest Greenland. Anthropologica II(2):1–12.

Walter, Heinrich
1973 Vegetation of the Earth. New York: Springer-Verlag.

Walters, Carl
1971 Systems Ecology: The Systems Approach and Mathematical Models in Ecology. *In* Fundamentals of Ecology. E. Odum. Philadelphia: Saunders.

Ward, Michael
1975 Mountain Medicine: A Clinical Study of Cold and High Altitude. New York: Van Nostrand Reinhold.

Watson, P. J., S. LeBlanc, and C. Redman
1971 Explanation in Archaeology. New York: Columbia University Press.

Watt, Kenneth
1968 Ecology and Resource Management. New York: McGraw-Hill.

———

1973 Principles of Environmental Science. New York: McGraw-Hill.

Way, Anthony
1976 Morbidity and Postneonatal Mortality. *In* Man in the Andes. Paul T. Baker and M. Little, eds. Stroudsburg, Pa.: Dowden, Hutchinson and Ross.

———

1978 General Health. *In* The Eskimo of Northwestern Alaska: A Biological Perspective. Paul L. Jamison, S. L. Zegura, and F. A. Milan, eds. Stroudsburg, Pa.: Dowden, Hutchinson and Ross.

Webb, Walter Prescott
1931 The Great Plains. Boston: Ginn and Co.

Webber, P. J.
1974 Tundra Primary Productivity. *In* Arctic and Alpine Environments. J. D. Ives and R. G. Barry, eds. London: Methuen.

Wedel, Waldo
1961a Prehistoric Man on the Great Plains. Norman: University of Oklahoma Press.

———

1961b Some Aspects of Human Ecology in the Central Plains. *In* Studies in Human Ecology. George Theodorson, ed. New York: Harper & Row.

———

1975 Some Early Euro-American Percepts of the Great Plains and Their Influence on Anthropological Thinking. *In* Images of the Plains. B. W. Blouet and M. P. Lawson, eds. Lincoln: University of Nebraska Press.

Weihe, W., ed.
1963 The Physiological Effects of High Altitude. Oxford: Pergamon Press.

Weiner, J. S. and J. A. Lourie, eds.
1969 Human Biology: A Guide to Field Methods. Oxford: Blackwell IBP Handbook, No. 9.

Weiss, Mark and A. E. Mann
1975 Human Biology and Behavior. Boston: Little, Brown.

Went, F. W. and N. Stark
1968 Mycorrhizae. Bioscience 18:1035–1039.

West, Oliver
1972 The Ecological Impact of the Introduction of Domestic Cattle into Wildlife and Tsetse Areas of Rhodesia. *In* The Careless Technology. M. T. Farvar and J. P. Milton, eds. Garden City, N.Y.: Natural History Press.

Weyer, Edward M.
1932 The Eskimos: Their Environment and Folkways. New Haven, Conn.: Yale University Press.

Wheatley, P.
1971 The Pivot of the Four Quarters. Chicago: Aldine.

Whelpton, Pascal
1954 Cohort Fertility. Princeton, N.J.: Princeton University Press.

White, Gilbert, ed.
1974 Natural Hazards. New York: Oxford University Press.

White Leslie
1943 Energy and the Evolution of Culture. American Anthropologist 45:335–356.

———

1949 The Science of Culture. New York: Free Books.

Whitmore, T. C.
1975 Tropical Rain Forests of the Far East. Oxford: Clarendon Press.

Whittaker, R. H.
1970 Communities and Ecosystems. New York: Macmillan.

Whittaker, R. H. and G. E. Likens
1975 The Biosphere and Man. *In* Primary Productivity of the Biosphere. H. Lieth and R. H. Whittaker, eds. New York: Springer-Verlag.

Wiesenfeld, Stephen
1969 Sickle-Cell Trait in Human Biological and Cultural Evolution. *In* Environment and Cultural Behavior. Andrew P. Vayda, ed. New York: Natural History Press.

Bibliography

Williams, Sue R.
1973 Nutrition and Diet Therapy, Second ed. St. Louis, Mo.: C. V. Mosby Co.

Wilson, Edward O.
1975 Sociobiology: A New Synthesis. Cambridge, Mass.: Belknap.

Wilson, Edward O. and W. Bossert
1971 A Primer of Population Biology. Stamford, Conn.: Sinauer Associates.

Winterhalder, B., R. Larsen, and R. B. Thomas
1974 Dung as an Essential Resource in a Highland Peruvian Community. Human Ecology 2(2):89–104.

Wissler, Clark
1926 The Relation of Nature to Man in Aboriginal America. New York: Oxford University Press.

Wittfogel, K. A.
1956 The Hydraulic Civilizations. In Man's Role in Changing the Face of the Earth. William L. Thomas, ed. Chicago: University of Chicago Press.

―――
1957 Oriental Despotism. New Haven, Conn.: Yale University Press.

Wolf, Eric and A. Palerm
1955 Irrigation in the Old Acolhua Domain. Southwestern Journal of Anthropology 11:265–281.

Wolman, Abel
1965 The Metabolism of Cities. Scientific American 213:179–190.

Woodburn, James
1968 An Introduction to Hadza Ecology. In Man the Hunter. Richard B. Lee and I. DeVore, eds. Chicago: Aldine Press.

―――
1972 Ecology, Nomadic Movement and the Composition of the Local Group among Hunters and Gatherers: An East African Example and Its Implications. In Man, Settlement and Urbanism. Peter Ucko et al., eds. Cambridge, Mass.: Schenkman Publishing Company.

Woodbury, Richard, ed.
1962 Civilizations in Desert Lands. Salt Lake City: University of Utah Press. Anthropological Papers, No. 62.

Woods, Frances J.
1972 Marginality and Identity. Baton Rouge: Louisiana State University Press.

Wulff, L. Y., et al.
1968 Physiological Factors Relating to Terrestrial Altitudes: A Bibliography. Columbus: Ohio State University Libraries.

Wyndham, C. H.
1966 Southern African Ethnic Adaptation to Temperature and Exercise. In The Biology of Human Adaptability. Paul T. Baker and J. S. Weiner, eds. Oxford: Clarendon Press.

Wynne-Edwards, V. C.
1965 Self-regulating Systems in Populations of Animals. Science 147:1543–1548.

Yellen, John E.
1976 Settlement Patterns of the !Kung. *In* Kalahari Hunter-Gatherers. Richard B. Lee and I. DeVore, eds. Cambridge, Mass.: Harvard University Press.

1977 Archaeological Approaches to the Present. New York: Academic Press.

Yengoyan, Aram
1968 Demographic and Ecological Influences on Aboriginal Australian Marriage Sections. *In* Man the Hunter. Richard B. Lee and I. DeVore, eds. Chicago: Aldine.

1976 Structure, Event and Ecology in Aboriginal Australia: A Comparative Viewpoint. *In* Tribes and Boundaries in Australia. N. Petersen, ed. Canberra: Australian Institute of Aboriginal Studies.

Yoshimura, H. and J. S. Weiner, eds.
1966 Human Adaptability and Its Methodology. Tokyo: Japan Society for the Promotion of Sciences.

Youngner, V. B. and C. M. McKell, eds.
1973 The Biology and Utilization of Grasses. New York: Academic Press.

Zegura, S. L.
1978 The Eskimo Population System: Linguistic Framework and Skeletal Remains. *In* The Eskimo of Northwestern Alaska: A Biological Perspective. Paul L. Jamison, S. L. Zegura, and F. A. Milan, eds. Stroudsburg, Pa.: Dowden, Hutchinson and Ross.

Zegura, S. L. and P. L. Jamison
1978 Multidisciplinary Research: A Case Study in Eskimo Human Biology. *In* The Eskimo of Northwestern Alaska: A Biological Perspective. Paul L. Jamison, S. L. Zegura, and F. A. Milan, eds. Stroudsburg, Pa.: Dowden, Hutchinson and Ross.

Zimmerman, C. C. and S. Russel, eds.
1967 Symposium on the Great Plains of North America. Fargo: North Dakota Institute for Regional Studies.

Zubrow, Ezra
1975 Prehistoric Carrying Capacity: A Model. Menlo Park, Cal.: Cummings.

Index: Name

Index: Subject

Index: Subject